BTEC Level 2
Building Better Results

endorsed by edexcel

BTEC First

Business

Dave Needham, Rob Dransfield,
John Goymer, Carol Sumner
Editor: Julie Coombes

DYNAMIC LEARNING

HODDER EDUCATION
AN HACHETTE UK COMPANY

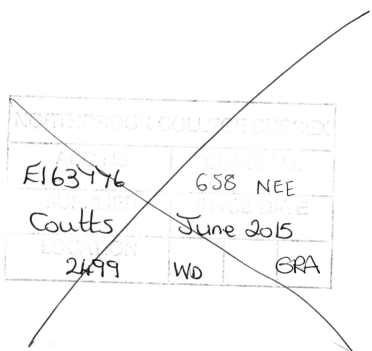

Orders: please contact Bookpoint Ltd, 130 Milton Park, Abingdon, Oxon OX14 4SB. Telephone: (44) 01235 827720. Fax: (44) 01235 400454. Lines are open from 9.00 – 5.00, Monday to Saturday, with a 24 hour message answering service. You can also order through our website www.hoddereducation.co.uk

If you have any comments to make about this, or any of our other titles, please send them to educationenquiries@hodder.co.uk

British Library Cataloguing in Publication Data
A catalogue record for this title is available from the British Library

ISBN: 978 0 340 99190 9

First Edition Published 2010
Impression number 10 9 8 7 6 5 4 3 2
Year 2014 2013 2012 2011

Artwork by Oxford Designers and Illustrators
Cover photo from © Stephen Strathdee/istockphoto.com
Typeset by Pantek Arts Ltd.
Printed in Dubai for Hodder Education, an Hachette UK Company, 338 Euston Road, London NW1 3BH

Contents

Customer relations in business

Business online

Exploring business enterprise

The marketing plan

Introduction

From September 2010 all learners registered on a BTEC Level 2 will be enrolled on the new specifications which sit on the Qualification Credit Framework (QCF). These new BTECs can act as stand-alone qualifications (as at present), form part of the Additional Specialist Learning alongside Diplomas or Technical Certificates within Apprenticeships.

As a present, the BTEC qualifications are made up of units, but the big change is that each unit is now allocated 'credits'. These credits, as well as building the BTEC qualification, form part of the Awards, Certificates and Diplomas of the Qualification Credit Framework (QCF) introduced by the Government as a way of rationalising and understanding the different types of qualifications that learners hold, what level they are and how they compare to other qualifications.

BTEC First qualification on the new framework will become Level 2 BTEC Firsts (QCF) and will be named as follows:

Level 2 BTEC Certificate (a new qualification)	consisting of 15 credits	equivalent to 1 GCSE
Level 2 BTEC Extended Certificate (previously called BTEC First Certificate)	consisting of 30 credits	equivalent to 2 GCSEs
Level 2 BTEC Diploma (previously called BTEC First Diploma)	consisting of 60 credits	equivalent to 4 GCSEs

What does this mean for teachers?

The features of the revised QCF BTEC Level 2 Firsts are that they retain the qualities of a current BTEC in that they are highly work-related. This book relates to the qualification by providing detailed work-related underpinning knowledge that supports learning and leads learners confidently towards assessment.

- Chapters have a common format. They introduce learners to the chapters via information on the learning outcomes through a section called 'What are you finding out'?
- Focussed areas of learning are provided by snappy 'did you know?' information and case studies.
- Learners seamlessly move towards pass, merit and distinction criteria via carefully crafted experiences encouraged through bite-sized information sessions and relevant activities.
- Discussion areas are introduced to provide collaborative learning experiences that encourage effective participation.
- Learning is enhanced by reflective tasks and activities encouraging practise on what has been learnt.
- Clear 'grading tips' focus learners on the necessary work for assessment.
- The chapters conclude with a valuable resource bank of Key Words and a copy of the BTEC specification grading criteria addressed within the chapter.
- The end of unit assignments assist teachers by covering whole unit assessment grading with learners placed in a scenario appropriate for their stage of learning.

What does this mean for learners?

BTECs are work-related and this book gives you information, advice and guidance that is up-to-date on how to achieve a Level 2 BTEC in Business at pass, merit or distinction.

- The topics chosen for study are up-to-date, interesting and relate to the assessment of the unit.
- Learning is provided in bite sized pieces that give you the knowledge you will require before answering the assignment.
- On many of the units you are given the chance to work with others or work individually.
- The units chosen have been very popular with previously successful learners.
- This book provides an exciting avenue to achieve your BTEC and move on a progression pathway within the business sector.

Julie Coombes
January 2010

Acknowledgements

The authors and publishers are grateful to the following for permission to reproduce illustrative material:

© Patryk Galka/ iStockphoto.com p1; HELLO! Ltd.p3; © Leabrooks Photography/Alamy p10; © Lightworks Media/Alamy p21; ©2009 photolibrary.com p29, p347; Martin Rickett/PA Wire/ Press Association Images p32; © Ingram Publishing Limited p43, p55, p264r, p391; Sage (UK) Limited p45; © Sean Prior - Fotolia.com p49; © Neil Fraser/Alamy p56; © Robert Wilkinson/Alamy p62; Christopher Furlong/Getty Images p75; © Klaus Tiedge/Corbis p87; © Stanislav Komogorov/ istockphoto.com p99; © Justin Kase zsixz/Alamy p114; Ricky John Molloy/Getty Images p119; Frantzesco Kangaris/Bloomberg News/Getty Images p122; Tony Metaxas/Getty Images p127; © Dennis MacDonald/Alamy p138; ©James Steidl/iStockphoto.com p153; © Chris Howes/Wild Places Photography/Alamy p175; ©Photodisc/Getty Images p178; © irishphoto.com/Alamy p184; © Comstock Images/ Photolibrary Group Ltd p187; © Tim Scrivener/Alamy p189; © Catherine Yeulet/iStockphoto.com p195; Alex Segre/Alamy p203; Shizuo Kambayashi/AP/Press Association Images p211; Jupiterimages/Getty Images p215; Comet p217; © Ingram Publishing Limited p225; © Robert Stainforth/Alamy p244; © Bananastock/Photolibrary Group Ltd p249; Lewis Stickley/ PA Archive/Press Association Images p250; © Errol Rait/Alamy p253; © PSL Images/Alamy p261; Johannes Kroemer/Getty Images p264l; Johnny Green/PA Wire/Press Association Images p276; © StephenBarnes Cars and Transport/Alamy p285; Tim Rooke/Rex Features p292; Pete Norton/ Getty Images p293; © Sebastian Duda/iStockphoto.com p301; comparethemarket.com p304; Chris Ratcliffe/Rex Features p310; © jamalludin din - Fotolia.com p338; PA Archive/Press Association Images p343; © Sue Cunningham Photographic/Alamy p349; © Picture Contact/Alamy p352; © Mark Bassett/Alamy p356; © Nicholas Sutcliffe/istockphoto.com p366; © British Retail Photography / Alamy p367; Matthew Fearn/PA Archive/Press Association Images p382l; Doug Peters/Doug Peters/ EMPICS Entertainment p382r; © B. O'Kane/Alamy p386; © Lenscap/Alamy p394; © Keith Morris/ Alamy p395; © 2010 Innocent p409.

Key: l = left, r = right

The authors and publishers are grateful to the following for permission to reproduce copyright material:

© Sunday Times 2009 / nisyndication.com p75; www.bettersoccercoaching.com p128; Plain English Campaign p182; RRC Training p190; © The Times 2008 / nisyndication.com p199; Best Companies Ltd p208; © The Times 2004 / nisyndication.com p219; The John Lewis Partnership p261: The Trafford Centre p265; Haymarket Business Publications Limited p309; B&Q p341; © Guardian News & Media Ltd 2009 p342; © Telegraph Media Group Limited 2009 p343; © Crown Copyright material is reproduced with the permission of the controller of HMSO.

Every effort has been made to trace and acknowledge ownership of copyright. The publishers will be glad to make suitable arrangements with any copyright holders it has not been possible to contact.

Unit 1

Business purposes

Chapter 1
The purpose and ownership of business

What are you finding out?

Nike and Timberland make shoes, Mars and Cadbury make chocolate and sweets, Oxfam is a charity providing famine relief. You will have heard of all or at least most of these organisations, but what exactly do they do and who owns them? In this chapter you will find out that organisations can have very different purposes. For example, Nike makes large profits from producing training shoes. In contrast, Oxfam doesn't seek to make a profit but to make money from its shops and donations from the public to relieve famine across the globe.

This unit explains the purposes of the main types of organisations in Britain and classifies them – for example, are they local, national or global, and are they are large or small? The unit also looks at the context in which business organisations operate, explaining how government affects business and how other factors such as the growth of new industries affect individual organisations.

This chapter will help you to:

- Understand the purpose and ownership of business.

Business purposes

The purpose of *Hello!* magazine is to provide a colourful, popular magazine with lots of articles about celebrity lifestyles.

The purpose of Walkers (crisps) is to provide convenient snack foods.

The purpose of Ryanair is to be Europe's number-one low-cost airline.

The purpose of HBOS is to be the world's leading bank, meeting the needs of business and private customers.

These organisations supply goods and services – crisps, cheap air travel and bank accounts. They usually do so at a profit.

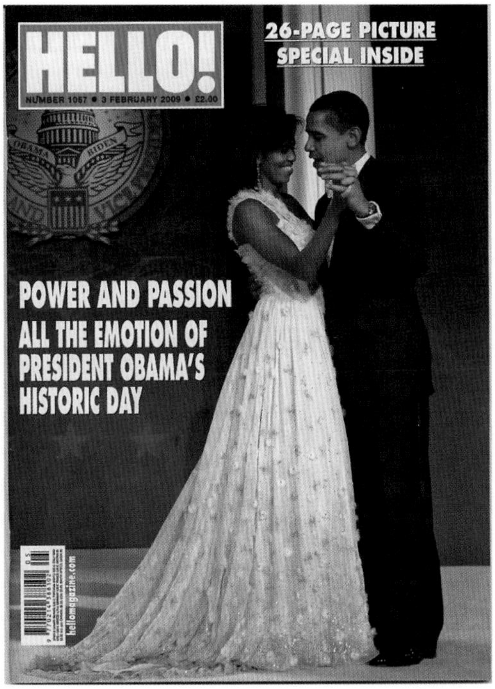

Hello! is a good example of a business that makes a profit.

In 2007 *Hello!* magazine made a profit of just over £850,000. In 2008 *Hello!* made a smaller profit of just over £700,000.

Task

What reasons can you think of that might have led *Hello!*'s profit to fall between 2007 and 2008?

What is a profit?

You might have thought that the profits at *Hello!* had fallen because it sold fewer magazines. However, this was not the case. In fact sales had increased by 3.3%.

In 2007 the money that *Hello!* made from selling magazines and money received from advertisers was £35.8 million. In 2008 this rose to £37 million.

So how does *Hello!* make a profit and what caused the profit to fall between 2007 and 2008?

To produce magazines like *Hello!* a company needs to:

- Employ journalists and photographers to prepare stories and to take photographs. It also needs an editor to put the stories in shape, working with page designers who lay out the pages. *Hello!* employs about 50 people.
- Pay a printing company to print the magazine and another company to transport the magazine to newsagents.

In addition, *Hello!* has to pay out other expenses to run the business, for example, electricity and gas bills, and the cost of renting offices.

You can now see how *Hello!* makes a profit by looking at the table below, which shows how a profit was made in 2008. It shows that the figure for profit is arrived at by taking away all the costs of preparing, printing and running the magazine from the value of the sales made during 2008.

Value of sales and advertising	Costs: wages, printing and transport, plus other expenses	Profit = Sales *minus* Costs
£37m	£36.3m	£37m – £36.3 m = £700,000

From these figures you can see how difficult it is to make a profit. The figure for profit is a lot lower than the money coming into the business.

(The reason why *Hello!*'s profits fell between 2007 and 2008 was that the costs of producing *Hello!* increased by more than the increase in sales and advertising.)

1. How much did *Hello!*'s sales and advertising receipts increase by between 2007 and 2008?
2. Can you calculate how much the costs increased by between 2007 and 2008? Explain how you worked this out.
3. What factors might affect *Hello!*'s ability to make a profit in 2009?
4. Why is it important for an organisation like *Hello!* to make a profit?

Why else do businesses supply goods and services?

Hello! is an example of a for-profit business. But not all businesses set out to make a profit. The main types of businesses are:

Not all businesses try to make a profit. Sometimes they have other motives.

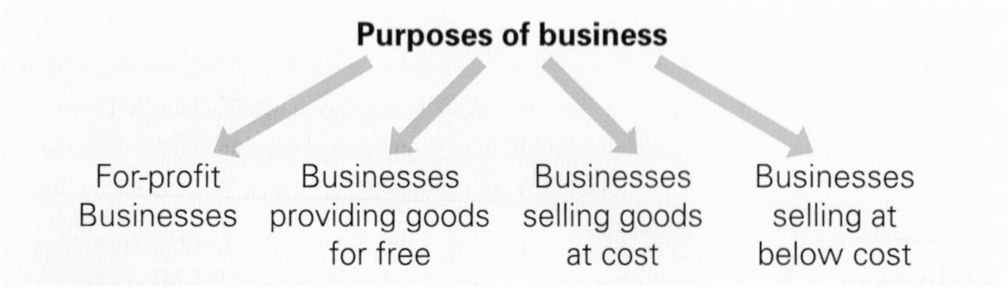

Figure 1.1 Purposes of business

Wikipedia

Wikipedia is an example of something that is provided for free. Wikipedia is a free online encyclopaedia. It was launched by an American called Jimmy Wales in 2001. The idea of the website was that anybody could contribute an article anywhere in the world. Anyone else could then add to the articles that are there. The idea was to create an online 'book' which would enable all human knowledge to be stored. People who work for Wikipedia are volunteers who give up their own time to produce something worthwhile rather than expecting to be paid.

1. Why do you think that some people set up organisations for purposes other than to make a profit?
2. What do you think that Jimmy Wales and people who make entries to Wikipedia get out of doing something that is not focused on profit?
3. What is a volunteer? Can you think of other organisations that depend on volunteers?
4. What sorts of activities would you be prepared to volunteer to do for the community?

There are many other products and services that are provided for free. A good example is soup-runs to feed the homeless on the streets of London and other large cities. Again, these services are provided by volunteers. Another example, is the **Samaritans,** a charity aimed at providing support for people who are contemplating experiencing feelings of distress or despair, including those which could lead to suicide. The Samaritans runs a 24-hour telephone helpline.

Rather than providing goods and services for free, an organisation could supply them at cost. Here an organisation would be seeking just to cover its costs.

For example, a community centre in a local village may organise a children's Christmas party at cost. The organisers work out that the cost of hiring a children's entertainer, buying in party food, buying presents for all the children and paying for the lighting and heating of the hall would come to £500. There are 50 children coming to the party, so the price charged for each child is £10.

Cost = £500

Money charged = £10 x 50 children.

Finally, a business may provide goods and services at below cost price. The business can do this only if the loss that it makes is covered by some other form of income.

Did you know...

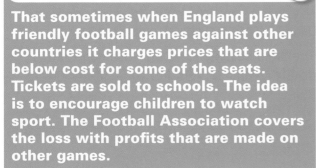

That sometimes when England plays friendly football games against other countries it charges prices that are below cost for some of the seats. Tickets are sold to schools. The idea is to encourage children to watch sport. The Football Association covers the loss with profits that are made on other games.

Who owns that business?

For-profit businesses

Have you ever wondered who owns M&S, or Tesco or Coca-Cola? These are well-known names that we are familiar with.

Today these businesses are owned by lots of different people called shareholders. Each shareholder is a part-owner of the business depending on how many shares they have. This type of business is called a plc.

Originally, however, large companies were usually set up by just one or a small number of people. M&S, for example, was started by Michael Marks who was a door-to-door seller of items that he charged only a penny for. The items included needles and thread, which he sold from a tray that he carried round with him. Jack Cohen, the founder of Tesco, was a market trader.

Sole traders are businesses owned by just one person. Working on their own, they make all the decisions themselves but they are able to take all of the profit. However, they only have a limited amount of funds to buy stock and premises.

Michael Marks eventually joined together with a partner, Tom Spencer. The two of them had more capital and could share out the jobs involved in running the business. Eventually they were able to run a number of market stalls in Leeds and the north of England. Eventually they bought their first shop.

A partnership usually involves the partners putting together a partnership contract that is kept by a solicitor. It sets out who is responsible for what in the business and how the profits will be shared. Partnerships usually consist of between two and 20 partners. Your local GP surgery is probably a partnership, and probably your vet and your dentist. Solicitors form partnerships, as do accountants. Builders and other groups of self-employed people may operate as partnerships.

Limited companies

Sole traders and partnerships are a good way of setting up a small local business. However, if you want to expand further afield you will need more funds. A good way of getting these funds is to invite other people to put money into your business. As we saw earlier, they are called shareholders.

Shareholders will be keen to enter your business if they think that it will be successful and make a profit. They will be reluctant to join if they stand to make losses when the business does badly.

To look after the interests of shareholders there is a legal protection called **limited liability**. A liability is a debt owed by one person or organisation to another. Limited liability limits the amount that a shareholder needs to pay out when a company makes a loss. Their liability is limited to the sum they have invested in shares in a business. This is very important. If I buy £500 worth of shares in a well-known company and it unfortunately 'goes bust', owing millions of pounds, all I will lose is a maximum of £500. In technical terms my liability is limited to £500.

All companies in Britain have limited liability and this is why shareholders are willing to buy shares.

There are two types of companies:

- Private limited companies (these have Ltd after their name)
- Public limited companies (these have plc after their name).

Private companies are ones where shares are sold privately only. Shareholders in the company choose a board of directors to run the business. The directors make day-to-day decisions. The directors choose a managing director who is the key day-to-day decision maker.

The board of directors decides who else can buy shares in the company. The board therefore has control over who owns the business. They will not sell shares to people who pose a threat to them. Private companies often start off as family

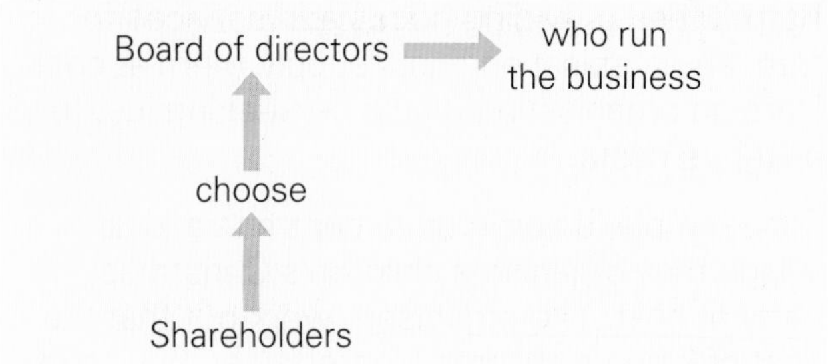

Figure 1.2 How a private company operates

businesses before bringing in trusted outsiders. Private companies can be very large. Some of the largest private companies in Britain include Iceland, Monsoon Accessorize, Fitness First, Alliance Boots and Countrywide (estate agents) – these companies all have Ltd after their names to show they are privately owned businesses.

When a company decides to expand further it may need to increase the number of shareholders. It can do so by becoming a public limited company (plc). Shares in a public company can be bought freely through the Stock Exchange and from other sellers of shares. For example, you could buy shares in a company simply by going into your bank. You can buy shares online.

The table below shows the advantages and disadvantages of different types of business organisation.

Sole trader	Partnership	Private company	Public company
Advantages			
Makes all the decisions	Usually between two and 20 partners	Can raise capital from shareholders	Can raise capital from a very large number of shareholders
Takes all the profits	More capital than sole trader	Directors decide who can be a shareholder	Shares are traded on the Stock Exchange
Easy to set up	Partners have different skills	Has limited liability	Name of the company widely known and has limited liability
Disadvantages			
No limited liability	Still quite small	Usually has access to less funding than a plc	Can be taken over by other people than the original owners
Only limited capital	Partners have to share profits	Requires quite a lot of paperwork to set up	Size may make it difficult to manage
Sole traders have to do all the management jobs themselves	Partners can fall out		A lot of paperwork and reports have to be produced

Figure 1.3 Advantages and disadvantages of different types of business organisation

Not-for-profit businesses

Charities and voluntary organisations

Two of the best-known types of not-for-profit organisations are charities and voluntary organisations. These organisations are not owned by anyone. They are supervised by trustees and volunteers.

To become a charity an organisation has to register with the Charity Commission. It will be recognised as a charity only if it meets one or more of a set number of purposes, which include:

- The relief of poverty
- The advancement of education
- The advancement of religion
- The advancement of health or the saving of lives
- The advancement of citizenship or community development
- The advancement of arts, culture, heritage or science
- The advancement of amateur sport
- The advancement of human rights
- The advancement of environmental protection or improvement
- The advancement of animal welfare.

The charity needs to demonstrate that its work will benefit the public.

A charity appoints trustees to manage and run the organisation. By law, trustees should not benefit financially from the charity unless the rules of the charity specifically state how. Trustees of a charity do not have limited liability. A charity needs to have a set of rules governing how it will run.

Activity

To find out more about how an organisation becomes a charity go to the Charity Commission website www.charity-commission.gov.uk. In particular look at the section of notes on 'registering as a charity'.

Examples of charities include:

- Children in Need
- Oxfam
- The Red Cross and Red Crescent.

Voluntary organisations

Voluntary organisations are ones that are made up of unpaid volunteers. Examples of voluntary organisations are the Alzheimer's Society, helping older people with dementia, and the Women's Royal Voluntary Service (WRVS). The Alzheimer's Society is both a voluntary society run by volunteers and also has charitable status, making it is a cross between a voluntary society and a charity. Branches of the WRVS can be found all over Britain and are made up of women who carry out a range of projects in local communities, such as visiting the elderly and helping with environmental projects. In addition, the WRVS provides a meeting place for women who organise a range of social events, competitions and talks on informative issues.

The differences between a voluntary organisation and a charity are listed below:

Voluntary organisation	Charity
	Registered with the Charity Commission
Run by unpaid volunteers	While it may have some volunteers, it also has many paid employees
Often less business-like in the way that it is organised	Nowadays, charities are highly organised along business lines

Charities and voluntary organisations do not make profits. When their income is greater than their costs, this leads to a surplus. The surplus is kept within the organisation for use in future years.

Cooperatives

Cooperatives are owned by cooperators.

The key to understanding cooperatives is the idea of **mutuality.**

- Cooperatives set out to provide mutual (shared) benefits to their members, i.e. cooperators.
- Cooperators work together at a task for their joint benefit.

Did you know...

That some of the first cooperatives in Britain were retail cooperatives. The first one to set up in Britain opened in Rochdale in Lancashire in 1844. Up to then workers in the local cotton mills were being paid in tokens, which they had to spend in mill-company shops where prices were high. A group of cooperators therefore joined together to set up their own shop. They bought the stock together and shared the profits out among themselves.

Activity

Carry out a search on Wikipedia using the term 'Rochdale Pioneers'. Find out who the pioneers were and what their objectives were in setting up the first cooperative retail society.

Today there are still lots of co-op shops in Britain. Most of these are small neighbourhood shops, although there are some giant supermarkets. The profits from these organisations are shared out among shoppers in the form of lower prices.

Another example of a cooperative is an agricultural co-op. Here farmers join together. They may help each other out at harvest time. They will send their crops to a cooperative warehouse. The cooperative will sell the produce to supermarkets on behalf of all the farmers. The farmers share out the money the cooperative makes according to how much they supply to the cooperative.

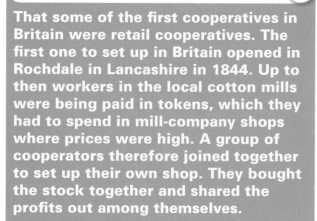

Retail co-ops	Wholesale co-ops
Shoppers are the cooperators and share the profits	Cooperative wholesalers buy goods from suppliers. The retail co-ops own the retail wholesalers.
Worker cooperatives	**Agricultural cooperatives**
Owned by workers who manage and run their own business	Owned by farmers who pool their crops and sell them through the cooperative

Figure 1.4 Types of co-op

Government businesses

Business activity that is government run is defined as taking place in the public sector. This contrasts with private sector activity which is carried out by private business (sole traders, partners, companies, voluntary organisations and charities).

The government owns a number of businesses such as Her Majesty's Revenue and Customs (to collect tax). The government makes sure that these businesses are run in the interests of the wider community. Funding for these businesses comes partly from the sales that these businesses make but also from taxpayers. These businesses therefore need to run efficiently.

Some government businesses are set up as 'public corporations', i.e. businesses run in the public interest. An example is the British Broadcasting Corporation – the BBC. The BBC is expected to provide high-quality news and programmes. Its funds come from producing films and programmes for sale to other television networks, and from the fees paid by television licence holders. If you have a television, you (or someone else in your house) will have to pay this fee each year.

In Britain today the government has far fewer public corporations than 20 years ago. Instead it has created public–private partnerships (PPPs). This is where government provides funds to businesses to run services on its behalf. High standards must be met by the private company to keep the government contract. An example of a PPP activity is the contract to maintain the London Underground.

Size of business

Businesses can be classified by size – small, medium and large. There are various ways of classifying business in this way:

1. By number of employees. In the European Union a business is defined as small if it has fewer than 50 employees. Using this definition, 99.3% of all British businesses are small. Medium-sized businesses are defined as having between 50 and 249 employees. Businesses with 250 or above employees are defined as large. The European Union also defines micro-businesses as having fewer than 10 employees.
2. Another way of defining small, medium and large would be by the value of sales a business makes in a given year.

Task

Classify the following businesses by size. The local newsagent employs two part-timers who work shifts two days a week, as well as four young people to deliver newspapers in the morning. In May, 2009 Shell UK employed 9,000 people in the UK and 104,000 around the globe.

Activity

How many people does your school or college employ? What size of enterprise would it be classified as?

Make the grade

P1 **P2** (This tip is designed to help you to show evidence of meeting P1 and P2.) Select and describe four different businesses to look at for purposes of comparison. One of these should be a very small local business such as a restaurant, café or newsagent. Another should be a partnership e.g. a vets', GPs' or builders' partnership. A third should be a very large public company that you can investigate on the internet, e.g. Unilever, Tesco, M&S. For small businesses you should research by speaking directly to the owner or writing a polite letter. Find out how many people are employed in the business, the area that customers come from, whether the organisation is part of something larger, the form of the organisation, e.g. sole trader, partnership, etc. Show how the type of business relates to size and scale.

Make the grade

M1 You should select two distinct businesses to compare to achieve M1. Find out what the purposes of these businesses are and who owns them. It would be helpful to make a contrast, e.g. between a small local and a large global business. You could also contrast not-for-profit and for-profit business.

The scale of business

Where do businesses operate? Do they just operate in your town or are they part of a much bigger company operating in a wider geographical area?

Next time you visit a large shopping centre in your nearest city, notice how many of the businesses situated there are not local businesses.

A local business is one that serves local customers only, e.g. people who live in part of Derby, such as a small corner shop or newsagents. The business is likely to have been set up by the owner using personal funds, as well as money borrowed from banks, family and friends.

A regional business is one that serves people in a particular geographical region, e.g. the north west of Britain, central Scotland, etc. There will be a number of businesses operating in your county or region; examples will include a regional hotel chain, regional newspaper or radio service. The business will operate on a regional basis for one of two major reasons:

- Because it is possible to control a business on this scale. It is possible for the management to keep in personal contact with local managers. Anything larger would require too much time and effort to control.
- The business is able to offer a product or service that appeals specifically to people living in a particular region, e.g. food targeted at local tastes, or news and programmes targeted at local populations (newspapers, radio and television).

Fieldwork

1. Make a list of 20 major stores and premises that you find in your nearest local town.
2. Classify these stores and premises according to the type of activity, e.g. clothes shop, café, bookshop, hairdresser, etc.
3. Identify whether they are one-off outlets or part of a larger chain. Research three or four of the chains on the internet to find out whether they also operate in other countries.

Types of business in the Westfield Centre

Westfield shopping centre

In the Westfield Centre in Derby there are a number of coffee shops, hairdressers, clothes shops, shops selling mobile phones, and restaurants. However, most of these – Monsoon, Costa Coffee, Starbucks, Toni & Guy, Zara, Topshop, Nando's, O2 – are part of large retail chains that you can find not only in shopping centres in Britain, but in many parts of Europe, the United States and the wider world. To find smaller local businesses in Derby you have to step outside the Westfield Centre – independent cafés, hairdressers, motor garages, bicycle shops and many others.

1. Are the retail outlets in your local shopping centre one-off stores or part of a larger chain?
2. Why do you think that shopping centres are dominated by chain stores?

A national business (in the case of a British business) is one whose market covers all or most of Britain. The business specifically limits itself to operating within the national market. Advantages of doing so are that the business is familiar with customer needs and requirements, no international paperwork or foreign currency exchange is involved, and distances to market are much lower.

Other businesses grow to become European businesses. They sell to many other countries within Europe. Britain is part of the European Union. This is a group of 27 countries (in 2009) containing about 500 million people. There are no taxes on British goods sold to these countries. The European Union is the best market for British-produced goods.

Many of the major brands that you are familiar with are produced by global companies. A global business is one that has operating units such as factories and retail outlets spread across a number of continents and whose products and services are recognised in most major cities across the globe. Examples of global companies are Shell and BP (oil, gas and petrol), Nestlé (food and health products), and Cadbury (chocolate, chewing gum, sweets). Global companies set out to gain customers across the globe and are able to spread costs (such as the cost of making an advertisement) over their sales of products across the globe.

Figure 1.5 Types of business

Did you know...

There are various levels of government business activity ranging from local to national activity. For example, your local government will either directly run or pay contractors to run services such refuse collection and street maintenance. National government organisations are responsible for the postal service run through the Post Office, as well as maintenance of rail track.

Classification of business

A useful way of classifying businesses is according to whether they are:

- **Primary businesses** – extracting raw materials.
- **Secondary businesses** – making finished goods.
- **Tertiary businesses** – providing a service for other businesses and for households.

Primary businesses

Primary businesses are at the first stage of production. They extract raw materials which will then often go into manufacturing goods. These businesses work in industries which include farming, forestry, fishing, mining and oil drilling. Farmers grow and harvest crops and farm livestock, while miners take out fuel and minerals from the ground.

Primary industries sometimes produce raw materials like iron ore (for making steel) and oil (for making petrol, plastics, etc.). Primary industries also produce final products such as fish or strawberries.

Secondary businesses

Secondary businesses are concerned with making and assembling products. Manufacturers (makers) use raw materials and parts from other industries. A semi-manufactured good is one that is only partly made. Most products go through several stages of production. Examples of manufactured products are iPods, muesli bars and lorries. Engineering is a good example of secondary industry. Engineers use maths, science, creativity and design to solve problems. Engineers work in many different industries, as shown in the table below.

Industry	Type of engineering work
Aerospace engineering	e.g. designing and building an aeroplane or spacecraft
Chemical engineering	e.g. refining oil into petrol
Civil engineering	e.g. designing and building a bridge or road
Electrical engineering	e.g. designing electrical systems for a classroom
Computer engineering	e.g. improving internet search engines
Mechanical engineering	e.g. designing an engine for a high-speed train

Construction is another important secondary industry involved with the building of houses, shops, factories and many other buildings.

Tertiary businesses

Tertiary (also called service) businesses are particularly important in Britain today. Services give something of value to people, but are not physical goods. You can physically touch or see a sandwich, a car or a television set. You cannot touch or hold life insurance, a visit to the cinema or the protection offered by the police. These are all services. Other examples are banks and public transport.

Make the grade

M1 This tip enables you to cover M1. When you compare two contrasting business organisations, make sure that the contrast is as wide as possible. For example, it wouldn't be a good idea to compare Sainsbury's with Morrison's because they are too similar – they are food retailers, public limited companies and have similar market shares. You will be much better off comparing quite different organisations, e.g. a small organisation in the voluntary sector with a large multinational company.

It is possible to classify services according to who provides the service:

	Service provider		
	Private services	Public services	Volunteer/not-for-profit services
Description	Services provided by business with the intention of making a profit	Services provided by local and national government bodies	Services provided by the not-for-profit sector
Examples	Insurance, banking, car wash, cinema, estate agent	Bin collection, education (in the public sector), police and ambulance services	Home help, advice centres, somewhere to meet (e.g. for the lonely and homeless)

Key words

Business purpose – What a business is there to do – e.g. to grow fruit (a fruit farm), manufacture crisps, build bridges, sell insurance, etc.

Company – An organisation set up for a specific purpose. The company is separate in law from its owners.

Charity – An organisation that has registered with the Charity Commission to carry out defined charitable purposes such as to provide education or relieve poverty.

Not-for-profit organisation – One that seeks to operate as near to cost as possible and which does not make or distribute profit to those involved in the organisation.

Revenue – Money receipts from sales and other activities.

Shareholders – Part-owners of a company. They benefit by receiving a share of the company profit.

Assignment for Unit 1 – part 1

You need to demonstrate that you understand the ownership and purposes of and differences between the main types of business organisation in Britain.

You have been asked to provide a guide for potential owners of new businesses and those thinking of investing in existing businesses. This should explain how businesses are classified into sectors and how business purposes vary, as well as differences in scale and legal ownership. Make sure to explain the ownership and purpose of multinational businesses. Set out brief case studies of local, national and international businesses.

Part 2 of this assignment appears at the end of Chapter 2. In your assessment you will need to be able to do the following:

To achieve a pass grade you need to:	To achieve a merit grade you need to:	To achieve a distinction you need to:
P1 identify the purpose of four different business organisations	**M1** contrast the ownership and purposes of two different business organisations	
P2 describe the different types of business ownership, linking this to the size and scale of four different organisations		
P3 explain how businesses are classified, using local and national examples		

Chapter 2
The business context in which organisations operate

What are you finding out?

The business context consists of things outside the business that influence the decisions that it makes. This chapter looks at two of the main components of this business context:

1. The way in which government affects business through its handling of the economy.
2. Changes that are taking place that affect business.

The first part of the chapter examines the way in which government affects business. The second part looks at the impact on business of some important changes in the business environment.

This chapter will help you to:

- Understand the business context in which organisations operate.

Role of government

It is helpful to first look at the role of government in influencing business. There are three layers of government that affect British business:

1. European Union government – decisions made by the European Commission, Council of Ministers and European Parliament, the three main EU decision-making bodies.
2. National government – decisions made by Britain's government and approved in the House of Commons.
3. Local government – the local council in your area.

The table below shows the part played by government in making decisions at different levels by showing the types of rules made at each of the three levels. It also gives some examples of the rules and laws that affect business.

Government consists of groups of people who have been chosen by voters to represent them. These representatives are chosen at three levels:

1. **European Union level.** Britain is a member of the European Union. The EU consists of 27 other countries or 'member states'. The member states have given the decision-making bodies in the EU powers to pass laws and make decisions that affect businesses in every EU country. For example, there are rules governing the minimum wage and the maximum number of hours employees can work in a given time period. Some of the rules made within the European Union allow some countries to 'opt out'. For example, Britain chose not to enter the eurozone (countries using the euro).
2. **National level.** The British government creates rules, including laws, about what businesses can and cannot do. For example, companies and charities must register before they can begin their operation. There are laws about how they should treat consumers and employees. In Wales, Scotland and Northern Ireland, there are regional assemblies that also make important decisions that affect business in these countries.
3. **Local level.** At a local level, citizens can vote for local representatives – referred to as councillors. Local councils raise money from business property and private housing in the form of rates. The local council passes local laws, for example about Sunday trading in local markets, and road use.

Government	At European Union level	At national level	At local level
Makes decisions ...	Regulations and other rules are created by European Union decision-making bodies	Laws created by Parliament	Local rules created by local councils
... that affect business	For example, setting a minimum wage that businesses must pay their employees, setting out pollution controls and environmental standards that must be met	For example, setting out how businesses and charities must register and the paperwork they have to create	For example, covering opening hours of nightclubs and discotheques

Figure 2.1 Role of government

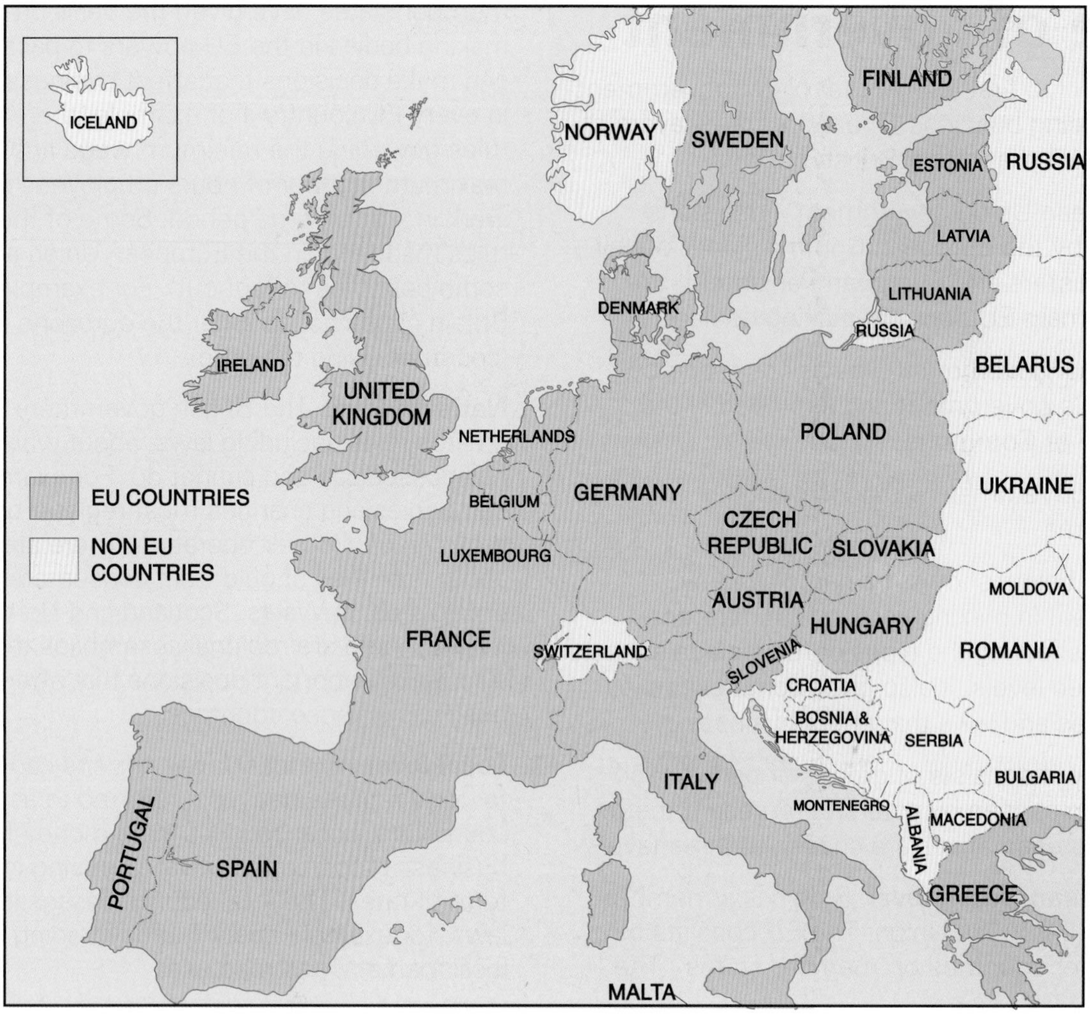

Figure 2.2 The European Union

> **Did you know...**
>
> **That in Britain the political party with the most elected Members of Parliament can form the government. It proposes new laws which have to be voted on and approved by Parliament.**

Government policies and actions

Government policies and actions affect business in many different ways. For example, government spending on a particular activity can help a business to be successful – e.g. when a bed manufacturer wins a contract to supply beds to the National Health Service. In Britain the government produces thousands of pages of rules each year setting out what businesses can and cannot do. These rules are called regulations. To see how government affects business it is helpful to examine some major government policies and activities:

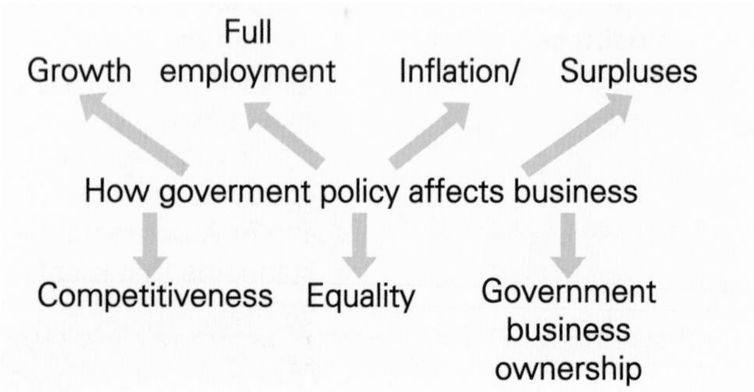

Figure 2.3 How government policy affects business

The economy consists of four main groups: government, businesses, employees (people who work for businesses) and consumers (people who buy goods). There is considerable overlap between these four groups.

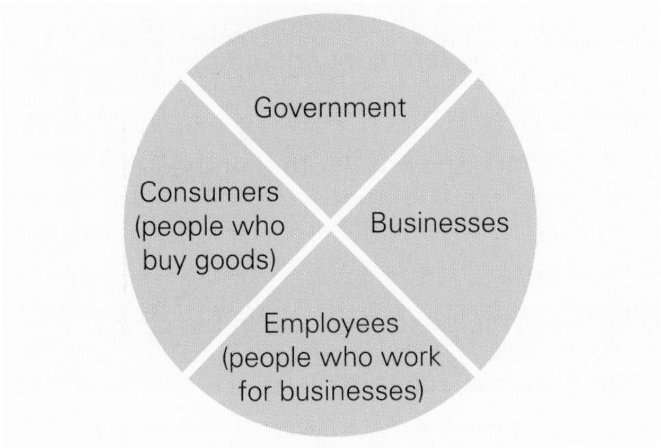

Figure 2.4 The four main groups in the economy

Government economic policy is designed to provide the best possible economic environment for each of these groups. In this unit we are particularly interested in how government policy affects business. Government policy affects business in each of the following areas:

Growth

Government policy seeks to grow the economy. Growth refers to increases in the total number of goods produced. The more goods that are produced, the more people are employed. They earn more income. They spend more, and so on. Growth is measured by GDP – gross domestic product.

GDP = The total value of goods produced in a country in a given year.

The government works closely with business to try and create policies for growth, e.g. trying to make sure that business taxes are not too harsh for small businesses, and providing grants for certain business activities such as investing in new technologies.

Local government seeks to encourage growth of local business, for example by creating new development sites for new factory, office and retail building.

Growth of GDP in the UK 2007–09

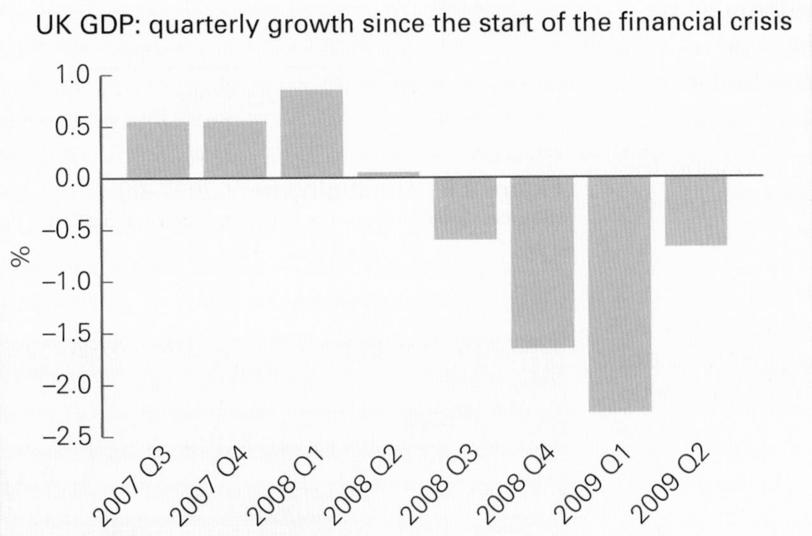

Figure 2.5 Growth of GDP in the UK 2007–09

Figure 2.5 shows changes in Britain's GDP between 2007 and 2009. This was a period of real concern for the government. In 2007 GDP was growing. People in Britain were better off and more goods were bought and sold. However, in 2008 there was a financial crisis when people around the world lost confidence in the banking system. Banks cut back lending to business. Businesses cut back on the quantities of goods they made and sold and laid off workers. The British government stepped in to try and halt this fall in GDP. The government invested billions of pounds into British banks in return for shares. The government encouraged banks to start lending again to businesses that were suffering.

1. What does the chart show happened to GDP in the periods shown? (Note that the chart divides years into three-month periods – quarters.)
2. Why is a fall in GDP a bad thing for business?
3. What is economic growth? Was the economy growing in the periods shown in the chart?
4. Why does the government get involved in trying to grow the economy?

Activity

Look through national and local papers to find examples where national and local government are encouraging business development in your local area. How are they encouraging business? Make notes of this to support your assignment tasks.

Full employment

Full employment exists in an economy when everyone who wants a job is employed. Availability of jobs is closely related to the growth of the economy.

The chart shows that 8% of people looking for jobs in the UK were unemployed by the period May–July 2009.

The problem of rising unemployment for business is that as people lose jobs there is less spending in the economy. On the positive side, it is easier for business to find employees with suitable skills to work for them.

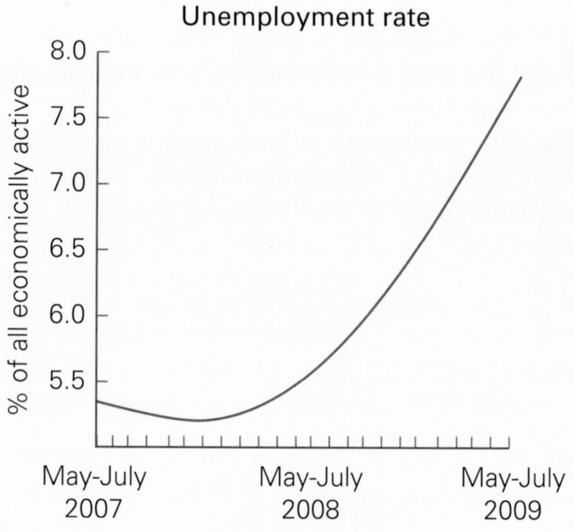

Figure 2.6 Unemployment 2007–09
(**Source**: Adapted from the Office for National Statistics figures)

Did you know...

That creating jobs is a major government policy. During periods of high unemployment the government will increase its own spending to try and provide work in the public sector. Government also provides grants and business advice available to businesses so that they can create more jobs.

Activity

What is the current level of unemployment in the UK? Go to National Statistics Online and then click on the theme Economy on the left-hand side of your screen. You can then choose Labour Market and from the sub-menu – People not in employment. From this you will be able to see the latest unemployment figures. Also take a look at what is happening to Youth Unemployment. How is the current level of unemployment likely to affect business?

Make the grade

P4 To achieve P4, your work needs to demonstrate that you recognise the role of government in creating a business climate through the use of incentives to business, such as cutting business taxes or providing local incentives such as regional development grants. A regional development grant is a sum of money made available by government to businesses, for example to create jobs in areas of high unemployment.

Inflation/deflation

Businesses make contracts to supply goods at a date in the future. This is easy to do when prices are stable or rising slowly at a predictable rate. It is a lot more difficult when prices are rising quickly and without a clear pattern of change.

Inflation refers to general increases in price levels in an economy. When there are general increases in price levels this can cause problems for business. Businesses can find that important costs are rising, e.g. the cost of raw materials or fuel. During periods of inflation employees will demand higher wages (again a cost for business).

One of the main government targets then is to try and make sure that inflation is kept under control.

In Britain inflation is measured by the Consumer Price Index (CPI). Changes in the CPI show changes in general price levels.

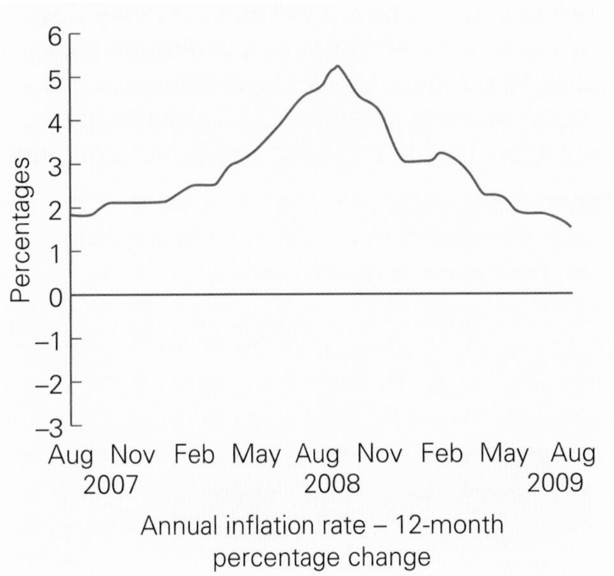

Figure 2.7 Annual inflation rate 2007–09

Figure 2.7 shows the CPI for the UK between August 2007 and August 2009. You can see that from August 2008, inflation had fallen from about 5% to under 2% by August 2009. Steady prices make it possible for businesses to make predictable contracts.

The reverse of inflation is deflation. This is when average prices start to fall. Whilst this may be a good thing for consumers, it is not good for business. Falling prices can lead to falling profits. Prices usually fall when consumers are not spending so much.

The ideal situation is therefore when prices are rising very slowly in a predictable way.

Activity

Find out what the current level of inflation in Britain is as measured by the CPI. What is the likely effect going to be on businesses in your local area?

Surpluses and deficits

A major way in which the government influences the economy is through its budget. The budget is a plan that the government makes each year. The plan sets out how the government will raise money and how it will spend money. The main way of collecting money is through taxes, including business taxes. Government spends money on many different activities including education, health, transport and the environment.

When the government spends more than it taxes, then it will run a deficit – putting more into the economy than it takes out.

When the government spends less than it taxes, then it runs a surplus.

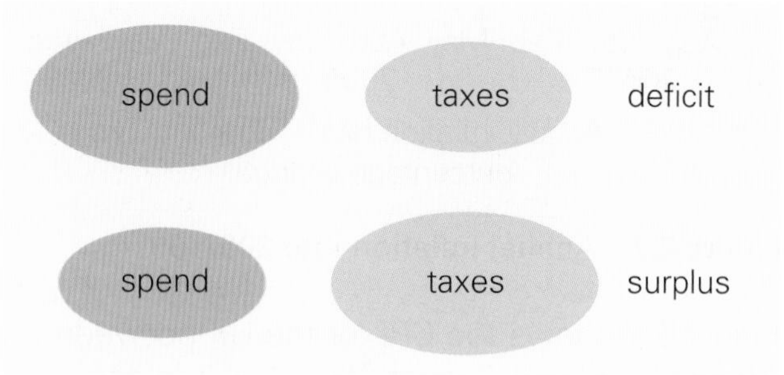

Figure 2.8 Deficit and surplus

Government surpluses and deficits have a knock-on effect for business. When the government runs a deficit it puts more money into the economy – so everyone has more to spend. For example, in the recession in 2009 the government ran huge deficits in an attempt to create more spending in the economy.

However, as we have seen, if there is too much spending in the economy this can cause inflation. At times like this it would make sense for the government to run a surplus to take some spending out of the economy.

Activity

Study national newspapers to find out whether the government is currently running a surplus or deficit. What are the likely effects for businesses in your area?

Competitiveness

It is important for Britain's businesses as a whole to be competitive. Competitive businesses are able to sell their goods and services overseas and at home in the face of competition from foreign firms.

The government supports business to be competitive in a number of ways, including:

1. By providing fast-moving motorways and train services.
2. By supporting the development of a new information technology structure including current efforts to improve broadband computer connections.
3. Through education and training initiatives.

The government is committed to creating a skilled workforce in order to make British business more competitive in world markets. An important part of this involves creating new vocational qualifications.

Did you know...

The Leitch Report published at the end of 2006 set targets that more than 90% of adults are skilled to GCSE level or to vocational equivalents by 2020. In addition, the number of apprenticeships would increase to 500,000 a year and 40% of the population would have a university degree by 2020.

Businesses are able to benefit from having suitably qualified employees.

Equality

Another government policy is to deal with issues of inequality. In Britain and other countries there is a substantial difference in income between the rich and the poor. Statistics produced by the government's Department for Work and Pensions in 2009 showed that inequality in Britain had risen in each year between 2006 and 2008, and that about 15% of state school pupils are now entitled to free meals because they come from low-income households.

Successive governments claim to be seeking to tackle inequality but the gap between the rich and the poor has continued to grow over the last 20 years. A government policy to reduce inequality is to tax people on higher incomes and businesses that make larger profits. Businesses sometimes see taxation as a burden. Some people argue that high taxes discourage business activity because they raise business costs. The money receipts from taxation are used to pay for services such as health, education and unemployment benefits. Taxes are one way of redistributing income from the rich to the poor.

Government business ownership

We saw earlier (page 9) that the government owns a number of businesses such as the Royal Mail and the BBC. The government appoints the BBC Trust with the responsibility for supervising the running of the BBC independently of direct interference by government.

We also mentioned private–public partnerships, which involve government and business working together.

Some public sector activities involve services provided directly by government departments – such as the Prison Service and Her Majesty's Revenue and Customs. Each year the government sets targets for its departments to meet.

The government can take over businesses when they get into trouble. For example, Railtrack, the company responsible for looking after Britain's railway lines and stations, was taken over by the government in 2007 because it was failing to keep up with the high quality standards required for the rail network.

The Forestry Commission

The Forestry Commission is a government department. It seeks 'to protect and expand Britain's forests and woodlands and to increase their value to society and the environment'. The Commission employs 3,000 staff.

The Forestry Commission contributes to wealth generation in many other industries. For every £1,000 raised from timber and forestry, another £3,000 is generated in the UK economy from associated products and services, for example, tourism, paper and food.

The Forestry Commission is a government department which seeks to protect and expand forests and woodlands. It employs 3,000 people.

1. Using the search term 'government department', see if you can find other examples of government departments.
2. Is the Forestry Commission a small, medium or large business? Explain your answer. What is the scale of operations for the Forestry Commission?
3. Why do you think that the Forestry Commission is run by the government rather than by a private business organisation?
4. What contribution does the Forestry Commission make to employment in the UK and to the growth of the UK economy?

Business environment

The business environment is made up of all the changes taking place outside a business that affect it. We have already seen that wider changes in the economy and the impact of government actions to control the economy are key influences. For example, in 2009 the government introduced a 'scrappage' scheme for cars older than ten years. People who traded in their old cars for new ones received a government payment of £1,000 matched by a further payment of £1,000 by the car retailer. This was part of a government initiative to increase spending on cars at a time of recession that was particularly hard-hitting for car manufacturers.

Trends

A trend is the general direction in which something tends to move over a period of time. For example, over the last 50 years there has been a general movement upwards in the GDP of the UK. In the shorter term, there are variations in the rate at which GDP grows. For example, in 2008 there was an economic recession. A recession occurs when there is a fall in GDP for two successive quarters (three-month periods). But generally over the period 1960–2010 there has been an upward trend in GDP.

In the previous section we identified the growth of the economy as being a major factor affecting business.

In examining the growth of the economy it is important to look at:

- changes in employment
- changes in income
- changes in output and spending

These are closely related.

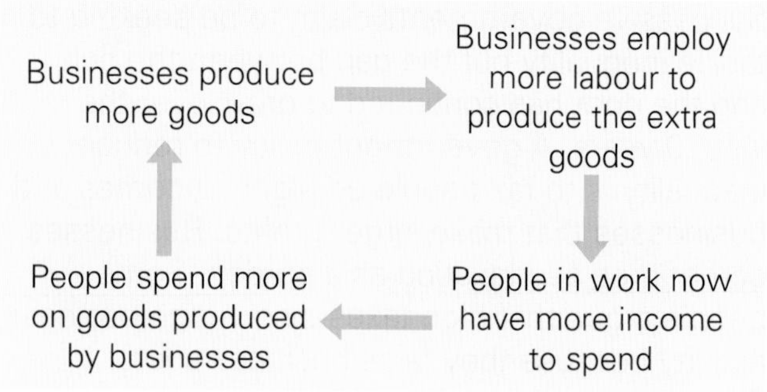

Figure 2.9 How growth affects the economy

It is therefore important to identify trends in GDP to find out whether the economy is growing or not.

Figure 2.10 illustrates the trend in GDP in the UK over the 50-year period leading up to 2008. What do you notice about the long-term trend?

Activity

What has been happening to GDP recently in the UK? Carry out some research in national newspapers to find a story about the growth of the economy and GDP. How is this likely to affect businesses? Also look at your local paper for stories about the growth of the local economy. What are job prospects like in your local area? Are people spending a lot of money in the shops – or are shops closing down?

Markets

All businesses need to have a good understanding of their market. A market is any situation in which buyers and sellers come into contact. This could be in a street market, a shopping centre or online retailers.

From the point of view of the individual business, the market consists of:

- other businesses that supply it with goods and services
- customers who buy their goods and services
- competitors with whom they compete to make sales.

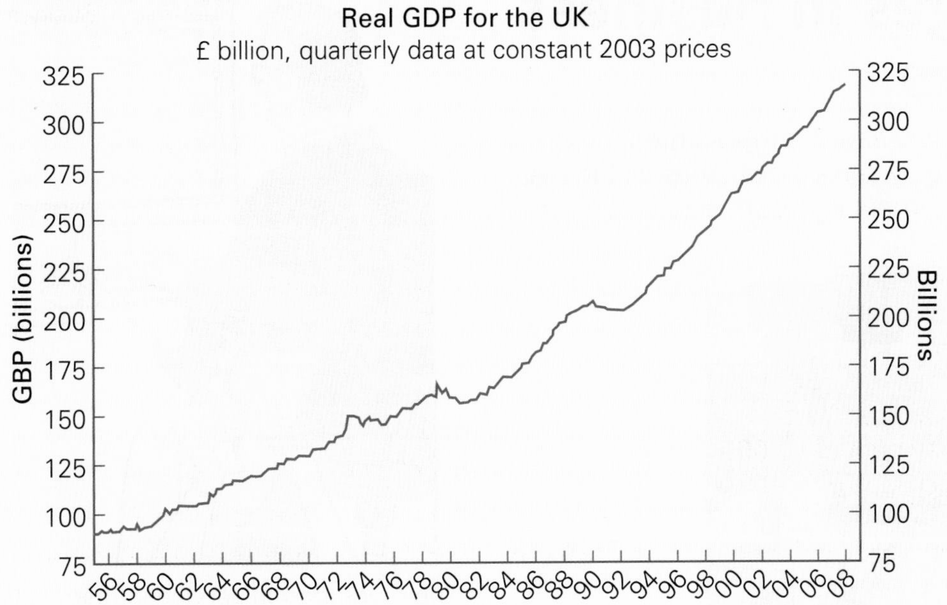

Figure 2.10 UK GDP from 1956–2008

Take, for example, your local Tesco supermarket. Managers there are concerned with getting supplies – e.g. fresh fruit and vegetables – often from local farmers, as well as branded goods from suppliers all over Britain. Managers are also concerned to provide the goods that shoppers are looking for, together with high-quality customer service. Managers also keep an eye out for the prices charged and offers made by their competitors – other supermarkets and other retailers.

Tesco is in direct competition with other supermarkets that supply a highly similar range of goods and services. They are in indirect competition with other retailers, e.g. clothing suppliers and delicatessens.

Tesco managers must constantly keep an eye on what rivals are offering to tempt customers away from them. At the same time, the managers must make sure that they keep in touch with customers and the types of things they are looking for. For example, Tesco has been very successful by offering a wide range of organic fruit and vegetables in line with the desires of many customers looking for healthy foods. Tesco's Computers for Schools campaign is also very successful. Shoppers are given vouchers that they can give to their local school, enabling the school to acquire computers.

Fieldwork

Working in a small groups, investigate a local business that operates in a competitive market. Which local businesses are competing directly and which indirectly in this market? Direct competition involves firms producing or selling similar or identical goods and services, e.g. two service stations that are close together. Indirect competition involves competitors who are competing for a slice of the consumer's spending but are producing different products. For example, a cinema is in indirect competition with a restaurant or night club. You can find out how competition affects a business either by observation or by talking to a manager at one of these competing organisations. How do the competitors compete in the market, for example, on price, range of products offered, or other aspects of competition? Write up your fieldwork in the form of a short report setting out how difficult it is for a local business to compete in the chosen market.

Changes in business sectors

The 20th century saw the replacement of manufacturing by service industries as the main type of employment in the UK economy.

The 20th century saw the decline of many of the UK's traditional heavy industries, leading to job losses in coal, shipbuilding, textiles, motor car manufacture, and many other industries.

There was a rise in service and leisure industries

The revolution in service industries has been accelerated by the use of ICT

At the same time as there were job losses in manufacturing, there were gains in the service industries such as retailing, hotel and catering work and the leisure industries.

These new service industries involve employees working closely with customers – for example, in face-to-face contacts, over the telephone and through electronic contacts such as email.

The revolution in the service industries has been speeded up by the use of information and communication technologies, which have helped to bring people into much closer contact than ever before.

Today it is common practice to refer to the 'new economy' as consisting of firms that make frequent use of internet technology and telecoms. Typical jobs in the new economy are desktop publishers, web designers and software architects, as well as call-centre workers and employees in leisure and health clubs.

UK employment

The table below compares UK employment in a range of industries in July 2007 and June 2009.

Industry	June 2007 (000s)	June 2009 (000s)
All	31,471	30,997
Agriculture, forestry and fishing	455	488
Mining, energy and water supply industries	187	191
Manufacturing industries	3,187	2,885
Construction	2,245	2,170
Distribution, hotels and restaurants	7,009	6,816
Transport and communications	1,849	1,854
Finance and business services	6,608	6,409
Education, health and public administration	7,954	8,193
Other services	1,976	1,991

The statistics outlined above are extracted from the Office of National Statistics, Labour Market Statistics for September 2009. They relate to a period in which the UK was experiencing a recession.

1. How many people were employed in services in 2009? You will need to total up this figure.
2. How did service-sector employment compare in terms of numbers employed in June 2009 with the remainder of the economy?
3. Give three examples of primary industries for which figures are shown in the table. How important was primary-sector employment in the UK economy?
4. In which industries did employment increase and in which industries did it decline between 2007 and 2009? Why do you think this was?

Make the grade

P5 **M2** **D1**

To achieve P5 you need to examine changes in employment, income and growth in the local economy. A good source of information for this will be your local newspaper, which will give an overview of how your local economy is changing and the types of new job opportunities that are available (as well as job losses). You local Job Centre will also provide you with details of current changes in the local labour market. The local Chamber of Commerce or Junior Chamber will provide details of prospects for business in your area. National labour market statistics showing growing and declining sectors of the economy are provided online by the Office for National Statistics, Labour Market Statistics, Table 5(2) Workforce jobs by industry.

To achieve M2 you need to look at how the national and local economies have changed over time. What have been the main trends in terms of economic growth (i.e. changes in GDP) and changes in numbers employed in different industries? To find out information about changes, carry out an internet search identifying Labour Market Statistics (available from the Office for National Statistics).

To achieve D1 you should look at how a particular business in your area has changed in response to the business environment. What changes have taken place in the business environment? Why have these changes come about? And how has this affected the business? For example, today's supermarkets have become one-stop shops, for food, petrol and a range of other items. This change has partly resulted from the way in which people like to shop today – getting all of their items cheaply in one big shop. However, there are other factors that have created this change, e.g. local planning authorities encouraging the development of new shopping areas in out-of-town development locations.

Did you know...

That in the north east of England many industries such as shipbuilding and coal went into decline in the 1970s and 1980s. National and local government provided incentives for the Japanese manufacturer Nissan to build a car plant there. This created a range of new businesses supplying services to the car plant, as well as creating jobs for Nissan workers.

Follow-up information

To research information about the economy, you should access:

- National Statistics Online. A particularly useful publication that you will be able to access electronically using this source is 'Labour Market Statistics'. You will be able to find out statistics related to employment and unemployment.
- In addition, if you access National Statistics Online, you can access data about GDP and growth. When you enter the National Statistics site you will see a menu on the left-hand side. Click on the heading National Accounts – this will show you details of National Income, Expenditure and Output.
- Also, if you click on Economy, you will be able to access figures for the Consumer Price Index (CPI).

Keywords

Budget deficit – Situation where the government spends more than it takes in tax revenues.

Budget surplus – Situation where the government raises more in taxes than it spends.

Consumer Price Index (CPI) – Method used to calculate the general increase in the level of prices.

Council of Ministers – Body made of up of senior politicians (Ministers) from the European Union countries.

Deflation – A general fall in the level of prices.

European Commission – Body made up of senior European Union politicians (commissioners) who are responsible for suggesting major EU laws in specific areas, e.g. education, health, etc.

European Parliament – An elected body made up of politicians selected by voters in particular regions of the European Union.

Full employment – A situation where everyone seeking work in a particular area is in employment.

Growth – Ongoing increases in GDP (gross domestic product) so that more goods are produced and more spending money is generated.

Inflation – A general increase in the level of prices.

Public sector – Part of the economy that is owned by the government on behalf of the population.

UK Parliament – The body responsible for making political decisions of national importance.

Assignment for Unit 1 – part 2

You need to demonstrate that you understand and can explain the various areas of growth and decline in the different sectors of the economy. Here you are simply required to examine areas of growth and decline in the primary, secondary and tertiary sectors. In addition, you should outline the impact of government decisions as a major external influence on business activity. Also, you need to explain changes taking place in your local business environment. To achieve a distinction grade you will need to evaluate how well one organisation has responded to the changing business environment.

In the guide that you have been preparing for local business owners you need to set out clear sections showing the evidence set out in the assessment grid below:

To achieve a pass grade you need to:	To achieve a merit grade you need to:	To achieve a distinction you need to:
P4 outline the role of government in creating the business climate	**M2** compare areas of growth or decline in the primary, secondary and tertiary classification of business activities	**D1** evaluate how an organisation has responded to changes in the business environment
P5 explain the characteristics of the local business environment		

Unit 2

Business organisations

Chapter 3
Setting business aims and objectives

What are you finding out?

We live in a world of organisations. They influence almost everything we do and are a very necessary part of our lives. For example, we may listen to the radio when we get up in the morning. Your breakfast might be cereal provided by a famous branded organisation. You might catch a bus to school or college. And, of course, your school or college is an organisation as well. These organisations have reasons for existing and these are represented through their aims and objectives.

This chapter will help you to:

- Understand about the aims and objectives of different kinds of business organisations.
- Understand the difference between an aim and an objective.
- Describe how the purposes of businesses relate to how they set aims and objectives.
- Write realistic aims and objectives for businesses.
- Compare the aims and objectives of different kinds of businesses.
- Make judgements about whether organisations are meeting their aims and objectives.

Aims and objectives

How often do you think about what you want to do when you leave school or college? You may want to stay on in education. You might want to get a job, take your driving test, or buy a flat and move away from home. If you are adventurous, you might want to go travelling. All of these are your personal aims. They are things that you want to work towards. In other words, they are your personal targets. To make them happen you will probably have to work very hard. That is simply your way of making your future happen.

It is possible to look at any organisation and think about what it is trying to achieve. Every organisation, by its very nature, exists to serve different groups of people. In serving these people, decision makers within an organisation need to think about how it serves them. In other words they need to set a direction: a way of making the future happen as they would like it. This would be where they would want to go.

Task

Think about the nature and type of aims and objectives that your school or college probably has.

1. **What is your school or college trying to achieve?**
2. **In what ways do the objectives of your school differ from the objectives of any other business?**
3. **How might the school measure whether it is achieving its objectives?**

The hierarchy of aims and objectives

One of the problems with discussing where an organisation wants to go is that different people and different organisations use different terms. One way of understanding the meaning of all of the words that are used to describe business objectives is to set them out in a **hierarchy**, which shows the relative meaning of each type of word or statement. At the top are the broader statements about where organisations wish to go. Then, as you go down the hierarchy, from a mission or vision to aims and objectives, each of the statements becomes more precise. This is because they begin to identify specific targets that organisations want to achieve. For example:

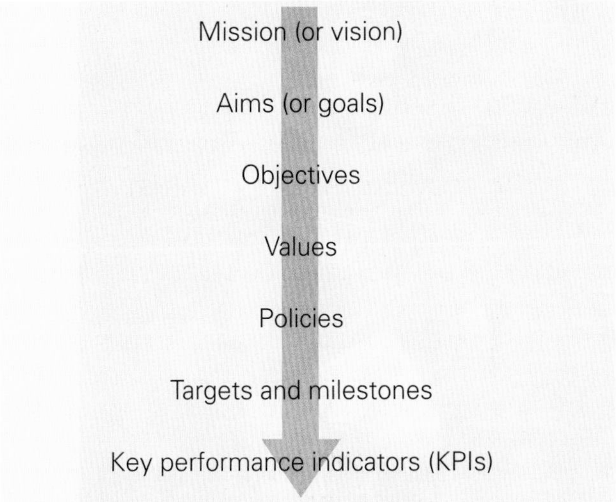

Figure 3.1 A hierarchy of business terms used for setting aims and objectives

Mission

A mission (or a vision) is a broad statement of where an organisation wants to go. Sometimes a vision or a mission might sound a bit idealistic. For example, Coca-Cola's mission is to:

- refresh the world
- inspire moments of optimism and happiness
- create value and make a difference.

The difference between aims (or goals) and objectives

When we think about goals we think about footballers like Wayne Rooney, Fernando Torres and Didier Drogba. During a match the mission of the team will be to win the match, but in order to do this, the team have to score goals. **Aims** or goals are therefore more specific than a

mission. However, in order to score (or achieve) a goal, the football team may need to put in place a number of **objectives**. These might include getting the ball to the winger or stopping the opposition's midfield playmaker. In business an aim (or a goal) is a broad statement about where an organisation wishes to go, while an objective is a much more specific target.

Even Wayne Rooney will have aims and objectives to meet

For an organisation, an example might be a sandwich business which has the aim of providing 'high-quality products at reasonable prices for its customers'. That aim would help employees and customers to instantly know about what that business was attempting to achieve. Aims will then provide the base upon which more specific objectives can be constructed. So, an aim:

- Would be a broader and more long-term statement than an objective.
- Should be communicated to employees and customers alike.
- Informs interested parties about where an organisation wishes to go.
- Would not be specific.
- Provides an understanding of the direction an organisation is taking.
- Creates the base upon which more specific objectives can be constructed.

Make the grade

P1 When you are using this for P1, make sure that you are able to define the difference between aims or goals and objectives.

Did you know...

One of the objectives of the BBC has been to reduce the volume of repeats on BBC1 from 8.5% towards a target of 5%.

Objectives

As we have seen, objectives are much more specific and purposeful than aims. Objectives are often expressed in numbers such as percentages, just like the BBC objective above. Objectives are precise statements. These statements are in line with mission or vision and aims or goals of an organisation. One way in which objectives are constructed is by using the acronym SMART. This ensures that objectives are:

1. **Specific** – they should identify what they want to achieve, such as 2,000 customers coming to a restaurant in a week.
2. **Measurable** – an organisation should be able to measure whether it is achieving its objectives or not. If only 1,500 customers come to the restaurant, then it is clearly not meeting its objective.
3. **Achievable** – the objectives set must be realistic. There is no point setting objectives that cannot be achieved.

4. **Realistic** – objectives must be sensible. If the restaurant has not got enough tables to seat 2,000 customers in a week, then there would be no point in setting it as an objective.
5. **Timebound** – there should be a sensible time over which objectives can be achieved.

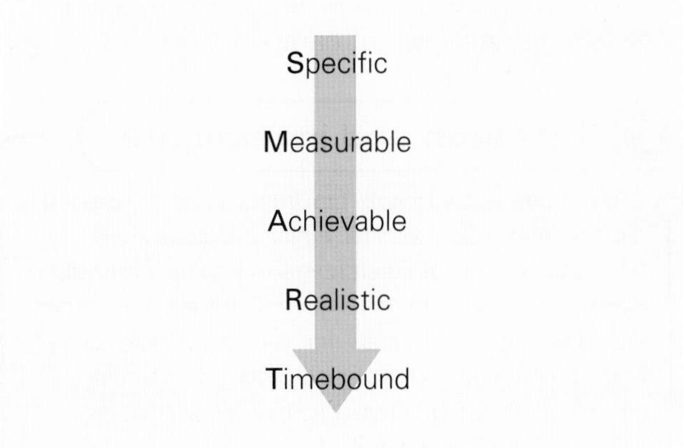

Figure 3.2 SMART objectives

The SMART framework helps organisations to construct objectives meaningfully. In doing this it helps a business organisation to evaluate whether it has successfully achieved its objectives.

Once the objectives are in place, the next question is: What actions need to take place in order to achieve its objectives? Some organisations have **values**. Expressions of values are deeply held beliefs that determine what an organisation does and what it does not intend to do. For example, Asda has three values. These are:

1. Respect for the individual.
2. To strive for excellence.
3. To provide good service for customers.

Sometimes, it is necessary to translate objectives into **policies**. These influence how an organisation is managed. Policies are statements that guide the decision makers within an organisation. For example, an equal opportunities policy would provide help to those who recruit new employees.

As a result of the objectives, the organisation will have some specific targets. These targets can be shared with individuals across a business organisation. **Milestones** are particular types of targets. Every milestone is dependent upon each other and has to be achieved in order. Once one milestone has been achieved, the next milestone can be approached. For example, an organisation may set itself the target to make as much money by a particular date. Once this has been achieved, it may then seek to serve markets elsewhere. Sometimes these targets or milestones might be turned into **key performance indicators (KPIs)**. This means that people within an organisation have something very specific to work towards. This helps them to know and understand whether they have been successful or not.

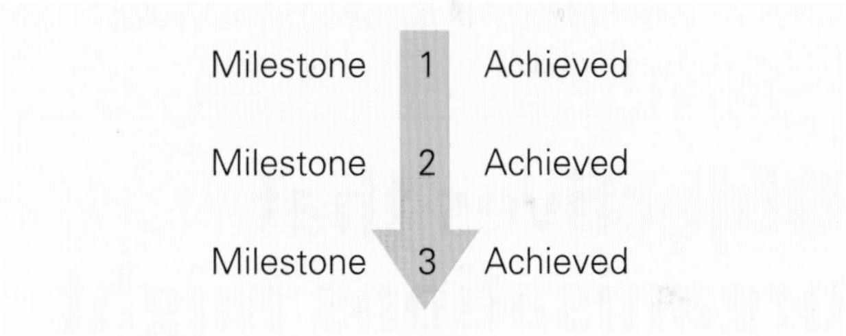

Figure 3.3 Achieving milestones in order

Fieldwork

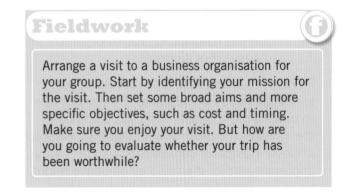

Arrange a visit to a business organisation for your group. Start by identifying your mission for the visit. Then set some broad aims and more specific objectives, such as cost and timing. Make sure you enjoy your visit. But how are you going to evaluate whether your trip has been worthwhile?

London 2012

The London Organising Committee for the Olympic Games and Paralympic Games, known as LOCOG, is planning and organising the Olympic Games for 2012. Their vision or mission is to 'to use the power of the Games to inspire change'. One of their business objectives is to 'have 100% of spectators travel to the Games by public transport, by cycling or on foot'. LOCOG's values are designed to provide a quality framework for how the Games are organised. For example, when people join the organisation they are told to behave within the spirit of the games.

1. Use the case study above to illustrate the differences between a mission, business objectives and business values.
2. To what extent might the aims and objectives for the Olympic Games be different from those of a Premiership football club?

Objectives that organisations might have

The objectives that businesses might have depend upon a range of factors. They will also depend upon the nature and type of organisation that a business is. For example:

1. Private sector organisations provide goods and/or services for the public. They might aim to make a profit. Their objectives could be to identify specific profit targets that they want to achieve. Customer service may also be a very important aim for them. So an objective might be to answer a telephone within ten rings.
2. Public sector businesses are owned by the state. They provide a range of services for individuals across the country. A main aim for a local authority might be to provide high-quality education provision for young people in schools. Their specific objectives might relate to the number of young people achieving certain grades.
3. Charities try to support needy causes. The aim for a charity would relate to the amount of support they provide for people. They might then set themselves objectives that relate to elements of care.

Research and investigate

Use the internet to find out mission statements, aims and objectives for two organisations in the private sector, two in the public sector and for two charities. In what ways are the mission statements of each group of organisations a) similar, and, b) different?

Different types of aims and objectives

You will have seen that organisations are likely to have many different types of business aims and objectives. It is in fact very difficult to identify what all of these aims and objectives are likely to be. However, they might include:

a **Profitability** – for most organisations in the private sector, profits are very important. They may aim for profit maximisation (this is where the profit objective is the most important objective for an organisation and they may want to make as much profit as they can). In order to achieve this, they will usually set, as an objective, a particular amount of profit that they expect to make within, for example, a 12-month period.

b **Customer service** – for some organisations in many industries, customer service performance targets are their most important business objective. For example, organisations like First Direct, HSBC's online bank, use customer service to distinguish themselves from their competitors. Similarly, many airlines compete on the basis of customer service. For example, some customers think Singapore Airlines provides the best service, while others prefer Emirates.

c **Market share/value** – the percentage of the market that a business controls is very important for many organisations, as is the value of their sales. Market share or value provides a fairly precise indication of how well an organisation is performing in comparison with their competitors. In 2007 the value of Somerfield's sales fell by 4%, while Tesco increased the value of its sales by 9%.

d **Positioning** – many organisations are very concerned about their image. This is how people think about them. For example, if you hear the name Topshop, you might respond very differently from how you feel when you hear the name Next or John Lewis. By having the right image, organisations can **target** the customers they want to sell to.

e **Growth** – this is particularly important for many organisations. They will constantly target growth so that they can sell more goods and services and hopefully achieve their aim of increasing their profitability. For example, Primark had 66 UK stores in 1994. Today it has 136 stores, as well as a large number of stores in Ireland and other parts of Europe. However, not everybody wants their business to grow. A local newsagent might be happy with the size of his or her business. If the business got larger there may be more risks and they might lose some control of the organisation.

f **Public responsibility** – being responsible is very important as an aim for many businesses. For example, the Co-operative Group works with a number of charities and **pressure groups** and is determined to be viewed in a very positive light. Some organisations are also very involved with **corporate social responsibility**.

g **Joint ventures** – some organisations seek to build strong relationships with other organisations in order to further achieve shared aims and objectives. For example, building strong partnerships with suppliers may be important. Similarly, an organisation that supports **franchises**, such as McDonald's, would want to develop good relationships with **franchisees**.

h **Innovation** – to be ahead of their competitors, many organisations will constantly need to aim to innovate. The iPod and iPhone have become iconic products for Apple. The difficulty is if you have been that successful with new innovations, what comes next?

i **Environment** – increasingly, business organisations like to show that they are responsible corporate citizens that have the aim of looking after the environment. This might mean saving energy, recycling and using fewer resources. We often hear of businesses that try to be sustainable. This means meeting the needs of customers today while respecting the needs of future generations. For example, Corus have recently had the objective of increasing steel packaging recycling in the UK to 55%.

Make the grade

M1 Remember to use this for M1. You must be able to compare two different organisations and explain why the aims and objectives of each organisation are very different.

Fieldwork

Identify a public sector organisation, a private sector organisation and a charity in the area in which you live. Create a mission statement for each of these organisations and then make a list of probable aims and objectives that each might have.

The important thing about setting aims and objectives is that they:

a identify a way forward for an organisation
b help managers within that organisation to develop strategies that enable it to achieve its objectives
c provide a way of evaluating whether that organisation has been successful or not.

Imagine that you are playing for a football team. You are taking on the team at the top of the league. One of your objectives for the game might be not to lose by more than the odd goal. What do you do at half-time if you are 4–0 down? Not all actions are successful. If a business sets objectives and is not achieving them, then it might have to change them. In 2009 the UK was in the depths of a recession. Many organisations will have changed their business objectives during this time to reflect the more difficult business environment in which they were operating.

Task

Think about what you want to achieve within your working life.

1. **What is your mission? Construct a broad statement that helps others to understand what you want to achieve.**
2. **Identify three short-term specific objectives (within three years) and three long-term broader aims (within ten years) that identify what you hope to achieve.**
3. **Construct four key performance indicators that would help you to know whether you are keeping on track in achieving your ambitions.**
4. **If you are not achieving your key performance indicators, what decisions might you have to take?**

Fieldwork

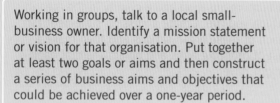

Working in groups, talk to a local small-business owner. Identify a mission statement or vision for that organisation. Put together at least two goals or aims and then construct a series of business aims and objectives that could be achieved over a one-year period.

Did you know...

Increasingly, organisations are setting themselves environmental aims and objectives. Find out whether your school or college has any aims and objectives associated with the environment.

Task

Look at the following mission statements. What do they all have in common? How similar are they to each other and how different are they from each other? Think about how they provide direction for each organisation. What does each mission statement tell you about each organisation and where it wants to go? (Relate this to all of the reasons that illustrate why different types of business have different aims and objectives.) Why are each of the mission statements so very different from each other?

Amway: 'Through the partnering of Distributors, Employees, and the Founding Families and the support of quality products and service, we offer all people the opportunity to achieve their goals through the Amway Sales and Marketing Plan.'

WHSmith 'aims to be Britain's most popular bookseller, stationer and newsagent'.

The National Coal Mining Museum for England 'aims to keep coal mining alive by collecting and preserving the industry's rich heritage, creating enjoyable and inspiring ways to learn for people of all ages, backgrounds and abilities'.

South London Healthcare Trust: 'Our mission is to achieve excellence in all that we do. We want South London Healthcare Trust to be the first choice for clinical care for patients through South London and the South-East of England; and to attract the best and the brightest among Directors, Managers, Doctors, Nurses and Healthcare workers.'

Alliance Boots: 'Our mission is to become the world's leading pharmacy-led health and beauty group. We seek to develop our core businesses of pharmacy-led health and beauty retailing and pharmaceutical wholesaling across the world and become a significant player in many major international markets.'

Optical Express Group: 'We lead in the global elective healthcare industry through utilising the most advanced technologies, scientifically analysing our clinical outcomes and by working with pioneers, innovators and opinion leaders in the healthcare industry'.

Thorntons: 'It is Thorntons mission to deliver Chocolate Heaven to the world.'

Measuring performance

Once an organisation has set a direction through its aims and objectives, it is important to know whether it is successfully moving forward in that direction. Mission statements and objectives are about trying to make the future happen. That is not always easy! Remember that setting business objectives helps managers within an organisation to measure its performance. They also help others who have an interest in that organisation, such as shareholders, to understand what the organisation is doing and how successful it has been.

In January 2009 Waterford Wedgwood plc, which had a number of companies in Ireland, was placed in **receivership**. This is a type of bankruptcy. It means that an organisation has serious financial issues. The company is associated with many different lifestyle products. These are very expensive products. When a business runs into problems, it is clearly not achieving its business objectives. There may have been many reasons for its failure. In 2009 the world was going through a recession. In a recession fewer people may have been buying expensive lifestyle products. They tend to want to buy cheaper products. Waterford Wedgwood's market share and value might have fallen. This means that it might not have as many customers wanting its products. Clearly, profitability went down. Other products might have come on to the market. For example, its competitors might have introduced cheaper alternatives. Perhaps the company was not introducing new products to meet changing customer needs. What it meant for Waterford Wedgwood was that it needed to change its mission and set new business objectives to reflect all that was happening to the business.

So how do you assess whether a business has met its business objectives? This is not an easy thing to do. The starting point is to undertake some research. If you are looking at a large business, the first thing to do is to read its Annual Report. The next thing to do would be to look at newspapers, press releases and find out more about what has happened to that business in recent months and years. You can do this by using the internet. If you are looking at a small business, perhaps the best thing would be to talk to the owner or a manager of the business. Interview them. They may not be willing to provide you with confidential information like profits and market share. However, they should be able to tell you in broad terms how their business is performing. Remember that it is important to evaluate how that business is performing in terms of its business objectives.

Make the grade

D1 Use the internet to find out as much as you can about a national business that has recently been in the news. Comment on whether you think that the organisation has been successful in meeting its aims and objectives. Provide reasons to support the points that you make. This can help you to achieve D1.

Discussion...

If a business does not set objectives, it will never be successful. Do you think that this is likely to be true?

The Recommendations

The Recommendations are a recently formed band from Richmond in North Yorkshire. Members of the band describe their music as a mixture of rock and power pop, although some of the music they play is commercial funk. The mission of the band is to 'enlighten entertainment in North Yorkshire with a mixture of music and fun'. Their two main aims are to always create their own music that appeals largely to young people locally. Their objectives include:

- the need to make £1,000 per week
- to play at least eight venues each month
- to move away from being a supporting band and become a band of first choice
- to launch a CD in their first year and have it reviewed in the music press
- to play at least four festivals in their first year.

The Recommendations had an interesting year. They managed to get an agent and had their first CD released. Although it sold very few copies, it was reviewed twice. They played at two festivals, one of which was in the south east. They are still largely a support band and they have, from time to time, struggled to find enough work.

1. Reconstruct The Recommendations' mission statement.
2. Evaluate the extent to which the band has met its business objectives.
3. Rewrite more realistic objectives for the following year.

Key words

Corporate social responsibility (CSR) – Commitment by an organisation to behave ethically and support and help the local community and society at large.

Franchisee – Person licensed to trade using a well-known name.

Franchise – A business that has the name of another organisation and is authorised to sell products or provides services for a fee.

Hierarchy – A structure or system that has a number of levels.

Pressure group – Organisation formed by people with a common interest, who get together to further that interest.

Receivership – Type of bankruptcy. A company is reorganised by a receiver, who is appointed by a court.

Stakeholders – Individuals or groups affected by the decisions of an organisation.

Target – Focusing efforts upon attracting particular groups of customers.

Assignment

You must demonstrate that you can set business aims and objectives.

Helping friends

Knowing that you are taking a business qualification at Bloomsbury Regional Technical College, you have been approached by several friends who would like you to help with the setting up of their businesses. You enjoy business because the subject constantly changes and you can see the relevance of all that you are learning. You can also apply what you are learning to different contexts.

a) Alice is thinking of setting up a small restaurant in a village two miles from the town centre. The setting is attractive. Her restaurant will only cater for a maximum of 36 customers, for whom she wants to serve gourmet food.

b) Perminder wants to create a small charity that locally supports children with cerebral palsy. She represents a network of 30 parents who experience the illness and she wants to make sure that the charity can provide them with many of the resources and experiences they require in order to make their lives more comfortable.

1. You meet both Alice and Perminder for a cup of tea. Explain why organisations need aims and objectives. **(P1)**
2. Describe to Alice and Perminder how they could use their aims and objectives. As you do so, explain the purpose of setting SMART objectives. **(P2)**
3. Produce a mission statement for Alice for her business as well as for Perminder's charity, alongside a series of objectives. **(P3)**
4. Compare the objectives that you have created for each business. In what way are they similar and in what way are they different? **(M1)**
5. Using the Internet, find out as much as you can about a national business that has recently been in the news. Look at press releases that mention this business, and read the financial press to find out what they have said about the organisation. Find their mission statement, goals and objectives and then match these with what has been stated about the organisation. Comment upon whether you think that the organisation has been successful in meeting its aims and objectives. Provide reasons and justification to support the points that you make. **(D1)**

In your assessment you will need to be able to do the following:

To achieve a pass grade you need to:	To achieve a merit grade you need to:	To achieve a distinction you need to:
P1 define aims and objectives	**M1** compare the aims and objectives of different businesses	**D1** assess whether a selected organisation meets its aims and objectives
P2 describe the purpose for a business in setting aims and objectives		
P3 write aims and objectives for a selected business		

Chapter 4
The main functional areas in business organisations

What are you finding out?

In order to meet their aims and objectives, businesses need to organise and structure themselves. This helps them to operate efficiently. Structuring a business may mean dividing an organisation into functions. For example, a human resources department would be there to look after employees. An accounting or finance function would be there to monitor the money that is earned or spent by the business. Increasingly, organisations have an ICT function that has specialists who are able to monitor the computer network and carry out various activities that ensure it runs efficiently.

This chapter will help you to:

- Understand why organisations need to divide themselves into functions.
- Describe the functional areas in different and contrasting business organisations.
- Explain how functional areas are linked within an organisation.
- Compare functional areas within an organisation.
- Show how functional areas relate to each other within an organisation.
- Illustrate how functional areas help organisations to achieve their aims and objectives.

Functional areas

Imagine all of the activities that have to be performed by people working for business organisations. In a broad sense, some individuals may work in offices dealing with paperwork and administration. Others may be involved in recording and monitoring finances within a business. Some people may work in customer service. Others may actually be producing products for a manufacturing business. The range of types of jobs and activities that individuals undertake is almost endless. The different areas or parts of the business in which individuals work are known as its functions. It is these **functional areas** of an organisation that determine how an organisation has been divided up. In effect, they are the parts of a business organisation or its departments. Each department will have a specialist function and will employ staff with expertise in that function.

Organisations are divided up into functional areas so that specialists can work together. This helps to make activities more efficient. For example, some individuals may work in production or operations. They need to work closely together, as the actions of one individual or member of the team may depend heavily upon the actions of another person. Similarly, it will be important for the accounting and finance people to work together. This will help them to develop an overview of how the business is operating.

The functional areas or departments within a business will usually depend upon the type of business. For example, a school will have very different departments from that of a business manufacturing handbags.

The departments that a business has will link closely with the aims and objectives of that organisation. For example, a customer service department will clearly intend to monitor customer satisfaction. The marketing department will be concerned about market share and value of all of the sales generated by the organisation. Research and development will be concerned with innovation, and human resources may be helping the business to recruit staff and meet its growth targets.

Task

Think about any organisation that you may have knowledge of. It may be a business that you work for or it could be an organisation for which you have had a placement. It may even be your school. List the functional areas of that organisation. Think about how each of these functional areas differs.

Did you know...

The impressive title of 'Frontline customer support facilitators' has been used as another name for call-centre workers!

Figure 4.1 The functional areas of business organisations

Make the grade

P4 Remember to use these for P4. Read about the functional areas and then describe the functional areas in two different business organisations. Remember that all organisations are different. So try to identify the differences between the functional areas in each of your chosen organisations.

Operations/Production

The word '**operations**' is a slightly more modern word than the word 'production'. When we think of production we instantly conjure up in our minds workers who make things. The term 'operations' moves away from that slightly old-fashioned factory-floor focus. Yes, people who are involved in manufacturing are involved in operations. However, most people today work for organisations that provide a service. They may be processing data, talking to customers on a daily basis or directly involved in providing some form of service such as serving customers in a retail environment. As these workers are part of the main or **core function** of the business, they are involved in operations.

You can imagine that, in the modern workplace, many operations are no longer concerned with old-fashioned manufacturing. For example, many organisations are concerned with providing customers with a service, such as a supermarket, or dealing with customer queries over the telephone, such as in banking and insurance. It is therefore probably more sensible to talk about operations than production.

So, in the broadest sense operations (or production) is a functional area within a business organisation. It is this functional area that carries out the main activities of the organisation, such as manufacturing or processing activities, that meet the needs of customers. These are its core activities and it is these that provide customers with the goods or services that they require.

In a business that produces physical products, a manufacturing business, operations involves turning raw materials through a range of stages until finished goods are produced.

It is important to monitor operations to make sure that customers get finished products of an appropriate standard.

Manufacturing business → turning raw materials into goods

Service business → organising resources to meet customer needs

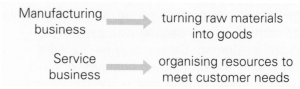

Figure 4.2 Types of operational function

In service industries, the operations function involves organising resources so that the final consumer gets the best value and quality. The finished good might be a haircut, a night out, a visit to a leisure park, visiting a golf course, or a thousand and one other services on offer. When physical products such as bicycles are manufactured, raw materials are required; employees may need to be organised into teams; tools and equipment may be necessary; and quality procedures need to be checked. In the same way when services are provided, materials, machinery and accommodation may be required; employees will also need to be organised into teams; tools and equipment may be necessary; and again quality procedures will need to be checked.

Quality is a very important part of the operations function. Today organisations emphasise the importance of **total quality management** (TQM). This is where the customer appears at the centre of the operations process. Everything each employee does is designed to 'delight' customers by closely meeting their needs.

There are many elements associated with production or operations. For example, these may include:

a Operations planning and scheduling – these involve making sure that resources are always provided in the right place at the right time where they can be used to either make goods or provide customers with the service they require.

b Control of operations – this involves monitoring operations within an organisation.

c Managing people and resources – within the work environment team leaders need to manage workers and resources to ensure that customer needs are met.

First Direct

First Direct is part of the HSBC bank. It provides online banking services and has been operating for more than 20 years! It provides a range of banking services such as current accounts, credit cards, savings accounts, insurance and loans. However, what is different about First Direct is that it provides these services in three ways. This is through the use of the internet, the telephone and text messaging. To meet the needs of more than a million customers it has more than 3,000 employees.

First Direct's main route to meeting customer needs is via their website. The website is easy to use. This helps customers to complete their transactions. First Direct was the first bank to develop a platform for iPhone banking. It is now possible for their customers to get their balances sent to their mobile phones. Call centres also support customers and work 24 hours a day, seven days a week, 365 days a year.

1. What is First Direct's operational function?
2. What roles might employees have as part of this function?
3. How does the operational function meet the needs of First Direct's customers?

Marketing

The marketing function is about meeting customer needs. Organisations do this by:

- **a** trying to identify the sorts of products and services that customers want
- **b** anticipating how customers might like these products and services
- **c** producing products and services that meet customer needs.

A marketing department will have two main functions. The first function will be to investigate customers' needs and wants. This will involve carrying out what is called 'market research'. Market research involves finding out about markets and customer needs. This involves discovering the answers to questions such as what customers want, where they want it, how they like it and what price they are willing to pay. In all business organisations there needs to be close cooperation between marketing and operations/production. This is so that the wishes of consumers can be closely tied in with product development.

The second function of an organisation is to produce a suitable **marketing mix**. This includes the range of strategies used to serve its customers. In its simplest form it is sometimes known for learning purposes as the four Ps.

The marketing mix

The first element in what is known as the marketing mix is **the product**. Once organisations have a product, then all of the other elements in this marketing mix can be engaged in order to meet customer needs. These may include developing the **pricing** for the product or service provided, working out how to **distribute** (place) goods to the customers, as well as how to **promote** them.

Task

Identify two market-leading products. These may be in markets such as tomato sauce, chilled ready meals, packet soups, pet food or confectionery. The purpose of this activity is to undertake a competitive audit. Use a matrix like the one below to make comparisons:

	Product A	Product B
Product	• Features • Benefits • Design • Brand • Other elements	• Features • Benefits • Design • Brand • Other elements
Price	• High price • Market price • Low price	• High price • Market price • Low price
Place/ distribution	• Availability • Types of outlet	• Availability • Types of outlet
Promotion	• Advertising • Sales promotions • Publicity and image	• Advertising • Sales promotions • Publicity and image

Finance and accounts

The accounts department must keep a record of all money paid in and out and make these records available so that **accounting statements** can be prepared. Accounts are usually kept and monitored by bookkeepers. These are individuals responsible for recording what is happening within the daily running of the business. Software packages, such as Sage, are more usually used to record transactions.

Sage

Based in Newcastle-upon-Tyne, Sage supplies business software to businesses around the world. Much of this software is designed to help business organisations manage their day-to-day finances.This might include payroll packages for paying wages. It also includes bookkeeping packages for both small and large organisations that enable businesses to record information and deal with their customers and their suppliers. For example, Sage Instant Accounts helps bookkeepers to record financial transactions and update their records and documentation, such as **invoices**, to their customers.

1. Why would an organisation use a software package?
2. What might the role of a bookkeeper be when using such a package?

Within the finance and accounts department, there would be two main subdivisions. These are:

a **The financial accounting function** is responsible for keeping records of financial events as they occur. Accounts need to be kept of all money paid to or by a company and records need to be kept of all debtor and creditor transactions. Debtors are customers who owe money to the business. Creditors occur where purchases have been made on credit. The company owes money to its creditors. The payment of wages will also be part of this function. This involves calculating and supervising the payroll. Data for these calculations might be generated by a whole series of other departments responsible for recording the work carried out by employees.

b **The management accounts function** has the responsibility of analysing figures from the present in order to use a range of tools to make predictions about the future. Management accountants will break down figures, to extract information about a company's present performance and about what sort of improvements can be made in the future. One of the techniques that they use is budgetary control systems. These set targets for achievements and allocate spending to various parts of a business.

Research and development (R&D)

In any well-run organisation, research and development (R&D) aims to further the business by creating new and better products. R&D will also aim to improve operational processes, develop new ones and provide expert advice to the rest of the business. This flow of new products, services and processes helps an organisation to remain successful.

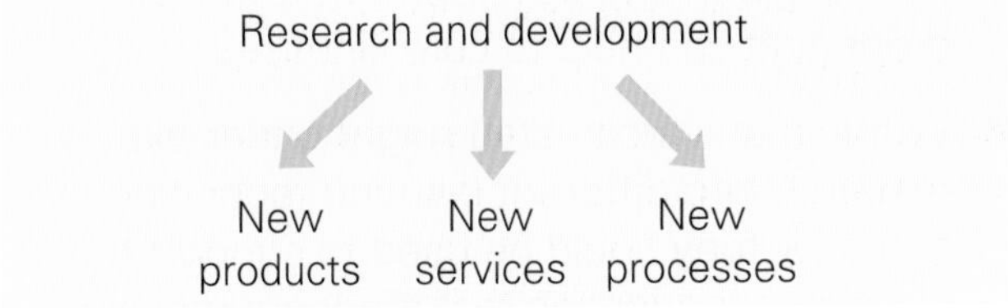

Figure 4.3 The influence of R&D

Did you know...

Within the UK the two companies that dominate research and development are in the pharmaceutical and biotechnology sector. They are GlaxoSmithKline and AstraZeneca.

Some research does not pay for itself in the short term. Many businesses allocate 5–10% of their research budgets for what are termed '**blue-sky**' investigations. This is often unrealistic, investigative and creative research into new areas. Usually there is no immediate short-term commercial value for this type of research. However, blue-sky research does help to build the expertise of research staff, generate adventurous new ideas and take an organisation's thinking further forward. In this way, it can help towards longer-term solutions as it stretches the minds of scientists and provides them with a deeper understanding of their work. Blue-sky research can also lead to some unexpected spin-offs. For example, it might create chance discoveries that could not have been predicted.

There may be many different types of research. For example:

- In the food industry nutritionists might work alongside top chefs in order to create new flavours that can be made into ready-made fresh foods.
- In the motor industry engineers would work alongside marketers and product developers to create new functions for vehicles.
- In the pharmaceutical industry scientists will use research and development to develop drugs that can help to cure illnesses.
- Within a university staff might undertake research into different learning technologies and how they could be used to support the learning experiences that students receive.

Did you know...

HM Revenue and Customs provides relief against taxation for certain types of research and development.

Discussion...

Could it be argued that all research and development is a good thing?

Human resources

The human resource management function used to be known as the **personnel function**. It covers a variety of activities involving perhaps the most important resource within an organisation, that is, its employees or its people.

There are many different types of work covered by the human resource function. For example, it could include the following:

a **A policy-making role** – this would involve establishing the major policies involving people within the workplace. As a role it helps to establish and create the sort of workplace that individuals would prefer to work within.

b **A workforce planning role** – the human resource management role will involve identifying both the number of employees and their roles within the workplace. Employees from this function will be involved in interviewing and appointing staff.

c **A welfare role** – this is concerned with looking after people at work and meeting their needs. This might include providing canteen facilities or supporting staff in times of illness.

d **A training/educational and development role** – this would involve supporting other functional managers in developing their staff. For example, new staff would normally go through an **induction programme** that helps to welcome them to the organisation so that they become familiar with their new role. Training helps to develop staff and make them more professional. Some training might be on-the-job. This is training that is undertaken within the workplace while the employee is working. Usually a trainer or an instructor would support a member of staff undertaking on-the-job training. Some training might be off-the-job. This is training away from the workplace. This might take place in a college or with a training provider. A variety of different techniques such as simulation or case studies might be used with the expectation that they will help to develop the employee in the longer term.

e **A bargaining and negotiating role** – those working with human resources will act as an intermediary between different groups and interests within the organisation. For example, they will help to provide a forum so that **trade unions** and management could exchange views.

f **An administrative role** – this is concerned with the payment of wages or the supervision of health and safety across an organisation.

g **A motivational role** – employees expect to be treated in a particular way while at work. For example, they would want to be treated fairly and with respect. **Motivation** involves using a variety of factors that help to stimulate staff to work hard while in the workplace. Motivation might include humour, encouraging staff to take a pride in their work or providing staff with job responsibilities.

Did you know...

The Chartered Institute of Personnel and Development is the professional body within the UK for those involved in the development of people within the human resource function.

Administration

All large organisations depend upon their administrators. Dealing with enquiries, communicating messages, maintaining files and producing documents for the workforce are all part of the administrative function.

Effectively administrators service the work of an organisation. Many organisations have a central office that is responsible for controlling key administrative functions. This department might handle the filing of materials, deal with the business's mail, handle reception duties as well as dealing with phone calls and emails. Any form of data handling is also a key part of the modern administrative function.

Administrative functions vary considerably between one organisation and another. For example, a junior administrator might come into work and be expected to file documents, send faxes to customers and deal with email enquiries. They may also deal with ordering travel documents and arranging **itineraries** for meetings. Administration involves ordering supplies such as stationery or new equipment.

Administration as a function helps an organisation to run smoothly and without problems. For example, telephones will be answered quickly. Mail gets delivered around the organisation. The reception area and those involved in administration convey a suitable image of the organisation for clients. Paperwork or files do not get lost or mislaid.

Clearly, in the modern workplace there is a close link between the administrative function and the use of information and communications technology (ICT). This is because ICT is used to obtain, process and disseminate information.

Customer service

It is easy to forget that just about every moment of a day you are a customer. If you do not sleep well it could be the fault of a bed that had been purchased. The toothpaste, shampoo and soap you use in the morning reflect the purchases made by either you or members of your family. If they do not perform in the way you would like, then you may buy other brands. Similarly the breakfast items have all been purchased, and you may become a customer again if you catch a bus to school or work. Customer service has become increasingly important as a way of winning customers and distinguishing the activities of some organisations. For example, financial institutions and airlines try to adopt a quality-service approach that makes them different from their competitors.

Customer service is associated with developing bonds with customers in order to create long-term relationships that lead to advantages for all groups. However, customer service is something that does not just happen. It is a process that involves pre-transaction, transaction and post-transaction considerations. Emphasis on customer service will change from one product to another. For example, when manufacturing goods such as bread or shampoo, customer service may involve developing strong customer relationships with many of the large retailers. In a pure service industry, such as hairdressing or insurance, there are no tangible goods, and so customers will view nearly all the benefits they get on the basis of the service they receive.

Matching service with your own workplace experience

In a service environment it is important for staff to understand what customers want as well as what they require. Queries or complaints from customers can be used to develop priorities for improvements to products and processes. The cost of poor customer service may have a direct impact upon sales. If a business develops a poor reputation for customer service it will not meet customer expectations.

1. What are the problems and issues that arise when working in an environment where customer service is important?
2. Comment upon at least two of the areas that would be necessary for training customer service staff.

Most organisations have staff working within the customer service function. Customers have certain expectations when they purchase a product or use a service. For example, they expect staff:

- to know about products and services and to be able to deal efficiently with an enquiry
- to know what customers want
- to be able to support customers when they make decisions
- to know how to provide products or services in the best possible way.

Staff within customer services deal with a whole range of enquiries, situations, complaints and issues. They need to be able to answer queries, deal with customers professionally and also resolve issues where they materialise.

Sales and purchasing

Sales

It could be argued that during every day of our lives we are in one way or another involved in selling. This might be through persuading a friend to accompany you to a sports event or a relative to buy something from you. What you are doing is using a relationship to sell your ideas to somebody else, something that is the responsibility of the sales team within a business organisation.

Sales are an important process for organisations as they generate income. As a function, sales has a close link with marketing and in some instances the sales function will be included with that of marketing. This is because it is the marketing department that is involved in all of the activities that lead up to the generation of sales in the first place. Sales are therefore the culmination of all of the marketing activities that have taken place beforehand.

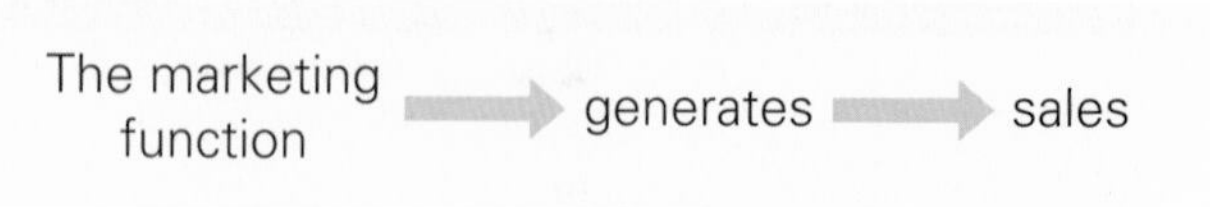

Figure 4.4 The marketing function

No matter how good a business's products are, if they do not sell, all of the effort producing the products or developing the service has been wasted. The role of those working in sales is to identify a way of matching the needs of consumers with the goods or services on offer.

Sales match very closely with the objectives of a business. For example, there may be specific sales targets that have been identified for sales staff. These might be in terms of the value of the sales made, or the volume of products that have been sold.

Sales are a cornerstone of an organisation as this is where individuals deal directly with their customers. At its very basic level and for a small business such as a retailer, sales may simply involve serving or supporting customers with the choice of products. In a world where businesses sell to other businesses, sales may involve providing customers with samples as well as technical advice and specifications that support the sales process. The role of selling will therefore vary from business to business. Sales can be one of the most expensive parts of the **promotional mix**. There are many techniques in this mix to communicate with customers, but getting them to finally agree to buy some products or services is the role of the sales function.

The purpose of having a sales function is therefore to 'push' products into a market. The sales function will keep records of customer transactions, which should be tracked and updated. Sales staff operate as a vital link between an organisation and its customers. The size of a salesforce will be determined by factors such as revenue and workload. Often large and widespread markets will need to be served by a large workforce. Sales might be broken up into a series of territories, each of which might be supervised by a small sales team. Selling can be quite expensive and some organisations provide their sales staff with **commission** as well as a salary.

Purchasing

One of the most important functions of any business organisation is that of purchasing. This function is sometimes called procurement. Purchasing involves making sure that a reliable flow of materials is acquired in order to facilitate the smooth running of the business. Whether a business is producing goods or supplying services, it needs materials. It might simply be stationery for the office, light bulbs, pens and other stationery or printer cartridges.

The role of telesales operators

Telesales operators are trained to sell products over the phone. There is a huge range of products that are sold in this way, such as gas and electricity or financial services. Some telesales operators might use a script that helps them to tell customers about all of the details related to their products. They may describe the product and explain the benefits of the products for customers. After having done this, they may take an order and arrange a delivery. Follow-up dates for further calls may be arranged. Telesales operators may be given a target number of calls to deliver.

1. Name three advantages and three disadvantages of working in telesales, selling over the phone.
2. What sort of skills might a telesales operator require?

Purchasing also involves acquiring raw materials that could be used to manufacture or contribute towards finished products or services. Materials are usually a key ingredient for any product or service that is supplied for customers. Having a source of reliable suppliers is very important for a business.

Having a good relationship with suppliers is usually considered to be very important. The organisation making the purchase will have certain expectations, not just in terms of price but also in terms of reliability. Suppliers might also have to provide products that meet certain defined specifications.

Sometimes products are produced on the basis of **just-in-time**. This is based upon a very simple idea. Finished products are produced just-in-time for them to be sold, rather than weeks or months ahead. In other words, the parts and components for a product arrive just when they are needed. This means that businesses can operate with small levels of stock. To make just-in-time work properly, those involved in purchasing need to work very closely with suppliers so that there is an exact match between supplies and the date for which they are required. A key element in enabling this process to work is the need for very high quality supplies. In fact, quality issues are always a key element in choosing suppliers.

The prices associated with purchases are of particular importance for those working in procurement. Sometimes discounts are provided by suppliers, particularly where large orders are placed. The flow of purchases has to be constantly monitored. For example, it is important to check that the correct products have been sent from the supplier. Where products that are received are faulty, they may have to be sent back as returns.

Distribution

Distribution is the process of making goods or services available for those who want to buy them. It could include:

- the process of moving goods and services to the place where they are wanted;
- the channels through which the products are made available.

Distribution may involve a single step or any number of steps. For example, a local baker may make bread and supply it directly to his or her customers. In contrast, a furniture superstore might supply chairs and tables that are manufactured in Hong Kong, and these may have passed through the hands of a number of organisations and been stored a few times before they reach their final destination. The **channels of distribution** offered by organisations for final consumers constantly change in order to become more convenient for customers. For example, Amazon has become a huge online seller, not just of books and DVDs, but of a wide range of products that meet consumer needs. Tesco has invested heavily in local convenience stores within communities. Supermarkets are today delivering groceries to customers to save them from having to visit stores. A considerable amount of shopping today takes place in retail parks rather than city centres.

In the manufacturing sector the channels of distribution used by organisations may involve transporting products from one organisation to another. This may even involve sending them overseas. We only have to look at the commercial vehicles on our roads to realise that the function of distribution is going on around us all of the time. In fact, it is often something that we take for granted.

Logistics is the process of managing the movement of materials and goods within and between organisations. This is an important part of what is known as physical distribution management. This is the management of the movement of products until they reach the final consumer. The distribution function will involve individuals in managing the movement and storage of products.

ICT

ICT stands for information and communications technology. Over the past 20 years ICT has literally transformed the way in which organisations are able to do business. Today even the smallest of businesses will have some kind of ICT function. The ICT function plays an increasing role in meeting customer needs both accurately and precisely.

Most organisations will have computers that are linked together in what is known as a network. Linking computers together in a local network is undertaken by a server. These computers may also be linked to printers, photocopiers, scanners and a range of other machines. It has become very easy to rely upon ICT. Staff may depend upon their computers for email, for using networked databases that have replaced traditional filing systems, and for using the internet. Computers have also replaced a whole host of standard operations between an organisation and its customers.

Within the ICT function staff will need to maintain the network and ensure that all of the applications are working correctly. They may constantly be involved in updating the system as new applications become available and also in dealing with crises when a system has a fault or is affected by a computer virus. At the same time it is always important to think about how ICT integrates all of the other functions. Businesses will want to be working efficiently. As individuals review how ICT helps parts of an organisation, it may be possible to identify other functions and applications that could make the business more efficient.

Purpose of functional areas in supporting the objectives of businesses

It is essential that the functional areas of an organisation are combined effectively if an organisation is to meet its objectives. The last thing any manager wants to happen is for functional managers to pull in different directions. When this happens these managers would be at odds with what the business would want to achieve. For example, those involved in marketing might want to take risky decisions about products, while financial managers would have assessed the risks and might argue that there was not a clear argument for investment.

Make the grade

P5 Remember to use this for P5. Look to see how functional areas link within one organisation. For example, try to find out how more than one functional area uses ICT, or find out how those in managerial accounts set budgets for each of the functional areas.

In the previous chapter we looked at business aims and objectives. The best way of getting the various functions of an organisation to pull in the same direction is to create a clear set of business objectives that can be translated into functional objectives. This means that each business function is then driven by the organisation's objectives.

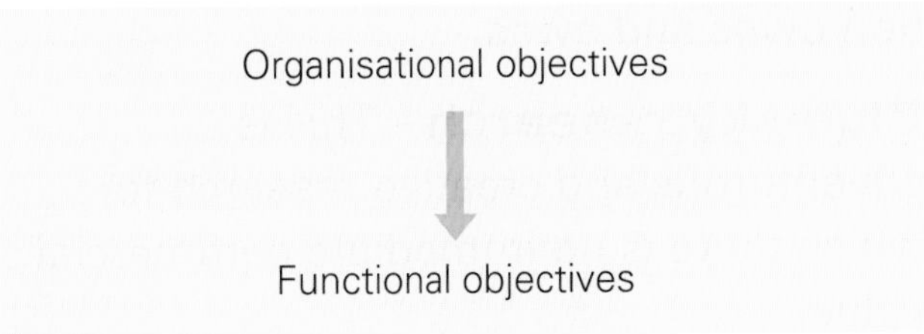

Figure 4.5 Hierarchy of objectives

Functional areas cannot work on their own. They have to work with and alongside each other. In modern organisations there is far more integration of the functions than ever before. The prime driver of this change has been an increasing focus on the customer.

For example, the use of ICT enables every functional area to share the same information. This pooling of information means that each area can work collaboratively and improve the quality of its decision making. For example, databases containing client information can be used by finance and accounts to find out more about customers and the regularity of their payments, by marketing to research the buying habits of customers, by administration, which handles the paperwork related to customers, and by sales staff when dealing with customer queries.

Working together enables functional areas to:

- use and share information about customers
- develop new markets
- create new products.

It is the ICT function that enables information to be shared and for organisations to create an appropriate response.

Every organisation may have slightly different functional areas. This is because of the industry they may be in or because of how it has structured itself around its customers. For example, Syngenta, a large plant-science business, has structured itself around research and development, global supply that includes manufacturing, human resources, sales and marketing, finance and information systems.

Make the grade

M2 Remember to use this for M2. Find out about the interaction of two functional areas within a business. Look to see how the interaction of functional areas are used to support wider business objectives.

Discussion...

Look at each of the functional areas of a business. Can you identify instances when certain functional areas might not want to work together?

Key words

Accounting statements – These are sometimes called the final accounts and will include a profit and loss account which records all of the trading activities of an organisation, as well as a balance sheet which will show what an organisation owns and owes.

Blue-sky research – This is adventurous and creative research for which there is no immediate commercial value.

Channels of distribution – Different ways and systems through which organisations transfer products and services until they reach their customers.

Commission – Fee generated for sales staff through undertaking a sales transaction.

Core function – The main activities of a business organisation.

Functional areas – The specialist parts or departments of a business organisation that people work within such as marketing, purchasing, administration or customer service.

Induction programme – 'Welcome' training provided for new staff that helps them to become familiar with their role.

Invoices – Document issued to a customer by a seller when goods have been sold on credit.

Itineraries – Plan, usually for travel arrangements; identified times and places of events.

Just-in-time – An idea from Japan that reduces the need to hold large supplies of stocks. It involves matching the ordering of products with the precise dates on which they are required.

Logistics – Process of managing the supply and movement of products.

Marketing mix – Range of strategies used in order to meet customer needs.

Motivation – Factors that stimulate individuals to be interested in working hard while at work.

Operations – The functional area within an organisation that is involved in planning and carrying out a whole range of activities that meet the needs of customers.

Personnel function – This is the former name of the human resources function.

Promotional mix – Range of activities designed to communicate with customers and meet their needs.

Total quality management (TQM) – Management process designed to meet customer requirements first time every time.

Trade union – Organisation that represents the interests of workers.

Assignment

You must understand the main functional areas in business organisations.

Finding out about functional areas

This assignment involves undertaking an internet search in order to find information about two different kinds of businesses. Clearly, for sufficient information to be available about businesses, they are likely to be quite large. Perhaps the starting point might be to undertake a search using key words like 'functional areas', 'business departments' or to use specific departments like 'operations', 'sales and purchasing' or 'customer service'. Although finding out about business organisations is a skill, often dependent upon using the right search words, it is becoming easier. When you think that you have enough information about two very different kinds of businesses, attempt the following tasks.

1. Describe briefly each of the functional areas in these two businesses. Explain briefly what they do. As you do so, describe the differences between the functional areas in one organisation and those in the other, and think of reasons why they differ according to business. **(P4)**
2. For each organisation that you are using, explain the links between the functional areas within these organisations. For example, how might sales link to accounts and to customer service? Provide as many examples and links as you can. **(P5)**
3. The purpose of functional areas is to provide a mechanism by which organisations can meet their business objectives. Use a range of selected examples from the organisations you have chosen that help to illustrate that functional areas work together to meet business objectives. Produce some notes for a discussion that makes a comparison between the nature and type of functional areas used within each of the organisations. **(M2)**

In your assessment you will need to be able to do the following:

To achieve a pass grade you need to:	To achieve a merit grade you need to:	To achieve a distinction you need to:
P4 describe the functional areas in two contrasting business organisations	**M2** compare the interaction of functional areas and how they relate to each other in two selected businesses to support the business objectives	
P5 explain how these functional areas link in one of these organisations		

Unit 3

Financial forecasting for business

Chapter 5
Costs, revenue and profit in a business

What are you finding out?

All businesses have something to sell, whether that is a product such as Apple's iPod or a service such as a stylist at Toni & Guy cutting your hair. The money received from selling the product/service is called revenue. In producing that product/service, a business has to meet certain costs, for example the cost of raw materials such as the environmentally friendly glass in the iPod Nano or the shampoo used at Toni & Guy. Profit is calculated by deducting the costs from the revenue. As most businesses aim to make as much profit as possible, they aim to maximise their revenue and reduce their costs.

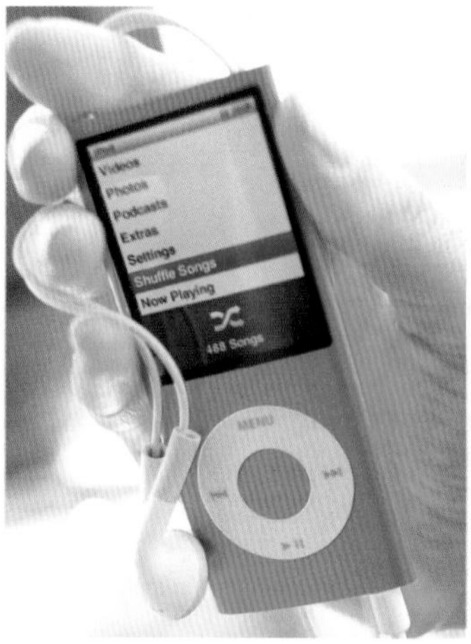

The cost of the environmentally friendly glass used in the iPod Nano is included in the sale price

This chapter will help you to:

- Understand the difference between revenue, costs and profit.
- Distinguish between start-up and operating costs and fixed and variable costs.
- Identify the different types of revenue.
- Outline the differences between gross and net profit.
- Explain the importance of costs, revenue and profit for a business organisation.

Revenue

Revenue is the total amount of money received by a business for goods sold or services provided during a certain time period. Revenue is also known as **turnover** or sales revenue. The amount of revenue received by a business will often depend on its size. For example, the total revenue received by New Look for the year ended 28 March 2009 was £1,322.6 million, whereas Tesco (UK and International) received £54,327 million for the same period.

Different types of revenue

Businesses often earn revenue from more than one source. For example, the table below shows the revenue received by Tottenham Hotspur FC for the year ended 30 June 2008.

Source	£ (000)
Gate receipts (Premier league)	18,274
Gate receipts (Cup competitions)	10,341
Sponsorship & corporate hospitality	27,778
Media & broadcasting	40,329
Merchandising	9,723
Other	8,343
Total revenue	**114,788**

Source: Tottenham Hotspur plc Annual Report 2008

Businesses can also receive revenue from renting out premises.

Some businesses also receive **income** from other sources, such as interest on money invested. For example, Marks & Spencer received £14.6 million in interest from the bank and other financial institutions in the year ended 28 March 2009.

Make the grade

P2 Remember, for P2 you must be able to identify the different types of revenue for a given business or a business of your choice.

Task

Find out the total revenue for one year for three different businesses. Hint: Look for Corporate Information or Financial Results on the websites of different businesses.

Did you know...

Despite the global recession, the total revenue received by Cadbury plc rose from £4,699m in 2007 to £5,384m in 2008. So... people are still eating chocolate!

Calculating revenue

Revenue is worked out by multiplying the amount sold (quantity) by the price it is sold for.

Revenue = quantity × price

For example, if Manchester United sold 100 season tickets for their south stand at £798 each, that would be:

Revenue = 100 × £798
Revenue = £79,800

Task

Calculate the revenue for the following businesses:

1. **Sofa.com sells 640 sofas at an average price of £740 each.**
2. **Sandra, the mobile hairdresser, styles 35 people's hair, charging them an average of £30 each.**
3. **Hull City FC sells 100 adult season tickets for its west stand for £450 each, 20 family season tickets for its west stand at £410 each, 2,500 adult season tickets for its south stand at £400 each and 50 adult season tickets for its east stand at £410 each.**

Most businesses seek to increase their revenue. To increase revenue, a business needs to either sell more goods/services or sell its goods/services for a higher price.

Costs

Costs are what a business has to pay out. There are different types of costs: **start-up costs** and **operating costs**.

Start-up costs arise when a business is first set up. They are an investment in the business and the money is spent to buy the assets (things a business owns) that the business needs. For example, a new manufacturing business would need to purchase machinery for the factory and a new retailing business would need to buy shop fittings and cash registers.

Operating costs (costs for the day-to-day running of the business) are divided into **fixed costs** and **variable costs** and, similarly, **indirect costs** and **direct costs**.

Fixed costs are those costs that *do not* change when the business changes the amount it produces or the number of customers it serves. These costs will remain the same over a set period of time. For example, easyJet had to pay £9.1 million for aircraft and passenger insurance in the year ended 30 September 2008. This amount would have been based on the expected number of passengers and aircraft that would be in use for that year and the amount paid would not change throughout the year.

Typical fixed costs are the rent a business pays for its premises and maintenance costs for the upkeep of buildings.

Variable costs are those costs that *do* change when the business changes the amount it produces or the number of customers it serves. For example, easyJet had to pay £708.7 million for fuel in the year ended 30 September 2008. The amount of fuel needed depends on how many planes fly and how many passengers are on each plane. If each plane carried more passengers than expected, more fuel would be needed and if each plane carried fewer passengers than expected, then less fuel would be needed; therefore the amount of fuel needed changes if the number of passengers change.

Typical variable costs are the costs of raw materials and the wages of staff involved in the production of a good.

When calculating profit, a business needs to work out its **total costs**.

Total costs = fixed costs + variable costs

Make the grade

P1 Remember, for P1 you must be able to identify the difference between start-up and operating costs and fixed and variable costs for a given business or a business of your choice.

Task

Swizzels Matlow Ltd produces a range of confectionery products. Divide their costs into fixed or variable costs:

Insurance	**Production workers' wages**	**Sugar**
Flavourings	**Managers' salaries**	**Telephone**

Costs can also be divided into indirect and direct costs. These are not different costs from fixed and variable costs; this is simply another way of classifying the operating costs of a business.

Indirect costs are those costs that cannot be directly traced back to the item being produced, for example the rental cost for business premises and managers' salaries. Indirect costs are often known as overheads and are often fixed costs.

Direct costs are those that can be directly traced back to the item being produced, for example the raw materials used to manufacture the item and the wages for the people who made the product. Direct costs are the same as variable costs.

Most businesses seek to reduce their costs. There are many ways to reduce costs, for example buying cheaper raw materials or using less electricity.

Task

Outline three other ways in which a business might reduce its costs.

Profit

Profit is what is left of the revenue after all of the business costs have been taken away.

Profit = revenue – total costs

For example, if a business received revenue of £75,000, had fixed costs of £22,000 and variable costs of £25,000, then its profit could be worked out as follows:

Profit = revenue – total costs
Profit = £75,000 – (£22,000 + £25,000)
Profit = £75,000 – £47,000
Profit = £28,000

Most businesses aim to make as much profit as they can and therefore try to increase their revenue and reduce their costs

Task

Simple profit calculations:

1. **For the year ended 30 September 2009, Brooks Builders Merchants received £210,000 in revenue, had fixed costs of £70,000 and variable costs of £95,000. How much profit did they make?**
2. **Last week, Peter's ice-cream business sold 5,000 items at an average price of £1.20 per item. He had to pay £1,200 for the stock of items, £70 for fuel for his ice-cream van, £30 in wages for his Saturday assistant, £10 insurance and £35 site fee for selling ice cream at the local car-boot sale. How much profit did he make?**
3. **Lucy, the mobile hairdresser, is going to style eight ladies' hair for a wedding. She will charge them an average of £45 each. Lucy will need to use products (such as shampoo, conditioner and hairspray) costing approximately £4.30 per person and will have the following additional costs: fuel £8, car insurance £7 and sharpening of scissors £5. Calculate the profit she will make.**

Businesses need to calculate their **gross profit** and their **net profit**. Gross profit is sales revenue minus **cost of sales**. Cost of sales is what it costs the business to buy in the stock that it sells or the direct costs of making the stock that it sells. For example, cost of sales for Marks & Spencer would be the cost of buying in all of its stock of food, clothing and household goods from the manufacturers who make these goods. For Swizzels Matlow, cost of sales would be the cost of the raw materials, labour and energy required to manufacture the confectionery.

Gross profit = sales revenue – cost of sales

Gross profit is not the 'final' or operating profit the business has made as it does not take into account all of a business's other **expenses** (operating costs). To find out the operating profit that a business has made, it has to calculate its net profit. Net profit is therefore gross profit minus expenses such as overheads.

Net profit = gross profit – expenses

The term 'operating profit' is used by companies to mean the profit they have made on their normal, day-to-day trading activities, and is calculated in exactly the same way as net profit.

The example below shows Marks & Spencer's gross profit and operating profit calculations for the period ended 28 March 2009.

	£m
Revenue	9062.1
Cost of sales	(5690.2)
Gross profit	3371.9
Selling and marketing expenses	(2074.4)
Administrative expenses	(570.1)
Other operating income	41.5
Operating profit	768.9

Source: Marks & Spencer Annual Report and Financial Statements 2009

Note: Brackets are used to show amounts that should be deducted.

Make the grade

P3 Remember, for P3 you must be able to outline the difference between the gross and net profit for a given business or a business of your choice.

Profit and loss accounts

To calculate gross and net profit, businesses draw up profit and loss accounts.

Example

Alice runs a small bed and breakfast in the Peak District. During the year ended 31 March 2010, she received £23,500 in revenue and her costs were as follows: food £3,250, laundry £1,750, heating and lighting £2,240, business rates £2,300, insurance £1,200, telephone £600 and advertising £375.

Using this information about Alice's revenue and costs, we can calculate her gross and net profit. We do this by creating a profit and loss account:

Profit and loss account for the period ended 31 March 2010

	£	£
Revenue		23,500
Cost of sales		
Food	3,250	
Laundry	1,750	5,000
Gross profit		18,500
Expenses		
Heating and lighting	2,240	
Business rates	2,300	
Insurance	1,200	
Telephone	600	
Advertising	375	6,715
Net profit		11,785

Alice's profit and loss account shows that she made gross profit of £18,500 and net profit of £11,785. If Alice had made a loss instead of a profit, the bottom line of the account would read Net profit/(loss) and the amount would be in brackets to show that it is a negative figure.

Task

Prepare profit and loss accounts for the following businesses:

1. **Sammy Jones has an old-fashioned sweet shop in Lincoln. During the year ended 31 March 2010, he received £260,000 in revenue and had the following costs: stock of sweets £78,000, staff wages £1,550, heating and lighting £1,200, business rates £1,800, insurance £1000, telephone £200 and advertising £575.**
2. **Jennifer Paris works from a small workshop in Buxton designing and making wedding dresses to order. During the year ended 30 April 2010, she received £110,000 in revenue and had the following costs: fabric, lace and thread £18,000, repairs to sewing machine £150, heating and lighting £1,000, business rates £700, insurance £400, telephone £540, courier and postage charges £875 and advertising £1,175.**

Company profit and loss accounts

The profit and loss account shown above for Alice is a typical example of a profit and loss account for a sole trader or partnership. However, company accounts are slightly different in that they do not have to show as much detail; for example, expenses are usually categorised as either administration expenses or selling and marketing expenses. Company profit and loss accounts are now known as income statements and the way in which company accounts are set out is governed by law, so all companies must use the same format.

Task

Examine the extract from the income statement for Clinton Cards plc and answer the questions below:

Consolidated income statement for Clinton Cards for the 53 weeks ended 3 August 2008

	£000
Revenue	465,029
Cost of sales	(428,873)
Gross profit	36,156
Other operating income	90
Administrative expenses	(45,903)
Operating profit/(loss)	(9,657)

Source: Clinton Cards Annual Report and Financial Statements 2008

1. **How much gross profit did Clinton Cards plc make for the 53 weeks ended 3 August 2008?**
2. **Explain how gross profit is calculated.**
3. **Did Clintons' make a profit or a loss in the period shown?**
4. **Explain, in full, two ways in which Clinton Cards could improve upon their performance for 2008.**

Research and investigate

Use the internet to find the consolidated income statements for Next plc and Debenhams plc and compare their revenue, gross and net profit. Which business is the more profitable? Note: make sure that you compare income statements for the same year.

The importance of costs, revenue and profit for a business organisation

To maximise profit is one of the main aims of most businesses. This is especially true of public limited companies as they need to keep their shareholders happy by returning dividends to them (dividends are a payment to shareholders from company profits). Profit is a reward for the investment of time and money into a business and is necessary for a business to grow.

In order to make a profit, a business needs to generate as much revenue as possible; without revenue, a business will not be able to exist. When an economy is in recession, the revenue for many businesses falls and therefore these businesses may make a loss and stop trading.

Similarly, in order to make a profit, a business must control its costs. Many businesses generate healthy amounts of revenue but then make a loss because their costs are too high. Clinton Cards, as shown above, is a good example. Although they generated revenue of £465,029,000, they still made a loss because their cost of sales was very high.

British Airways

The fortunes of the airline industry are very dependent on the state of the economy. When the economy is booming (businesses are doing well and the demand for goods/services is rising), many new budget airlines start up and are able to generate revenue. However, when the economy is in recession (businesses are not doing well and the demand for goods/services is falling), only the strongest competitors survive and even some of the larger airlines find themselves in financial difficulty.

During 2008, airlines not only suffered the effects of global recession, they also faced rapidly rising costs due to the rise in oil prices, which increased the amount they had to pay for their fuel. Two airlines that went out of business as a direct result were Oasis (in April 2008) and Zoom (in August 2008).

Even the larger airlines were finding it difficult to make a profit in 2008–2009. After facing record losses, British Airways, in a desperate attempt to cut costs, asked its staff to work without pay for one month. BA chief executive Willie Walsh and his chief financial officer, Keith Williams, attempted to lead by example by stating they would give up their wages for July 2009.

See the table below for extracts from British Airways Group consolidated income statement for the years ended 31 March 2008 and 31 March 2009:

	2009 £m	2008 £m
Traffic revenue: Passenger Cargo	 7,836 673	 7,600 615
Other revenue	483	543
Total revenue	8,992	8,758
Expenses: Employee costs Fuel and oil costs Other costs	 2,193 2,969 4,050	 2,165 2,055 3,660
Total expenditure on operations	9,212	7,880
Operating (loss)/profit	(220)	878

Source: British Airways Annual Report and Accounts 2008/09

1. British Airways experienced a small rise in revenue between 2008 and 2009. Explain why some other airlines may have experienced a fall in the amount of revenue they received.
2. British Airways experienced a sharp increase in costs between 2008 and 2009. Outline one factor that caused the costs to increase.
3. Using the financial information in your answer, explain why it is important for British Airways to try and reduce its costs.
4. To what extent do you agree with BA's decision to ask staff to work for free for one month?

Make the grade

M1 Remember, for M1 you must explain the importance of costs, revenue and profit for a given business or a business of your choice.

Discussion...

Many new businesses employ a large number of staff in anticipation that they will be busy, and then find that the staff have very little to do. Discuss the effects this may have on a business's profit.

Key words

Cost of sales – What it costs the business to buy in the stock that it sells or the direct costs of making the stock that it sells.

Direct costs – Those costs that can be directly traced back to the item being produced.

Expenses – Indirect costs.

Fixed costs – Costs that do not change when the business changes the amount it produces or the number of customers it serves.

Gross profit – Sales revenue minus cost of sales.

Income – Monies received by a business.

Indirect costs – Those costs that cannot be directly traced back to the item being produced.

Net profit – Gross profit minus the expenses of the business.

Operating costs – Costs for the day-to-day running of the business.

Profit – What is left of revenue after all of the business costs have been taken away.

Revenue – The total amount of money received by a business for goods sold or services provided during a certain time period.

Start-up costs – Costs that arise when a business is first set up.

Total costs – Fixed costs plus variable costs.

Variable costs – Costs that change when the business changes the amount it produces or the number of customers it serves.

Assignment

You must demonstrate that you know about costs, revenue and profit in a business organisation.

The business organisation

Peter and David have a love of olives and in 2008, when they returned from their holiday in Greece, they decided to open a small shop selling olives, olive oil, peppers, garlic and olive-based products. They named the business Olive Oyl and it started trading on 1 September 2008.

To be able to start the business, Peter and David both put in £6,000 of their own money. They used this start-up capital as follows:

- £5,000 for the shop fittings (shelves and display stands)
- £1,000 deposit on the property (repayable once the business leaves the premises)
- £1,000 for the first two months' rent
- £50 for a cash register
- £1,000 for insurance
- £1,400 for stock
- £100 for till rolls, bags and carrier bags
- £50 for stationery
- £500 on advertising and promotion
- £100 on cleaning materials
- £1,800 paid into a business account to be used as working capital.

In their first year of trading, they sold goods from the shop to the value of £30,000. They also found that they could supply businesses with small plates of olives for office parties and received extra revenue from this activity totalling £1,500.

At the end of their first year of trading, the business made a gross profit of £20,000 and a net profit of £9,800.

Produce a report for Peter and David to provide them with the following information.

1. (a) State the difference between start-up and operating costs.
   (b) Peter and David started their business with £12,000. Of the costs they had when they started the business, identify those which are start-up costs and those which are operating costs.
   (c) State the difference between fixed and variable costs.
   (d) Identify the fixed and variable costs that Peter and David will have to pay during their first year of trading. **(P1)**
2. Identify the different types of revenue a business can receive and state the sources of revenue that Peter and David have. **(P2)**
3. Peter and David made £20,000 gross profit and £9,800 net profit. Explain to them what gross profit is and what net profit is and why there is a difference between them. **(P3)**
4. Peter and David love olives and are enjoying running their business but they do not fully understand the financial side of the business. Explain to them the difference between revenue, costs and profit and explain why each is important for their business. **(M1)**

To achieve a pass grade you need to:	To achieve a merit grade you need to:	To achieve a distinction you need to:
P1 identify the difference between start-up and operating costs, variable and fixed costs	**M1** explain the importance of costs, revenue and profit for a business organisation	
P2 identify the different types of revenue		
P3 outline the differences between gross and net profit		

Chapter 6
Break-even analysis

What are you finding out?

Most businesses aim to make a profit, therefore they need to be able to work out the point at which they are earning enough revenue to meet all of their costs because, after this point, they begin to make profit. Break-even point is the point at which total revenue equals total costs. Break-even analysis works out the volume of sales required to generate enough revenue to cover the total costs. If a business sells more units than it requires to break even then it will make a profit; however, if it sells fewer units than it needs to break even, then it will make a loss.

This chapter will help you to:

- Calculate break-even point.
- Construct a break-even chart.
- Show the impact of changing costs and revenue on break-even point.
- Make judgements about the role of break-even analysis in the effective management of a business's finances.

Break-even analysis

Break-even point is reached when a business sells enough units of output for its **total revenue** to equal its **total costs**, which will result in the business making neither a profit nor a loss.

Break-even point is when total revenue (TR) = total costs (TC)

For a business to be able to calculate its break-even point, it must have the following information available:

- The selling price per unit.
- The **fixed costs** for the period in which it wishes to calculate its break-even point.
- The **variable costs** per unit.

With this information, the profit or loss at each level of output can be calculated and the data can be used to create a **break-even chart**.

For example, CoolMobile Ltd makes fun cases for mobile phones. Each case sells for £6. The fixed costs per year are £10,000 and the variable costs are £2 per case. The maximum amount of covers that CoolMobile can make in one year is 6,000.

We can now use this information to calculate fixed costs, variable costs, total costs, total revenue and profit/loss at different levels of output. To do this, we need to remember the following from Chapter 5:

- Fixed costs do not change when the business changes the amount it produces.
- Variable costs change when the business changes the amount it produces.
- Total costs = fixed costs + variable costs.
- Revenue = quantity × price.
- Profit = total revenue – total costs.

Break-even point is the number of units a business needs to sell for its total revenue to equal its total costs. From the table below, we can see that if CoolMobile sell 2,500 covers, it will have total costs of £15,000 and total revenue of £15,000, therefore the break-even point for CoolMobile is 2,500 units of output, or, in this case, 2,500 cases.

Break-even point is also the level of output at which a business will make neither a profit nor a loss. From the table above, we can see that at 2,500 units of output, CoolMobile has a profit/loss of zero.

Profit/loss at each level of output for CoolMobile Ltd					
Units of output (cases)	Fixed costs (£)	Variable costs (£)	Total costs (£)	Total revenue (£)	Profit or loss (£)
0	10,000	0	10,000	0	(10,000)
500	10,000	1,000	11,000	3,000	(8,000)
1,000	10,000	2,000	12,000	6,000	(6,000)
1,500	10,000	3,000	13,000	9,000	(4,000)
2,000	10,000	4,000	14,000	12,000	(2,000)
2,500	10,000	5,000	15,000	15,000	0
3,000	10,000	6,000	16,000	18,000	2,000
3,500	10,000	7,000	17,000	21,000	4,000
4,000	10,000	8,000	18,000	24,000	6,000
4,500	10,000	9,000	19,000	27,000	8,000
5,000	10,000	10,000	20,000	30,000	10,000
5,500	10,000	11,000	21,000	33,000	12,000
6,000	10,000	12,000	22,000	36,000	14,000

Figure 6.1 Profit and loss for CoolMobile Ltd at different levels of output

Task

Using the table on page 67 as a guide, construct a table for the following business to show the profit/loss at every level of output and then state the number of units required to break even:

Simon Broadbent makes dessert, which he sells to a local restaurant. Each dessert sells for £2.50. His fixed costs per year are £1,500 and the variable costs are £0.50 per unit. The maximum amount of desserts that Simon can make in one year is 1,250. Hint: your units of output should begin at zero and increase by 250 units each time.

Make the grade

P4 Remember this for P4. This is one way in which you can calculate break-even, using given data to show the level at which total revenue equals total costs. However, it is better to use this data to construct a break-even chart.

Constructing break-even charts

Once we have the data we need set out in a table, such as for CoolMobile, we can use this data to construct a break-even chart. To construct a break-even chart we need to plot three sets of data: fixed costs (FC), total costs (TC) and total revenue (TR) on a graph. See Figure 6.2 below.

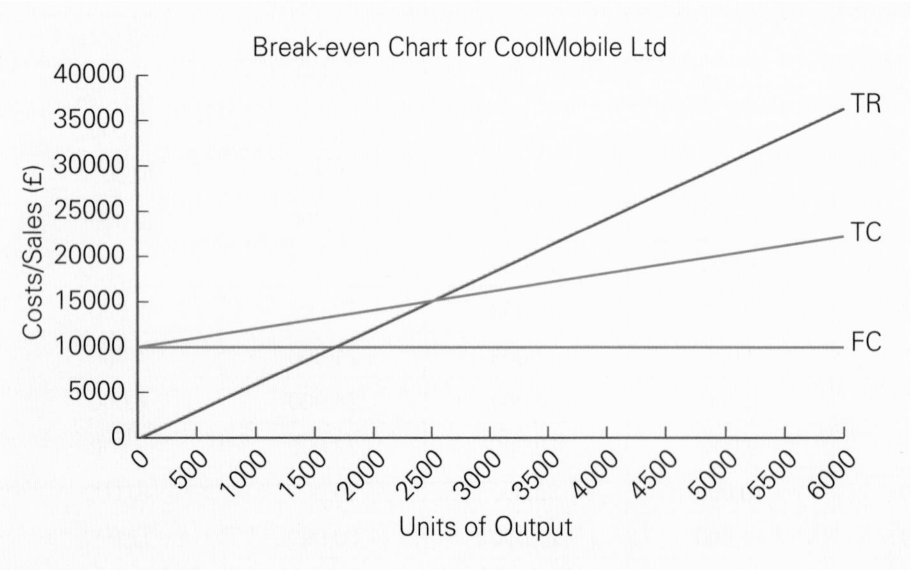

Figure 6.2 Break-even chart for CoolMobile Ltd

Remember, break-even point is the number of units a business needs to sell for its total revenue to equal its total costs. We can clearly see on the chart that the lines for total costs (TC) and total revenue (TR) cross at 2,500 units of output. Therefore, the break-even point for CoolMobile is 2,500 units of output.

As break-even point is the point at which total costs equal total revenue, there is no need to plot the line for variable costs but it is standard practice to plot fixed costs.

Break-even charts can be hand-drawn using graph paper or produced on computer using spreadsheet software.

Task

Examine the break-even chart for CoolMobile and answer the following questions:

1. **Why does the total cost line begin at £10,000 and not at zero?**
2. **Why does the total revenue line begin at zero?**
3. **What is the value of total revenue at the break-even level of output?**

Task

Using graph paper, ruler and pencil, construct a break-even chart for Simon Broadbent, using the table of data you created earlier. Here are some hints to help you complete the task:

- **To plot the X axis, you need to allow for the minimum and maximum units of output.**
- **To plot the Y axis, you need to look at the data for revenue as this will give you the maximum amount required for the costs/sales data.**
- **Fixed costs will be a straight line.**
- **Coloured pencils will be useful to distinguish between fixed costs, total costs and total revenue.**

Does your chart show the correct break-even point?

Now try creating the break-even chart for Simon Broadbent, using spreadsheet software and following the instructions below:

1. **Open spreadsheet software and copy the data from your table into a new worksheet.**
2. **Highlight the data for fixed costs, total costs and total revenue (not the headings) and click on the chart wizard icon.**
3. **Under 'Chart Type', select Line and then select the first graph shown and click Next.**
4. **You should now be looking at the data range, click on the Series tab and in the 'Name' box type FC for series 1, then select series 2 from the 'Series' box and name this TC, then select series 3 and name this TR.**
5. **Click on the box for 'Category (X) axis labels' and this will take you back into your spreadsheet. Highlight the units of output data (but not the heading) and this should show in the pop-up box, then close this box and click Next on the series window.**
6. **Select the 'Titles' tab and type in a title for your chart, label the X axis 'Units of Output' and the Y axis 'Costs/Sales (£)'. Click Next**
7. **Select 'as object in' and click Finish. You will notice that your chart is not quite as it should be, so now you need to format it.**
8. **Right click on one of the numbers on the X axis and click on Format Axis and select the 'Scale' tab and remove the tick from the box that says 'Value (Y) axis crosses between categories'. Now click the alignment tab and set the alignment of the text so that it is vertical, and click OK. Your chart should now have the total revenue originating at zero.**

9. To remove the grey background, right click on it, select 'Format Plot Area' and then 'None', and click OK.

10. To remove the gridlines, click on one of them they will all be highlighted (black box at the end of each one), and then press delete on your keyboard (you can do the same for the border).

Your break-even chart for Simon Broadbent should now look like this:

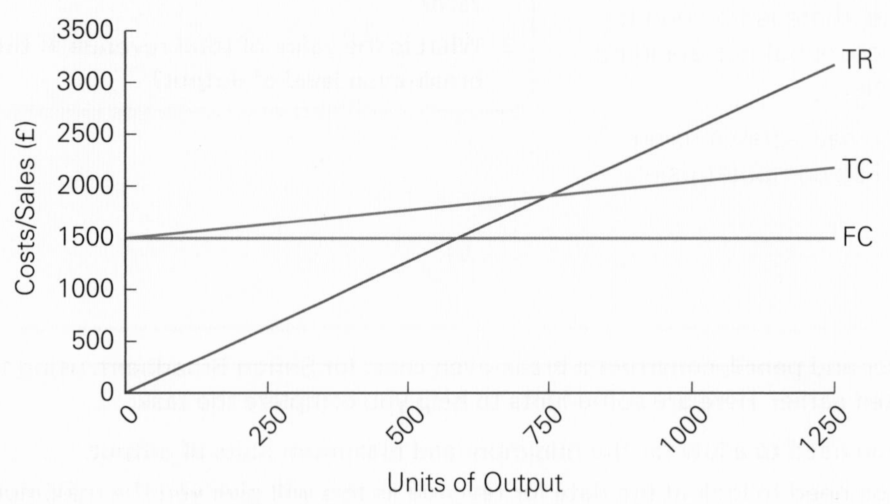

Figure 6.3 Simon Broadbent's break-even chart

Make the grade

P5 Remember this process for P5. You must provide evidence that you can present the break-even point for a given business in an annotated graph.

Margin of safety

Margin of safety is the amount by which demand can fall before a business makes a loss. For example, if CoolMobile were selling 5,000 units of output, then their sales could fall by 2,500 before they start to make a loss. Margin of safety is therefore the desired/current level of output minus the break-even level of output, so, in the case of CoolMobile, it is 2,500 units (5,000 – 2,500).

Margin of safety can be shown on a break-even chart. Figure 6.4 shows CoolMobile Ltd's margin of safety.

Task

If Simon Broadbent was selling 1,100 desserts per year, what would his margin of safety be? Show this on your break-even chart.

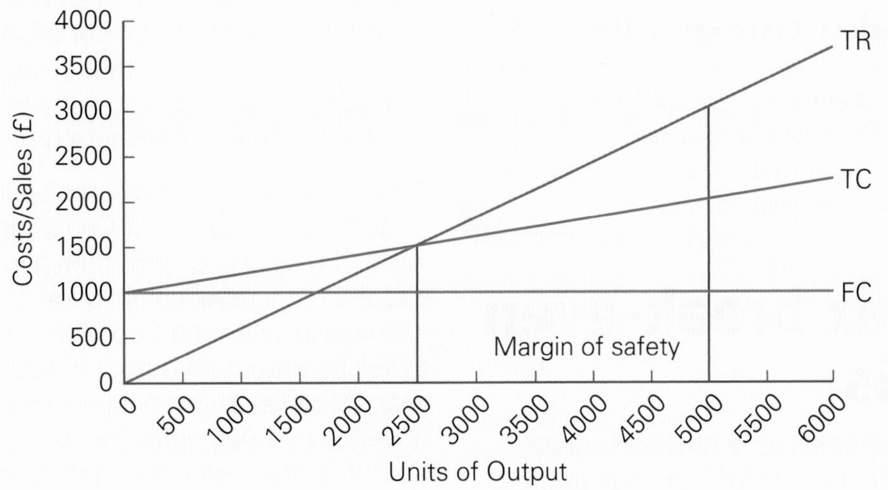

Figure 6.4 CoolMobile Ltd's margin of safety

Using a formula to calculate the break-even point

The simplest way to calculate break-even point is to use the formula:

$$\text{Break-even point (BEP)} = \frac{\text{fixed costs}}{\textbf{contribution per unit}}$$

Contribution per unit = selling price – variable costs

We can calculate the break-even point for CoolMobile Ltd using this formula:

$$\text{Break-even point (BEP)} = \frac{\text{fixed costs}}{\text{contribution per unit}}$$

$$\text{BEP} = \frac{10{,}000}{6-2}$$

$$\text{BEP} = \frac{10{,}000}{4}$$

BEP = 2,500 units (cases)

Task

Use the example above to answer the following questions:

1. **Claire's Chocolates makes handmade chocolates. Each chocolate sells for 80p and has variable costs of 20p. The fixed costs for the business are £18,000. How many chocolates does Claire's need to sell to break even?**
2. **Buxton Tours Ltd run open-top bus tours of the town. Each ticket for a tour sells for £8. The variable costs of each tour are £3 per passenger and the fixed costs for each trip are £125. How many passengers need to go on each tour for it to break even?**
3. **Sue and Bob produce terracotta pots. The labour costs for each pot are £1 and the raw materials for each pot cost £1.50. The fixed costs are £12,000 and the pots sell for £6.50. How many pots need to be sold for Sue and Bob to break even?**
4. **Dairy Friends produce their own ice cream. The ice cream is sold in one-litre cartons. The fixed costs are £24,000 and the variable costs for each litre of ice cream are £2.50. How many litres would Dairy Friends need to sell to break even if their selling price per litre was:**
   a. **£8.50?**
   b. **£10.50?**

> **Make the grade**
>
> **P4** Remember the formula for P4. You must show that you can calculate break-even using given data to show the level at which income equals expenditure.

Complex break-even analysis

The revenue and costs for a business do not often remain constant for long periods of time. A business may change its prices and this will affect the revenue it receives, or a supplier may change its prices and this will affect the costs of the business.

In order to effectively manage its finances, a business needs to be able to find out the effect of changes in revenue and costs on its break-even point. This aids decision making.

Using the example of CoolMobile, the managers of the business want to know what the effect would be on their break-even point if they lowered their price to £4 per case in order to be more competitive with their rival, FunMobile. To find out, a new revenue line is plotted on the break-even chart: see Figure 6.5.

This shows that the new break-even point would be 5,000 units (cases). If CoolMobile could only sell 5,000 cases per year then it would not make a profit; but a reduction in price may result in an increase in sales and CoolMobile may be able to sell its maximum output of 6,000 cases per year. However, this would only leave a margin of safety of 1,000 units (6,000 – 5,000) and therefore the business might consider a price reduction to £4 per case to be too great a risk.

CoolMobile may think that a better way to compete with their rival FunMobile would be to spend more on advertising their products. This would lead to an increase in marketing costs, which would be a fixed cost to the business (as it is not dependent on the number of cases produced). To find out the effect of spending an additional £2,000 on advertising, a new break-even chart can be constructed: see Figure 6.6.

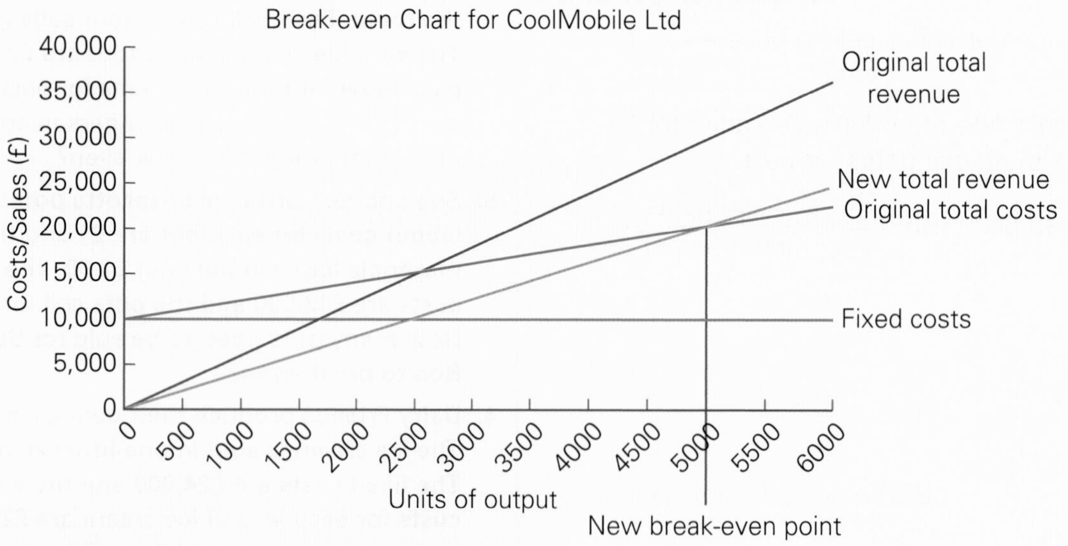

Figure 6.5 Break-even chart with new break-even point

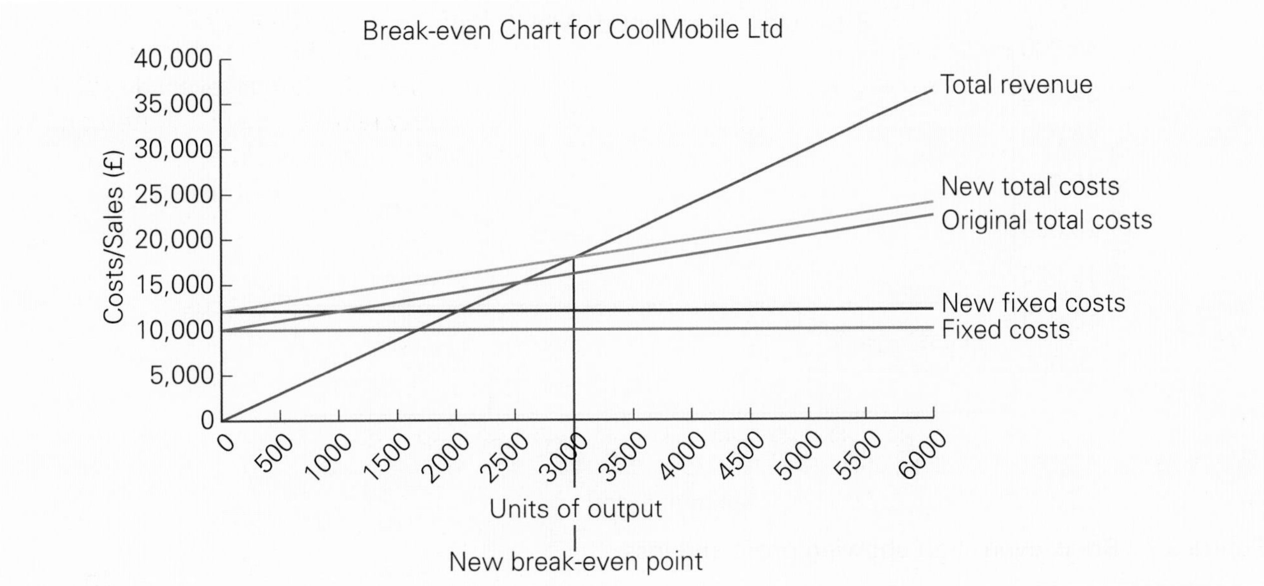

Figure 6.6 Break even chart with advertising costs

This shows that the new break-even point would be 3,000 cases. If CoolMobile continued to sell 5,000 cases per year, then it would make less profit, but more advertising may result in an increase in sales and CoolMobile may be able to sell its maximum output of 6,000 cases per year. This would give a margin of safety of 3,000 units (6,000 – 3,000) and therefore the business might consider an increase in spending on advertising to be worthwhile.

However, it would need to look at the levels of profit to be made. The level of profit (or loss) can be read from the chart by measuring the distance between the total costs and total revenue lines and reading this from the Y axis. If the business produced and sold 5,000 cases with no increase in advertising, it would make £10,000 profit; but if it produced and sold 6,000 cases as a result of an increase in advertising, then it would make £12,000 profit.

Figure 6.7 on the next page (using the new fixed and total costs) shows the levels of output at which a profit will be made (where the total revenue line is above the total costs line) and the levels of output at which a loss will be made (where the total costs line is above the total revenue line).

Some changes to costs are beyond the control of a business. For example, a landlord might increase the rent, a supplier may increase prices or there may be an increase in the national minimum wage that would cause labour costs to rise. For each of the above changes, a new break-even chart could be constructed to show the effect on the break-even point for a business.

Make the grade

M2 Remember this for M2. You must demonstrate the impact of changing cost and revenue data on the break-even point of a given business.

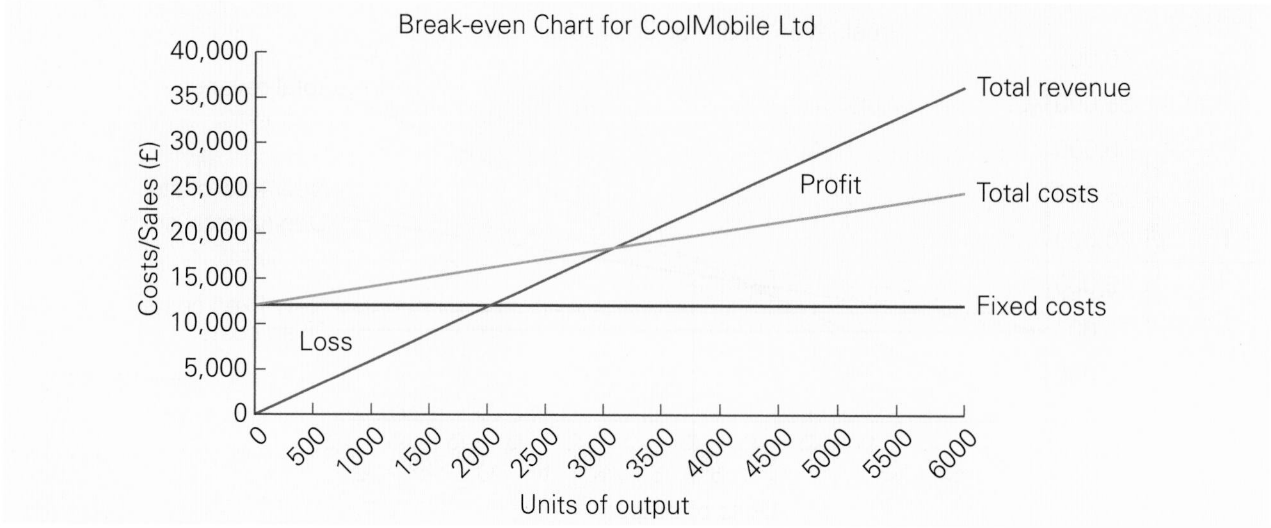

Figure 6.7 Break-even chart showing profit and loss

Task

Using your data for Simon Broadbent as a starting point, create new break-even charts to show the effect on Simon's break-even point of the following changes. In each case, state the new break-even level of output.

1. **An increase in the price Simon sells his desserts for to £3.50.**
2. **An increase of £500 in the rent Simon pays for his premises.**
3. **An increase in the average cost of the raw ingredients Simon uses in each dessert, causing variable costs per unit to rise from 0.50 to £1.**

The importance of break-even for the effective management of finance

In calculating the break-even point, a business is finding the level of output at which total revenue is equal to total costs. This means that if a business produces and sells this level of output, it will generate enough revenue to pay all of its costs. If a business did not calculate its break-even point, it may be that, although it is selling products and generating revenue, this revenue is not enough to meet the costs of the business because the business is not aware of how many products it needs to sell. This situation would lead to losses being made, and eventually the business would have to stop trading.

It is very important for new businesses to calculate the level of output required to break even as there may be limited finance available to sustain continuous losses caused by operating below the break-even level of output. For example, if you were considering setting up a new business washing cars and you needed to wash ten cars per day to breakeven but market research showed that you were only likely to wash five cars per day, then you would know that you were not going to cover your costs and would therefore make a loss. As a result of calculating your break even point, it is likely that you would not go ahead with the business.

It is also important for existing businesses to calculate the break-even point for any new products that they are planning to produce. Although an existing business may have the financial resources to support a product that was operating below the break-even point, it would not wish to do this for a long period of time. Calculating the break-even level of output helps a business to determine the level of financial support that a new product may need.

Calculating break-even also helps a business manage its finance effectively by allowing it to:

- Calculate the effect of a change in price.
- Calculate the effects of changes in costs.
- Estimate the level of output it needs to produce and sell to meet targets for profit.
- Provide evidence to a bank or other financial institution in support of a request for a loan.

Make the grade

D1 Remember this for part of D1. You must be able to evaluate the importance of break-even for the effective management of finance for a given business.

Discussion...

Any entrepreneur considering starting a new business should first calculate the likely break-even point. Discuss.

Jaguar Land Rover

Tata, the Indian parent company of Jaguar Land Rover (JLR), is to take greater management control of the British car maker after withdrawing from talks over government financial support. The business asked for assistance when the credit crunch and recession triggered a collapse in sales.

Tata Motors is said to have brought in senior executives to work alongside JLR's team to improve cash management and lower the company's break-even point. They will be helped by consultants that specialise in the automotive industry who will advise the loss-making British car maker on how to cut costs.

It is thought that JLR's research and development programme and its plans for new models, including a new sports car and small Land Rover, will not be cut.

Source: 'Tata Motors tightens reins at Jaguar Land Rover', by Dominic O'Connell, *Sunday Times*, 16 August 2009

1. Why might the 'collapse in sales' caused by the credit crunch and recession have led to the business asking for financial support from the government?
2. Explain what is meant by 'lower the company's break-even point'.
3. Explain how cutting costs will help to lower JLR's break-even point.
4. To what extent will greater management control of JLR's finances help to support its research and development programme?

Key words

Break-even chart – A line graph showing total revenue, total costs and fixed costs and each level of output, and which enables the break-even point to be identified.

Break-even point – The level of output at which total revenue is equal to total costs and neither a profit nor a loss is made.

Contribution per unit – Selling price minus variable costs.

Fixed costs – Costs that do not change when the business changes the amount it produces or the number of customers it serves.

Margin of safety – The amount by which demand can fall before a business makes a loss.

Total costs – Fixed costs plus variable costs.

Total revenue – The total amount of money received by a business for goods sold or services provided during a certain time period.

Variable costs – Costs that change when the business changes the amount it produces or the number of customers it serves.

Assignment

You must be able to prepare a break-even analysis.

The business organisation

Mel plans to set up a small restaurant selling vegetarian food. Her fixed costs will be £10,000 per year. Market research indicates that a typical customer will pay £8 for a meal at the restaurant and Mel knows that variable costs per customer, such as ingredients and staff costs, will be £4.

1. Mel would like to know how many meals she will need to sell in a year to meet her costs. Calculate her break-even point. **(P4)**
2. Mel would like to see her break-even point on a graph so that she can see the difference between total costs and revenue above and below the break-even point. Create a break-even chart for Mel that is fully labelled and annotated to show the information she needs. **(P5)**
3. a) Mel is considering raising her prices. This would mean that a customer would be paying £9 on average for a meal. Create a new break-even chart for Mel to show the original total revenue, the new total revenue and the two break-even points.

   b) The national minimum wage is increasing and this will increase Mel's variable costs per customer from £4 to £5. Mel would like to know the effect of this change if she kept her average price at £8 per meal. Create a new break-even chart for Mel to show the original total revenue, the original total costs, the new total costs and the two break-even points. **(M2)**

4. Write a short report for Mel explaining:
   - what you have calculated for her.
   - why it is important to know the break-even point for a business.
   - how calculating the break-even point will help her to effectively manage the finances of her business. **(D1)**

To achieve a pass grade you need to:	To achieve a merit grade you need to:	To achieve a distinction you need to:
P4 calculate break-even using given data to show the level at which income equals expenditure	**M2** demonstrate the impact of changing cost and revenue data on the break-even point of a selected business	**D1** evaluate the importance of break-even for the effective management of business finance
P5 present the break-even as an annotated graph showing break-even		

Chapter 7
Cash flow forecast

What are you finding out?

All businesses have money moving through them on a daily basis; they receive money and they pay money out. For example, AA Driving School instructors receive money from learner drivers for their lessons and they have to pay money out for fuel each day. This movement of money through a business is known as its cash flow. The management of cash flow is very important to a business – if the driving school did not have the money available to purchase fuel, lessons could not take place and then the business would be unable to continue. Businesses therefore need to plan their cash flow and they do this by using cash flow forecasting.

This chapter will help you to:

- Prepare a cash flow forecast using monthly data.
- Analyse the implications of regular and irregular cash inflows and outflows for a business organisation.
- Evaluate the importance of cash flow for the effective management of business finance.

Cash flow

Cash flow is the movement of money through a business or organisation. **Cash inflows** are amounts of money coming into a business and **cash outflows** are amounts of money leaving a business.

Cash inflows can come from:

- revenue
- loans
- interest received on money invested
- rent received for premises
- the sale of **assets** such as machinery
- grants: for example, money received from the government
- the owners of the business.

Cash outflows can be for:

- fixed costs such as rent and salaries
- variable costs such as raw materials and wages
- the purchase of assets
- payment of taxes
- value-added tax (VAT) payments
- loan repayments
- interest payments
- dividend payments (payment of a share of the profits to shareholders).

For example, in 2008, National Express had cash inflows from the sale of tickets, from selling property, plant and equipment and from interest received. It had cash outflows for taxation, to buy plant and equipment and to pay dividends to shareholders.

Businesses often experience cash flow problems. This happens when their demands for cash outflows are greater than their cash inflows. This is usually as a result of customers not paying for goods and services on time or not paying at all, but it can also arise if the business does not keep its costs under control.

> Did you know...
>
> **More than half of Britain's small businesses fail because of cashflow problems.**

Cash flow forecast

A **cash flow forecast** is an estimate of the cash inflows and outflows for a business or organisation over a future period of time. Businesses use cash flow forecasts to help them manage their cash flow. Using a cash flow forecast can show a business when it might be short of cash and this enables the business to put measures in place to prevent this from happening, for example, arranging an **overdraft** for a short period of time.

Cash flow forecasting is especially important for businesses that have irregular inflows or outflows of cash. For example, a small hotel in Skegness will have more cash flowing in during the summer months than it does in the winter months; a construction company will have a lot of cash outflows when building houses and then large cash inflows at the end of the project when the houses are sold. Businesses such as these need to manage their cash very carefully. If the construction company ran out of cash while building the houses, it would not be able to pay its suppliers or its workers. This could mean that suppliers refuse to deliver any more raw materials and that workers are laid off. All of this would result in the building work stopping and may cause the company to stop trading.

Task

1. **Name a business that you think could have irregular inflows or outflows of cash (this could be a local, national or international business).**
2. **Discuss the consequences for this business of failing to manage its cash flow effectively.**

If a construction company runs out of money, work will come to a halt

Make the grade

M3 Remember this task for M3. You must analyse the implications of regular and irregular cash inflows and outflows for a given business or a business of your choice.

Preparing a cash flow forecast

To prepare a cash flow forecast, a business must be able to estimate what the cash inflows and outflows will be over a future period of time. Businesses base their forecasts on what has happened in the past and upon factors that are likely to affect their cash flow in the future.

Example

Peter Graham runs a small hotel in Brighton called Chez Peter. Using the information he has given us below, we can prepare a cash flow forecast for the six months from June to November (see the next page).

At the beginning of June, Peter will have £400 in the bank. Every month Peter knows that he will have to pay £1,200 rent and £250 for business rates. In June, he will have to pay for repairs and maintenance, which he estimates will cost £850. In July, he will have to pay an insurance premium of £600.

Peter predicts that his revenue for the six months will be: June: £2,600; July £5,600; August £8,400; September £2,500; October £1,300 and November £500. He knows that the cost of purchases, such as food and toiletries for the guests, is usually 20% of revenue, and heating and lighting will be 10% of revenue from June to September and 20% of revenue from October to November.

Every November, Peter rents out his function room for one weekend to the hotel next door for a special event. For this, he receives rent of £200.

From preparing this cash flow forecast, we can see that Peter will have a cash shortage in June of £80. Peter will therefore need to take steps to avoid this happening; for example, he could arrange an overdraft with his bank for the month of June or he could negotiate with tradesmen to pay for his repairs and maintenance over a two-month period.

Chez Peter

Cash flow forecast for Chez Peter from June–December						
	June (£)	July (£)	Aug (£)	Sept (£)	Oct (£)	Nov (£)
Cash inflows						
Revenue	2,600	5,600	8,400	2,500	1,300	500
Rent						200
Total cash inflow	2,600	5,600	8,400	2,500	1,300	700
Cash outflows						
Rent	1,200	1,200	1,200	1,200	1,200	1,200
Business rates	250	250	250	250	250	250
Repairs and maintenance	850					
Insurance		600				
Purchases	520	1,120	1,680	500	260	100
Heating and lighting	260	560	840	250	260	100
Total cash outflow	3,080	3,730	3,970	2,200	1,970	1,650
Net cash flow	–480	1,870	4,430	300	–670	–950
Opening bank balance	400	–80	1,790	6,220	6,520	5,850
Closing bank balance	–80	1,790	6,220	6,520	5,850	4,900

Notes:

- Net cash flow = total cash inflow – total cash outflow.
- Closing bank balance = opening bank balance + net cash flow.
- The opening bank balance for each month is the closing bank balance for the previous month.

Because cash flow is the movement of all money through a business, it does not just represent revenue and costs. For example, a cash inflow could be a loan to the business, but this is not revenue. Similarly, a cash outflow could be a loan repayment, but this is neither a fixed nor variable cost for a business. Therefore, as profit = revenue – total costs, a cash flow forecast cannot be used as a means of forecasting profit or loss. In the example above for Chez Peter, the closing bank balance of £4,900 in November is not profit, it is simply the amount that he will have in the bank at the end of November if his cash flow forecast proves to be correct.

Make the grade

P6 Remember this task for P6. You must be able to prepare a 12-month cash flow forecast using monthly data for a given business or a business of your choice.

Task

Using the example above, prepare a cash flow forecast for the following business for six months from February to July:

Platts Builders Ltd has purchased a plot of land in Lincoln and has planning permission to build 12 houses. It plans to start the work on 1st February when the project manager estimates that it will have £40,000 in the bank. The company is borrowing £250,000 from the bank and this will be paid into their account in early February.

The project is expected to last for six months. In the first month, £80,000 will need to be spent on building materials and £15,000 on wages. From March to June, building materials will cost £110,000 per month and wages will be £12,000 per month. In the final month, July, building materials are expected to cost £70,000 and wages £11,000.

In February, there will be an insurance premium of £3,500 to pay, and every month there will be interest charges to pay of £1,800 and other expenses amounting to £1,100 per month.

The project manager estimates that there will be three houses ready to sell by April at a price of £160,000 each and a further three houses ready to sell in May for the same price. However, the market is a little slow, and the houses are expected to take two months to sell.

Using ICT to prepare a cash flow forecast

Cash flow forecasts can be prepared using spreadsheet software. For example, the cash flow forecast for Chez Peter was prepared using Microsoft Excel. Figure 7.1 is a screen shot showing the formulas used.

Using spreadsheet software to prepare a cash flow forecast is useful for a business because possible solutions to any cash shortages can be modelled. For example, for Chez Peter, we could split the costs of the repairs and maintenance between June and July and very quickly see the effect this would have.

Task

If you have completed the cash flow forecast for Platts Builders using pen, paper and calculator, do it again now using spreadsheet software.

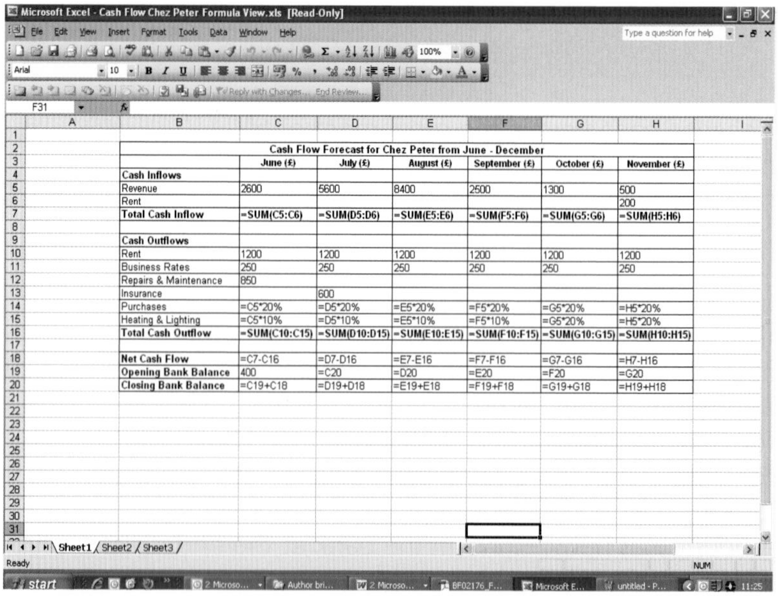

Cash Flow Forecast for Chez Peter from June - December						
	June (£)	July (£)	August (£)	September (£)	October (£)	November (£)
Cash Inflows						
Revenue	2600	5600	8400	2500	1300	500
Rent						200
Total Cash Inflow	=SUM(C5:C6)	=SUM(D5:D6)	=SUM(E5:E6)	=SUM(F5:F6)	=SUM(G5:G6)	=SUM(H5:H6)
Cash Outflows						
Rent	1200	1200	1200	1200	1200	1200
Business Rates	250	250	250	250	250	250
Repairs & Maintenance	850					
Insurance		600				
Purchases	=C5*20%	=D5*20%	=E5*20%	=F5*20%	=G5*20%	=H5*20%
Heating & Lighting	=C5*10%	=D5*10%	=E5*10%	=F5*10%	=G5*20%	=H5*20%
Total Cash Outflow	=SUM(C10:C15)	=SUM(D10:D15)	=SUM(E10:E15)	=SUM(F10:F15)	=SUM(G10:G15)	=SUM(H10:H15)
Net Cash Flow	=C7-C16	=D7-D16	=E7-E16	=F7-F16	=G7-G16	=H7-H16
Opening Bank Balance	400	=C20	=D20	=E20	=F20	=G20
Closing Bank Balance	=C19+C18	=D19+D18	=E19+E18	=F19+F18	=G19+G18	=H19+H18

Figure 7.1 Chez Peter cash flow forecast

Cash flow management

Businesses need to avoid cash flow problems. If a business is short of cash, it will be unable to pay its suppliers who, in turn, will refuse to supply any further goods or services. This can then lead to a poor **credit rating**, resulting in other suppliers refusing to supply goods on **credit**. Similarly, a business that is short of cash may be unable to pay its staff, which may result in those staff being made redundant or looking for jobs elsewhere. Severe cash shortages lead to businesses failing.

As cash flow is the movement of cash through a business, to avoid cash flow problems, a business could speed up cash inflows, increase the amount of cash available by finding additional funding or decrease or delay cash outflows, or put in a combination of these measures. The table below shows the actions a business could take:

Unfortunately, some of these actions can have negative effects. If customers are given shorter credit periods, they may choose to take their business elsewhere, and smaller businesses may be reluctant to constantly remind customers that they owe them money for fear of losing their business. Cutting costs by using cheaper suppliers may mean compromising on the quality of the goods supplied, which may affect the quality of the end product and affect sales. Delaying the purchase of assets or selling assets may prevent a business from expanding or accepting new orders, and taking out a loan or an overdraft attracts costly interest payments.

Make the grade

D1 Remember this task for D1. You must be able to evaluate the importance of cash flow for the effective management of the finance of a given business or a business of your choice.

Actions a business can take to improve its cash flow		
Speed up cash inflows	**Decrease/delay cash outflows**	**Find additional funding**
Negotiate shorter credit periods for customers	Negotiate longer credit periods with suppliers	Arrange an overdraft with the bank
Send out reminders to customers who owe money	Cut costs; for example, find a cheaper supplier	Take out a bank loan
Offer a discount to customers if they pay for their goods/services promptly	Delay the purchase of assets, such as new machinery	Sell assets, such as land

Task

Examine the cash flow forecast you prepared earlier for Platts Builders Ltd and answer the following questions:

1. **Outline the problems shown by the cash flow forecast.**
2. **Explain three possible courses of action that Platts Builders could take to avoid the problems you have outlined.**
3. **To what extent might the cash flow forecast be unreliable?**
4. **Evaluate the importance of the cash flow forecast for the effective management of Platts Builders' cash flow.**

Discussion...

Good cash flow is more important to a business than making a profit. Discuss.

The Maypole Hotel Group

In February 2009, hotel operator the Maypole Group revealed that it was in talks with its lenders after doubts were raised over its future. This came as a result of disappointing trading at the end of 2008, which was considerably below expectations and the equivalent period in 2007.

The group, which owned six hotels in the UK, admitted that it was experiencing 'significant pressures' on its cash flow and was in discussions with its bankers with a view to agreeing a solution. It was hoping to reduce costs and was considering options for fundraising to ensure that the company could continue to trade.

The company was founded in November 2003 and owned the 32-bedroom Wroxton House hotel near Banbury in Oxfordshire, the Lifeboat Inn and Old Coach House, in Thornham, Norfolk, and the Wayford Bridge Hotel in Norfolk.

Source: 'Cash flow problems hit Maypole Hotel group' by Gemma Sharkey, www.caterersearch.com, 19 February 2009

1. Identify the likely cause of the Maypole Group's cash flow problems.
2. Outline ways in which a hotel group could reduce costs.
3. Explain two ways in which the hotel group could raise a significant amount of finance in order to overcome its cash flow problems.
4. To what extent would the preparation of cash flow forecasts for the six-month period from September 2008 to February 2009 have been of benefit to the hotel group?

Key words

Assets – Items a business owns that generate income.

Cash flow – The movement of money through a business or organisation.

Cash flow forecast – An estimate of the cash inflows and outflows for a business or organisation over a future period of time.

Cash inflows – Amounts of money coming into a business.

Cash outflows – Amounts of money leaving a business.

Credit – Providing a period of time in which to pay for goods or services rather than asking for immediate payment.

Credit rating – A judgement made about how safe it is to provide a business with goods on credit.

Net cash flow – Total cash inflow – total cash outflow.

Overdraft – An arrangement with a bank to borrow money up to an agreed maximum amount. The amount borrowed may change daily.

Assignment

You must be able to create a cash flow forecast.

The business organisation

Mel plans to take over a small restaurant selling vegetarian food. However, she needs a cash flow forecast for the business for her first year to present to the bank so that she can get a loan to help her refurbish the business premises.

She has provided the following information for the first year of trading (January to December):

- Mel is prepared to put £1,500 cash into her business in the first month to help meet her expenses.
- Every month Mel will have to pay £500 rent and £100 in business rates to the council. In January she will have a £500 insurance premium to pay.
- She predicts sales in the first month, January, will be £1,000 while the cost of ingredients will be £400. Staff costs will be £100 and electricity £100. To get the business off to a good start, Mel will spend £200 on advertising.
- In February, Mel expects to have more business and predicts sales of £1,200. She expects ingredients to cost £500. Staff costs will be £200 and electricity £150. She will spend £50 on advertising.
- Mel expects March and April to be busy months and predicts sales of £2,000 per month, with the cost of ingredients being £750 per month. Staff costs are expected to be £250 per month and electricity £250 per month. She will spend £100 per month on advertising.
- In May, June and July, sales are expected to be £1,500. Ingredients will cost £600, staff £250, electricity £100 and advertising £100.
- In the remaining five months of the year, Mel forecasts sales of £2,000 per month and expects ingredients to cost £750 per month, staff to cost £250 per month, electricity to be £250 per month and advertising to be £100 per month.

1. Prepare Mel's cash flow forecast. **(P6)**
2. a) Once people get to know about Mel's business and she has loyal customers, Mel expects her cash inflows to increase and become more regular. Analyse the implications of this on Mel's business.

   b) Mel cannot be sure of her sales predictions. Because her business is a restaurant, she could lose sales if a new restaurant opened nearby. Analyse the implications for Mel's business if her cash inflows became irregular.

   c) Every month, Mel will have to pay her rent and rates regardless of how much sales revenue she might receive. Analyse the impact of these regular payments on Mel's cash flow.

   d) Mel may find that there are some items (such as linen and cutlery) in the business that need to be replaced. This would cause irregular outflows of cash from her business. Analyse the impact of these irregular payments on Mel's cash flow. **(M3)**
3. Write a short report for Mel explaining the importance of cash flow for the effective management of her business finances. **(D1)**

To achieve a pass grade you need to:	To achieve a merit grade you need to:	To achieve a distinction you need to:
P6 prepare an annual cash flow forecast using monthly data	**M3** analyse the implications of regular and irregular cash inflows and outflows for a business organisation	**D1** evaluate the importance of cash flow for the effective management of business finance

Unit 4

People in organisations

Chapter 8
Job roles and functions in organisations

What are you finding out?

At some stage in our lives we've all been told we need to 'get organised'. There is a very strong possibility that every member of your class has been instructed by someone to get their bedroom 'sorted out' – in other words, 'organised'.

What does being 'organised' mean? Think about the things that add up to getting anything organised. Things are in their right place. There are places for things and these places are arranged properly in the room. Being organised means having some form of organisation so that a purpose is achieved. Have you ever been driven mad because you couldn't find your shoes? In a sense, every bedroom needs organisation so that it serves its proper function.

Business organisations are of course different, but the basic principle is the same. Organisations have people doing job roles in particular structures, to serve certain functions. They could work in departments. In each separate department, or section, things are arranged to achieve something.

This chapter will help you to:

- Understand job roles within different organisational structures.
- Understand how organisations can have different structures.
- Create basic documents concerned with recruiting to a particular job role.
- Complete an application process for a specific job.
- Match your own skills and knowledge to possible job opportunities.
- Compare job roles and structures in organisations.
- Make judgements about job roles within particular contexts.
- Make judgements about the effectiveness of recruitment in an organisation.

Job roles

Could your bedroom do with some organisation?

Imagine your favourite movie. In that movie, actors play 'roles' that fit in with the storyline. In organisations, people perform roles that fit in with the aims and objectives. Whilst they are not acting as such, they are behaving in ways that the organisation requires. They relate to each other according to the needs of the business.

Just as you would (reluctantly!) set about organising your bedroom by tidying up and putting things away, a business organisation is arranged carefully so that its overall aims and objectives can be achieved. Chapter 3 tells you that organisations can have many different aims. Some exist to make profit for shareholders. Others exist to provide services that we all need such as health or education; others work on a voluntary basis.

One thing that all organisations have in common is that they provide employment for people. An organisation needs to employ people to carry out the different roles that exist within it. (Later we will see how this can be done effectively.) It is a characteristic of organisations that people have to fit in to a structure. An organisational structure is a framework that helps a business organisation achieve its purposes.

Hierarchy

A typical structure is arranged in a **hierarchy**. A hierarchy is where there are different levels of authority from top to bottom. In other words, the person at the top can take bigger and broader decisions about things than people lower down. For example, he or she can set the 'direction' of the organisation – hence the term 'director' used for those at the top.

The following is a classical structure for a private commercial **company**, working to make profits for shareholders. Remember that not all private businesses have this structure. For example, a fish and chip shop might be run by one person (a sole trader) and he or she might have a very small organisational structure:

Director(s)

At the top level is the person, or people, who make strategic decisions that give the business its overall direction – **directors** work together to agree big decisions. A 'strategy' might be to enter new markets or to target different customers.

Task

Together with a classmate, list three different types of local business organisation. For each one, identify three 'strategic' types of decision that might have been taken. Example: a local supermarket might have taken a decision to relocate to your area.

Directors make decisions that can affect everyone in the organisation. They are said to have a wide 'span of influence and control'. Every function in the organisation can be affected by the decisions taken by directors. If the directors of a business decide to purchase a costly new automated machine to change a production process, many people in the business might be affected. Production staff could at the very least have their jobs changed. They could even be made redundant. Finance staff might have to find the money to fund the investment. Human resources will have to deal with staff affected, by providing training.

Because the impact of these decisions is so wide-ranging, only top people such as directors in the structure have the **authority** to make them. Note that this is not the same for every organisation. Some organisations allow people lower down a hierarchy to make big decisions. This is called '**delegation**'.

Apart from making strategic decisions, directors can also make decisions about overall policy. A policy is something that applies across a whole organisation. There might be a policy about 'acceptable use of IT', about holidays, about sickness pay and maternity and paternity leave. Once again these are big issues for all staff.

Task

See if you can find out in your school or college who decides on policy. Write out your own statement explaining the differences between a 'strategy' and a 'policy'.

Manager(s)

The next level down in a classic hierarchy is day-to-day management. Managers usually run the various functions in an organisation, based on the strategy and policies set by directors. But what is a 'function'?

Some typical functions in organisations are:

- Finance
- Marketing
- Human resources
- Production
- Sales
- IT
- Customer service
- Distribution.

All organisations are structured according to certain functions. A 'functional area' in an organisation consists of a group of people whose work is focused particularly on that function. So a manufacturer is likely to have a 'production' function, a 'sales' function and possibly a 'maintenance' function, among others. Functions in an organisation are governed by what the overall purpose of the organisation is. For example, your school or college is unlikely to have a 'sales' function, or a 'production' function. It will have a science department, however, and most companies will not.

Some people would say they do 'produce' something and they also 'sell' something – what do you think?

A company that manufactures window frames certainly *does* produce a physical product.

Managers are held accountable to directors and shareholders for their performance. This means they are answerable to them. Most managers have performance targets they must meet. This is one reason why managers often have SMART objectives (see Chapter 3). They are specific, measurable, achievable, realistic and related to a period of time. This means that more senior people can monitor and check their performance.

Make the grade

M1 You can use the information on the next page about the Sekura Group to help you achieve M1 when you compare job roles and functions.

Sekura Group

Sekura is a northeast-based manufacturer of uPVC windows, doors and conservatories. The business is organised in a classical hierarchy with a managing director, Mr Charles Hill, working with a small number of other company directors. Mr Hill and his directors make key decisions and the rest of the workforce have to be guided by these.

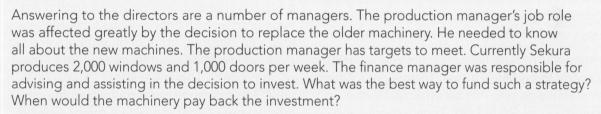

Recently, Sekura invested over one million pounds in equipment and machinery to transform the manufacturing process. This decision was taken to improve speed of production and to cut out waste.

Answering to the directors are a number of managers. The production manager's job role was affected greatly by the decision to replace the older machinery. He needed to know all about the new machines. The production manager has targets to meet. Currently Sekura produces 2,000 windows and 1,000 doors per week. The finance manager was responsible for advising and assisting in the decision to invest. What was the best way to fund such a strategy? When would the machinery pay back the investment?

Other managers, such as sales and marketing, all have targets for their functions. How many products need to be sold? Which markets to target? Where to sell and how to promote? Each manager leads a team of staff to assist the company in achieving its aims and objectives.

1. In the Sekura context, explain the difference between a strategy and a policy.
2. What is meant by a business 'function'? How does Sekura benefit from having specialist functions?
3. List at least three other responsibilities that managers will have in Sekura.

Motivating staff

A vital part of any manager's job role is to supervise and *motivate* staff. A manager cannot do everything alone. This is why it is so important to recruit the right people into job roles. Good managers are able to give their staff clear targets for a period of time. Then they guide and support staff so that they are motivated to do their jobs well.

To be 'motivated' means that you work hard to do the best you can. A skilful manager is one who gives staff the desire to work. A poor manager has the opposite effect: staff are *demotivated*. This means they don't try their best. Sir Alex Ferguson of Manchester United is known as an extremely motivational manager because his players really work hard for the team. To have top skills is one thing, but add to this top motivation as well and you have a very good chance of success.

Managers create **motivation** by offering rewards such as salary bonuses, giving praise and recognition, by offering promotion and career progression opportunities. All employees like to feel recognised and valued. A good manager does this well.

Task

Find out how many of your classmates have part-time jobs. Do some research to find out whether they work for a manager who 'motivates' them, or who 'demotivates'. Find out why in each case and make a note of the reasons.

Recruitment and dismissal

Managers are usually responsible for recruiting new people to work in the business. This is a very important task. Careful recruitment means that the right people, with the appropriate skills to carry out a job role, are employed. We will see various ways of doing this in the next chapter.

Recruitment means firstly deciding on whether a job needs to be filled. It then means considering how suitable people can be attracted to the organisation to do that job. Then, where a job should be advertised and how the job should be described. Prior to recruitment, managers often have to think about the education, experience and training needed by new staff.

Dismissal means ending a person's contract with the organisation: giving them 'the sack'. Dismissal can be the result of disciplinary action or it could be caused by a capability problem. Managers supervise staff and appraise how they are performing in a job. If a member of staff has targets to meet and fails to do so, sometimes it is the manager's unpleasant task to dismiss them. The sales function can be especially hard in this respect. A car salesman who regularly fails to sell his quota of cars in a month is highly likely to face dismissal.

Allocation of work

Managers hold an important role and they are one of several people within organisations who give employees their daily tasks to complete. Skilful managers arrange tasks so that a workload is fairly distributed between staff. On a daily basis employees can be given instructions by managers on what to do. This is often called 'line management'. As we will see, almost all job descriptions state that a job holder must carry out all reasonable tasks as allocated by the manager.

Task

Write a statement explaining what problems can arise if a manager does not allocate job tasks on a fair basis.

An organisational structure creates **lines of command**. This means that managers control only their own functional area. For example, a finance manager in a business should not walk onto a shop floor in a production context and start ordering production workers around. In all organisations, authority follows a 'line of command'. This means that usually only your 'line manager' can rightly give you your instructions. Other managers might well be senior in the organisation but they are not expected to control or supervise staff members who do not answer to them directly.

Task

Discuss with a classmate the idea of 'line management'. Why might it cause problems in a medium-to-large organisation if all managers had the authority to give tasks to anyone they chose?

Managers as communicators

Communication is the difference between a really effective manager and a poor one. Communication means getting a message from A to B exactly as it is intended. There is clarity and understanding.

Communication skills

Naim Mahmood is manager of a pizza business. His management style is very direct. One day he spoke to a female member of his staff to allocate her tasks for the morning. Before he got down to the real business, Naim began the conversation by asking, 'Have you been eating garlic?' Then he listed five or six things he wanted to have done before lunchtime. The woman in question did not hear the first four things that Naim said because she was so embarrassed and upset by his opening comment.

Mr Mahmood left the premises that morning confident that he had given clear instructions to his staff. On his return he was furious that some of his instructions had not been carried out.

1. In your opinion, is the employee at fault or Mr Mahmood? Justify your view.
2. What has happened in this case to the manager's communication? How could he have done things better?

Good managers can say things clearly, they can write things down clearly and they have a sympathetic understanding that people need to know what to do. In the past there have been many extremely knowledgeable and well-educated managers who were not able to communicate. This could be the difference between success and failure in an organisation.

Managers must communicate in many ways. They can communicate face to face, in writing, via email, by phone, memorandum or report. Managers have to attend meetings. It is crucial that managers can negotiate with other managers and directors so that everyone understands the issues and problems that a departmental function might have.

Task

Work with one of your classmates and create a two-columned table listing the various methods of communication a manager in a large organisation will have to use in their job role. For each method, give an illustration of the context in which this form of communication will be used.

Example

Communication method	Context
Face-to-face meeting	This method is best used when detailed instructions need to be given. This means that the member of staff can ask questions

Planning and decision making

Managers have to plan ahead. If you ask your school or college's head or principal, you will find that they plan ahead by examining the numbers of pupils or students that are likely to come to the school or college next year.

In a private business, managers often look at sales trends or market trends in order to plan ahead. Managers are expected to forecast how things are going to change. In the Sekura Group case study earlier, managers will have planned ahead to take account of the impact of the investment in new equipment. They will have considered things like staff, costs, disruption and training.

Decision making in organisations is expected of all managers. An organisational structure, as we saw earlier, gives some people the right to make decisions. A good manager makes decisions quickly based on the best interests of the overall organisation. The reasons for decisions should be understood by everyone and they should be taken fairly and sensitively, especially when people are affected. A lack of decisions can cause any organisation to fail.

As an example of the above, imagine a business where a manager knows a major supplier is having difficulties. However, the manager ignores this information and fails to make any decisions on seeking alternative suppliers (e.g. of raw materials). The supplier goes bankrupt and stops trading. The absence of a proper management decision has placed the business in jeopardy.

Make the grade

M1 Think about decision making in a hierarchy when you are working to achieve M1. If a decision has to be made *very* quickly, is it helpful to have to wait until a more senior manager is on the scene? What can a manager do to get around this problem?

Problem solving

In every job role there are problems to solve. Managers have responsibility to make sure their functional section of the organisation does its job. So a sales manager who finds that sales are falling must try to act to stop the decline. Here are some problems a typical manager in a business might have to face:

- A person calls in sick and there is work to be done.
- A customer has a serious complaint.
- A supplier cannot deliver on time because of a dispute.
- The IT system has failed because of a computer virus.
- A member of staff has been caught stealing.
- A machine has developed a fault.
- Two members of staff have had an argument.

Every manager is paid to deal with problems. Good managers learn to anticipate problems and sort them out quickly.

Supervisors/team leaders

Organisations often appoint 'supervisors' to look after a group of employees carrying out their job roles. As an example, today, there are many care support services provided for elderly people. Support workers are appointed to visit old people in their homes and help them with basic everyday things such as shopping and housework. In this context, the supervisor is also a support worker but has extra responsibility for managing a group of staff. This might mean allocating work or helping with a problem case.

Operatives

An '**operative**' is the term used to describe people who carry out the basic day-to-day work. This could be giving personal support as described above; it could be on the shopfloor in a factory or a shop. In many organisations people work in offices doing basic clerical duties.

It is very important to realise that at *all* levels people do job roles that are vital to the organisation. People on the shopfloor in a factory are essential to the business. Whilst a structure shows different levels of power, authority and pay, everyone has a role to play in the success of an organisation.

Task

On your break, or at lunchtime, make a note of the people in your school or college carrying out basic job roles at 'operative' level. This might include cleaners, refectory or canteen staff, porters or drivers. How important would you say they are to the organisation?

Fieldwork

Together with one or two of your classmates, either arrange to visit a business organisation or search for an appropriate online business. Using a table listing the various kinds of job role, try to identify the main features of the roles as they operate within the structure of the organisation. When you have completed your visit, create a short presentation to give jointly to the rest of your class.

Organisational structures

Earlier we commented that a fish and chip shop may well be owned by one person. He or she is a sole trader carrying full responsibility for running all aspects of the business.

The smaller the business, usually the flatter the structure. Being 'flat' means that there are not many layers in the hierarchy.

A flat organisational structure: Bells Fish & Chips

Graham Kennedy runs Bells fish and chip shop. This is a busy and successful takeaway food shop just outside Durham. Graham runs this business as a sole trader. However, he employs eight staff.

The structure of Graham's organisation is very flat. There is:

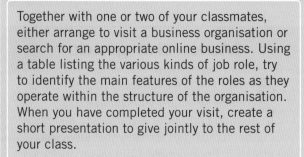

On a day-to-day basis Graham can give instructions and guidance to his staff. If there is a problem, he can deal with it. If a member of staff has a problem, they can talk to Graham. All of the functions of the business, whether they are finance, maintenance of equipment, advertising, sales or recruitment, can be handled by Graham. On a day-to-day basis, this structure performs only two functions – production and sales. Bells is a very informal organisation.

'I take all the risks and I make all the decisions,' says Graham.

One member of staff, Margaret, has worked in the shop for years. When Graham is not around, Margaret runs the shop.

1. Bells has a **flat structure**. What advantages does this give to the organisation?
2. Is Graham's job is made easier by having a flat structure? Are there any disadvantages?

A hierarchical structure

Large organisations often have **tall structures**. There are many levels of authority from top to bottom. A complex plc can have a board of directors, then a multitude of functional divisions dividing the work up horizontally. These can be based on typical functions such as marketing or finance, or they could be based on product or geographic area.

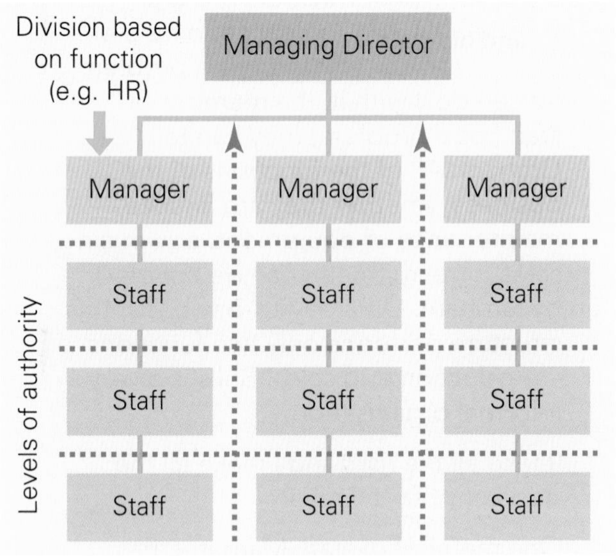

Figure 8.1 A typical 'tall' hierarchy

Research and investigate

Access the website of the multinational company AkzoNobel at www.akzonobel.com. Click on the site link to 'organisation'. With a classmate, summarise the way this company is structured and prepare a report for the rest of your class.

In a tall hierarchy, the (horizontal) levels from top to bottom show the distribution of authority. The divisions from top to bottom across the structure (vertical) show how the work of the structure is divided up into functions or specialist areas.

There are virtually no limits to the complexity and diversity that organisational structures can take. Organisations can be structured according to departmental functions such as finance, or according to divisions, such as 'polychemicals' (AkzoNobel).

Task

Find out how your school or college organisation is structured. Draw up a chart to illustrate the structure and write your own comments about whether you feel it is a tall or a flat hierarchy.

Make the grade

M1 When you are examining your school or college structure you can use this information to contribute towards M1 and show your understanding of the way that job roles are affected. For example, who takes decisions about the organisation's IT system? How are people consulted about it?

Make the grade

D1 You can use the following case to work towards D1 to help show the ways in which job roles can be affected by the structure of the organisation.

The Vice Principal is annoyed

Trimdon College of Further Education is a very large organisation employing over 650 staff on four sites. The structure broadly looks as shown in Figure 8.2.

One of the Vice Principals had made it clear to a head of faculty that a particular course should be run at a short-term loss because it was considered important for the local area and she had agreed this with the local council. However, it turned out that the faculty concerned had not been able to run the course because of a shortage of full-time staff. A head of department had felt unable to take staff off another full-time programme because it would have caused a problem.

The VP wanted to know why she had not been informed of this and was very annoyed.

1. Would you say Trimdon College is a 'tall' or a 'flat' structure? Justify your response.
2. Do you think that the problem experienced by the Vice Principal is caused by the structure?
3. What would you suggest the VP could have done differently to avoid this problem?

Board of governors
↓
2 vice principals
↓
7 heads of faculty
↓
Heads of academic departments
↓
Teaching staff
↓
4 heads of service:
- Marketing
- Human resources
- Management information system (MIS)
- Estates and Facilities

↓
Librarian
↓
IT support
↓
Exams centre
↓
Administration and reception
↓
Caretakers and cleaners

Figure 8.2 Hierarchy of Trimdon College

Matrix structures

While a classic organisational structure divides work up into specialities such as human resources and is based on a top-down hierarchy, a matrix structure brings people together to work on particular **projects**. A team leader manages a project and people join the team until the project is complete.

For staff this means that they may work for more than one team. The functions of finance, marketing, HR, etc. still exist, but now the specialists serve the teams.

A matrix structure works well when the organisation operates on project lines. So if staff are working on a particular product development, this is a project team. Alternatively, a group doing research into the effects of drugs on disease might work in a project team. In both cases a matrix allows them to focus on something with the support of other functions.

Make the grade

M1 **D1** The information on matrix organisations could help you to explain the relationship between job roles and organisational structure for M1 and D1.

Key terms

Hierarchy – An organisation where there are several layers of authority and decision-making power, with the greatest at the top.

Director – A top-level executive able to make major decisions.

Strategic – Affecting the general aims and direction of a business.

Span of influence and control – The range of things a director or manager can affect within an organisation.

Authority – The formal (or informal) ability to take decisions.

Delegation – Where authority to take decisions is formally handed down to a lower level.

Functional area – A department, section or division of an organisation existing to handle a specific thing, such as finance or marketing.

Line of command – The people in a hierarchy to whom a person answers.

Flat structure – Where there are few if any layers of authority.

Tall structure – Where there are many layers of authority.

Assignment

You are working as an assistant to a management consultant. She knows that you have just left full-time education and has asked you to help her to prepare to give a presentation on organisational structures. You decide to use a real organisation that you are familiar with.

You have the following information to prepare:

1. a) Describe the main job roles that occur at different levels in the organisation.
   b) Describe the typical functions in the structure where job roles are carried out. **(P1)**
2. Identify at least two different organisational structures used within other business organisations. **(P2)**

To achieve a pass grade you need to:	To achieve a merit grade you need to:	To achieve a distinction you need to:
P1 describe the main job roles and functions in an organisation	**M1** compare the main job roles and functions in two organisations and explain how they may differ in different organisational structures	**D1** analyse the relationship between job roles, functions and an organisation's structure, using appropriate illustrative examples
P2 identify different organisational structures used within business organisations		

Chapter 9
Documentation for specific job roles

What are you finding out?

Building a successful organisation depends to a very large extent upon getting the right people into the right jobs. Of course, this has two aspects to it – the people and the jobs. Both have to be carefully considered. In this chapter you will find out that jobs are not just 'advertised'. There is a careful process of thinking about the job role that needs to be carried out.

Think of it like this...

Imagine you are responsible for planning, organising and running a fashion event that will have rock bands, vintage clothes sales stands, a DJ and lighting and dancing – among other things. Obviously there are many things to think about and plan. How important is it that you get together a strong team? Would you:

- Get the first half dozen pals you came across to 'lend a hand'?

Or:

- Think about who would be better at doing certain tasks and discuss with them what needs to be done?

The answer is obvious, of course. You would give certain tasks to the people you knew would do them best. Organisations do this by making sure that all jobs are properly considered.

This chapter will help you to:

- Understand the ways in which job descriptions can be drawn up.
- Understand the ways in which person specifications can be drawn up.
- Understand the contents of a job description.
- Understand the contents of a person specification.
- Produce a detailed and relevant job description and person specification for a specific job.
- Analyse how effective recruitment to jobs helps an organisation succeed.

Documents for filling a job role

Every **job role** within an organisation needs to be carefully considered before the **recruitment process** is started. An organisation that merely replaces staff, without adequately considering things about the job, is likely to be heading for trouble. This is one of the reasons why medium-to-large organisations usually employ human resources managers (HRM) to deliver a *professional* HR function. Even a small business often buys in external HR consultancy services to support it in dealing with staff.

These are some of the things that HR managers need to consider before recruiting to a job:

- Is the job role still needed? It is possible that a particular job role has changed due to technology or external factors.
- If the job is needed, does it still consist of the same tasks?
- What kind of person will be best suited to do this job?

These things are all helped by some important documents that help to form the background to the process of selecting the right person for a job. Two important documents are:

- Job description
- Person specification.

Drawing up a job description

As the name of the document suggests, a job description is a systematic way of detailing the tasks that make up a specific job, the context in which the job is done and the title, grade and sometimes salary that are attached to it.

A job description can be drawn up in a number of ways. These are discussed below.

Job description created by departmental staff

In this method, the HR department supplies a template for the job role to the manager and staff of the (potentially) recruiting department. The manager and staff draw up the list of tasks involved in the job and its place in the structure.

Here is a sample *of part* of a job description:

Job description
Post title: ICT & e-Learning Support Technician **Post Number: UXXXX** **Grade: Business Support Pts 12–15** **Responsible to: The Senior ICT & e-Learning Technician** **Responsible for: ICT & e-Learning technical support**
Overall objectives of the post Provision of ICT & e-learning 'helpdesk' and technical support service for all users of the college information & communication systems technology.
Key tasks of the post 1. To be responsible for the provision of a helpdesk service for all users of the school's ICT hardware, systems and services. 2. Receive and log enquiries, ensuring appropriate actions and responses are provided within prescribed timescales. 3. Acting as a first line of support for all user problems. 4. Resolve an increasing percentage of reported problems directly, over the phone, with minimal escalation or referral to others. 5. Install ICT hardware, software and other equipment. 6. Maintain the asset database. **General** 1. Undertake any other duties in line with the grade, which may be required within the needs of the service as required by the Head of ICT.

Task

With a classmate, design and carry out a small survey in which you ask people to list the key tasks of their job role. If you can, see if you can find out how much they are aware of their own job description and whether or not they feel it should be amended.

There are advantages in creating the document in this way.

- The detailed tasks required from a job role can be worded appropriately and accurately.
- All tasks required by the department can be included.
- Changes to the list of tasks can be made according to the manner in which a job role may have evolved.

When a departmental manager is satisfied with the tasks listed for the job, the HR function can then create the official job description. This will be in the format that applies across the whole organisation.

Make the grade

D2 Think about this case and remember your responses to the questions when you analyse how effective recruitment contributes to an organisation's success for D2.

Job description created by the existing job holder

There are several reasons why a job in a particular organisation might become available. These include:

- resignation
- dismissal
- promotion
- retirement
- maternity leave.

In many cases managers will look to try and save cash by not filling a vacant post. This often means that other staff members within the organisation are given extra tasks to do.

Aztec Print & Design

Aztec Print & Design is a rapidly growing printing and design company. The business employs 52 people in its factory and falls into a category known as SMEs (small to medium-sized enterprises). Aztec was established 15 years ago by Mike Lee, who left school with few qualifications. From starting with only a guillotine to cut paper in a single room, Mike developed Aztec to a situation where the company now boasts many high-profile clients.

Aztec can print magazines, posters, programmes (including for Premier League clubs), leaflets, newspapers – in fact almost anything.

Recently, right in the middle of a very busy period, one of Aztec's administrative staff left the business to take up another post. Mike and one of his partners, Lee, took out an old advertisement for the office job and sent it off to the local paper. They were surprised to receive over 80 applications for the job. However, working very late one evening, both Mike and Lee became very disillusioned because few of the candidates could handle the kind of computer work that was needed; the few who could lived many miles away.

'What did we do wrong?' moaned Mike. 'We'll have to start again.'

1. In your own words explain what Aztec did wrong in this situation.
2. Outline the ways in which a carefully prepared job description would have helped.
3. Draft a short report to Mike explaining what you would recommend.

In normal circumstances the creation of a vacancy means that someone has to be found to fill an existing post. An excellent way of discovering the details of what this post involves and gaining a good insight into the role is to invite the current post-holder to list the tasks of the job and the qualities needed. This can work well because the existing post-holder knows as well as anyone what is required of a job role. The greater the experience of the post-holder, the more of an insight they can give.

Job description created by interviewing existing post-holder

In this method, the person doing the job is interviewed face to face about the tasks, responsibilities and context of the job role. This is a real opportunity for the HR function (or any manager) to discover the nature of a job. Some organisations use '**exit surveys**' to find out a person's true feelings about the job and the company they are leaving.

Task

Discuss with a classmate the advantages of using existing post-holders to find out about a job. Can you see any problems in the method? Write out a list of the advantages and possible problems.

Contents of a job description

You can see from the above example that a typical job description lists the important tasks involved in a job.

Here is a further example:

Job descriptions can contain the following features:

- Job title
- Job location
- Description of the organisation's business
- Purpose of job
- Main tasks
- Standards required
- Pay and benefits
- Promotion prospects
- Lines of reporting.

Job description

Post title: Maintenance Assistant

Post Number: UXXXXX

Grade: Business Support point 3

Responsible to: Maintenance Supervisor

Responsible for: Cleaning Staff

Overall objectives of the post

To supervise a team of cleaners and undertake the cleaning of the establishment to ensure a comprehensive cleaning service is provided in compliance with school requirements and Health & Safety regulations.

Key tasks of the post

The post holder is responsible for:

1. Assisting in ensuring that the school is maintained to a high level of cleanliness, both internally and externally, and actively carrying out cleaning duties as required.
2. Assisting in the supervision of cleaning staff and ensuring that they carry out their duties safely, efficiently and effectively.
3. Undertaking the opening and closing of the college premises and maintaining security.
4. Ensuring that gullies and downcomers on the roof are inspected and cleared on a regular basis.
5. Assisting in the efficient and economical operation of the heating system.
6. Assisting in the removal of rubbish from school grounds and ensuring that approaches and walkways are free from snow and ice.
7. To act as a First Aider and maintain a first-aid qualification.

General

1. All staff are responsible for the quality of their own work and for the operation of all relevant parts of the school's quality system.
2. It is expected that all staff participate in identifying their own professional development needs and in appropriate professional development activities to meet the school's mission and objectives.

We can see from the above examples that most of the above are included. In these examples, however, 'promotion prospects' are not. In this case it will be up to a **job candidate** to enquire about this.

Task

For each of the example job descriptions shown above, try and identify the item that corresponds to the list of features shown on page 103. Discuss with a classmate whether you feel these job descriptions are adequate or whether they could contain more information.

Why do you feel it is necessary to include 'lines of reporting' in the job description?

Research and investigate

Work with a small group of classmates and collect as many examples of job descriptions as you can. Work together to identify the features or content that they all have in common; then list the differences.

Produce a short presentation to give to the rest of your class, entitled 'Job descriptions – uses and variations'.

Person specification

We saw earlier that there are always two aspects to whether a job role really contributes to an organisation's success; the job itself and the person holding the job. HR staff and departmental managers could spend hours, days or weeks structuring and creating the most fabulous job role; however, if the person appointed to it does not possess the personal qualities required to fulfil that role, then there are problems.

It is the role of another document – the person specification – to detail carefully the characteristics needed of someone to fulfil a particular job. (Note that a person specification is sometimes called a 'job' specification or a 'human' specification. These terms refer to the same thing.)

Contents of a person specification

A person specification is designed to detail the sort of person who would ideally be capable of doing a particular job role. This shows how important it is to get the job role specified correctly. Managers could easily appoint the wrong person (see Aztec case study above) and the wrong kind of applicant could apply.

A person specification is traditionally based on a seven-point plan that was devised by Professor Alec Rodger of the National Institute of Industrial Psychology.

The structure is shown in the table below:

1. Physical make-up	What health, physique, appearance, bearing, speech (exclude discriminatory features such as accent) are needed for the job?
2. Attainments	What education, training, experience, achievements are required?
3. Intelligence	What cognitive ability, learning capacity, analytical ability, and ability to synthesise are needed?
4. Special aptitudes	Are there any special abilities, such as construction, equipment, dexterity, mathematical, IT ability, required in the role?
5. Interests	Would particular intellectual, practical, active, social interests help in doing the job?
6. Disposition	Are maturity, self-reliance, and compassion, humour required?
7. Circumstances	Is geographical mobility (excluding discriminatory factors such as age, children, marital status, etc. – unless specifically relevant to job) required in the job role?

The following is an example of a person specification:

Person specification	**Assessment criteria**	
Post title: Post number Grade Department:	Candidate name: Time of interview: Salary:	
Comments:		
Essential requirements	**Desirable requirements**	**Interview comments**
Education and training Reasonable standard of general education	• First-aid certificate • NVQ Cleaning Science • Knowledge of COSHH • SIA holder	
Relevant experience Experience of maintenance, security services and cleaning		
Aptitude and skills Trustworthy, hardworking, able to work with minimal supervision	• Handyman skills • Security skills	
Disposition Flexible and adaptable		
Circumstances • Suitable to work with children • Lives close to work • Must be willing to take majority of annual leave during school closures	Lives within 30 mins of school	

Task

Look back at the example job descriptions earlier in this chapter. You should be able to easily match the person specification above with one of those documents.

Make the grade

D2 You could consider the example documents you have seen when you respond to the D2 criterion 'how effective recruitment contributes to an organisation's success'.

Applying for jobs

A business organisation can succeed only if it is able to attract and recruit the right kind of people to fill its job roles. Many large organisations spend a great deal of time and effort in considering local labour market conditions before they decide to locate (or relocate) in a particular area. Nissan located in Sunderland because having researched the area they knew there was a suitable supply of labour.

We can look at recruitment and selection in two ways: from the point of view of the recruiting organisation and from the viewpoint of applicants.

We have seen above that the organisation must:

- analyse the job role
- describe the job role
- specify the qualities of a person needed to do the job role.

In addition, the organisation needs to think about the following questions:

- How shall we appoint? (internal or external candidate)
- What is the best way to recruit? (attract good candidates)
- How shall we advertise the post? (press?)
- How shall we select the best candidate?

Documents used by organisations in the application process

Many organisations use their own application forms – either paper ones or online. An online form is one that is available via an organisation's website and it can be completed, edited and submitted online. It is always wise to keep your own copy!

Business organisations must consider the ways in which they want applications to be presented. Application forms, CVs, letters of application are all valid means of applying for a job.

Application forms

Application forms, whether online or on paper, are designed so that information about candidates can be gained and then easily compared. Application forms ask a standard set of questions covering the following:

- Personal details
- Educational background
- Experience and employment history
- A personal statement.

Recruiting organisations have to be careful to ask questions that actually relate to the job. Anti-discrimination law prevents employers asking irrelevant questions. For example, is it relevant whether a person is married or single? Is it relevant whether they are 25 or 45?

The wording on application forms must be simple, clear and well written. To attract good candidates, the organisation must present a good impression.

Curriculum vitae (CV)

This should be a carefully structured document prepared by the candidate. The words themselves come from Latin, roughly meaning 'the course of (my) life'. Recruiting organisations often specifically ask for CVs. They give a quick

Research and investigate

Investigate the websites of at least four organisations with websites. Navigate to the 'careers' link. For each organisation, summarise the application process and write a statement outlining the advantages or disadvantages of an online application process.

reference to the important facts and effectively tell a story about a person's personal, educational and work life so far.

A typical CV looks like this:

Curriculum vitae	
Personal details Name: Address: Tel No: Date of birth:	
Education 2007-2009 2002-2007	 Trimdon College of FE Esh School
Academic qualifications BTEC First Diploma in Business BTEC National Certificate in Business GCSEs	 Distinction DM award English C History C Business Studies B IT D CDT D Maths E Science E
Work experience 2007-2009 Part-time employment at Barclays Call Centre, Duxford Park	
Personal statement I am a friendly person and I am able to get along with people from many backgrounds. I have an excellent telephone manner and I feel I am able to communicate well with people. In my spare time I enjoy music and socialising with my friends. I am very interested in vintage fashion and collect accesories and clothes. I am reliable and trustworthy. **Referees** 1. 2.	

Figure 9.1 A CV

Task

If you have already created your own CV, read through it and update it. Exchange your own CV with a classmate's and make constructive comments that will help improve them both. If you have not yet created a CV, create one now.

Letters of application

A good letter of application should relate carefully to the job being applied for. It is usually a bad idea to have a standard letter that is sent to every recruiting organisation. Employers can tell if you do this and many find it insulting that you have not taken the trouble to write a specific letter to them.

Plan the letter and give it a structure such as this:

- *Paragraph 1 – why are you interested in this job? What attracts you to this organisation?*
- *Paragraph 2 – what qualities do you have that make you good for the job? How might your past experience help you?*
- *Paragraph 3 – what educational experiences have you had that will help? What are your strengths?*
- *Paragraph 4 – say you would welcome the chance of an interview and that you will be available. Say how you can be contacted.*

Task

An administrative job is advertised in a local company. Applicants need to be IT literate, have experience of dealing with customers and have good telephone manner.

Write a suitable letter of application for the post.

It should be obvious why employers prefer to see letters that actually relate to the job that they have available. They want you to be the answer to all their needs. It is up to you to convince them in your letter that you could be and that you should be shortlisted and interviewed.

Make sure you are well prepared for an interview

Preparing for an interview

An invitation to attend for interview is the signal that your initial application has been good enough to interest the employer. You are on a 'shortlist' of people who are considered potentially suitable for the job. Now you have to prepare for the interview.

Think about the following before you attend for an interview:

Dress – All organisations will expect you to dress appropriately. This means in a business manner; smart casual, if not a suit.

Research – What does the organisation do? (Products, services)

Questions to ask – Think about things that you would like to know. An interest in career opportunities is good.

Questions to expect – Why do you want this job? What makes you feel you would be good at it? What personal skills (e.g. IT) do you have that will help? You could be asked to expand on something that is in your CV. This is why it is important to make sure that you are honest and truthful in your statements.

Your aim at interview is to send messages that you are a suitable employee. Your appearance, attitude, ambition, hopes, interest and enthusiasm should all come across. How can you send these messages to add to what the interviewers already know?

Body language

Non-verbal messages almost always override verbal messages.

You can check this out for yourself by trying some simple experiments with some of your class, or your friends or relatives.

- Tone of voice – try saying something very commonplace (such as 'How are you doing?') but in an aggressive, sharp tone. See how often people pick up on this and ask if something is wrong.
- Set up a conversation with someone but when the discussion is started never look the other person in the eye.
- Set up an interview situation with at least three people acting as the 'panel'. Then ask another three people to act as candidates. Brief the three candidates as follows:
  - First candidate sits upright with hands clasped between his/her knees and always looks down.
  - Second candidate sits leaning casually back in the chair with arms folded, legs outstretched and crossed.
  - Third candidate sits upright with hands resting on his/her lap, feet together.

Ask observers to comment on the impression given by each candidate. How did the posture of each 'candidate' affect how you felt?

Body language is a major thing in interviews. What you should have seen is that one candidate looked frightened and timid; another looked as if he/she couldn't care less and the third looked interested and alert.

Key terms

Job role – A series of tasks carried out by a paid employee.

Recruitment process – The means of attracting candidates to apply for a job.

Exit survey – questioning people when they leave an organisation.

Job candidate – Someone who has applied for a job.

Labour market – People available to work, and their skills, qualifications and profiles.

Assignment 1

You are working as an assistant to a management consultant. You have been asked to help prepare materials for a job role that is to be advertised shortly.

The post is ICT support technician and you have been asked to prepare the following:

1. Using your own knowledge and investigation of a real job role as an ICT technician, draft a basic job description and person specification for the post your company needs to fill. **(P3)**
2. If you can find more detailed information on the general role, offer relevant additional information and more detail to the job description and person specification. **(M2)**
3. In additional notes to go with the documents, analyse how effective recruitment contributes to an organisation's success. **(D2)**

You might find it helps to try to find example job descriptions and person specifications for jobs done in your school or college.

Assignment 2

A job has been advertised for an administrative assistant in your local council. The job involves data input, using IT software and dealing with members of the public, by telephone as well as face to face.

1. Complete a suitable application form for this post. (Use a sample application form to complete this task).
2. Prepare to be interviewed for the post.
3. Carry out a role play of an interview for the position. **(P4)**

Role play guidance

You should organise your class into groups making sure that everyone has the chance to be interviewed and to act as interviewer. The groups should be:

- Interview panel (4–6 people)
- Observers (need an observation sheet to help with comments)
- Candidates

You will need questions for candidates. It is not important if others see the questions. The important point is that everyone experiences an interview.

To achieve a pass grade you need to:	To achieve a merit grade you need to:	To achieve a distinction you need to:
P3 produce a basic job description and person specificarion for a specific job	**M2** produce a detailed and relevant job description and person specification for a specific job	**D2** analyse how effective recruitment contributes to an organisation's success
P4 complete an application and interview for a specific job		

Chapter 10
Preparing for employment and planning career development

What are you finding out?

This unit has shown you that organisations take great care to ensure that job roles are properly and accurately described. It has also shown you that the process of recruiting people into job roles is helped by carefully prepared documents.

In this chapter you will learn how to relate your own personal knowledge and skills to possible job opportunities. You will learn to use appropriate sources of information and advice.

This chapter will help you to:

- Prepare a personal audit of your own skills and knowledge.
- Understand different types of employment.
- Access reliable sources of information and advice.
- Understand career development strategies and opportunities.

A personal audit

When people or businesses carry out an 'audit', they do a systematic, careful check in order to investigate evidence about how things are. There are many kinds of audit.

A '**personal audit**' of skills and knowledge is a careful check to see where a person stands in relation to either the whole job market, or in relation to a particular job. In considering a particular job that is advertised, a person might send for further details. On reading the job description and person specification, they might be confused about whether they could do the job. Here is where a personal skills and knowledge audit might come in useful.

The structure of a personal audit

There are many ways of carrying out an audit of skills and knowledge. Here is one way of doing it:

Do a self-assessment based upon eight groups of questions, with specific questions in each group. Rate how you feel about each question from 1 (strong agreement) to 4 (strong disagreement).

- **Communication – reading**
  - 'I feel confident about my reading'
  - 'I can select information'
  - 'I can summarise'
  - 'I can find information'
- **Communication – writing**
  - 'I can reproduce my ideas in writing'
  - 'I can write reports'
  - 'I always check my spelling'
  - 'I can plan things I write'
  - 'I can make notes'
- **Communication – oral**
  - 'I can explain things to new people'
  - 'I can give presentations'
  - 'I can take a discussion forward'
  - 'I can listen'
- **Teamwork**
  - 'I can work in a team'
  - 'I am sensitive to people'
- **Problem solving**
  - 'I can break a task down'
  - 'I enjoy a challenge'
  - 'I think about alternatives'
- **Personal effectiveness**
  - 'I can organise myself'
  - 'I know my strengths and weaknesses'
- **Numeracy**
  - 'I can do calculations with confidence'
  - 'I can do graphs'
  - 'I can handle statistical data'
- **IT**
  - 'I can use a word-processing package'
  - 'I can use a spreadsheet'
  - 'I can use the internet'

Task

With a classmate, look at each of the eight groups of questions above and see if you can add more questions so that there are at least SIX questions in each group. Discuss the ways in which you would judge the level of confidence of someone who had completed this audit. (For example, you would probably judge someone scoring 48 (the best assessment of each section based on six questions) as '*highly* confident'.)

There are other categories that you could add to a personal skills audit. These could include technical or practical questions. The idea is to see how confident you feel about these things. Of course, the more confident you are, the better you are likely to come across at interview.

Fieldwork

In your previous work in the unit, you will have come across some job descriptions and person specifications. Choose a job and see if you can match your own personal audit to a particular job opportunity.

Types of employment

Employees can be appointed to organisations based on a number of different employment patterns. This is set in an '**employment contract**'. You may have a part-time job yourself, so you will be well aware of the difference between full- and part-time employment.

There is no standard definition of what full- or part-time work means in terms of the hours at work. Depending on the contract of employment, some employees work longer than others.

Did you know...

According to the Office of National Statistics, in December 2008, full-time workers in the UK averaged 37.0 hours. Part-time workers averaged 15.5 hours.

Full time

Normally a full-time worker is someone who works on a permanent basis for an employer for more than 35 hours per week.

Part time

A part-time worker is someone who works permanently for an employer for fewer than 35 hours per week.

Permanent work

An employee can work on a permanent contract, meaning that he or she is committed to work for the organisation until the contract is ended by either party.

Temporary work

A temporary worker is usually employed for a fixed term for a limited period; this could be six months, a year or occasionally longer.

Seasonal work

This is where an employee works only during a particular season; it is typical in the hotel and hospitality industry.

Unpaid or voluntary employment

Voluntary workers are those who work for a particular cause or purpose and not for an agreed rate of pay.

Did you know...

According to the Office for National Statistics, in June 2009 the total number of people in employment in the UK was 24,919,000.

Out of 24,919,000 people working in the UK in June 2009, 6,457,000 were working part-time.

Out of 6,457,000 part-time workers, 22% were men and 78% were women.

Sources of information and advice

There are many sources of information, advice and guidance on job opportunities. The two most obvious sources are:

- Job advertisements – newspapers, trade magazines
- Word of mouth.

Fieldwork

Carry out a search of your local press. Collect local job advertisements and create a table showing the main categories of information the adverts usually show. Also show in the table the different methods of application required by employers.

Employment and government agencies

Jobcentre Plus is a part of the Department for Work and Pensions.

Their aim is to:

- help more people into paid work
- help employers fill their vacancies; and
- give people of working age the help and support they are entitled to if they cannot work.

Job adverts

Junior Office Administrator

EgO Windows & Doors Ltd

We are a leading manufacturer of UPVC windows and doors. We are looking to recruit a flexible and enthusiastic Junior Office Administrator for our St Georges site at Algarth.

Candidates should be numerate and possess good communication and IT skills. Familiarity or experience with MS Office software applications such as Excel, Word and Access will be an advantage.

Hours of work will be 9 till 5 Monday to Friday. Occasional weekend work is expected.

Apply in writing enclosing a suitable CV to Mrs J Reynolds, EgO Windows and Doors Ltd, St Georges Industrial Park.

Receptionist/Clerk

Brinkburn Leisure Centre

Brinkburn Leisure Centre is a state of the art leisure facility serving the needs of Brinkburn. The facility consists of full sized swimming pool, a childrens play area, gymnasium and fitness areas, cafe and bar.

We are looking to recruit a full time Receptionist/ Clerk. Duties will include Reception, customer queries, membership applications and general clerical duties including the maintenance of the membership database.

Candidates should have excellent IT and people skills and be capable of working under pressure within a team.

Shift work is required to include alternate weekend work. Hours are 7 am till 2 pm or 2 pm till 9 pm.

1. What are the advantages for a business in advertising a job in the press?
2. Summarise the information given to potential candidates. What else could be included? Write a summary saying what things would encourage you to apply for either job.

Job Centre Plus offices are located in most towns and cities and advisors can be contacted via call centres too.

Careers advice

Making a decision about a career is obviously a very important step. Even in a world where the pace of change is fast, you could place yourself in a very good position by an informed choice of career. There are many good sources of advice. Some of these are listed in the Fieldwork box.

Fieldwork

Visit at least three of the following sources of online careers advice and prepare a summary of the kinds of service provided for people:
www.connexions-direct.com
www.connexions-direct.com/jobs4u
www.direct.gov.uk/careersadvice
www.direct.gov.uk/youngpeople
www.careers-gateway.co.uk

Other sources of advice for young people can be much nearer home. Your school or college tutors can often point you in the right direction. Most schools and colleges have their own professional careers advisory service. Your own friends and family can often be a realistic and valuable source of help. After all, they know you better than anyone.

Career development

There are a number of ways that organisations can help you to make a good start in developing your career. Note that a 'career' is different from just a 'job'.

Task

In what ways is a 'career' different from a 'job'? Write a summary of the main differences, in your opinion.

Induction

When you start a job for the first time you will undergo an induction period. You may already have experienced induction, either in a part-time job role or in college or school.

'Induction' means to absorb you into the organisation. Although you may have researched an organisation thoroughly before attending an interview, you really need to be inside to get to know how an organisation works.

An induction will usually cover areas such as:

- health and safety
- disciplinary and grievance procedures
- rules and regulations
- structure of the organisation
- welfare
- training opportunities/needs
- performance reviews
- personal development opportunities.

Training needs

Training in the initial stages of a new job is usually in-house. This means it is carried out within the organisation, either in a specialist training centre delivered by specialist trainers, or it takes place off-site at a college or training centre.

Training needs are often identified through a process of continual professional development (CPD). Staff can be required to undertake either 'certified' training; this is where a qualification or certificate is awarded; or un-certified, where the training does not attract a qualification.

Performance targets

A job role is often measured in terms of specific targets. For example, a sales person will be expected to achieve a specific number of sales in a month or other period. The SMART objectives relating to a job allow a manager to review performance at the end of a year. This is usually done in a 'Performance Review Meeting'. These are held annually and the information gained from them is used to plan the following year.

During review meetings, both sides (i.e. the employee *and* the manager) are expected to contribute. It should not be a one-way conversation. The employee expresses his or her feelings about the job and the manager about the performance of the employee within it. Sometimes a job role can be adjusted.

During review meetings, members of staff can request training. Alternatively, the manager may suggest training to help the employee develop further. From this kind of discussion, a **Personal Development Plan** can emerge.

Fieldwork

Investigate what is meant by the term 'work–life balance'. Create a short presentation explaining its meaning and importance.

Flexible working

Some contracts allow flexible working. This is where the employee does not work set hours such as 9 a.m. till 5 p.m. but instead is able to work their 37-plus hours during the hours that suit them best. Modern mobile technology increasingly allows people to work from home.

Key terms

Personal audit – A self-check of skills and knowledge.

Employment contract – Written statement of terms of employment.

Induction – The formal process of settling someone safely into an organisation.

Career – Usually lifelong occupation backed by qualifications (e.g. doctor).

Job – A paid weekly position sometimes unskilled or semi-skilled.

Review meeting – Annual one-to-one look back over a year's work and a look ahead to the next year.

Assignment

You have been asked to consider your own career development. In order to do this properly you decide that there are certain things you must do.

Task 1

- Investigate job opportunities in your area and if necessary beyond. Look for 'administrative' posts; clerical; data input; receptionist; or customer-services-type roles. However, consider any roles you may find interesting.
- Match your current level of knowledge and skills to one of these opportunities by using appropriate sources of information and advice. You could look at careers advice information, or carry out an audit of your IT skills. **(P5)**

Task 2

Produce a personal career development plan that relates to this job role. For example, if you took a job in the office of a local council, what kind of training might you get? What are the different grades? What specialist careers could you try for (social work, finance, HR etc)? **(P6)**

To achieve a pass grade you need to:	To achieve a merit grade you need to:	To achieve a distinction you need to:
P5 match current knowledge and skills to possible job opportunities, using appropriate sources of information and advice		
P6 produce a personal career development plan.		

Unit 7

Verbal and non-verbal communication in businesss contexts

Chapter 11
Using non-verbal communication skills

What are you finding out?

Communication takes place in businesses every minute of every day. Much of this communication is verbal and non-verbal rather than written. To be effective, all forms of communication must be clear and must give a positive impression of a business to its customers. Non-verbal communication skills are about the way in which you convey messages and interact with others – your interpersonal skills. Good non-verbal communication skills are very important as it is very easy to give the wrong impression. You therefore need to learn good non-verbal communication skills and be able to demonstrate these skills in different business settings.

This chapter will help you to:

- Demonstrate appropriate interpersonal interactions in a business context.
- Explain how interpersonal interaction skills are used to support business communication.
- Discuss the importance of effective interpersonal interaction skills in a given business situation.

Conveying a professional image

It is important for businesses to have a positive image with customers and other businesses that they deal with. It is also important for **colleagues** to be able to communicate with each other effectively on a daily basis. Poor **communication** leads to errors and misunderstandings. As an employee, you represent the business you work for and you must also be able to work with others. You therefore need to convey a professional image when you are at work. This means that you should:

- Dress appropriately.
- Pay care and attention to personal hygiene.
- Have sound organisational skills.
- Have good **time-management** skills.
- Behave in a professional and businesslike manner when dealing with colleagues and customers.

Appropriate dress

The way you present yourself affects the impression people you deal with form of you and the business you work for. If you look as if you don't care about your appearance, then other people will think that you do not care about your job or the service you are providing. They will not have confidence in your ability to do your job properly, which means that any message you are trying to convey may not be communicated effectively.

You will be judged by your appearance but the way you dress will vary according to the industry you work in. You would not expect an accountant and a road sweeper to wear the same clothes or pay the same amount of attention to the neatness of their clothing; but the way you look and present yourself must be appropriate to the environment you work in.

The way you dress therefore needs to be appropriate for the type of business that you work for and the job that you do. If you work in an office environment, then your dress should be smart and your clothes should be clean and neatly pressed. If you are working in an environment in which you meet and greet customers on a daily basis, then again your clothes should be clean and neat at all times. However, the style of your clothing will depend on the business you work for. If you work in a themed restaurant, for example, then your clothing will be expected to match that theme. If you work for a clothing retailer, then your style of clothing might be expected to match the style of that sold and it is likely that you could be asked to wear clothes from the current range in stock, if appropriate.

Make sure you dress appropriately for your work

Many businesses and organisations provide a uniform for staff members, which has a number of benefits to the organisation itself and to the individuals wearing the uniform. These include:

- Presenting a professional image.
- Allowing staff to be easily recognised.
- Providing a sense of belonging (being part of a team).
- Being functional and providing protection.
- Providing staff with clothes for work.

In some organisations, wearing a uniform is essential. You wouldn't expect police officers on the beat, for example, to be wearing their own clothing, as this would make them impossible for the public to recognise and would make it difficult for them to carry out their duties.

If you are provided with a uniform, you still have the responsibility of looking after it and ensuring that it is washed and pressed regularly, and you must wear it correctly so that you look smart. The box on the next page shows some of the uniform guidelines for female cabin crew working for British Airways.

British Airways cabin crew

Dressing appropriately is about more than your clothing. You also need to ensure that your hair is clean and tidy and, if appropriate, tied back. Female cabin crew working for British Airways must have their hair styled away from the face and are allowed to wear only one hair accessory, a plain scrunchie or an Alice band.

You must also ensure that you follow your employer's guidelines on the amount of jewellery you may wear. Some businesses or organisations will allow you to wear only a wedding ring.

Make-up is another part of your personal presentation that you must take great care over. Again, many businesses set their own guidelines but, if they don't, you must ensure that make-up is natural looking and that you do not wear too much.

Did you know...

One of the reasons that female cabin crew wear make-up is because of the intensity of the aircraft lighting. Just like actors in the spotlight!

Fieldwork

Arrange to visit two large businesses and interview the human resources managers to find out what their dress codes are for their employees.

Personal hygiene

It is important to take care with personal hygiene when you work with others. Poor personal hygiene can be offensive to colleagues and customers. This means that it can be very difficult to convey messages effectively if the person you are speaking to does not want to stand and listen to you. Imagine trying to work alongside somebody with poor personal hygiene on a daily basis – you probably would not communicate effectively with that person. This would mean that you were unable to do your job properly.

If you work in a situation in which you are in close contact with colleagues and customers, you need to ensure that you shower regularly, use appropriate toiletries, such as deodorants, and keep your hair, hands and nails clean.

Cap

- Must be placed horizontally on the head above the brow line with the coat of arms badge centralised at the front.
- Must always be worn when in public areas, except where politeness or safety demands its removal.

Wrap

- May be worn over the uniform coat or with the uniform suit.
- Should be worn with the British Airways speedmarque showing.

Coat

- May be worn fully buttoned or unbuttoned with the uniform.
- Must not be draped over shoulders or thrown over one shoulder.
- If worn buttoned the belt must be fastened, tied in a knot to the frontside of the coat or tied at the back. If worn unbuttoned the belt must be tied at the back.

Jacket

- May be worn fully buttoned or fully unbuttoned with uniform.
- Must not be worn draped around shoulders.
- Must always display relevant name badge and brevet.
- Collar must not be worn turned up.

Shirt

- Must be fully buttoned, and worn with the uniform tie or clip-on cravat.
- Shirts with long sleeves must be fastened at the wrists.
- Must never be worn outside skirt, trousers or culottes.
- Must not be worn with the collar turned up.
- Must always display relevant name badge when worn without the uniform jacket, coat or cardigan.

Clip-on cravat/tie

- A choice of clip-on tie, standard tie and clip-on cravat is available.
- The tip of the tie should touch the belt buckle.
- The navy cravat and ties must be worn at all times.

Skirt

- The hemline must be on the knee.

Trousers

- The hemline of the trousers should sit approximately 1″ (25 mm) below the ankle and must not touch the ground.

Source: Information requested via email to British Airways.

Figure 11.1 Uniform guidelines for British Airways female cabin crew

Sound organisational skills

How well organised you are in your work says a lot about you. If you are disorganised and your work area is untidy, you will be sending the message to others that you are not very capable. This means that customers and colleagues may not have confidence in your ability to do your job.

To convey a professional image, you must spend time organising yourself and your work area. This means making time to file documents and information in appropriate places so that when you need something, you know exactly where to look.

Start by clearly marking files and the drawers of your filing cabinets. This is best done with printed labels. Then sort your filing out alphabetically and then by date. Anybody then entering your work area will gain the impression that you are competent and well organised.

If you use a computer in your work, it is essential that you create appropriate folders and use file names that will help you recognise and find the information you need easily. You will not present a professional image if you cannot find information when you are asked for it.

You also need to ensure that telephone numbers you use on a regular basis are kept beside the telephone and that addresses and contact details for people you regularly communicate with by letter or email are kept in an appropriate file or address book.

If you work with equipment, it is just as important to keep it in good order as it is to keep your work area in good order. Imagine if you worked in a fast-food restaurant and the cash till and trays were grubby; this would suggest that you were not much bothered about the job or your customers.

How organised you are therefore sends messages to those you work with about you as a person and your ability to do your job. If you create a poor impression of yourself and the business you work for, your business may lose customers and you may lose your job.

Bridget's organisational skills

Bridget has been working for a large furniture retailer for two months. Part of her job is to complete written agreements with customers who want to purchase furniture on credit. Due to her poor organisation skills, the following has happened:

a Bridget had asked a customer to return to the store with some form of identification so that she could photocopy it and attach it to the customer's agreement. When the customer returned, Bridget could not find the agreement and had to ask the customer to spend another 30 minutes with her while she completed a new agreement.

b Bridget's manager, Dan, asked her for the agreement completed for Mrs Featherstone as he needed to amend it. It took Bridget over an hour to find the agreement as it had been filed under S instead of F.

1. Outline the impression that the customer may have formed of:

   a Bridget

   b the business.

2. Describe the effect that Bridget's dealings with the customer may have on the business.
3. Describe the impression that Bridget's manager may have formed of her.
4. Explain the actions that Bridget's manager may take as a result of Bridget's mistakes.

Good time management

Good time management starts with good timekeeping. If you are constantly late for work, you will have difficulty in completing tasks on time throughout the day. You are also likely to lose your job!

Good time management is linked to sound organisation skills. Well-organised people usually manage their time well, as they know exactly what they must do in a day and allocate time to each task. People with poor time-management skills are late for meetings, fail to complete tasks by the deadlines set and therefore create a poor impression.

To manage your time effectively, you need to be able to **prioritise**. This means that you look at the tasks you must complete and select those that are most important or have the closest deadlines. These are the tasks you must allocate time to first. Some people list all the tasks they must complete on a 'To do' list and then allocate a level of importance to each task in order to help them prioritise.

Example:

To do list	Priority (1 – very important; 2 – quite important; 3 – less important)
Meeting with Mr Curtis at 10 a.m.	1
Prepare report for finance manager	2
File correspondence	3
Reply to customers' enquiries	1
Send samples to photographer	2
Discuss new brochure with assistants	2

Having a prioritised 'To do' list will help you set yourself goals. Setting goals for what you want to achieve in a day is another effective time-management tool. It is also very motivating to achieve those goals.

Poor time management often stems from **procrastination**. You procrastinate when you put off the tasks that you should be doing. This may be because you choose to do tasks you are more comfortable in doing, you have failed to prioritise your tasks or because you feel unable to complete a task and don't know how to get started. Procrastinators tend to find other things to do as soon as they sit down to a task, such as making a cup of coffee or checking their emails. To avoid procrastination, set yourself goals, ask someone else to check on you or make yourself a **schedule** and stick to it.

Schedules are simply a timetable, a plan of what you will do and when. You must first plan as priority tasks the things you absolutely have to do, and then all other tasks. However, it is also important to plan in some contingency time (time for unexpected events) and time to take a break.

You need to choose a method of time management that suits you, but remember that if you manage your time well, you will do your job effectively and create a good impression. This will convey the message to others that you are competent and can be relied upon.

Task

Make yourself a schedule for the completion of your assignment for this unit. You will need to plan in time for the following:

- **lessons**
- **research**
- **assessment of your practical skills**
- **writing your assignment**
- **contingencies.**

Professional and businesslike manner when dealing with colleagues and customers

Your **interpersonal skills**, the way you communicate and interact with other people, greatly affect the impression that other people will gain of you. When you are at work, you must behave in a professional and business-like manner when dealing with colleagues and customers. This means that you need good interpersonal skills, which include positive behaviour and attitude, being **courteous** and confident, and using positive body language.

Ignoring customers is inappropriate behaviour

Behaviour and attitude

Your behaviour and attitude towards colleagues and customers count. You must be able to work and communicate with colleagues and they with you; therefore you need to behave in a business-like manner. In customers' eyes, you represent the business you work for and if you behave inappropriately, customers will form a poor opinion of you and the business you work for.

If you worked with somebody who was difficult to approach, often in a bad mood and who spent a lot of time complaining about the business and the work, you would probably feel quite demotivated and would not enjoy going to work. On the other hand, working with people who are very positive about their work and the business they work for can make your job very enjoyable.

For customers, it can be very off-putting to be served by staff who are obviously uninterested in them and the work they are doing. If you were waiting to be served in a cafe or restaurant and the staff all stood talking to one another rather than serving you, you would have every right to feel annoyed. Similarly, if staff serving you in a shop or a bank are chewing gum rather than talking to you, you might also feel that you were not a valued customer. Each of these examples shows inappropriate behaviour by employees, and yet many of us have experienced similar situations. It is therefore very important to have a positive attitude and show customers that you are interested in them.

Simple ways to behave professionally towards others include:

- Greeting people with a smile.
- Listening carefully to what they have to say.
- Responding positively to their requests.
- Ignoring distractions when being spoken to.
- Being friendly and showing concern.

The way you speak to colleagues and customers is also important. The language you use when communicating with customers should be straightforward and easy to understand. It is especially important not to use technical terms or jargon that are specific to your business, and you should avoid the use of slang (local terms) and colloquialisms (words/phrases appropriate to familiar conversations) such as 'innit?' instead of 'isn't it?' and 'mate' or 'duck'. When speaking to colleagues, you should treat them with respect and be courteous. It isn't always appropriate to speak to others in the workplace in the same way that you would speak to your friends.

Task

In pairs, practise greeting one another and enquiring about each other's days. When you have each taken a turn, discuss what you could have done better.

Courtesy and confidence

Good manners cost nothing and if you remember to be polite when you speak to colleagues and customers and always say please and thank you, then, usually, colleagues and customers will be courteous to you and will form a good impression of you.

It is also courteous to show interest in what colleagues and customers have to say and, if appropriate, show concern. It is the way in which you communicate that will be remembered more than you what you actually say and so you must ensure that you convey the appropriate emotion.

You must also speak confidently when you communicate with colleagues and customers. Greet people in a clear and confident manner as this makes them feel welcome and lets them know that you are available to assist them. You will develop confidence in your workplace as you develop your knowledge and skills in your job and become more familiar with the business and its products or services.

Did you know...

Words account for less than 10% of a message's impact. The rest comes from non-verbal cues.

Body language

You may be saying the right words but your body language may be saying something else. Your body language could spoil any message you wish to convey as it may display a lack of confidence, disinterest or aggression. The correct use of open body language will help you to communicate effectively. Open body language means using facial expressions, gestures and a stance that are friendly and welcoming to the person you are communicating with.

Someone showing good body language

Your facial expressions must show that you are interested in what colleagues or customers have to say and that you have understood what has been said; this means that you must display appropriate emotions. You must also make eye contact as this shows that you are listening to the other person. Yawning and looking around the room when others are speaking to you will show that you are not interested in what the other person is saying.

Open gestures and stance include uncrossed arms and legs, facing the person you are speaking to, standing or sitting straight, leaning forward slightly and generally being relaxed. Open body language makes expressive use of your hands and arms, for example, using open palm gestures when speaking.

Closed body language, such as folding your arms, crossing your legs and putting your head down, should be avoided as it generally implies that you want to be left alone.

Make the grade

P1 **M1** Remember this for P1 and M1. You must be able to demonstrate appropriate interpersonal interactions in a given business context and be able to explain how interpersonal interaction skills are used to support business communication.

Task

Work in groups of four. Two group members should complete the task while the other two observe and then swap over. One person should convey the message below using closed body language and the other should convey the same message using open body language. The observers should feed back to the group on how effectively the message was conveyed in both instances.

Message: 'Good morning. Today, I would like you to meet with Mrs Smith, write a report about the meeting and then hand that report in to me by four o'clock. When we meet, I would then like to have a chat about customer complaints.'

Better Soccer Coaching

On Better Soccer Coaching's website, there are 'Six steps to better non-verbal communication'. The advice for soccer coaches states, 'Encourage your players and boost morale with these body language signs and tactics:

Face

Smiles, grimaces, nods and winks all contribute to creating rapport and giving instant feedback.

Hands

Indicators of shape, size, direction, numbers. They are also a universal feedback mechanism – applause, thumbs up, high fives.

Eyes

Eye contact intensifies and personalises interaction.

Body

Look interested, be interesting.

Mouth

Even the mouth is a non-oral method of communication. Silence is a powerful tool to elicit answers from the quietest groups.

Space

Be intimate, not intimidating. Don't crowd players, but close proximity creates unity and a connection.

Source: www.bettersoccercoaching.com

1. State the benefits to a soccer coach of following the advice above.
2. Explain how open body language will improve the effectiveness of communication between a coach and their team.
3. To what extent will effective communication between a coach and their team improve the performance of a football team?

Make the grade

D1 Remember your answers to the case study for D1. You must assess the importance of effective interpersonal interaction skills in a given business situation.

Discussion...

Non-verbal communication has more impact on the effectiveness of the message being conveyed than what is actually said. Discuss.

Key words

Body language – Describes how we communicate with others using our posture, facial expressions and gestures.

Colleagues – Fellow workers or members of staff in the same business.

Communication – The process by which information is exchanged.

Courteous – Polite, well mannered and considerate.

Interpersonal skills – The skills needed to communicate and interact with and to relate well to other people.

Prioritise – To arrange tasks in order of importance.

Procrastination – Putting off/delaying tasks.

Schedule – A timetable; a plan of what you will do and when.

Time management – A range of skills, tools and techniques used to manage time when accomplishing specific tasks, projects and goals.

Assignment

You must be able to use non-verbal comminucation skills.

Verbal and non-verbal communication in business contexts

This assignment must be completed when you are on work placement or when you have arranged to spend the day with a business of your choice.

When working for your selected business, you must demonstrate appropriate interpersonal interactions. You must present, as evidence, a log, signed by the person managing you, to show that you:

1. Dressed appropriately for work
2. Demonstrated sound organisational skills
3. Demonstrated good time management
4. Behaved in a professional and businesslike manner when dealing with colleagues and customers
5. Behaved in a positive manner and demonstrated an appropriate attitude to the work set and towards colleagues and customers.
6. Behaved in a courteous and confident manner, using positive body language. **(P1)**

Produce a short report in which you:

1. Explain how the interpersonal interaction skills of the staff are used to support business communication in your selected business. **(M1)**
2. Discuss how important it is for staff in your selected business to demonstrate effective interpersonal interaction skills in a typical working day or transaction. **(D1)**

To achieve a pass grade you need to:	To achieve a merit grade you need to:	To achieve a distinction you need to:
P1 demonstrate interpersonal interactions in a business context	**M1** explain how interpersonal interaction skills are used to support business communication	**D1** assess the importance of effective interpersonal interaction skills in a given business situation

Chapter 12
The purpose of verbal communications in business

What are you finding out?

An organisation needs to create the communication channels that most effectively help it to be successful. One way of doing this is through verbal communications. The communication of information and ideas can be likened to transferring water by bucket from the tap in the kitchen to dry plants in a garden. A good bucket will not let any of the water escape, so that the job is carried out in an efficient way. However, if the bucket is leaky and has holes, the further the distance from the tap to the plants, the less efficient the system will be. This is why organisations need to use communication channels that best help tehm to achieve their business objectives.

Transmitter (sender) → Oral communication → Successfully received → Meeting business objectives

Figure 12.1 The communication process

Communicating verbally is something that we do daily. It is a form of interaction between two or more people and, in its simplest form, may involve straightforward conversation. A key element in any form of verbal interaction is for one or more people to understand what the other person is saying. Some individuals are very good at expressing themselves and can make a discussion interesting, focused and exciting. Think of teachers you have had who have made their lessons exciting though the quality of their verbal communication. Verbal communications can therefore be considered a skill. This is because some individuals are very articulate and express themselves well to an audience. Skilled communicators often use humour when they speak, they change the pitch and pace of their delivery and are sensitive to their audience's needs.

This chapter will help you to:

- Understand the purpose of verbal business communications.
- Appreciate how verbal business communications could be used in at least four different business contexts.
- Identify and explain a range of situations in which verbal business communications are used.
- Discuss how verbal communications can be used effectively in different situations.

Precise verbal communications

Verbal communications are part of our everyday lives; from the moment we get up until the moment we go to bed, our thoughts are structured by our language. Almost everything we do involves some form of verbal communication. Sometimes communications bring us bad news and sometimes good news. The important thing to remember in verbal communications is to identify the correct words to use. By doing this, verbal communications become precise. They help the person that you are talking with to understand exactly what you mean. In business this is particularly important as it means that people are not guessing what you want or feel but, instead, know exactly what you want or how you feel.

Purpose of verbal communications

Verbal or oral communications describe interactions using the spoken word. Being able to communicate orally within a business is very important. Oral communications should be clear and precise. This is to ensure that the message or communication made through the conversation is understood by both parties to the conversation. Clear verbal communications are a valuable tool. They help to ensure that the actions of employees are all focused on a business achieving its business objectives.

In every type of organisation in which individuals work, employees will need to communicate verbally with others. Think about some of the situations in which individuals might communicate verbally. For example, imagine that you have just got a job with an organisation. There would be so much to learn on your first day. You would want to find out about procedures and what you are required to do. You may be allocated a **business mentor**, whose role is designed to support you while you learn your job role. You may wish to ask your mentor some questions such as: 'Who is my line manager?' 'Where do I find new stationery?' and 'How do I apply for holiday leave?' All of these will involve some form of verbal communication. By communicating effectively on your first day, you will be preparing yourself much better for the role that you will have to undertake.

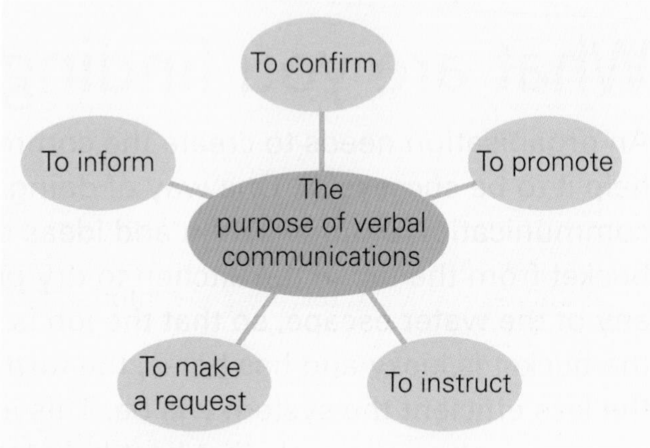

Figure 12.2 The purpose of verbal communications

Task

This is a simple but very useful communication task that will help you with your verbal communications. Work in groups of two, possibly with somebody you might not know terribly well. Each person should, over a five-minute period (total ten minutes), find out as much about the other person's interests and hobbies as they can. Having done so, each individual in turn should then use what they have discovered to describe the person that they interviewed and relay this back to the group.

When the task has been completed ask yourselves the following questions:

- **Did they ask the right questions?**
- **How did they feel about relaying everything back to the class?**
- **Could they remember everything that they learned about the other person?**
- **Does confidence play a part in verbal communications?**
- **Are some individuals just naturally better at communicating verbally than others?**
- **To what extent are verbal communications a skill?**

Using verbal communications to inform

Within a work environment, individuals need information. There are many different types of information that they might require. For example, they might want to find out about customer details, changes to working procedures, how to operate a new piece of software, new working arrangements, or find out about changes to the office. Although some of these details could be communicated in writing, they might also be transmitted through conversation.

When communicating, it is important that the person receiving the information knows exactly what the person communicating the information means. The last thing they want is some kind of misunderstanding. Communicating verbally might add precision to the message and also provide the opportunity for the communicator to receive some **feedback** to their message.

Using verbal communications to confirm

Unlike some written communications, verbal communications are more usually a two-way process. Verbal communications might be used to confirm that particular policies are being introduced by a business. They might also be used to confirm that an arrangement has been made or that an agreement has been reached. In other words, they are, in a very precise way, letting individuals know for certain that something is happening or taking place.

Using verbal communications to promote

It is easy to forget that we are all salespeople of our own ideas. You probably find that even within your own conversation you sometimes say 'Well, how about…?' 'Wouldn't it be a good idea to…?' or 'Have you thought about…?' Verbal communications are a creative form of communication. They allow the user to think in a variety of ways about the sort of response that they would like to make, so that they enable the individuals to promote their ideas and thoughts.

Using verbal communications to make a request

There are many instances within a workplace in which one person, usually the more senior, has to request another person to undertake a task or an activity. For example, they might ask them to pick up a package from the postroom, or to prioritise a particular job. Sometimes individuals need to be sensitive when asking or requesting others to do something. They would want to give them something that they would be happy with and prepared to do.

Using verbal communications to instruct

Instructing individuals is not just directly informing them what to do. It is also about helping them to get on with something by showing them how to do it. For example, an employee may know about some procedures but be unsure about how they work. When instructing them to carry out such a role, the person doing the instructing will also be supporting them and making sure that they have the knowledge to carry it out. Instructing is an efficient way of learning. In the office environment individuals are therefore learning by doing things or undertaking tasks. It is important that everybody in a work environment is able to undertake what they are asked to do. It is also useful for them to understand why they are being instructed to undertake certain work procedures.

Make the grade

P2 Remember to use this towards P2. Talk to somebody who works for a business organisation. Find out in what circumstances they use each of the above ways of communicating with others within their workplace. Ask them in what context they use each of the purposes when dealing with others.

The staff development day

As office manager, Daljinder really enjoys it whenever she organises a staff development day. She finds that on these days staff have time to discuss issues that have arisen within the workplace. It also provides them with an opportunity to contribute their ideas to the management of the office. There is also a clear purpose to such days. Daljinder wants to find out whether everybody is happy within their role and she wants to use her staff development days to help, support and motivate staff. Sometimes when changes are taking place within the office she feels that she has to give life to such changes that make individuals feel good about them. Staff development days are also used to inform staff of new working arrangements.

1. How do Daljinder's actions relate to the purposes of verbal communications?
2. If you were a member of staff working within Daljinder's office, what would you personally expect from the staff development day?

Did you know...

It has been said that your voice is one of the tools of your trade.

Task

Find out about the communication systems within your school or college. Ask your teacher/lecturer to tell you about how information is communicated and shared. Interview a senior member of staff and try to find out about the effectiveness of the various forms of communication.

Business contexts in which verbal communications take place

No matter what form of communication takes place within an organisation, it is important that it is effective. When designing communication systems within a business, it is important to consider how people work and that the best systems for ensuring that good communication links are set up.

Formal and informal oral communication

There are two ways in which oral communication takes place within organisations. This is either through **formal communication** or through **informal communication**. Formal communications within an organisation are communications that take place through recognised channels. In the context of oral communications, this might mean communication at meetings or staff briefings, as well as through presentations. Formal communications are likely to be used more within a very large organisation. In a big business, fewer people know each other and so it may be necessary to set up systems where staff can talk and communicate. Informal communications are communications that take place, but not through the officially recognised networks of an organisation. For example, it may simply involve discussion within the staff dining room, or talking to a colleague while at the photocopier. Small organisations are likely to be more informal, quite simply because there are fewer staff.

Both formal and informal communications are important in supporting how an organisation operates. The formal functions are stated and are part of the systems within the business. For example, in staff meetings individuals would be able to communicate how they feel about changes that might affect them. However, just as important is the way in which staff communicate with each other on an everyday basis within a workplace. Staff talk to each other all of the time. This is generally good for an organisation. It is a way that they can provide each other with help and support. They can provide information for each other, make their points clearly and help to solve problems. If individuals do not speak to each other, they might not be able to support key initiatives that are happening at work. Research into the nature of communications within organisations indicates that it is important to have both formal and informal oral communications. For example, management may break information to employees through meetings or team briefings, but the full understanding of what management has had to say might come about only through informal discussion between team members. Most managers recognise the importance of informal communications.

Telephone contact

One of the most frequent forms of oral communication is through using the telephone. The great benefit of the telephone is that it is fast and allows people who might find it difficult to meet in person to converse. A telephone may be both a formal and an informal form of communication. For example, when a caller from the outside calls an organisation, the telephone call may be the first form of contact with that business. It is important to make a good impression in that first call. The caller should also be put at ease. For formal telephone calls, the person taking the call should have all of the necessary information to hand and know how to deal with issues that affect that caller. In a more informal way, talking on the telephone is a quick and efficient way of exchanging information and ideas. Although there is no written evidence of the call, it is a quick way of dealing with an issue. However, if the issue is a long and complicated one that requires detailed information, perhaps the best way is to use a communication mechanism that involves writing information down.

Task

In a school or college setting most of the formal communications take place within lessons where teachers/lecturers will deliver a presentation or some other form of learning to their students. This would be the more formal element of oral communications. However, think about other things that you do or other activities you undertake within your lesson. Identify where informal communications take place and explain how you learn from informal communications.

Did you know...

A good way to develop your voice is to take relaxation, breathing and voice exercises. Put your hands at the side of your rib cage and then breath in through the nose, breathing deeply. Sigh out through the open mouth and throat and then push all of the air out of your lungs. Do this ten times.

Meetings

Meetings take place within nearly all organisations. Smaller meetings are likely to be more informal than larger meetings. For example, if a team of six members who work together have a meeting, they will know each other well and most, if not all, members of the team will probably contribute to the discussion. In very large meetings there will be an **agenda**. There will also be a chairperson who will manage the meeting. Reports may be read out at the meeting and there may be quite a few documents associated with the running of the meeting. Meetings therefore involve verbal and written communication methods.

Task

Give a description of a meeting that you have attended. The meeting might have been held at a place you work at. It could have been at school, at a formal meeting of people, such as an assembly, or it could have been a school or college council that you might have been a member of. Explain whether the meeting was formal or informal. What was the purpose of the meeting? What type of communication methods were used? Explain what the meeting achieved.

Formal meetings	Annual General Meeting of a large company Staff meeting in a large organisation Team briefing Meeting with clients/customers
Informal meetings	Meeting of a small team Unplanned meetings between staff

Type of meeting context

Technical enquiries

Having the information necessary to deal with a technical enquiry is important. For example, if you phone a school or college to find out the term dates, you would expect somebody to have those details on hand. Within a business setting technical enquiries might include:

- queries about products
- requests for prices and quotations
- questions about delivery and reliability
- enquiries about the business.

The list is almost endless. It is important that staff are trained properly to deal with technical enquiries. It does not look good for a business if a member of staff cannot deal with any questions about technical enquiries. Technical enquiries might be on the phone or delivered in person when visiting a customer. Because of the nature of technical enquiries and the fact that in most cases they require a one-to-one response, they are usually formal oral communications. However, many customers might want the oral communication to be supported with a written statement.

Did you know...

BT has customer-service call centres in India that employ more than 11,000 people.

Communicating with a supervisor/ colleagues and customers

Oral communications take place much of the time within a busy business environment. There is a whole range of individuals or groups that you may be communicating with. Some of these individuals might be within an organisation, while some might be outside the organisation.

Internal communications are communications within an organisation. No matter what role an individual undertakes within an organisation, he or she will work closely with others, such as a supervisor or colleagues. Whenever you work closely with individuals there are constantly different situations in which you communicate. For example, we can match many of the types of communication against the purpose of verbal communications (see table below).

Communicating with supervisor and colleagues	To inform	You are told that a new colleague is starting work next Monday
	To confirm	The new working arrangement will start in a fortnight
	To promote	You tell your supervisor that you feel that the working space you are using is too small and that you need a bigger desk
	To request	You ask if you can have next Friday off work
	To instruct	You instruct a new colleague to complete the totals of some invoices and show them what to do with the information

People within organisations often have to communicate verbally with others outside a business. These are **external communications**. One of the most important groups of people to communicate with are an organisation's customers. When communicating with customers it is important to be knowledgeable and be able to refer to appropriate information. It is important that in these instances customers come away with a good image of the company.

Communicating orally with customers

Kathryn is concerned about the quality of verbal communication between her organisation and its customers. She is worried that sometimes her staff are a little bit too informal and are not particularly good at sticking to the point. This, she feels, wastes the time of the customers as well as that of her employees. She is also concerned that some staff are a little bit negative on the phone and that this puts off some customers. She has considered monitoring calls and also investing in training.

1. Make a list of rules and guidelines for communicating with customers.
2. In the longer term, how could Kathryn improve the quality of dialogue between her employees and her customers?

Complaints

One of the most difficult situations for any employer to be put into is to deal with a complaint. Complaints should be effectively dealt with and customers or others should be listened to. If somebody is not happy with a product or a service, there is nothing worse than for their complaint to be passed from one person to another. This creates a bad impression of the organisation, may cause a lot of personal anguish and wastes time. If an employee does not deal sympathetically and well with a complaint, then the customer may not return and further business will be lost.

Oral presentations

An oral presentation

Many people within business organisations are expected to give oral presentations. This is not just a discussion between colleagues or a meeting. An oral presentation involves making a presentation to a group of people. Planning and preparation are particularly important. You may want to create a **PowerPoint** presentation. Speaking as you think is not always easy. Something that you say in front of an audience cannot simply be erased. It is also sometimes difficult to keep the interest of an audience over a period of time. However, an oral presentation provides an opportunity to get some interaction with an audience. For example a speaker may take questions.

Task

Working in groups of three or four, prepare a presentation called 'Preparing for work'. The presentation should last around 15 minutes.

Key words

Agenda – A list of things to be considered and discussed.

Business mentor – Employee whose role is to help, support and counsel new staff in a way that positively helps them within their new role.

External communications – Communication with individuals outside a business organisation.

Feedback – A response from individuals to a message.

Formal communication – Communication that takes place through organised and recognised channels and lines of communication.

Informal communication – Communication that takes place through less rigid channels of communication and through which everybody has a chance to contribute.

Internal communications – Communications within an organisation.

Motivate – To encourage individuals and provide them with an incentive.

PowerPoint – A graphics presentation package from Microsoft.

Assignment

You must understand the purpose of verbal communication in business contexts.

Verbal communications within the workplace

The office in which Peter and Daljinder work has recently been restructured. The purpose of the change was to enable individuals to take on more responsibility. Instead of instructions always coming from the office manager, the changes were designed to enable staff to take charge of their role and take many decisions on their own. It was felt that by doing this staff would be happier with the work that they undertake. However, to be able to deal with the changes, it is important that verbal communication takes place within the office at a variety of different levels.

1. Peter and Daljinder are thinking about the purpose of business communications. Working in pairs, make a list of why oral communications are necessary in different business contexts. Provide examples of four different contexts in which oral business communications could be used. **(P2)**
2. Peter and Daljinder have been asked to make a list of the different ways in which oral communications could be used within the office in different business situations. List all of the purposes of oral communications within the restructured office. Alongside each of the different purposes, identify different situations that could be used to meet such needs. For example, if somebody is ill and their work needs to be covered urgently, staff would need to be informed. Role play a team briefing within your classroom for which your teacher will provide you with feedback. As part of the role play, explain the role of staff within the new office. At the end of the role play, comment upon what you feel to be your strengths and weaknesses in making presentations within a briefing. **(M2)**

In your assessment you will need to be able to do the following:

To achieve a pass grade you need to:	To achieve a merit grade you need to:	To achieve a distinction you need to:
P2 explain, using examples, the purpose of verbal business communications in four different business contexts	**M2** discuss how verbal communications can be used effectively in business situations	

Chapter 13
Using verbal communications in business contexts

What are you finding out?

Speaking is an important part of all of our lives. It is something that we simply take for granted. As we saw in the last chapter, communicating verbally has many functions and purposes and we appreciated that it has a key role in different business contexts. Although communicating orally is very important, we emphasised that it is a skill as well because some individuals are better at speaking and are more articulate than others.

Figure 13.1 Conversation is a two-way process

Conversation is a two-way process. A conversation cannot take place if the people doing the speaking are not also listening. So to communicate orally, individuals need both speaking and listening skills. Sometimes we need to communicate with somebody on a one-to-one basis. At other times we may be expected to communicate with a group of people, perhaps within a meeting.

This chapter helps you to:

- Demonstrate how to use both speaking and listening skills in one-to-one and group business contexts.
- Review your own speaking and listening skills in a one-to-one and group business context.
- Identify your strengths and weaknesses in a one-to-one and group business context.
- Assess the effectiveness of your speaking and listening skills in supporting operations in a given business context.

Listening skills

It is not easy to be a good listener. Can you think of any situations when lengthy instructions have been read out to you in an uninteresting way? Trying to remember everything that somebody has said can be very difficult. By being a better listener within a workplace, it is possible to improve the way in which you perform your role.

Listening involves three steps:

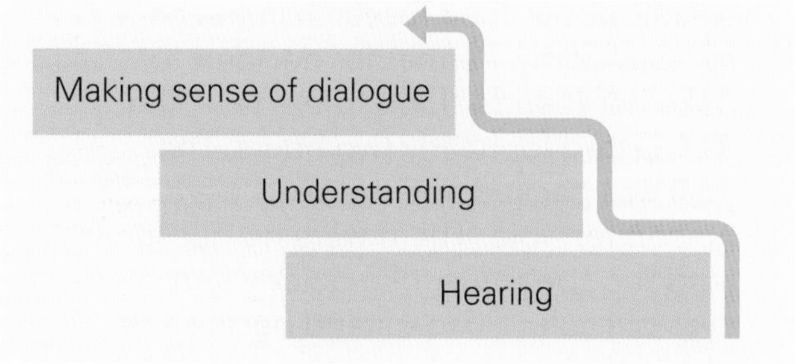

Figure 13.2 The three steps of effective listening

The first step in listening is to hear what somebody has said, unless you are deaf. Deaf people hear by lip-reading what is being said. For example, you may have been told that on Friday a visitor from one of your client's businesses is coming to the office and that they will be there from 10 a.m. until 4 p.m. If you can remember that and perhaps make a note that this is happening, then you have successfully heard what has been stated. The next element of listening involves understanding. Having heard this message, you may want to put it into context. As they are visiting the office, you may want to prepare for the visit. For example, you may book a meeting room and obtain a copy of their file. And now you need to make sense of the dialogue. So why are they visiting your office? Does that mean that they have further requirements? Is there an issue with the service that you are providing?

Listen and understand instructions given verbally

A good listener is an **active listener**. Active listening is a structured way of listening to a speaker. Not only does it involve listening, it also involves analysing the speaker's behaviour and body language. Active listeners look for clues. They focus upon the speaker and what they are about to say. They do not allow their mind to wander. Doing this allows the listener to learn more about what the speaker is trying to communicate.

> Did you know...
>
> **If you are finding it difficult to concentrate on what somebody is saying, repeating what they have said in your mind helps to reinforce the message. This also improves your powers of concentration.**

As a listener, you need to show the person speaking that you are listening. This might involve:

- Giving your full attention to the speaker.
- Concentrating.
- Responding to the speaker from time to time.
- Using a name as part of your response and being positive.
- Using facial expressions to show that you understand what is being said.
- Listening for the main ideas from their dialogue.
- Providing feedback on some of the comments.
- Asking questions.
- Occasionally using body language or cues, such as a nod, to show that you understand what they are saying.

Task

Trying to remember what has been said is not easy. This task is designed to develop your listening skills. Sitting in a circle facing each other, the first person starts by saying, 'I went into town and went to the supermarket to buy a loaf of bread.' The second person repeats this sentence and adds another product until a point is reached where individuals fail to remember the dialogue. Sometimes it is possible to start this with a letter association such as a product beginning with a, then a, b and so on.

Task

Working alongside a partner, talk to them for at least two minutes about your favourite interest. Having used active listening skills and, without taking notes, they should then summarise what you have said.

As with all forms of communications, there are some barriers that can make listening more difficult. These might include:

- A failure to understand some of the language of the speaker. For example, the speaker might use jargon or technical terms that not everybody knows.
- Confusion caused by the speaker's dialect or accent.
- Bias or prejudice of the listener. They may simply interpret what is being said into a form that fits their own views.
- A limited attention span. Sometimes if a speaker talks too long or speaks with little emphasis and a single tone, they can be difficult to listen to.
- Noise, such as that within a busy office or from roadworks, can limit the ability of the listener to concentrate. It may simply interfere with their thinking and concentration.
- Worry or concern about what the speaker is saying may make it difficult for the listener to take everything in.
- Presenting too many concepts in a complicated way for the listener.

Finding out about the universe

Perminder is interested in astronomy. Recently she noticed that a famous speaker was visiting her local university to talk about their research in the area of astronomy. Perminder decided to take her friends along to the talk. The talk lasted for nearly two hours. The hall was packed and the seats were uncomfortable. There were no questions and the speaker spoke quickly and was difficult to understand because of the technical words that they used. As Perminder was sitting close to the back of the hall she had difficultly hearing the speaker. She was also distracted by the noise of the traffic outside. For Perminder, the whole experience was disappointing and she had to apologise to her friends.

Within a business environment, there are many different situations in which individuals have to listen.

Communications that require listening skills

Face to face	Using technology
• Direct conversations • Meetings • Staff briefings • Presentations • Staff meetings • Interviews	• Telephone landline • Mobile phone • Video conference • Voicemail • Skype • Answering machine

Task

Rate yourself as a listener somewhere on the scale from 1 to 10. 10 would be excellent and 1 very poor. Explain why you rate yourself in such a way. If you have rated yourself badly, why do you think that you are such a poor listener? If you have rated yourself well, why are you such a good listener?

It might be very difficult in a busy work environment, with a lot to do, to have to listen to instructions. A good active listener may make a mental note of any changes in ways of working. In contrast, a poor listener may not hear all that is being said or may simply interpret the instructions in their own terms. They may simply do what they think has been said.

Did you know...

Spoken words only account for around 30–35% of what is being said. The rest is translated through non-verbal communication.

Interpret instructions and task requirements correctly

It can sometimes be difficult to interpret instructions. For example, instructions might be complicated and difficult to understand. Technical words could be used. The instructions might be **ambiguous**. This means that what has been said could be interpreted in several different ways. The speaker communicating the instructions might speak very quickly.

To cope with instructions that are not being presented well, it is important to listen intently. Listening skills are very important. It may be necessary to ask questions to clarify any words that you do not understand or to find out what is required. It might be necessary to take notes from their dialogue as this then provides the listener with something that they can come back to later.

One way of interpreting information is to use what is known in journalism as the five Ws and one H. These are generally considered to be useful series of questions for information gathering. The five Ws are: 'Who', 'What', 'When', 'Where' and 'Why?', and these are then followed by 'How'.

For example, as you listen to somebody, you may think:

Who – are the messages targeted at? Who might be affected by the work and who will undertake it?

What – will the work entail? What details do you need to know in order to complete the work?

When – does everything need to be completed by?

Where – are the resources necessary to complete the work?

Why – is the work necessary?

How – will it be undertaken?

Make notes

As you listen it may be useful to make some notes. It is important that your notes are legible and that they can be referred to and used later. Notes are particularly good for reminding you what you have to do in response to the speaker. What you are doing is using your list to work out a series of priorities based upon the dialogue of the speaker. Listing could help you to:

1. Identify all of the tasks that you might have to undertake.
2. Think about the timings of these activities.
3. Schedule what you need to do and put them into order.
4. Think about resource requirements.

Reflection

Listening to somebody for a long period of time may involve quite a lot of concentration. You may be taking notes, but at the same time you will be thinking as you interpret their dialogue. Many questions may go through your mind. For example, what does the speaker want you to do? Is there anything you need to consider? What are you thinking about in response to what they are saying? These thoughts are as a result of your own reflections about what the speaker is saying. You will have feelings about the sort of message that the speaker is trying to communicate. There may be elements that you agree with, areas that you may have difficulty completing, or you may disagree with some of what the speaker is saying. We all have thoughts and our reflections are a response to or an interpretation of what we are hearing.

Seek clarification where appropriate

Sometimes speakers can be a little bit ambiguous or their dialogue might be a little bit confused. If they are explaining something complicated or if they talk too quickly, the message may be lost. There is nothing wrong with asking for clarification. By asking for clarification you are simply asking the speaker to make something easier to understand. If instructions are not clear, it is easy to make mistakes within the workplace and these will cost the business money.

Did you know...

Gerald Ratner was the former chief executive of the Ratner Group, a major British jeweller. In a key speech he once said that some of his earrings were 'cheaper than an M&S prawn sandwich'. After that speech his firm's value plummeted by £500 million and his business nearly collapsed. People were certainly listening that day!

An office working at full capacity

Claire has been an office manager for the last 12 months. The office processes data across the organisation and also provides a whole host of supporting services. Since she joined the business, turnover sales have doubled, but she has the same number of staff. Claire feels that her office is running at full capacity and she is worried that the sheer volume of work having to be completed is going to affect its quality. She was recently invited to a meeting with the director in charge of administration, who informed her that the business was in the process of acquiring one of its competitors. She was told by the director that the administration for the competitor would have to be undertaken by her department.

1. What might Claire be thinking?
2. Would you expect Claire's response to be to simply accept that her office would take on extra capacity?

One-to-one communication

One-to-one verbal communication involves one person communicating with another person. It can be a very personal form of communication and is the form of communication that we commonly practise and experience probably daily throughout our lives, and often with people we are very close to.

In a work situation one-to-one verbal communication might simply involve talking to a colleague or a customer. Conversation that is one-to-one is usually informal. However, if an individual is being interviewed by another, or being appraised through recognised channels, then it will become more formal.

Task

Speaking clearly is not always easy. Sometimes words are difficult to pronounce and sometimes combinations of words may sound complicated. Practise the following voice exercise.

'Who would know ought of art must learn and then take his ease.'

Methods of conveying messages or series of instructions

There are a number of situations in which messages or instructions need to be conveyed. For example, an employee might be told to give a message to another member of staff when they arrive in the office. You may be having a one-to-one discussion with your employer or simply talking to a colleague about a work-related issue. Often messages may be conveyed verbally over the telephone or **Skype**.

One of the clear advantages of conveying messages on a one-to-one basis is that it is possible to use a lot of personal qualities. This might be because you know somebody, or because the one-to-one conversation is face to face. For example, it is possible to show consideration and empathy as part of your dialogue. You may be sympathetic with the reaction that an individual has to the message that you are being asked to convey, particularly if you know that they might not like it. So, as you deliver the message, the tone of your voice and facial expression can show that you are aware of their feelings as they receive the message.

When delivering messages it is important to speak accurately. It is also important to say exactly what you mean. Speaking within a workplace is not like having a conversation with a friend. It involves choosing words precisely so that the exact meaning of a message or nature of an instruction is properly conveyed.

When delivering messages it is also useful to be sincere. This means being yourself and trying to put people at ease. Eye contact and facial expressions can help. This helps to show that you mean what you are saying and are genuinely interested in an individual's response to a message. Although this is not always easy when conveying messages, it helps if you can relax. People who relax are able to express themselves more naturally.

Task

Think of somebody you know who has good speaking skills. What are those qualities and how does that make him or her better at the communication of messages?

There are some situations in which it may be difficult to convey a one-to-one message. For example, there may be a lot of noise within an office, or there might be some sort of media playing. Similarly, you may need to convey a message that has some personal element that you would like to keep private. In this situation

In some situations conveying a message may be difficult

and, in order for the one-to-one message to be conveyed, you may need some privacy. It may be possible to use a meeting room or an enclosed office in order to convey the message.

Relaying one-to-one messages over the telephone requires a different skills set, mainly because you cannot see the person you are talking to. The starting point with any call is to clarify who the caller is, as well as what the purpose of the call is. It may be difficult to hear the caller and you may have to ask them to spell certain words. If the call is a long-distance overseas call, you may have trouble hearing what they say, or there might be a slight time delay. Taking or relaying a message accurately is important so that the key element is fully understood and recorded.

As with any form of one-to-one conversation, in feeling empathy with the person you are speaking to, the conversation may wander or become prolonged and time might be lost. As one-to-one conversations tend to be informal, it is also possible for them to waste time and affect workloads.

Did you know...

A recent survey by Microsoft revealed that employees waste as much as 35% of their working hours while in the office.

Discussion...

How might reducing time wasted within an office impact upon staff morale?

Messages to suit different situations

Messages need to be tailored to different situations. For example, some messages might be confidential. On a one-to-one basis, it might involve an office manager talking to an employee about their appraisal, or it could be about their yearly bonus. Clearly, this involves information that both parties would not want anybody else within their work environment to hear. So, when conveying this message, it would be better to talk in a closed environment such as a meeting room or a private office. In contrast, when dealing with a day-to-day issue that is not confidential, then talking to somebody within an open office would not be a problem.

When communicating with somebody else on a one-to-one basis, different emphasis needs to be placed in different circumstances, and this is perhaps where a variety of very human qualities comes into play. For example, if an office manager has an urgent job that he or she wants to get finished, then they need to emphasise that it needs to be finished quickly and pass on their enthusiasm to members of the office. In contrast, if a member of the office has just received some bad news, the office manager would need to be sincere and sympathetic. Perhaps somebody is upset at how their job has changed; in this circumstance the office manager would have to sell their new role and motivate the individual to convince them of their need to move forward in their thinking. Representing oneself in a sincere way depending on different situations is not always easy. Some people have a natural talent for communicating with both **empathy** and enthusiasm.

In some situations it is better to meet somebody face to face than discuss an issue with them over the telephone. This is particularly important if the issue is confidential or there is a need to have a protracted discussion with somebody. On the other hand, however, by using a telephone, it is possible to reach another person quickly and resolve an issue or get the information required relatively quickly.

Task

Make a list of all of the qualities required by a manager who shows empathy.

Working in a group situation

Communicating individually with others is only one aspect of communication within an organisation. As organisations grow, there are many situations where, instead of meeting with individuals individually, it becomes necessary to meet others in group situations. These situations might include meetings, staff briefings, group activities, training sessions, formal presentations, committees, team meetings and so on.

Did you know...

It has been said that a camel is a horse designed by a committee!

Task

Think about your experience of meetings. Think about a group that you have belonged to. What advantages did meeting as a group have over simply meeting individually? What could the group decide that meeting individually would not allow them to decide?

In the modern workplace, analysing a problem alone might not take into account all of the skills and knowledge of those likely to be influenced by any decision that is made. Group discussion is **inclusive** and helps to make staff feel that they are valued. When staff are valued they may be more receptive to change as they feel that both their feelings and views have been taken into account. It also makes them feel more professional. It is for this reason that it is argued that group decisions simply have to be better than decisions taken by individuals.

Make relevant contributions to a discussion about business tasks

Regardless of what a group discussion is about, group discussion will produce more and better suggestions than just a single individual working on their own. Where groups contribute to decisions:

- The more members there are, the more minds and knowledge there are to draw on.
- It is easier to find a solution.
- Ideas are recorded.
- Better suggestions are made.
- Responsibility for the decisions that are made are shared.

So what sort of contributions should individuals make within groups?

Meetings

Nearly all employees at all levels within an organisation will spend some time attending meetings. Meetings are held to deal with issues, problems and areas of concern within an organisation. They provide an opportunity for a group of people to use their specialist backgrounds, experiences and knowledge to contribute to a range of matters. Some meetings are simply informal gatherings in which no formal records are kept. In contrast a formal meeting may involve lots of procedures.

- The features of a formal meeting are as follows:
- The meeting is called by a notice or **agenda.**
- Conduct in the meeting depends upon formal rules.
- Decisions are often reached by voting.
- The proceedings are recorded in **minutes**.

A notice of a meeting will be accompanied by or followed by an agenda. This is a list of topics to be discussed at the meeting. It will normally be sent in advance to those invited to attend the meeting so that they can consider all of the topics.

A **chairperson** has certain duties and powers at a meeting. They make sure that the meeting is properly conducted, they keep order and work through the agenda. Shortly before the meeting starts the chairperson makes sure that there is a **quorum**. The chairperson will make sure that everybody has an agenda and will introduce the new members. If any apologies are received from those unable to attend the meeting, this is recorded. If minutes from the previous meeting have been circulated, then those at the meeting will be asked to approve that they are a correct record of events at the last meeting. At this stage any matters arising from the minutes will be discussed. The chairperson will then work through each of the agenda items in turn. **Any other business** is the last agenda item and this enables areas to be discussed that have not been itemised on the agenda.

Examples of good and bad contributions

Good contribution	Poor contribution
Listening to others before using creative ideas that actively relate to and contribute to the discussion	Speaking at length and repetitively in a way that does not interest other members of the group
Getting to the point and being articulate about the views that you express	Being vague and ambiguous and confusing members of the group with dialogue
Preparing for the meeting, taking notes from other contributors and then making a measured and thoughtful contribution	Interrupting others and negatively affecting the mood of the meeting with poorly presented points
Asking questions that clarify and help others to understand what has been said	Not listening when others are speaking and then not contributing in a way that takes into account the views of others
Being flexible and accepting that others have made some good points	Refusing to accept the views of any other person
Speaking clearly and being articulate about your views	Annoying others with comments and making personal views about other contributions
Being constructive with ideas and seeing the bright side of the discussion	Wasting time, enjoying talking but not willing to take any form of action

Did you know...

Group pressure, sometimes known as 'mob psychology', can influence individuals in group situations to agree with poor decisions.

At the majority of meetings you attend you will probably be a participant. The following is a useful guide:

- Scrutinise the agenda.
- Research areas of interest and obtain relevant reading materials.
- Plan out, either in your mind or by making notes, what you might wish to say.
- Listen to what others have to say before speaking yourself.
- Timing is important. Make sure the points you make fit the discussion.
- Do not ramble on.
- Be tactful and do not deliberately upset anyone.
- Be assertive.
- Make your contribution coherent.
- Be ready for some form of opposition by trying to anticipate the response you might receive to the points you are making.

Tips for speaking well

Pace	The larger the audience, the slower you should speak. Use pace to emphasise the points you wish to make
Pitch	High-pitched voices tend to sound harsh. Breath deeply and try to lower the pitch of your voice
Volume	Do not shout! Your voice should be loud enough so that everybody can hear you
Tone	The tone of your voice helps you to express feeling and empathy
Pausing	Sometimes speakers can pause for effect
Breathing	Breathing exercises can be used to prepare you for a talk

Team briefing

Everybody, in one way or another, is a member of a team within the workplace. Sometimes the teams may be very small, and sometimes they might be large. A briefing provides an opportunity to pass on information that is of interest to the team and something which might influence their actions within the workplace. For example, most secondary schools will have a team briefing. The purpose of the briefing is to pass on critical information for staff about what is happening within the school that day. For example, there may be some important visitors to the school or certain areas of the school might have been declared out of bounds. The briefing provides the opportunity not just for the headteacher to contribute, but also other members of staff who may have important information to pass on.

It is also useful to make notes at a briefing so that information can be acted upon. The advantage of a briefing is that an opportunity exists to discuss how any changes might affect staff and their roles within the workplace. Team briefings provide the opportunity for everybody to contribute news and also discuss activities.

Make the grade

M3 Remember to use this for M3. When it comes to communicating, we all have strengths and weaknesses. The word 'audit' means the evaluation of a person or a system. For M3 you need to audit your own speaking and listening skills. Think about how speaking and listening skills differ between talking with individuals on a one-to-one basis and talking within a group. Identify your strengths and weaknesses within each situation. Explain why you feel that you have got strengths in each instance and also why you feel you have weaknesses in certain areas. Discuss what you intend to do to minimise your weaknesses.

Respond appropriately to others

There are clear protocols that influence the ways in which individuals should respond in certain situations. For example, often when students make presentations or when a guest speaker finishes, it is appropriate for those listening to applaud the speaker as well as to thank them for their talk. The use of the word 'please' is also important when asking individuals for their thoughts or to do something.

Within the workplace there may be accepted ways in which people respond to each other, both in a one-to-one situation as well as within a group. For example, there may be a certain way of dealing with a supervisor or a senior manager. It is also important to try to be positive. For example, providing positive feedback for individuals who have just completed a task helps them to feel appreciated and valued.

Confidentiality is another key issue within a response. Every organisation has issues that should be kept confidential.

Did you know...

The worst-kept secret is that Levi Roots would like to challenge Boris Johnson at the next election for the Mayor of London!

Move a discussion forward

Within a meeting, it is helpful if individuals are precise and that the response of others builds on the suggestions that have been made. Sometimes when agreement is not reached, it is possible to go to a vote.

Make the grade

D2 Remember to use this for D2. Search the internet on sites such as YouTube to find and listen to individuals involved in business who have inspirational speaking and listening skills. Explain what makes an inspirational speaker. Look at the personal qualities that they have and evaluate why they are good at speaking to audiences.

Key words

Active listener – Making a real effort to hear the words of the speaker as well as how a message is being communicated.

Agenda – A list of itemised areas to be discussed at a meeting.

Ambiguous – Open to a whole range of meanings and interpretations.

Any other business – This is usually the last item on the agenda for a meeting where other issues have already been discussed.

Chairperson – Somebody who controls and directs the proceedings of a meeting.

Empathy – Identifying and understanding another person's feelings and thoughts.

Inclusive – Takes into account everybody's views and includes everybody likely to be influenced by a decision.

Minutes – Written record of the proceedings of a meeting.

Mob psychology – Individuals within a group are influenced though peer pressure by the majority element.

Quorum – Minimum number of people required to attend a meeting before it can take place.

Skype – Internet telephone and videophone service.

Assignment

You must be able to use verbal communications in business contexts.

Learning to communicate within a business context

You have just joined a company. You have been appointed as a junior salesperson, a post that requires good verbal communication skills. One of the processes that you go through when you join a new organisation is that of training. The training helps you to develop the skills necessary to undertake the role for which you have been appointed.

1. For this task you need to work in pairs. You have been asked to interview the other person to find out as much as you can about your job role. You want to know about working hours, tea and lunch breaks and facilities, holidays, as well as what the job might entail. One of the pair should take the role of the experienced member of staff and the other that of a new member of staff. Discuss these issues for ten minutes and then change over and swap roles. **(P3)**
2. This activity needs to be carried out in small groups of five or six. Before carrying out this activity, you need to undergo some preparation. Each member of the group should identify, make some notes for and then be prepared to talk about one of the themes itemised below:
   - the venue of the office Christmas party
   - the need for sales staff to be provided with company mobile phones
   - last year's sales reports
   - the need to buy a new photocopier
   - how to improve customer service
   - why the office requires some new office chairs.

   Each person should speak for around three or four minutes. After each person has spoken, other members of the group should demonstrate their listening skills by each asking at least one relevant question. **(P4)**
3. Having undertaken the small-group activity, identify the strengths and weaknesses of your verbal communication skills for both one-to-one discussion and speaking and listening in a group context. Summarise, by indicating what sort of training you might require to improve your communication skills. **(M3)**
4. For this activity learners need to draw upon a case study. The case study should come from a media source such as a television programme in which two individuals are talking within a business situation. By referring to specific examples within the case study, identify and discuss how effective the conversations you have observed have been. For example, have they achieved their purpose? **(D2)**

In your assessment you will need to be able to do the following:

To achieve a pass grade you need to:	To achieve a merit grade you need to:	To achieve a distinction you need to:
P3 demonstrate speaking and listening skills in a one-to-one business context	**M3** carry out a review of your speaking and listening skills in both a one-to-one and a group context, identifying your strengths and weaknesses	**D2** assess the effectiveness of speaking and listening skills in supporting business operations in a given business context
P4 demonstrate speaking and listening skills in a business-group context		

Unit 8

Business communication through documentation

Chapter 14
Purpose of written communication in business contexts

What are you finding out?

Within all businesses, a great deal of communication takes place each and every day. Good communications are essential to the running of a business, otherwise employees would not know what to do, customers may not feel valued and managers would not be aware of how the business is performing. Each day communication will take place between colleagues and between a business and its stakeholders. Much of this communication is written and the style and format of the written communication will depend on its purpose and the business context in which it is used. Colleagues may email each other in an informal way, for example, or a formal letter on headed paper may be used to inform customers about problems with their accounts. You will find out about the different purposes and importance of written communications and the methods of written communication that are used in different business contexts.

This chapter will help you to:

- Identify the purposes of written business communications.
- Describe appropriate methods of written communication in different business contexts.
- Explain the importance of written communication in specific business contexts.

The purposes of written business communications

There are many purposes in business for using written communications. Above all, a written communication provides a record for a business of the information that has been exchanged, who it was exchanged with and when, even though the primary purpose of the communication may have been to inform, confirm, promote, make a request or to instruct.

It is important for businesses to keep records of communications, as clarification of information may be needed at a later date. For example, a customer may claim to have been quoted a different price for goods, or a member of staff may make an enquiry about their rate of pay. If communications are written and copies are kept, then it is easy for a business to check details and maintain good relationships with its employees, customers, suppliers and other **stakeholders**.

To inform

Businesses frequently need to use written communications to give out information. This could be internally to keep staff informed or externally to stakeholders outside the business.

Internally, businesses need to inform their employees about the aims and objectives of the business, working practices and health and safety, the products or services the business supplies and the terms and conditions of their employment. It is essential that all employees know the aims and objectives of the business to ensure that everyone is working towards a common goal. Similarly, businesses must make sure that all employees are knowledgeable about their products or services so that they can pass on information to customers.

The flow of information within a business is also essential to decision making. Written communications, such as **reports**, are used to keep managers informed about the performance of the business so that they can direct staff and plan for the future.

Externally, a business needs to use written communications to pass on information to a number of different stakeholder groups. Letters can be used to give customers information; for example, banks write to customers to let them know if there is a problem with their accounts. A company's shareholders receive information about the performance of the company in the form of an **annual report**, and government departments are sent financial information.

To confirm

Businesses often use written communications to confirm arrangements. Letters may be sent to customers to confirm bookings, emails may be sent to suppliers to confirm meetings, and letters may be sent to employees to confirm appointments or promotions. A travel agency or tour operator, for example, will confirm holiday arrangements by sending out letters or tickets to customers, and theatres will send out confirmation of advance bookings for seats. Most businesses write to prospective employees to invite them for interview and to confirm the time and date; then they will send a letter to the successful candidate confirming their appointment.

To promote

Businesses use a wide variety of written communications to promote themselves and their products or services. A business can make use of externally produced written communications, for example, by placing an advertisement that has been created by an advertising agency into a newspaper or magazine, or it can create its own promotional material, such as leaflets or flyers. In using promotional material, the business hopes to attract customers.

A business can also use written communications to promote an internal event to staff. Emails or a poster on a noticeboard, for example, could be used to promote a staff social event or an activity in aid of a charity.

Most workplaces will have a staff noticeboard

To make a request

Businesses may need to make requests of their customers. Businesses such as banks and building societies, for example, may write to customers to invite them to visit the branch to discuss their accounts or may ask them to send in some documents to help process a transaction.

Businesses also make requests of their suppliers. Sending an order for goods is making a request to a supplier to supply certain quantities of products and if a business needs to select a supplier that meets its needs, it may make a request to a number of different suppliers to attend meetings and make presentations about the products they have to offer.

Internally, managers may request that colleagues attend meetings by circulating **agendas**, and requests may be made by departments for photocopying or stocks of paper and other stationery.

To instruct

Written instructions can be found everywhere, in boxes with new products, on the walls of offices and factories, next to photocopiers, even on your cereal box (open this end)! Businesses produce an endless array of written instructions because they need to make sure that they comply with the law, ensure the health and safety of their employees and customers and to make sure that employees have the information they need to be able to carry out their jobs effectively.

Businesses try to protect themselves by providing customers with the information they need to use a product correctly. If customers fail to follow the instructions provided, then a business cannot be held liable for any damage. Businesses also provide instructions to help customers get the maximum benefit and enjoyment from the product they have bought. However, many people do not bother to read instructions, relying instead on trial and error!

Ensuring the health and safety of employees and customers is essential and all business premises must have instructions on what to do in an emergency and must display instructions in each room showing where the nearest exit is and the location of the fire-assembly point.

Providing written instructions is also an essential aid to businesses when training their staff and many businesses provide training manuals. If a job involves lifting, then businesses, by law, must ensure that employees are given instructions on manual handling.

Make the grade

P1 Remember this for P1. You must be able to identify, using examples, the purposes of written business communications in four different business contexts. This information will help you to look for and identify the different purposes that your chosen business has for using written communications.

Task

State the purpose of each of the written communications below.

Memo

To: All staff in Accounts

From: S Ahmed

Date: 29/1/10

Re: Recycling

Please place all waste paper in the new green bins for collection at 4 p.m. today.

ABCO Ltd
SunnySide
Derby

2 February 2010

Mr A Jones
16 Maria Street
Derby
DE4 8JS

Dear Mr Jones

We are delighted to confirm your promotion from administrative clerk to office manager effective from 1 March 2010.

May we take this opportunity to congratulate you and we hope that you will continue to enjoy working for us.

Yours sincerely

S Sullivan & K Freeman

S Sullivan & K Freeman
Personnel Managers

Task

Find out the different purposes that your school has for using written communications to communicate with your parents.

Appropriate methods of written communications in different business contexts

There are many methods of communicating in writing and each could be handwritten, transmitted electronically or word processed. They include letters, memoranda (**memos**), reports, emails, notices, agendas, **minutes**, company newsletters and magazines, **purchase orders** and **invoices**.

The method of written communication a business chooses to use must be appropriate to the particular business context it is to be used in. For example, it would not be appropriate to send a memo to a customer as memos are intended for internal use only. The different business contexts are:

- Formal
- Informal
- Communicating with **subordinates**
- Communicating with supervisor
- Communicating with colleagues
- Communicating with suppliers
- Communicating with customers
- Handling complaints
- Confidential.

Letters

Letters are a formal method of written communication and can be used in a number of business contexts including to communicate with subordinates, supervisors, suppliers, customers and to respond to complaints. Not all letters are confidential but letters from managers to their subordinates usually are.

Memos

Memos are a form of communication used internally and can be used to communicate with subordinates, colleagues and supervisors. They are usually shorter than letters and are used to pass on or request information. Memos can be confidential because they contain information about the internal workings of a business. If the contents of a memo are confidential, then the memo will usually be marked as 'Confidential'. The term 'leaked memo' usually refers to the contents of an internal memo that have been discussed inappropriately with people outside the business, for example with newspaper journalists.

Reports

A report is a formal method of written communication using a set format that is usually used to pass on information internally. Subordinates may be asked to produce reports for managers, or colleagues in different departments may produce reports for each other on certain aspects of the business that they may be working together on. Reports are usually used to identify problems and present possible solutions or to report on performance or progress.

Although most reports are produced within a business, external bodies, such as consultants and auditors, can be asked to produce reports for the managers of a business about its performance or how to improve its performance.

Reports that are intended to be confidential are marked 'Confidential' but generally it is not appropriate to discuss the contents of a report with people outside the business.

Emails

Emails can be both formal and informal and are used in almost all business contexts. The essential difference between a formal and an informal email is the language used; formal emails are far more polite. Informal emails can be sent between colleagues to pass on or request information but, generally, formal emails are used to communicate with supervisors, suppliers and customers. Many businesses now invite feedback, including complaints, from customers via email and will respond by email.

Confidential information should not be sent by email. Emails can be easily intercepted or misdirected, and, once received, can very easily be forwarded and therefore read by people they were not intended for.

Notices

Noticeboards can be used for formal and informal communication within a business. Formal notices that may appear on a noticeboard include advertisements for internal jobs, information from trade unions and hours of work for part-time staff. Informal notices include information about staff social events and staff news items such as a forthcoming wedding or the birth of a baby. Noticeboards are used when information is for everybody to see and therefore it would be inappropriate to pin confidential information to a noticeboard!

Agendas

An agenda is a notification to those attending a meeting of the topics that will be discussed at that meeting in the order that they will be discussed. It is a formal method of written communication used for formal meetings. Everyone who is expected to attend a meeting will be given or sent an agenda.

Minutes

Minutes are a formal record of a meeting. At every formal meeting, somebody attends to take the minutes. This person records who has attended the meeting, the main points of what was discussed and what actions need to be taken and by whom. Minutes of meetings should be given only to those who attended or who were invited to attend the meeting and managers of the business who may request them.

Company newsletters and magazines

Company newsletters and magazines are formal methods of communicating with all employees, though they often contain informal news items such as an employee's wedding or a staff social event. Generally, they inform employees about what is happening within the business, about any awards the business or the staff have received and include messages to staff such as ways to save paper. Many well-known businesses, such as Cadbury and John Lewis, for example, have company magazines or newsletters.

Purchase orders

A purchase order is a formal method of written communication that is sent by a business to a supplier to order goods. A purchase order lists the description, quantity and price of each type of good that the business wants, and commits the business to buy the goods from the supplier. A purchase order is an official document and businesses need to keep them on file.

Invoices

An invoice is the same as a bill. Once a supplier has sent goods ordered out to a business, it will also send an invoice, which shows the description, quantity and price of the goods sent and the total amount that the business needs to pay for the goods. It will also tell the business how long it has in which to pay for the goods; for example, many suppliers allow businesses 30 days in which to pay. An invoice is an official document and businesses need to keep them on file.

Make the grade

M1 Remember this for M1. You must be able to describe appropriate methods of written communication in different business contexts for a given business or business of your choice.

Fieldwork

Arrange to visit, or write to, a number of large businesses and ask for their company newsletters or magazines. Look for similarities and differences between them and the way they are used to communicate information to employees.

Task

Select the most appropriate form of written communication for the following:

1. **To inform an employee of his new rate of pay.**
2. **To tell all employees about the date of the Christmas party.**
3. **To inform all sales staff of price reductions.**
4. **To order a new supply of paper for the photocopier.**

The importance of written communication in specific business contexts

Written communications provide a record for a business of the information that has been exchanged, who it was exchanged with and when, and this can be extremely important to the efficient running of a business. Imagine that all communications were verbal and to find anything out, employees had to depend on each other's memories – this would be like a game of Chinese whispers in which everyone might give a different version of events.

The method of written communication is also very important as it must be appropriate for its purpose. If customers started to receive memos instead of formal business letters, the image of the business would suffer as the business would seem unprofessional and disorganised. Appropriate, well-written communications will present a good image for a business, suggesting that it is well run.

In some business contexts, written communications are essential. Records are needed of formal communication between employees, between a business and its suppliers and, in some cases, between a business and its customers.

Communication between employees

Employees must know what the aims and objectives of the business are and, if appropriate, what their targets are, and although this information can be communicated verbally, it needs to be made formal by being communicated in writing. This way, employees know that it is official and part of their job to meet these expectations.

For the day-to-day workings of a business to be effective, employees often need to be given updated information or discuss ways in which a business can move forward. For these reasons, employees meet. If records of these meetings were not kept, in the form of minutes, employees might eventually forget what was discussed and any actions they needed to take. It is therefore important that employees receive a copy of the minutes of a meeting in which they were involved.

Similarly, reports are important to the efficient running of a business because they contain information about current issues and the performance, or desired performance, of the business. Managers need the information contained in reports to be able to make decisions and carry out their jobs effectively. For example, if a production manager did not know that the output of the business had fallen on certain days due to problems with machinery, then they would not investigate the situation and take the appropriate actions needed to sort out the problems.

Letters to employees are an important record for the employee and the business. These are used to confirm the dates of commencement of employment, rates of pay, status within the business (for example, a confirmation of a promotion), any special requests made and/or granted (such as additional holiday), and also to record any disciplinary action that may have been taken.

Company newsletters and magazines may be viewed as less important to the running of a business than, for example, reports, but they have an important role. They make employees feel part of a team and an important part of the business, which motivates employees. Many company magazines and newsletters feature achievements by employees (both inside and outside the workplace) and also print contributions from employees, which can make them feel valued by the business.

Communication between a business and its suppliers

Written communications between a business and its suppliers are essential. Businesses must keep records of goods ordered and invoices as they form part of the accounting system of the business and help to prevent instances of fraud. If a business did not keep invoices, it would not know how much money had been paid out by the business for goods and then would be unable to calculate its costs and therefore its profits.

Communication between a business and its customers

A great deal of communication between a business and its customers takes place verbally but there are occasions when communication must be in writing.

Some businesses trade with other businesses and if their business customers order goods, then they need a purchase order. Purchase orders must be kept by the business so that they know what goods have been ordered and can issue correct invoices. If they did not, they would not know how much money was owed to them or received and would then be unable to calculate revenue and therefore profit.

Customers may write to a business to complain and, in these circumstances, it is often appropriate to respond in writing. This is particularly important if a complaint is about a health and safety issue or a claim against a business that may end up in court, as records of all communications between the business and its customer would need to be kept.

Written communications with customers are also important in terms of presenting a good image of a business. Badly written letters with grammar and punctuation errors that do not follow the correct format for a business letter will give customers a poor impression of a business.

Did you know...

Eighty per cent of complaints received by an organisation are likely to have poor communication as their root cause, either with the customer or within the organisation itself.

Make the grade

D1 Remember this for D1. You must be able to explain the importance of written communication in an organisation in specific business contexts. You might consider why a communication needs to be written rather than made verbally.

Task

Read the following conversation that took place between two employees and answer the questions that follow:

Manager: *Joe, phone J C Bloggs Ltd and ask them to send us some more paper.*

Joe: *How much paper do we want?*

Manager: *One hundred boxes.*

Joe: *OK. Can I speak to you about my pay first?*

Manager: *What do you want to know?*

Joe: *You told me last month that I would be getting an increase in pay but my pay was the same as before.*

Manager: *Sorry, Joe, I wasn't able to give you the pay rise as nobody is getting a pay rise at the moment.*

1. **State the form of written communication that should be used to order the paper from J C Bloggs Ltd.**
2. **Explain the importance of using written communication for this transaction.**
3. **When the original discussion about Joe's pay took place, what should Joe have requested to confirm his pay rise?**
4. **Discuss the importance of written communications between employees.**

The Red Lion Inn

Our Menu

Starters

Garlic muchrooms
Soup of the day with bred
Prawn cocktail
Soup of the day

Mains

Steak and kidney pie
Medallions of pork
Gammon steak
8oz steak

Deserts

Bread & butter pudding
Chocolate brownie
Ice créme sundae
Lemon meringue pie

We are located in a picturesque part of the peak district

Contact us on:

09876 456789

To make a booking

Open fires and comfortable seating.

The Red Lion Inn

Home of good food and beer

Visit us when you visit the Peaks

We are open all day everyday

The Red Lion Inn is a busy public house with rooms to let in a picturesque part of the Peak District. Most of its trade comes from selling lunch and evening meals to regular customers and tourists. The landlord and landlady have produced a leaflet to promote the inn, which they distribute to holiday accommodation and local retailers. The image above shows one side of the leaflet:

1. State the purpose of the written communication above.
2. State three ways in which this written communication could be improved.
3. Describe the impression that customers might form of the Red Lion Inn from reading this written communication.
4. To what extent is the quality of written communication used between a business and its customers important?

Discussion...

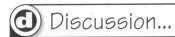

Only large businesses need to use written communications between employees; in small businesses, employees can speak to each other more regularly. Discuss.

Key words

Agenda – A notification to those attending a meeting of the topics that will be discussed at that meeting in the order that they will be discussed.

Annual report – A report on a company's performance produced at the end of each accounting year, which must be sent to every shareholder.

Invoice – A bill for goods or services.

Memo – A method for communicating brief messages within an organisation.

Minutes – A formal record of a meeting.

Purchase order – A document used to place an order for goods.

Report – A document that follows a set format used to pass on detailed information, usually about the performance of a business.

Stakeholders – Individuals or groups who are connected with or affected by the actions of a business.

Subordinate – An employee who is answerable to a specific manager.

Assignment

See Chapter 16, page 185

To achieve a pass grade you need to:	To achieve a merit grade you need to:	To achieve a distinction you need to:
P1 identify, using examples, the purposes of written business communications in four different business contexts	**M1** describe appropriate methods of written communication in different business contexts	**D1** explain the importance of written communication in an organisation in specific business contexts

Chapter 15 Completing and using business documents

What are you finding out?

All businesses use written communications but, in order for communication to be effective, a business must have systems in place to ensure that the correct messages are communicated to its employees, managers and other stakeholders. Any written communications must be accurate, consistent and well presented, especially if used to communicate with stakeholders outside the business. Poor communications that are poorly presented are likely to create a negative image for a business. Whether used internally or externally, it is important to use the correct method to communicate, especially if communication is formal, and to ensure that messages are clear, otherwise they may be misunderstood and ignored. To communicate in writing, different types of documents are used and for each method there is a recognised format that you can learn.

This chapter will help you to:

- Produce business documents of different types for internal communication in an organisation.
- Produce business documents of different types for external communication by an organisation.
- Compare your choice of internal and external documents with alternatives.
- Justify your choice of internal and external documents, explaining why each document is appropriate for its intended audience.

Documents and appropriate layouts

Documents used for written communication in business have a set format and follow certain rules. This ensures that communication between different businesses and between businesses and their **stakeholders** is effective because the information to be communicated is set out in a standard way and can be easily understood. Most business documents are printed on **headed paper**. This means that the name of the business and other details, such as the address, telephone number, email address and web address, will already be printed on the paper. This ensures that whoever receives the communication knows where it is from and is able to reply.

The main types of document used by businesses are letters, **memos**, **reports**, email, notices, **agendas**, **minutes**, **purchase orders** and **invoices**. Each of these documents follows a set format and set of rules that determine how it will look.

Letters

Even the smallest of businesses uses headed paper for its letters. This gives the business a professional image and makes customers and other businesses feel more confident in dealing with the business. However, even though a letter may be on headed paper, it can still create a negative image for a business if it does not follow the conventional format for a business letter or is poorly written. Business letters must therefore follow a standard format, be free from spelling and grammatical errors, use an appropriate font (Times New Roman or Arial) and font size (10 or 12) and be written in a formal style.

A business letter should contain:

- The name and address of the business (usually part of the headed paper).
- A reference (any reference number given by the business – this may be a file number, an account number or a customer number).
- The date the letter is written.
- Any special mark, such as 'Confidential' or 'Urgent'.
- The name and address of the recipient.
- A salutation (for example, 'Dear Sir' or 'Dear Mrs Jones').
- A subject heading or reference to show what the letter is about.
- The main body of the letter, in paragraphs.
- A complimentary close. ('Yours faithfully' if the name of the recipient is not known. 'Yours sincerely' if the name of the recipient has been used.)
- The signature of the person sending the letter (five lines of space should be left for the signature).
- The name and position (job title) of the person sending the letter.
- 'Enc' (short for enclosure) if the letter contains another document or 'Encs' (short for enclosures) if the letter contains other documents.
- 'cc' if copies of the letter are to be sent to anyone else, followed by the names of those people who will receive copies (for example, cc D Smith, M Jones).

Example

Figure 15.1 is an example of a fully blocked business letter, which is the most commonly used style. A fully blocked letter is typed with no punctuation in the address, date, salutation or close, and each part of the letter starts at the left-hand margin. Paragraphs are indicated by leaving a space.

4 March 2010

Miss Katie Buchan
33 Moorhouse Road
Manchester
M3 2BH

Dear Miss Buchan

Re: order no. 3423

Thank you for your order for ten costumes for your forthcoming play. I can confirm that the delivery date for the costumes will be 5 May. Should you require any changes to the design (copy enclosed), please let me know immediately. I'm afraid that we will not be able to make any changes after 9 April.

The final payment for the costumes must be made upon delivery and I can confirm that you will be invoiced for £815 plus VAT.

Once again, thank you for your order and please do not hesitate to contact me if there is anything that you need to discuss.

Yours sincerely

C Jenkins

Carly Jenkins
Head of Sales

Enc

CD Designs Ltd
Stockport Road, Manchester, M5 8PN
Tel: 0161 811 9800
www.cddesigns.co.uk

Figure 15.1 A fully-blocked business letter

Other styles that can be used are indented and semi-blocked. Letters using the indented style (generally used for hand-written letters) follow the normal conventions of punctuation and paragraphs are indented. Semi-blocked letters have some items indented, the date may be on the right-hand side and the subject heading could be centred.

Figure 15.2 is an example of a letter using the indented style.

Using the correct format for a business letter is important but there are other things to remember.

When writing a business letter, you must:

- Use simple vocabulary and avoid **jargon**.
- Use a logical sequence (the first paragraph should be short and state the purpose of the letter; the body of the letter should contain the relevant information relating to the purpose. The last paragraph should state what action you expect the recipient to take).
- Make sure that it is courteous.
- Check for spelling and grammatical errors.

4th March 2010

Miss Katie Buchan,
33 Moorhouse Road,
Manchester,
M3 2BH

Dear Miss Buchan,

Re: order no. 3423

Thank you for your order for ten costumes for your forthcoming play. We can confirm that the delivery date for the costumes will be 5th May. Should you require any changes to the design (copy enclosed), please let us know immediately. I'm afraid that we will not be able to make any changes after 9th April.

The final payment for the costumes must be made upon delivery and I can confirm that you will be invoiced for £815 plus VAT.

Once again, thank you for your order and please do not hesitate to contact me if there is anything that you need to discuss.

Yours sincerely,

C Jenkins

Carly Jenkins
Head of Sales

Enc

CD Designs Ltd
Stockport Road, Manchester, M5 8PN
Tel: 0161 811 9800
www.cddesigns.co.uk

Figure 15.2 An indented business letter

Task

Using the fully blocked style, write a letter to CD Designs Ltd to request changes to an order you placed on 10 May for 20 junior football kits.

Memos

Memos are used internally by businesses to communicate short messages. Many businesses use memo pads of pre-printed memos (similar to using headed paper), so that employees only have to fill in the details.

Memos vary in style according to the business but have the same format. Every memo will state who it is to and from, the date, the subject of the memo and then the content.

Task

Write a memo from the managing director to the finance manager to request copies of the accounts for February.

Example:

Memo

To: Amy Jones
From: Brian Cobb
Date: 29/1/10
Re: Samples

Could you please let me have a sample of each of the new fabrics so that we can photograph them for the sales catalogue.

Figure 15.3 Memo

Reports

A report is a formal method of internal written communication. The style of a report can vary from business to business and department to department, depending on its purpose, but a business report should contain the following:

- Title page – showing the subject of the report.
- Executive summary – a maximum of one page that summarises the issues and most important information or results plus any action steps recommended.
- Methodology – the research methods used.
- Introduction – what the report is about to cover and how.
- Main body – a logical development of the key facts and arguments.
- Conclusion – a summary of the main points and a clear conclusion.
- Recommendations – recommended actions based on the evidence presented in the report.
- Appendices – evidence supporting points referred to in the text, such as maps, tables, illustrations plus all sources and research information.

Business reports are formal documents and an appropriate font and font size should be used, for example, Times New Roman or Arial in font size 12. Page numbers should also be added and headers and footers can be used to ensure that the title and date of the report appear on every page.

If the standard format for a business report is followed and sub-headings are used throughout, then managers will find it easy to find the information that they need.

Email

Emails are used to communicate internally and externally. Although some emails between colleagues may be regarded as informal, generally business emails should be regarded as formal communications and should therefore follow certain rules.

It is important to be polite and use appropriate vocabulary in a formal email. For example, use 'would you' rather than 'can you' and 'I would' instead of 'I'd'.

Examples of formal and informal vocabulary:

Formal	Informal
Thank you	Thanks
I would like to apologise for ...	Sorry for ...
I would appreciate it if you ...	Can you ...
Would you happen to know ... ?	Do you know ...?
Unfortunately, I will not be able to ...	I can't ...
I am unable to say whether ...	I don't know whether ...
Could you ask ... ?	Can you ask ... ?

There is a great deal of information available on email etiquette, but here are the main Dos and Don'ts of formal emails:

Do	Don't
Be polite	Type in capitals (this is considered to be shouting)
Keep messages brief and to the point	Overuse punctuation (such as multiple exclamation marks !!!)
Add a meaningful subject in the subject line	Send abusive, aggressive or insulting messages
Use a proper structure and layout (short paragraphs and blank lines between paragraphs)	Use abbreviations or text speak
Use correct spellings and punctuation	Attach unnecessary files
Respond promptly	Use unusual fonts or formatting (as the recipient may not be able to read your email)
Include a signature	Discuss or send confidential information
Read through the email before you send it	Use 'Urgent' or 'Important' on the subject line (unless something is really very, very urgent)

It is worth remembering that emails can be forwarded, so if it would not be appropriate for a number of different people to read what you have written, do not send the message as an email.

Notices

Notices are generally a form of internal communication intended for many employees to see. Notices need to be short and to the point but with important information emphasised; for example, a notice about a meeting may have the date, time and place emphasised.

As notices are placed on noticeboards, they need to be clearly written or typed using an easy-to-read font and appropriate font size. Notices written in font size 10 can be a little difficult for some people to read! A clear heading is needed so that people do not waste time reading through notices that do not concern them.

Agendas

An agenda is a formal notification to those attending a meeting of the topics that will be discussed at that meeting in the order that they will be discussed. It is a form of written communication used internally.

An agenda should contain:

- The title of the meeting or name of the group who are meeting.
- The day, date, time and venue of the meeting.
- The heading 'Agenda'.
- A list of the topics to be discussed, which should include:
  - Apologies – this should appear as item 1 as it is apologies from those who cannot attend the meeting (to be read out by the chairperson).
  - Minutes of the last meeting – this should appear as item 2 so that those attending can check that the minutes of the last meeting are an accurate record of that meeting.
  - Matters arising – this should be item 3 as it is a discussion of any issues that have arisen from the minutes of the previous meeting.
  - Any items for discussion at this meeting.
  - **AOB** – this means any other business and it gives the people attending the meeting an opportunity to raise items for discussion that are not on the agenda.
  - The date and time of the next meeting.

Example:

ICT Committee Meeting
Friday 12/2/10, 11am, Room 16

Agenda

1. Apologies
2. Minutes of last meeting
3. Matters arising
4. Budget
5. Resources
6. AOB
7. Date and time of next meeting

Figure 15.4 An agenda

As an agenda is a formal document, it should be typed in an appropriate font (such as Times New Roman or Arial) and use a suitable font size (such as 10 or 12).

Minutes

Minutes are the notes taken at a meeting that become the formal record of the meeting. Once the minutes are typed up, they are copied and given to all those who attended and were invited to attend the meeting. A copy of the minutes of all meetings is also kept on file.

Minutes follow the same order as the agenda and will include:

- A list of those present at the meeting.
- A list of those who sent their apologies.
- Confirmation that the minutes of the previous meeting have been agreed.
- The main points of what is discussed at the meeting and contributions from individuals.
- Actions that need to be taken as a result of what has been discussed, with the name/initials of the person/people who will be responsible.
- Any decisions that have been made.

Example – an extract from the minutes of the ICT Committee meeting:

4. CG reported that there was £1,100 left in the buget. AP requested that the new budget for 2010–2011 be distributed by 1 March. CG to action.

5. AP requested additional cabling to enable the installation of two desktops in room 14. PD to action by 20/2/10.

Minutes are not copious notes of everything that was said at a meeting. They are a record of the main points, but they must be an accurate record as they will often be referred back to in order to find out what was discussed and who was responsible for taking any actions recorded.

Task

As a group, plan and hold a meeting to discuss how you will collect information for your assignment for Unit 8. One member of the group should write the agenda, another member should chair the meeting and another should take the minutes.

Purchase orders

Businesses constantly need to buy things, for example stock for resale, stationery for use by the business and items for use in the business such as desks and computers. When a business wishes to make a purchase, a purchase order must be completed and sent to the supplier. A purchase order is a formal method of written communication that commits the business to buy the goods.

Purchase orders differ in style from business to business but each purchase order should contain the same essential information:

- The name and contact details of the business.
- An order number (essential for record keeping).
- The date of the order.
- The delivery address (which may differ from the business address).
- The name of the supplier.
- A reference or catalogue number for each type of item ordered.
- The quantity of each item required.
- A description of each type of item required.
- The unit price for each item.
- The total amount for each type of item.
- A total quantity of items ordered (if appropriate).
- A total order value (before and after the addition of **VAT** if the business is registered for VAT).
- A signature to authorise the order.

Example:

Purchase order

Olive Oyl Ltd
Brutus Way
James Industrial Estate
Newark
Tel: 01636 785421

To: The Real Olive Company
Deliver to: Olive Oyl
16 Market Place
Old Town
PT12 8NU

Order No. 647
Date: 04/03/10

Reference No.	Description	Quantity	Unit Price	Total Price
3427	Extra virgin olive oil	10 litres	1.00	10.00
3876	Antonio olive oil	5 litres	0.50	2.50
3980	Grecian olive soap	20 bars	0.25	5.00
			Subtotal	17.50
			VAT	3.06
			Total	20.56

Delivery: By return
Signed: *J Smith*

Figure 15.5 Purchase order

Task

Using a computer, create a purchase order for your school to order the following from JC Supplies Ltd, Western Way, Coventry, CV4 5TH:

- **24 boxes of paper at £2.50 per box**
- **20 boxes of black pens at £5 per box**
- **100 exercise books at £2.50 per pack of 50.**

Use the current rate of VAT, today's date and create your own order number.

Save your work.

Invoices

All businesses sell goods or services and most need to send invoices to customers so that customers know how much they must pay for those goods or services. An invoice is a formal method of written communication that records the type and quantity of goods sold and the amount owed by a customer.

Invoices differ in style from business to business but each invoice should contain the same essential information:

- The name and contact details of the business.
- The invoice number.
- The name and address of the customer.
- The date.
- The payment terms (when the invoice should be paid, for example within 30 days).
- The customer's order number.
- The despatch date (date the goods were sent to the customer).
- The description, quantity, unit price and total price of each type of good supplied.
- The total amount that the business needs to pay for the goods (before and after the addition of VAT if the business is registered for VAT).

Example:

Invoice

The Real Olive Company
5–8 Elton Street
Bristol
BS2 9EH
Tel: 0117 954 7480
Fax: 0117 955 3515

To:	Olive Oyl Ltd	Invoice No:	000345
	Brutus Way	Date:	08/03/10
	James Industrial Estate	Order No:	647
	Newark	Despatch Date:	05/03/10

Reference No.	Description	Quantity	Unit Price	Total Price
3427	Extra virgin olive oil	10 litres	1.00	10.00
3876	Antonio olive oil	5 litres	0.50	2.50
3980	Grecian olive soap	20 bars	0.25	5.00
			Subtotal	£17.50
			VAT	£ 3.06
			Total	£20.56

Terms: Payable within 30 days.
Cheques payable to The Real Olive Company.

Thank you for your business

Figure 15.6 Invoice

Task

Using a computer, create the invoice to be sent to your school by JC Supplies Ltd for the order you placed earlier. The invoice number is 589000034. Save your work.

Make the grade

P2 **P3** **M2** **D2**

Remember this for P2 and P3. You must produce three documents of different types to support straightforward business tasks for internal communication in an organisation, and three documents of different types for external communication by an organisation.

For M2 and D2, you must also be able to compare and justify your choice of internal and external documents, explaining why each document is appropriate for its intended audience.

Task

Select the most suitable form of written communication to convey the following messages and give reasons for your choice:

1. **The marketing manager requesting an update on the progress of a new advertising campaign from his three marketing assistants.**
2. **Responding to a customer who has written in to complain about poor customer service.**
3. **To communicate the production figures for the month and present possible solutions to a fall in orders to directors ahead of a board meeting.**
4. **To let a customer know the amount that is owed for their recent order.**

Research and investigate

Use the internet to find examples of different business documents. This will help you to produce your own business documents.

Writing internal and external documents for business

When producing documents for business, as well as following set formats and conventions, you also need to know when it is appropriate to use technical language and graphical information, be prepared to draft and redraft your work, ensure consistency and fitness for purpose and be able to meet deadlines.

Technical language includes the use of business-specific jargon, data and equations. Generally, technical language will be used only in internal communications and externally to communicate with suppliers because the recipients are connected with the industry and will understand the terms used. If technical information needs to be communicated to customers or other stakeholders who may not understand business-specific technical language, then care needs to be taken to ensure that those reading the messages can understand them. Jargon, for example, can be used if an explanation of the terms used is included or if, the first time a term is used, an explanation is given in brackets. Some businesses send contracts containing technical language to customers, and to overcome any misunderstandings they include a glossary of terms at the beginning of the document.

Graphical information can also be considered to be quite technical and, again, is mostly used for internal communications, for example to show the performance of a business or product. Graphical information is most commonly found in business reports, but sometimes graphs are used in sales and marketing communications that are given to customers. If graphical information is to be used in external communications, then it must have a clear purpose and be easy to understand.

When preparing a business document, it is important to draft and redraft it to ensure that the message is clear and properly communicated. The accuracy of any information to be communicated must be checked and the format of the document must follow the set conventions so that the communication is fit for purpose. It would not be acceptable, for example, to send an order for goods to a supplier that had been written out on a memo. Similarly, it would be inappropriate to send a letter to a customer that had been hurriedly written and had not been checked for its use of language and spelling and grammatical errors.

It is also important to check, when working for a business, that any documents produced match the style and format used by that business. Consistency is important in creating a positive image for a business.

Finally, any written communication produced will be worthless if it misses its deadline. Business reports, for example, are often needed for meetings, so have to be produced in time, otherwise managers will not have the information they need.

Recording and reporting

Although the primary purpose of a written communication may have been to inform, confirm, promote, make a request or to instruct, written communications also provide a record for a business of the information that has been exchanged, who it was exchanged with and when. It is very important for a business to keep accurate and complete records of all transactions, formal conversations and meetings to enable the smooth running of the business and to comply with requests for information from shareholders and government departments.

If accurate records of transactions, conversations and meetings were not kept, it would be very difficult to make reports to management about the progress of the business or about any issues causing concern. This is particularly true of financial transactions, as without purchase orders and invoices, it would be very difficult to calculate revenue and costs and therefore impossible to create the accounts for a business.

The types of record that businesses need to keep include:

- Agendas and minutes – as a record of all meetings that have taken place and actions that have been agreed.
- Copies of letters.
- All financial documents, including purchase orders and invoices.
- Reports.

Business reports are used to keep managers updated about the performance of the business or about issues that have arisen and possible solutions, but reporting back to supervisors and line managers is also done verbally on a daily basis. However, many businesses also have systems in place for using written communications to make daily reports. A manufacturing business, for example, may have record sheets to record the daily levels of production, and retailers will have stock sheets to complete showing daily levels of stock.

Fieldwork

Arrange to interview the owner of a small business to find out what written communications the business uses for recording and reporting

Discussion...

It is more important for large businesses to keep records than it is for small businesses. Discuss.

IKEA supplies corruption case

On 11 October 2007, a supplier of goods to IKEA and two former IKEA staff were jailed. The supplier had set up a number of companies to supply goods to IKEA stores in the UK. However, IKEA had a policy that stated that it would not take more than 40% of the value of goods that a supplier was selling. This policy was designed to prevent suppliers relying on IKEA for too much of their business. In this case, almost everything this supplier produced was being sold to IKEA and this fact was hidden because the supplier was supplying goods through his various companies.

To help keep this fact from being discovered and to ensure that his companies' supplies and invoices would be approved, the supplier made corrupt payments to two IKEA executives in influential positions. Later, the corrupt payments were linked to the quantity of goods ordered. Eventually, the supplier was dictating what would be ordered by IKEA according to what goods he had available. These events took place between 1998 and 2000.

IKEA became suspicious about differences between the amount of goods invoiced to IKEA and the amount of goods received they had received and discovered the link between the supplier's companies. Following an internal inquiry, the case was referred to the Serious Fraud Office.

Source: Serious Fraud Office

1. State the documents that would have been used by the supplier and IKEA in their transactions.
2. Explain the reasons for using these business documents.
3. In relation to this case, discuss the importance to IKEA of keeping these documents on file.
4. To what extent does the recording of business transactions protect a business from illegal practices?

Key words

Agenda – A notification to those attending a meeting of the topics that will be discussed at that meeting in the order that they will be discussed.

AOB – Any other business.

Headed paper – Writing paper with the name and address of a business already printed on it.

Invoice – A bill for goods or services.

Jargon – Specialist terms that are associated with a particular industry or organisation.

Memo – A method for communicating brief messages within an organisation.

Minutes – A formal record of a meeting.

Purchase order – A document used to place an order for goods.

Report – A document that follows a set format used to pass on detailed information, usually about the performance of a business.

Stakeholders – Individuals or groups who are connected with or affected by the actions of a business.

VAT – Value added tax.

Assignment

See Chapter 16, page 185.

To achieve a pass grade you need to:	To achieve a merit grade you need to:	To achieve a distinction you need to:
P2 produce three documents of different types to support straightforward business tasks for internal communication in an organisation	**M2** compare the aims and objectives of different businesses	**D2** justify your choice of internal and external documents, explaining why each document is appropriate for its intended audience
P3 produce three documents of different types for external communication by an organisation		

Chapter 16
The importance of different methods of communication for different audiences

What are you finding out?

The type of document used for written communication depends not only on its purpose but also on who will receive it. Some forms of written communication are only suitable for communicating with those internal to the business, therefore if messages need to be sent to those outside the business, a method of communication that is fit for purpose must be selected. When communicating with those external to the business, especially a wide audience, then consideration must be given to the complexity of the language used to convey the message. If recipients cannot understand a message, then the written communication could not be considered to be fit for purpose. When choosing a method of communication, consideration also needs to be given to the level of confidentiality required and whether copies of the communication need to be kept on file by a business.

This chapter will help you to:

- Identify and describe appropriate methods of written communication to communicate with different audiences.
- Explain why one method of written communication is more appropriate than another in different business contexts.

Different methods of communication for different audiences

The main types of document used by businesses are letters, memos, reports, email, notices, agendas, minutes, purchase orders and invoices.

Letters are an appropriate method of communicating with any audience but their use depends on the message to be conveyed. It would not, for example, be appropriate to send an employee a letter to ask him to take his lunch hour a little earlier on a particular day, but it would be appropriate to send an employee a letter to confirm a promotion.

Memos are only appropriate for communicating short messages internally. Making a simple request would be an appropriate use of a memo but sending detailed instructions on how to operate a new system would not.

Reports are used internally by businesses to convey information on the performance of a business or issues that have arisen, along with possible solutions. Generally, a report will contain at least three pages of text and therefore is not suitable for conveying short messages or requests to employees.

Email is a very quick way to communicate with a number of different audiences. Generally, emails are more appropriate for communicating with internal audiences but many businesses also communicate with their suppliers and customers using email.

Notices are appropriate for communicating information to audiences that are internal to the business. Notices are used when large numbers of employees need to be made aware of information, and are used to communicate with staff on all levels.

Agendas and minutes are used to communicate with those internal to the business who have been invited to attend the meeting for which the agenda has been drawn up. It would not be appropriate to circulate the agenda and minutes of a meeting to all employees.

Purchase orders and invoices each have a specific purpose. Purchase orders are used solely to communicate between a business and its suppliers and invoices are used solely to communicate between a business and its customers.

Make the grade

P4 **M3** Remember this for P4 and M3. You must be able to identify and describe appropriate methods of written communication for different audiences.

Dealing with confidential matters

It is important to use appropriate methods of communication to convey **confidential** messages. Confidential matters arise internally, between a business and its employees, and externally between a business and its customers, shareholders, government departments and financial institutions.

Confidential information should be noted clearly

Between a business and its employees

To communicate information that is confidential between an employer and a specific employee, a letter marked 'Confidential' should be used. A confidential letter may, for example, be used to communicate a change in an employee's rate of pay because the pay or salaries of employees is information that should only be shared between the employer and the individual employee. Similarly all information about an employee's terms and conditions of employment is also confidential.

Some businesses use confidential memos to communicate information to employees. Information about new products or strategies may be circulated on internal confidential memos. However, because confidential memos are usually circulated to more than one employee, it can sometimes be the case that the contents do not remain confidential.

Business reports can also be marked confidential, if, for example, the contents are intended to be read by one or a small number of employees, such as the senior management of a business. Reports on the outcomes of the trial of a new product would be considered to be confidential, as would new strategies such as ideas for corporate rebranding. Although issues such as these can be discussed between employees, they are to be treated as confidential as the information would be valuable to competitors.

Between a business and its customers

To communicate confidential information between a business and its customers, it would be normal practice to use letters marked 'Confidential' or 'Private and Confidential'. Banks, for example, send statements and letters about customers' accounts out to them in envelopes marked 'Private and Confidential'.

Businesses also use invoices to communicate with customers. Invoices inform customers about the amount they owe for goods or services received. Financial transactions between businesses and their customers can be considered to be confidential and therefore invoices should be regarded as confidential documents that need to be kept secure.

Not all information that a business communicates to its customers is confidential but anything of a financial or personal nature should be treated as confidential and communicated in an appropriate way.

Between a business and its shareholders

Once a year, companies send annual reports out to their shareholders. Annual reports inform shareholders about the progress of the company and provide financial information to show how well the business has performed over the previous year. Although annual reports cannot be considered to be confidential, as they are freely available on the internet, the information is made available to shareholders first.

There are occasions when companies need to send confidential letters to their shareholders, for example when they need to invite them to cast a vote. Recently, shareholders in the Royal Bank of Scotland were asked to cast a vote on the bank's pay and pensions policy.

Between a business and government departments

All businesses have to communicate at some time with government departments. Businesses that are registered for value-added tax (VAT) have to send in VAT returns to Her Majesty's Revenue and Customs (HMRC) and companies have to submit their accounts to Companies House. To communicate financial information, it would be normal practice to use confidential letters. However, it is now becoming more common for government departments to use the internet to allow businesses to submit information to them using secure websites that have password-protected accounts.

'Peanut butter' memo reveals sticky situation at Yahoo!

In 2006, Brad Garlinghouse, a senior vice president at Yahoo!, wrote a confidential internal memo to other top executives. In it, he argued that the company must stop spreading a thin layer of 'peanut butter' across countless opportunities and instead focus on key areas, improve upper-management accountability and reorganise, including a reduction in staff by as much as 20%.

Although the memo didn't say anything that hadn't been said before, it did confirm the problems facing Yahoo!.

The contents of the confidential memo were leaked to *The Wall Street Journal* at a time when many thought that the web portal has lost its competitive edge. *The Wall Street Journal* posted it on its website, adding 'Yahoo! lacks a focused, cohesive vision which has made it reactive and eager to be everything to everyone.'

Source: Juan Carlos Perez, *IDG Newswire*, 28 November 2006

1. State the types of business documents that can be used for internal communication.
2. Describe alternative methods that Brad Garlinghouse could have used to convey his message to the other executives.
3. To what extent do you think that an internal memo is a suitable method of communicating confidential information?
4. Explain the likely consequences to Yahoo! of the contents of this memo appearing on *The Wall Street Journal*'s website.

Between a business and financial institutions

All businesses have bank accounts and therefore need to communicate with their banks. All communications between a business and its bank should be considered confidential and if written communication needs to be used, then this would normally be in the form of a confidential letter. However, online banking is now flourishing but again, secure websites that have password-protected accounts are used.

In addition to banks, many businesses have dealings with other financial institutions such as venture-capital businesses and insurance companies. Because the content of any communication may be financial, then it should be considered confidential and again, the most usual method of written communication would be confidential letters.

Data protection

People's personal information should always be treated as confidential; therefore, to send messages containing personal information, only methods of written communications that are suitable for conveying confidential information should be used: normally, letters.

Businesses that keep data containing personal information must comply with the **Data Protection Act 1998**. The Act states that all personal data shall:

1. Be processed fairly and lawfully.
2. Be obtained only for one or more specified and lawful purpose.
3. Be adequate, relevant and not excessive.
4. Be accurate and, where necessary, kept up-to-date.
5. Not be kept for longer than is necessary.

6. Be processed in accordance with people's rights.
7. Be kept securely.
8. Not be transferred to countries that cannot provide adequate protection.

Businesses, therefore, are bound by law to keep personal information secure, which means that it must be treated as confidential information.

Task

Access some company websites and click on the links that say 'privacy' or 'security and privacy'. Use the information to make notes on how the companies are making sure that their websites comply with the Data Protection Act.

The amount of detail in written communications

The degree of detail and the complexity of the language used in a written communication depend on the audience. If a business is producing written communications for a wide audience, such as its customers, it may need to keep the language simple and straightforward and use short words and sentences to ensure that customers can understand it. One way of checking how easy or difficult text is to read is by using the **Gunning Fog Index**.

To check the Gunning Fog Index of a piece of text, you need to:

1. Use an extract of 100 words.
2. Count the number of sentences.
3. Find the average sentence length by dividing the number of words (100) by the number of sentences.
4. Count how many complex words there are (words with three or more syllables, not counting words that begin with capital letters, such as place names).
5. Add the two totals together (the average sentence length plus the number of complex words).
6. Divide this number by 10 and then multiply by 4 – this is your Fog Index.

Example: If you average 20 words a sentence and 10 complex words (in 100 words), your total is 30. Divide by 10 (3) and multiply by 4 to get a Fog Index of 12.

The average person reads at level 9. The easy reading range is 6–10 and anything above 15 is getting difficult.

Using **SMOG** is another way of checking the readability of text. To use SMOG:

1. Select a page of text.
2. Count ten sentences.
3. Count the number of words with three or more syllables in the ten sentences.
4. Multiply this by 3.
5. Find the number closest to your answer from 1, 4, 9, 16, 25, 36, 49, 64, 81, 100, 132, 144.
6. Find the square root of that number.
7. Add 8 to get your SMOG level.

Example: You have ten sentences containing 40 words with three syllables or more. Multiply this by 3 to get 120. Select 132, the square root of which is 11. Add 8, making the SMOG level 19.

Most people will understand a readability level under about 10.

Did you know...

Analysis undertaken by the National Institute of Adult Continuing Education has shown the average SMOG scores for newspapers to be as follows:
***The Sun:* under 14**
***The Daily Express:* under 16**
***The Telegraph* and *The Guardian:* over 17**

Source: National Literacy Trust

Research and investigate

Log on to the National Institute of Adult Continuing Education's website and access their leaflet on Readability. Use the contents of the leaflet to check the readability of your own work.

If a business is producing communications for its customers, such as instruction leaflets or promotional leaflets, it may want to apply for the **Crystal Mark** to show that its communications are clear and easy to understand. The Crystal Mark was introduced by the Plain English Campaign in 1990 as a seal of approval to encourage organisations to communicate clearly with the public.

When awarding the Crystal Mark, the Plain English Campaign looks for the following:

- A good average sentence length (about 15 to 20 words).
- Plenty of 'active' verbs (instead of 'passive' ones).
- Everyday English.
- Words like 'we' and 'you' instead of 'the insured', 'the applicant', 'the society' and so on.
- Conciseness.
- Clear, helpful headings with consistent and suitable ways of making them stand out from the text.
- A good type size and clear typeface.
- Plenty of answer space and a logical flow (on forms).

Source: Plain English Campaign www.plainenglish.co.uk

It is in the interests of businesses to ensure that their communications can be easily understood as it will give them a positive image and avoid any misunderstandings with customers.

Fieldwork

Collect some promotional material from different businesses or collect leaflets from the tourist information centre. Check the leaflets to see if they have the Crystal Mark. If they do not, check them against the criteria used by the Plain English Campaign and decide if you would award the Crystal Mark.

Audit requirements for written communications

Many written communications used in business must be kept by businesses for a period of time or copies must be kept. This is because businesses need to keep records of their transactions for their own and legal purposes and also because there are occasions when business documents are needed as evidence, for example, for an **audit**.

An audit is an evaluation of an organisation or its systems and processes. For an audit to take place, a business must submit all relevant documents to an **auditor**. For example, a business could have a **social audit**. This would be a check of the extent to which a business is being **socially responsible** and considering the needs of its stakeholders.

A number of businesses produce corporate social responsibility reports. In order to produce these reports, they need documentary evidence of what the business has done to meet the needs of its stakeholders. In Waitrose's corporate social responsibility report of 2008, information has been included from the financial accounts, the company magazines and staff surveys.

The most common form of audit is a **financial audit**. This type of audit is a review of the financial statements of a business. All written communications that deal with financial transactions must be kept by businesses so that accounts can be prepared and, by law, large public limited companies must have their accounts audited. It is also a requirement of all companies that they submit their accounts to Companies House.

For large public limited companies to comply with the law, independent auditors must check their financial statements. The auditors must then make a report to the company's members as to whether the company has prepared its financial statements in accordance with company law and the applicable financial reporting framework. The report must also state whether a company's accounts give a true and fair view of its affairs at the end of the year.

PricewaterhouseCoopers LLP of London are the auditors used by Marks & Spencer. Here is an extract from the May 2009 auditors' report to the members of Marks & Spencer Group plc:

In our opinion:

- the financial statements give a true and fair view, in accordance with International Financial Reporting Standards as adopted by the European Union, of the state of the Group's and the parent company's affairs as at 28 March 2009 and of the Group's and the parent company's profit and cash flows for the year then ended;
- the financial statements have been properly prepared in accordance with the Companies Act 1985;
- the information given in the Directors' report is consistent with the financial statements.

Make the grade

D3 Remember this information for D3. You must be able to explain appropriate methods of written communication to different audiences and need to consider the requirements for copies of documents to be kept on file.

Task

Access the website for the John Lewis Partnership, search for social audit and find the corporate social responsibility report for Waitrose. Read through it and write down any other written documents you think would have been needed by the business to be able to produce this report.

Discussion...

Making sure that the message to be conveyed is clear and easy to read is the most important consideration for written business communications. Discuss.

HSBC loses customers' data disc

The HSBC Banking Group lost a computer disk with the details of 370,000 customers. Usually the information would have been sent electronically, but the usual electronic link had not been working and so the details were downloaded on to a disk. The disk was then sent by courier using the bank's normal postal service.

The details included on the disk included the customers' names, dates of birth and the level of their insurance cover. The customers' addresses and bank details were not included. The information was protected by a password but the details had not been encrypted. However, HSBC thought that the customers would only have a limited risk of suffering fraud as a result of the lost disk.

Source: BBC News

1. Describe suitable methods of communicating confidential information externally.
2. To what extent did HSBC comply with the Data Protection Act when putting details of its customers onto computer disc?
3. The data that was lost included details of customers' levels of insurance cover. This is financial data as it includes the amount that an insurer would have to pay out in the event of the death of a customer. Explain why all financial data must be kept secure by a business.

Key words

Audit – An evaluation of an organisation or its systems and processes.

Auditor – A person who carries out an audit.

Confidential – Private, not to be discussed with others.

Crystal Mark – An award given by the Plain English Campaign to show that written communications bearing the mark are clear and easy to understand.

Data Protection Act 1998 – Legislation to protect the rights of the individual about whom data is obtained, stored, processed or supplied.

Financial audit – Review of the financial statements of a business.

Gunning Fog Index – A readability test designed to show how easy or difficult a text is to read.

SMOG – Stands for 'simplified measure of gobbledygook'; a formula that gives a readability level for written material.

Social audit – A review of the activities of a business that affect its stakeholders.

Socially responsible – Acceptance of having duties towards all stakeholders.

Assignment for Unit 8

You must:

- Know the purpose of communication in business contexts.
- Be able to complete and use business documents for internal and external communication in an organisation.
- Know the importance of using appropriate methods of written communication depending on audience.

The business organisation

You are a business studies student on work placement in the administration department of a large insurance company. Your line manager has asked you if you will look at communications in the business and produce a report of your findings.

Know the purpose of communication in business contexts

1. Begin your report by identifying four different contexts (situations) in which the insurance company would use *written* communications. The contexts you can choose from are:
   - Formal
   - Informal
   - Communicating with subordinates
   - Communicating with supervisor
   - Communicating with colleagues
   - Communicating with suppliers
   - Communicating with customers
   - Handling complaints
   - Confidenial.

   Ensure that you include at least one formal and one informal context.
2. State, using examples, the purpose of using *written* business communications in each of the four contexts you have identified. **(P1)**
3. For each of the contexts (situations) you identified above, describe appropriate methods of *written* communications that the insurance company could use. **(M1)**
4. Explain why you think it is important that the insurance company should use *written* communications for each of the situations you have identified. **(D1)**

Be able to complete and use business documents for internal and external communication in an organisation

5. As part of your report, you need to provide good examples of written communication for the insurance company. You must therefore produce three different types of written communication that are suitable for *internal* communication. Your three documents must support a straightforward business task (for example, passing on simple instructions). **(P2)**
6. You must also produce three different types of written communication that are suitable for *external* communication. **(P3)**

7. As part of your report, make comparisons between your documents. Explain why some of the documents you chose may be suitable for *internal* and *external* communication whereas some may only be suitable for *internal* communication. **(M2)**
8. Now that you have made comparisons, you need to explain why you chose to use each document as a method of *written* communication. Your explanation must include the reasons why each of your documents is appropriate for the person or people you would send it to. **(D2)**

Know the importance of using appropriate methods of written communication depending on audience

9. In this part of your report, you must identify the different methods of written communication that the insurance company should use to communicate with different audiences. For example, you might begin by identifying the documents that are most appropriate for communicating with customers. **(P4)**
10. Now that you have identified appropriate methods of written communication, you should describe them. For example, if you have identified that a business letter is a suitable method to use to communicate with customers, you might now explain the main contents and layout of a business letter. **(M3)**
11. You must now explain your choices. For example, if you have identified that a business letter is a suitable method to use to communicate with customers, you must now explain *why* it is a suitable method. **(D3)**

To achieve a pass grade you need to:	To achieve a merit grade you need to:	To achieve a distinction you need to:
P1 identify, using examples, the purposes of written business communications in four different business contexts	**M1** describe appropriate methods of written communication in different business contexts	**D1** explain the importance of written communication in an organisation in specific business contexts
P2 produce three documents of different types to support straightforward business tasks for internal communication in an organisation	**M2** compare your choice of internal and external documents	**D2** justify your choice of internal and external documents, explaining why each document is appropriate for its intended audience
P3 produce three documents of different types for external communication by an organisation	**M3** describe appropriate methods of written communication to different audiences	**D3** explain appropriate methods of written communication to different audiences
P4 identify appropriate methods of written communication to different audiences		

Unit 9

Training and employment in business

Chapter 17
The rights and responsibilities of the employer and the employee

What are you finding out?

People are the most important resource in any business. Without people, a business is no more than buildings, equipment and furniture. It is people that generate ideas, make things happen and drive a business forward.

The employees in a business therefore need to be properly managed in order to get the best from them, and employers have responsibilities to their employees that they must fulfil. Employees have certain rights and it is the responsibility of each employer to meet these rights, for example ensuring that each employee receives their entitlement to holidays from work.

Employers also have rights and can expect employees to uphold the aims and objectives of the business, follow certain rules, respect the property of the business and do the jobs they have been employed to do.

This chapter will help you to:

- Outline the rights and responsibilities of employees in a chosen organisation.
- Explain the rights and responsibilities of employers and employees.
- Compare the rights and responsibilities of employers and employees.

The rights and responsibilities of the employer

Employers have rights and responsibilities. An employer's rights are what he or she can expect from an employee. For example, an employer can expect an employee to assist the business to make a profit if that is one of the aims of the business. An employer's responsibilities are the duties he or she has towards each person employed. For example, an employer has a duty to ensure that an employee is safe while at work.

The rights of the employer

Employers have certain rights. They have the right to expect employees to support the business aims, follow health and safety procedures, and use company equipment and time appropriately. Each employer also has the right to set down the **conditions of service** for each person they employ and to set the **disciplinary and grievance procedures** that should be followed within the business.

To support the business aims

The aims of a business are what it wants to achieve in the long term. Many businesses aim to make a profit or to provide excellent customer service. Businesses use their aims to enable them to set business objectives. Business objectives are medium- to long-term targets that employees can work towards. For example, in order to make a profit, an objective may be to increase sales by 10% within a two-year period.

When an employer employs people to work for the business, he or she has the right to expect them to support the aims of the business. If the aim of a business is to make a profit, then employees can be expected to help that business to make a profit. If an employee deliberately did something that would cause a business to lose money, then the employer would be within their rights to follow disciplinary procedures against that employee. Similarly, if the aim of the business was to provide excellent customer service and an employee was deliberately rude to a customer, that employee could expect disciplinary measures to be taken.

Follow health and safety procedures

All businesses should take responsibility for their workers' safety

Employers are responsible for the health and safety of their employees. However, an employer has the right to expect employees to follow health and safety procedures and, under the **Health and Safety at Work Act 1974**, employees have the following responsibilities:

- To take reasonable care of their own health and safety.
- If possible, to avoid wearing jewellery or loose clothing if operating machinery.

- To take reasonable care not to put other people – fellow employees and members of the public – at risk by what they do or do not do in the course of their work.
- To cooperate with their employer, making sure they get proper training and understand and follow the company's health and safety policies.
- Not to interfere with or misuse anything that has been provided for their health, safety or welfare.
- To report any injuries, strains or illnesses they suffer as a result of doing their job.
- To tell their employer if something happens that might affect their ability to work.
- If they drive or operate machinery, to tell their employer if they take medication that makes them drowsy.

An employer also has the right to expect employees to follow any training received. For example, if an employee has been trained in the correct way to lift boxes, then that employee is expected to use the methods he or she has been shown. Should any injury arise from not following the correct procedures, then an employer cannot be held to be responsible.

To use company equipment and time appropriately

Employers have the right to expect their employees to use the equipment that belongs to the business appropriately. This means that equipment should only be used as directed by the employer, for the jobs it was intended, and that it should not be used for employees' own purposes. For example, it would be inappropriate for an employee to use a piece of equipment belonging to the business to make something for personal gain. It would also be inappropriate to disregard safety instructions when using a piece of equipment.

Worker crushed to death in machine press

In February 2006, a Lincolnshire company was fined £75,000 and ordered to pay £13,300 costs by Lincoln Crown Court following the death of an employee in August 2004. The man was dragged into a machine press and crushed to death as he reached inside to free a blockage, inadvertently starting the machine up again.

The company admitted breaching the Health and Safety at Work Act 1974 by failing to ensure the worker's safety. The danger should have been clear and it was foreseeable that the lack of safety devices on the machine might result in catastrophic injury or death. The Health and Safety Executive prosecutor said that a metal plate costing just £100 would have prevented the accident.

Source: RRC Training (www.rrc.co.uk). Reproduced by permission

1. Who was responsible for the health and safety of this employee?
2. Explain the rights that the employer would have had in this case.
3. To what extent could both the employer and the employee have been at fault in this case?

Time should also be used appropriately. Most employees are paid for the amount of hours that they work and an employer can therefore expect employees to be carrying out the work for which they are paid during the time that they are at work. It would be inappropriate to conduct personal business during working hours. For example, many employees surf the internet during working hours to look for holidays or items they wish to purchase. This is an inappropriate use of both time and the equipment belonging to the employer.

To set conditions of service

It is the right of employers to set the conditions of service for their own employees. The conditions of service statement is a document that each employee receives when starting work for a business. Its sets out the terms under which each employee is employed and includes:

- The employee's place of work.
- The rate of pay and when wages/salary will be paid.
- Working hours.
- Holiday entitlement.
- Entitlement to sick pay.
- Pension arrangements.

Here is an extract from the *NHS Terms and Conditions of Service Handbook*:

'Staff will receive the entitlement to annual leave and general public holidays as set out in Table 7 below:'

Table 7: Leave entitlements

Length of service	Annual leave and general public holidays
On appointment	27 days + 8 days
After five years' service	29 days + 8 days
After ten years' service	33 days + 8 days

To set disciplinary procedures

A disciplinary procedure is a formal process that an employer must follow if an employee has failed to meet the terms of their employment contract. For example, if an employee is repeatedly late for work, an employer may wish to use the formal disciplinary procedure to get the employee to change their behaviour. If the employee does not change their behaviour, then following the disciplinary procedure will allow an employer to dismiss the employee fairly.

Employers have the right to set down their own disciplinary procedure for use in the workplace. However, the procedure must comply with the Employment Act 2002. According to the Act, the minimum steps that must be taken in a disciplinary procedure are:

Step 1: Statement of grounds for action and invitation to meeting

1. The employer must set out in writing the employee's alleged conduct or characteristics, or other circumstances, which lead him to contemplate dismissing or taking disciplinary action against the employee.
2. The employer must send the statement, or a copy of it, to the employee and invite the employee to attend a meeting to discuss the matter.

Step 2: Meeting

1. The meeting must take place before action is taken, except in the case where the disciplinary action consists of suspension.
2. The meeting must not take place unless:
   a) the employer has informed the employee what the basis was for making the allegations in the statement of grounds under step 1, and
   b) the employee has had a reasonable opportunity to consider his response to that information.
3. The employee must take all reasonable steps to attend the meeting.
4. After the meeting, the employer must inform the employee of his decision and notify him of the right to appeal against the decision if he is not satisfied with it.

Step 3: Appeal

1. If the employee does wish to appeal, he must inform the employer.
2. If the employee informs the employer of his wish to appeal, the employer must invite him to attend a further meeting.
3. The employee must take all reasonable steps to attend the meeting.
4. The appeal meeting need not take place before the dismissal or disciplinary action takes effect.
5. After the appeal meeting, the employer must inform the employee of his final decision.

Disciplinary procedures have different stages:

1. Verbal warning.
2. Written warning (if the verbal warning did not result in a change in the employee's behaviour or attitude).
3. Final written warning (if the written warning did not result in a change in the employee's behaviour or attitude).
4. Dismissal (if the final written warning did not result in a change in the employee's behaviour or attitude).

As each stage is used, the procedure must comply with the law as stated above.

In most cases in which an employee has failed to meet the terms of their employment contract, steps 1 to 4 above will be followed. However, gross misconduct by employees can result in the procedure for step 4, dismissal, being used straight away. Gross misconduct includes:

- fighting
- being drunk at work
- stealing
- harassing people
- subjecting people to racial abuse
- failing to obey reasonable management instructions
- bringing your employer into disrepute.

To set grievance procedures

A grievance procedure is a formal process by which an employee can raise a serious complaint about his or her treatment at work. Employers have the right to set down their own grievance procedure for use in their workplace. However, the procedure must comply with the Employment Act 2002. According to the Act, the minimum steps that must be taken in a grievance procedure are:

Step 1: Statement of grievance

The employee must set out the grievance in writing and send the statement or a copy of it to the employer.

Step 2: Meeting

1. The employer must invite the employee to attend a meeting to discuss the grievance.
2. The meeting must not take place unless:
   a) the employee has informed the employer what the basis for the grievance was, and
   b) the employer has had a reasonable opportunity to consider his response to that information.
3. The employee must take all reasonable steps to attend the meeting.
4. After the meeting, the employer must inform the employee of his decision as to his response to the grievance and notify him of the right to appeal against the decision if he is not satisfied with it.

Step 3: Appeal

1. If the employee does wish to appeal, he must inform the employer.
2. If the employee informs the employer of his wish to appeal, the employer must invite him to attend a further meeting.
3. The employee must take all reasonable steps to attend the meeting.
4. After the appeal meeting, the employer must inform the employee of his final decision.

Before grievance procedures are used, most employers encourage employees to discuss any issues or complaints they may have with their line manager.

Research and investigate

The Advisory, Conciliation and Arbitration Service (ACAS) issues a Code of Practice for employers on disciplinary and grievance procedures. The Code of Practice sets out in diagrams the steps employers should follow. Access the ACAS website (www.acas.org.uk), find the Code of Practice and find out what employers should do before they use their formal disciplinary procedure.

Did you know...

An Argos employee was sacked for having a Facebook entry that said bad things about his employer.

Source: Personnel Today

The responsibilities of the employer

Employers have certain responsibilities towards their employees. They have a duty of care towards employees and they must:

- Provide a safe workplace.
- Observe employment law and codes of practice.
- Observe employees' contracts.
- Provide procedures to protect relationships with employees.
- Provide liability insurance.
- Provide training.
- Adhere to EU directives.

Duty of care to provide a safe workplace

Employers have a duty of care towards their employees. This means that they must do all that is reasonable to ensure the health, safety and welfare of their employees while they are at work. To be able to do this, employers must carry out risk assessments to spot possible health and safety hazards.

The employer's duty of care forms part of the Health and Safety at Work Act 1974. To comply with this law and ensure that they provide a safe workplace, employers need to:

- Provide and maintain safe plant and equipment.
- Ensure safe use, handling, storage and transportation of any articles, substances and materials used during the course of employees' work.
- Ensure the health and safety of their employees by providing adequate information, instruction, training and supervision.
- Provide and maintain a safe working environment by the use of safe systems of work.
- Provide adequate welfare facilities such as toilets and first-aid facilities.

In large businesses, a member of staff who is trained in health and safety carries out risk assessments and is responsible for making sure that the employer complies with the law. In smaller businesses, this responsibility usually lies with one of the owners of the business.

Task

Find out more about risk assessments and undertake a risk assessment in your school.

To observe employment law and codes of practice

Employment law exists to protect employees, and employers must abide by the law. There are many different laws that make up employment law. These include:

- Equal Pay Act 1970 – stating that both sexes should have the same pay and conditions if they do the same work.
- Sex Discrimination Act 1975 – stating that there must be no discrimination between the sexes in relation to recruitment, promotion, dismissal or access to benefits, services and facilities.
- Race Relations Act 1976 (amended 2000) – stating that employers cannot discriminate on racial grounds.
- Disability Discrimination Acts 1995 & 2005 – stating that disabled people must not be treated less favourably than the able bodied and that employers must take all reasonable steps to make the workplace accessible.
- Employment Rights Act 1996 – covers many employee rights including: the statement of employment particulars, pay statements, time off work, maternity rights, termination of employment and redundancy provisions and payments.

Codes of practice are recommended practices that are created by employers' associations. Good employers will observe codes of practice and this, in turn, will improve their image. For example, ACAS produces a code of practice for employers on disciplinary and grievance procedures; this is intended to help employers to do what is required of them in the proper way.

To observe employees' contracts

An **employment contract** (or contract of employment) is an agreement between an employer and an employee which sets out their employment rights, responsibilities and duties. An employment contract does not have to be in writing but employees are entitled to a written statement of their employment terms (conditions of service) within two months of starting work.

The contract of employment between an employer and an employee exists as soon as an employee accepts a job offer; and when an employee starts work, this shows that they have accepted the job on the terms offered by the employer (even if they don't know what they are).

Both the employer and the employee are bound to the employment contract and it is the responsibility of the employer to honour the terms of the contract. For example, the employer must pay the employee according to the contract and honour any holiday entitlement given in the contract. In addition, an employer may not terminate the employment of an employee unless the contract ends, the required period of notice is given or the employer has followed the statutory **redundancy** procedures; neither must the employer change the terms of the contract without the employee's agreement.

To provide procedures to protect relationships with employees

Employers have a responsibility to ensure that procedures are in place to protect relationships with employees. These procedures include the disciplinary and grievance procedures. Disciplinary procedures are there to make sure that the employer deals fairly with each employee and does not take inappropriate actions. Grievance procedures are there to ensure that employees have a way of raising issues they are not happy with if they have not been resolved through discussions with their line manager or other managers.

Employers can also choose to work closely with **trade unions**. Trade unions are organisations that represent the interests of employees. Employees pay a subscription to belong to a union and the union will communicate with employers on behalf of employees. Unions will, for example, negotiate for pay rises and good working conditions on behalf of employees. Working closely with the unions is another way in which employers can protect relationships with employees, as it ensures that employers have taken account of the impact of their decisions upon their employees.

To provide liability insurance

Employers must have **public liability insurance** if members of the public or customers go to their premises. This insurance is there to compensate people who may be injured on the employer's premises. Similarly, employers must have **employer's liability insurance** which will enable them to meet the costs of damages and legal fees for employees who are injured or made ill at work through the fault of the employer.

To provide training

Training is about developing the knowledge and skills of employees. It is of benefit to employers to train their employees because skilled and knowledgeable employees can help the business develop and become more efficient and, therefore, become more competitive.

It is the responsibility of the employer to provide training for employees, especially in health and safety. There are different types of training, these are:

- induction training
- on-the-job training
- off-the-job training.

Induction training

This is provided for employees when they first start working for the business. It is an introduction to the business, the people who work there and its systems.

Induction training includes:

- An introduction to the business and its aims and objectives.
- Meeting the people the employee will be working with.
- Initial health and safety training.
- Instruction on what to do in case of fire or emergency.
- A tour of the workplace.
- What to do in case of illness.
- An introduction to procedures (for example, disciplinary and grievance procedures).

On-the-job training

A more experienced employee can advise in on-the-job training

This takes place in the employee's place of work in the place where their job is done. The training can either be in the form of a more experienced person watching the employee do the job and providing advice and guidance, or the employee learning the job by watching a more experienced person.

Off-the-job training

This takes place away from where the employee performs their job. This can either be at an external organisation, such as a college, or in another part of the place of work, for example, a training or meeting room.

Employees benefit from training as part of their personal development as it will help them to gain promotion.

Fieldwork

Arrange to visit a medium-to-large-sized local business and find out about the training that is offered to employees there.

To adhere to EU directives

In addition to complying with the law, businesses must also adhere to EU directives. **EU directives** are EU laws that member countries are required to translate into national law. For example, the EU directive on Equal Treatment in Employment and Occupation was incorporated into the following UK laws:

- The Employment Equality (Sexual Orientation) Regulations 2003
- The Employment Equality (Religion or Belief) Regulations 2003
- The Employment Equality (Age) Regulations 2006.

Member states of the EU are given a certain amount of time in which to translate EU directives into law but it is in the interest of businesses to adhere to EU directives even before they become national law. This is especially important if the business trades in Europe.

Make the grade

P1 **M1** Remember all of these rights and responsibilities of employers for P1 and M1. This will help you to explain the rights and responsibilities of the employer in your chosen organisation.

The rights and responsibilities of employees

Employees have rights and responsibilities. An employee's rights are what they can expect from their employer. For example, an employee can expect their employer to provide paid holidays. An employee's responsibilities are the duties they have towards their employer. For example, an employee has a duty to make proper use of equipment belonging to the business.

The rights of the employee

Employees have certain rights; some are **statutory rights** and some are non-statutory rights. Statutory rights are those that are laid down by law and employers must abide by the law. An employee's statutory rights include a contract of employment, the right not to be discriminated against, the right to work a limited number of hours, and holiday entitlement. Non-statutory rights are those an employee can expect from a reasonable employer and are often laid down in codes of practice. These include the expectation that an employer will have procedures in place to protect relationships between employees and employer; that an employer will follow codes of practice; and that an employer will recognise bodies, such as trade unions, that represent employees.

Contracts of employment

Once an employee accepts a job offer, then a contract of employment is formed. A contract of employment is a legally binding agreement between an employee and his employer. Employees therefore have the right to expect their employers to honour the terms of their contracts.

If an employer (or an employee) does not honour the contract of employment, then a breach of contract can be said to have occurred.
A breach of contract happens when the employer

(or employee) breaks one of the terms of the contract. For example, if an employer did not pay an employee's wages, then the employer would be in breach of the employment contract.

Anti-discrimination

An employee has the right not to be discriminated against by an employer. Employees may not be discriminated against on the grounds of sex, sexual orientation, gender reassignment, religion or belief, race (includes colour, nationality or citizenship and ethnic or national origin), age or disability.

An employer must not discriminate directly or indirectly. Direct discrimination is treating an employee less favourably than others. Indirect discrimination is applying a provision, condition or practice that disadvantages certain employees, for example when advertising a promoted position.

Under anti-discrimination laws, employees also have the right not to be harassed, intimidated or victimised. This particularly applies to a situation in which an employee may wish to complain about unfair treatment to an employer. The employee has the right to be treated fairly and equally at all times.

Working hours

Employees have rights under the **Working Time Regulations**. The Working Time Regulations cover the number of hours employees can be expected to work in the average working week, night work, rest breaks and days off.

Employees should not have to work more than 48 hours a week on average, unless they choose to.

Employees who work at night should not work more than an average of eight hours in each 24-hour period. (Night-time runs from 11 p.m. to 6 a.m.)

Adult employees (over 18s) have the right to a 20-minute rest break if expected to work for more than six hours at a stretch. Employees aged 16–18 are entitled to at least 30 minutes' break if they work longer than 4.5 hours. The break cannot be taken off one end of the working day – it must be somewhere in the middle and can be spent away from the place of work.

Employees have the right to a break of at least 11 hours between working days. For example, an employee finishing work at 7 p.m on Monday should not start work until 6 a.m on Tuesday.

Adult employees are entitled to one day off each week, or two days off every two weeks. Employees aged 16–18 are entitled to two days off per week.

Holiday entitlement

All employees have a right to at least 5.6 weeks' paid annual leave (holiday from work) if they work a five-day week. This entitlement may include bank holidays.

Part-time employees are entitled to the same level of holiday pro rata. This means that a part-time employee may take holiday at the rate of 5.6 times their usual working week. Therefore, for an employee who works three days per week, this would be 16.8 days per year.

However, employees do not have the right to take their holiday entitlement when they want, as an employer can control when employees take their holiday.

Procedures to protect relationships with employers

Employees have the right to expect procedures to be in place to protect their relationship with their employers. For example, if an employee is unhappy with something at work and has exhausted all the normal channels for discussing and resolving the cause of the unhappiness, then the employee should be able to use an established grievance procedure to have the issue resolved.

Similarly, if an employee has done something wrong at work, then he or she has the right to expect the employer to treat them fairly and follow an established disciplinary procedure for dealing with the issue.

Codes of practice

Employees have the right to expect fair treatment and good working practice from employers. If employers follow codes of practice relating to employment, then employees should find themselves in a good working environment with set procedures and systems for dealing fairly with each employee.

Representative bodies

Employees have the right to belong to a body that will represent them in the workplace. This can be a professional association or a trade union or both. For example, teachers belong to a professional association called the General Teaching Council and most teachers also belong to a trade union. The main teaching trade unions are the National Union of Teachers (NUT) and the National Association of Schoolmasters Union and Women Teachers (NASUWT).

A professional body works to improve standards and can provide support and advice for employees. A trade union represents the interests of employees to their employer.

Employees also have the right not to join a trade union and should not suffer unfair treatment from their employer for belonging or not belonging to a trade union.

The responsibilities of employees

Employees have certain responsibilities towards their employers. They should uphold the aims and objectives of their employer's business, follow the rules of their employer, adhere to the terms of their contract and respect property belonging to their employer's business.

Uphold business aims and objectives

It is the responsibility of employees to uphold the aims and objectives of the business they work for. Employers aim to recruit people whose outlook is similar to that of the business and expect their employees to work hard to help the business meet its objectives.

If employees fail to meet this responsibility, they may be in breach of their contract of employment and an employer would be within their rights to discipline any such employee. For example, if an aim of a business was to create good-quality products and an employee was consistently and deliberately producing shoddy work, then the employee may be in breach of their employment contract by not doing what they were employed to do.

Follow business rules

When employees begin working for a business, they should receive induction training, which includes being told the rules of the business and initial health and safety training. It then becomes the responsibility of employees to abide by the rules and follow all health and safety procedures. If an employee fails to abide by the rules of the business, then they may be subject to disciplinary procedures. If an employee fails to follow health and safety procedures, then the employer may not be liable for any harm that comes to the employee and, again, the employee may be subject to disciplinary procedures.

Marks & Spencer

Marks & Spencer sacked an employee who 'blew the whistle' on its plans to cut redundancy terms for staff. M&S insisted that it had no choice but to dismiss the worker, given that he had breached company rules by contacting *The Times* to reveal how the retailer wanted to cut redundancy terms by up to 25 per cent. (M&S watered down one of its proposals after *The Times* reported its plans.)

Speaking from his home, the employee said: 'I just think they have totally overreacted. It's totally unfair. They just expect staff not to talk about the company at all.'

An M&S spokesman said: 'The employee concerned broke the company's rules and regulations and deliberately leaked internal company information and made derogatory and speculative comments to the media, despite a variety of internal routes available to address any concerns.' M&S said it did not see the case as 'whistle-blowing' because it did not believe it was doing anything wrong.

Source: 'TUC Chief Brendon Barber attacks Marks & Spencer whistle-blower's dismissal' by Steve Hawkes, *The Times*, 4 September 2008 © The Times 2008 / nisyndication.com

1. In what way did the employee at Marks & Spencer break the business' rules?
2. The M&S spokesman refers to 'a variety of internal routes available to address any concerns'. What internal procedure is available to employees to raise any issues they have concerns about?
3. In this case, the employee was dismissed from his job. Explain the procedure that the managers at Marks & Spencer would have had to follow in order to dismiss the employee.

Adhere to terms of contract

It is the responsibility of employees to adhere to the terms of their employment contracts. For example, they should not expect to receive additional holiday entitlement or to work different hours from those specified in their contract. Employees must also perform the job role according to the **job description** given to them as part of their contract of employment.

Respect property belonging to the business

All employees should use any property belonging to their employer for its intended purpose and in the proper manner. For example, a single-purpose tool that is intended to be used for only one type of job may not be used to do another job because this could cause a health and safety risk. Property, tools and equipment should also be treated with respect and not misused or deliberately damaged, otherwise it would be within the rights of the employer to take disciplinary action against the employee.

Make the grade

P2 M1 D1

Remember all of these rights and responsibilities of employees for P2 and M1 and use them to help you achieve D1 – a comparison of the rights and responsibilities of the employer and employees in your chosen organisation.

Discussion...

An employer has more rights than an employee. Discuss.

Key words

Advisory, Conciliation and Arbitration Service – An independent organisation that aims to improve organisations and working life through better employment relations.

Code of practice – Recommended practices that are created by employers' associations as a guide to employers.

Conditions of service – A statement that each employee receives when starting work for a business, setting out such things as rate of pay, working hours and holiday entitlement.

Disciplinary procedure – A formal process that an employer must follow if an employee has failed to meet the terms of their employment contract.

Employers' Liability Insurance – Insurance taken out by employers to enable them to meet the costs of damages and legal fees for employees who are injured or made ill at work.

Employment contract – A legal agreement between an employer and an employee, which sets out the employee's employment rights, responsibilities and duties.

EU Directives – EU laws that member countries are required to translate into national law.

Grievance procedure – The method by which an employee can raise a serious complaint about their treatment at work.

Health and Safety at Work Act 1974 – The law that requires employers to ensure the health and safety of employees when at work.

Job description – A detailed statement of the nature of the job, which identifies an employee's tasks and responsibilities and usually forms part of the contract of employment.

Public Liability Insurance – Insurance taken out by businesses to compensate members of the public or customers if they are injured on their premises or injured while work is being carried out at a customer's premises.

Redundancy – Occurs when there is no longer a need for a particular job role to be fulfilled.

Statutory rights – Those that are laid down by law.

Trade unions – Organisations that represent the interests of employees.

Working Time Regulations – The law covering the amount of hours employees should work and entitlement to rest breaks and days off.

Assignment

You must know the rights and responsibilities of the employee and employer.

The business organisation

You should base this assignment on a business of your choice. A large business would be more suitable than a small business as you need to ensure that there are a number of employees. You must ensure that you seek permission from the managers or owner of the business as you will need access to the staff and other items such as company handbooks, contracts and policies.

For this assignment, you should produce a report.

1. a) Begin your report by writing a brief outline of the rights of the employer in your chosen business.

b) Your next section should be a brief outline of the responsibilities of the employer to his employees. **(P1)**

2. a) You should now outline the rights of employees at your chosen business.

b) Your next section should be an outline of the responsibilities of the employees. **(P2)**

3. a) Your report will need more depth. You should therefore *explain* the rights and responsibilities of your employer in your chosen business.

b) You must *explain* the rights and responsibilities of employees. **(M1)**

4. Finish your report by making a comparison between the rights and responsibilities of employer and those of the employees. In what ways are they the same and in what ways are they different? **(D1)**

To achieve a pass grade you need to:	To achieve a merit grade you need to:	To achieve a distinction you need to:
P1 outline the rights and responsibilities of employers	**M1** explain the rights and responsibilities of employers and employees	**D1** compare the rights and responsibilities of employers and employees
P2 outline the rights and responsibilities of employees in a chosen organisation		

Chapter 18
Motivating employees

What are you finding out?

Every business needs to manage its resources effectively. As employees are a business's most important resource, managers should aim to get the best out of them. Employees perform at their best when they are motivated and it is therefore very important that the managers in a business understand motivation theories and how to apply them in the workplace.

Managers also need to understand the value of teamwork and understand the satisfaction employees gain from contributing to the work of a successful team. Well-motivated employees who enjoy their jobs are more likely to stay with their employer; retaining skilled and experienced employees has many benefits for a business.

This chapter will help you to:

- Explain the importance of job satisfaction and teamwork in the workplace.
- Examine how employees can be motivated in the workplace.
- Analyse the relationship between motivation, teamwork and job satisfaction and how they contribute to organisational success.

Theories of motivation

Motivation is what causes people to behave in a certain way or to achieve goals, but can also be defined as the will to work. There are many theories on how to motivate people and many of these theories either originated in the workplace or have been applied to motivating people in the workplace. Theories range from 'money motivates', to identifying that people have a range of needs that must be met in order for them to be motivated. The most often studied motivation theories are those of Frederick Winslow Taylor, Elton Mayo, Abraham Maslow and Frederick Herzberg.

Frederick Winslow Taylor

Frederick Winslow Taylor is considered to be the 'father of scientific management'. **Scientific management** is a systematic method of determining the best way to do a job and specifying the skills needed to perform it.

Taylor started his career as an apprentice in a small machine-making shop and later became a machinist foreman (supervisor). As a foreman he wanted his men to give their best and to increase their production, but there was nothing in it for the workers if they did. Taylor therefore attempted to introduce **piece-rate** systems of pay; this meant that the workers would be paid for each unit or 'piece' that they produced. However, his idea was not popular with the workforce. The real problem, Taylor decided, was that no one knew how much it was reasonable to expect a man to do. If a standard or measure of work was suggested by the management, there was always plenty of room for argument and agreement was rarely reached.

Taylor therefore sought to find the standards that would serve as established measures of job performance. He focused his attention on the design of jobs, the standardisation of tools and machines, machine speeds, measurement of workers' capabilities, and the 'proper' integration of man–machines–tools–job (finding the right man for each job). He also argued that too much of a manager's job was being left to the workers; they had too much say in the planning of their work and how they performed their jobs.

Taylor therefore established the following principles of scientific management:

- Managers do all the thinking and planning by scientifically analysing every task that needs to be done. A worker is not required to think, just do.
- Tasks should be broken down into their smallest components to get maximum **division of labour.**
- There is only one 'right way to do a job' and one best worker for the job.
- The worker selected to perform the job must be trained to do it in the way specified by management.
- Workers are paid in proportion to their output.

In implementing this approach, Taylor expected **productivity** to increase because he believed that workers had been trained in the best way to do a job and would increase their output in order to increase their pay. He firmly believed that money would motivate employees to work harder.

Fieldwork

Arrange to visit two fast-food outlets to observe the way in which employees work. What evidence is there of the principles of scientific management being used?

Elton Mayo

Elton Mayo had been a follower of Taylor's scientific approach to management and was hired by businesses to conduct **work-study** investigations with a view to increasing efficiency. However, it was through a series of workplace experiments at Hawthorne in the United States that Mayo was able to show that worker productivity is influenced by far more than purely 'scientific' factors such as tools, methods and incentives. From Mayo's work came the **human relations** approach to management.

Mayo's work at the Hawthorne plant of Western Electric in Chicago became known as the Hawthorne Experiments. Mayo was called into Hawthorne to try to explain the findings of a previous test into the effects of lighting upon productivity levels. The lighting conditions for one work group had been varied, whilst those for another remained constant. The surprise was that whatever was done to the lighting, production rose in both groups. This proved that there was more to motivation and efficiency than being paid by output.

Mayo then conducted further experiments at Hawthorne. In one of the experiments, known as the Relay Assembly Test, six voluntary female assembly staff were separated from their workmates. Every twelve weeks a new working method was tried with the six women and their results were recorded and discussed with them. The working methods included:

- different bonus methods, such as individual versus group bonuses
- different rest periods
- different refreshments
- different work layouts.

Before every change, the researchers explained the new methods fully to the women and, almost without exception, productivity increased with every change. At the end of the experiment, the group returned to their original method of working (48-hour, 6-day week with no breaks) and output went up to an even higher level and the women claimed they felt less tired than they had at the start.

Mayo therefore proved that there was more to motivation than being paid by output and concluded that:

- working as part of a team is motivational
- communication between workers and managers influences morale
- workers are affected by the degree of interest shown in them by managers (known as 'the Hawthorne Effect').

The women who took part in the Relay Assembly Test had felt valued by the interest being taken in them and were therefore motivated to work hard.

Abraham Maslow

Abraham Maslow was an American psychologist who carried out research into human needs. His theory of motivation is called the Hierarchy of Needs.

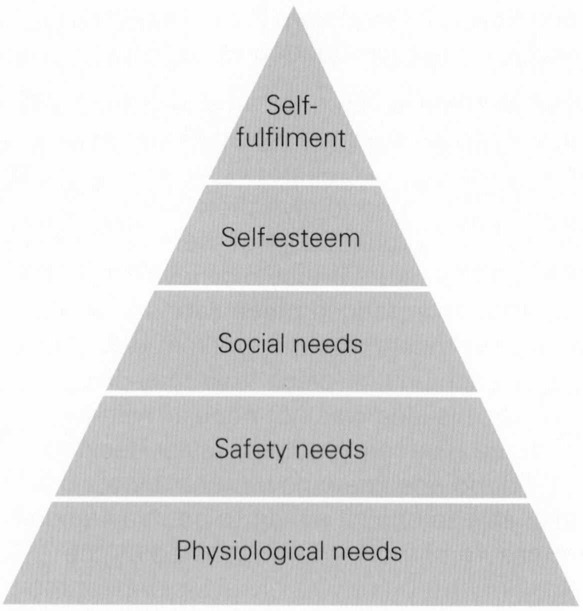

Figure 18.1 Maslow's Hierarchy of Needs

Maslow believed that everyone has needs that motivate them to do something but as a need is satisfied, it fails to motivate and therefore, the next need in the hierarchy would be the one that motivates. For example, if a person's physiological needs (for food and shelter) were met, then this need would not motivate a person, but the need for safety would motivate until that need was met. In other words, the 'unobtained' level of the hierarchy will motivate.

This theory could then be related to the workplace in order to motivate employees by using motivation strategies designed to meet the unobtained level in the hierarchy.

The diagram below shows Maslow's hierarchy of needs, with the type of need identified in a 'life setting' on the left and how this might relate to the workplace on the right.

Applying this theory to the workplace suggests that people may be first motivated to work because they need wages (to provide food and shelter). However, once this need has been met and an employee is earning a steady wage, then wages may not motivate the employee to continue to work hard. The second level in the hierarchy may then be the motivating factor, the need to feel safe and know that health and safety rules are being observed in the workplace. If so, then an employee may be motivated by social needs and this can be done in the workplace using teamwork. If social needs are met, then employees may be driven by the prospect of recognition and promotion.

According to Maslow's theory, the top level in the hierarchy, self-fulfilment (or self-actualisation), will always motivate (if the other needs are met) because this level is never fully obtained, as the human desire for achievement is limitless.

Frederick Herzberg

Frederick Herzberg was an American psychologist who developed a theory on motivation in the workplace is called the Two-Factor Theory. The two factors are 'hygiene factors' and 'motivators'.

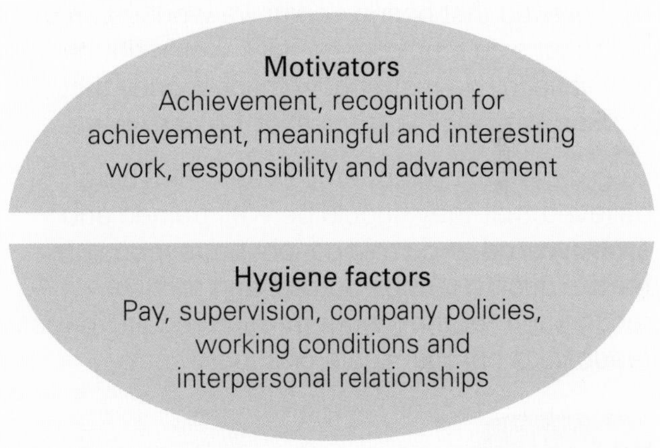

Motivators
Achievement, recognition for achievement, meaningful and interesting work, responsibility and advancement
Hygiene factors
Pay, supervision, company policies, working conditions and interpersonal relationships

Figure 18.3 Herzberg's motivators and hygiene factors of motivation

Figure 18.2 Maslow's Hierarchy of Needs – types of needs related to the workplace

Herzberg argued that the hygiene factors, such as pay and working conditions, do not motivate an employee to do a good job, but if the hygiene factors are not as they should be, then this will lead to an employee being dissatisfied at work and therefore difficult to motivate. If an employee is happy with the hygiene factors, then they are in a position to be motivated by the motivators.

Herzberg proposed that the motivators are achievement, recognition for achievement, meaningful and interesting work, responsibility and advancement. He strongly believed that workers should be allowed to think for themselves in the workplace and be given responsibility. He believed that boring, repetitive work that did not require an employee to think would not be motivational, no matter how much money that worker was paid – a reversal of Taylor's views.

To get the best out of employees, Herzberg believed that they should be well trained and **empowered** to do a good job, be responsible for the quality of their output, and receive recognition for their work through regular, direct feedback from managers or supervisors.

Task

Statements 1 to 4 below show different ways in which businesses try to motivate their employees. For each one, explain whose motivation theory you think it most relates to (Taylor, Mayo, Maslow or Herzberg) and why:

1. **Business A organises regular social events for its employees and has holiday homes that employees can use.**
2. **Business B runs a profit-sharing scheme. Every three months, employees receive a share of the profits of the business.**
3. **Business C organises its employees into teams and each team is encouraged to work with the community and support a local charity.**
4. **Business D says that they offer interesting, challenging jobs and that they provide opportunities for employees to broaden their horizons.**

Herzberg's theory has been applied in the workplace through approaches such as **job enrichment** and **total quality management.** Job enrichment means giving employees work on different levels to challenge them and allow them to use their skills and abilities. Total quality management (TQM) is an approach in which a culture of quality is adopted in the workplace – each employee is responsible for the quality of their output as they pass it on to the next employee, whom they must view as a customer.

Job satisfaction

Job satisfaction describes how content an employee is with their current job role.

The happier an employee is with their job, the more satisfied they are said to be.

Job satisfaction can be influenced by a number of factors, such as relationships with supervisors, the working environment and the nature of the work. However, having job satisfaction is not the same as being motivated, as an employee whose output is low may well be content with their job.

Many businesses aim to improve job satisfaction among their employees by using approaches such as **job design** and **ergonomics**, **job rotation**, **job enlargement**, job enrichment and **empowerment**.

Job design and ergonomics

Job design is all about deciding how the tasks required to complete a job should be divided or grouped into job functions. For example, should jobs be divided into small parts (division of labour) or should an employee have a complete unit of work?

Job design affects job satisfaction and motivation. Taylor, for example, believed in a high division of labour and thought that employees would be satisfied because they could generate a high output, which would increase their pay. Herzberg, on the other hand, believed that employees should have a complete unit of work and be responsible for the quality of their own output, which in turn would be motivational.

Ergonomics is the science of designing the job, equipment and workplace to fit the employee. Ergonomics is used to ensure that work tools and equipment do not cause injury and strain to workers and also to improve the productivity of employees. For example, in car manufacturing businesses, many of the employees on the assembly line have moving seats that can swing in and out of a car as it passes them on the line. This allows the employees to move in and out of the car to fit a part without having to constantly bend and helps to avoid back strain, while increasing the speed at which the employee can work. From an employee's point of view, this makes the job easier and more comfortable to do and therefore should improve job satisfaction.

Research and investigate

Using the internet, find out what ergonomically designed items are available for employees who work on computers every day.

Job rotation

Job rotation is a way of varying the work that employees do by moving them around different tasks. For example, an office worker might spend some time photocopying, some time typing and some time filing documents. Job rotation is said to increase job satisfaction because it adds variety to a job and means that an employee is not doing boring, repetitive work.

An added benefit of job rotation is that, in allowing employees to complete a range of different jobs, it means that they will be able to do the jobs of absent colleagues. This, in turn, should help to improve productivity.

Job enlargement

Job enlargement means introducing new tasks into a job role to enlarge it. The aim is to increase job satisfaction by giving employees new things to do to avoid boredom and complacency in a job role. Adding new tasks to a job role will often mean that the employee will need training and this helps to improve motivation by giving employees the opportunity to learn new skills.

Job enrichment

Job enrichment means giving employees work on different levels to challenge them. This is done by adding tasks that have more responsibility, which allows employees to use their skills and abilities. For example, a manager may delegate some of his work to an employee to allow that employee to take more responsibility and therefore gain job satisfaction.

Job enrichment is an application of Herzberg's theory on motivation – it gives an employee extra responsibility, interesting work and the opportunity of advancement.

Empowerment

Empowerment is allowing employees (and teams of employees) to make their own decisions about what they do and how they do it. For example, a team of employees may be given the task of preparing a banquet. If the team is given full responsibility for deciding the menu, the order in which things should be done and how they should be done, then the team is being empowered. Allowing employees the freedom to decide their own working methods will increase job satisfaction and motivation as it enables employees to use their abilities and take responsibility.

However, not all employees want to be empowered. Many do not want the responsibility of having to make decisions and some may find it difficult to work out the best way to complete tasks. For these employees, this can cause job dissatisfaction.

Medtronic

Medtronic, a company that makes medical devices such as pacemakers, aims to help the sick get better and its employees feel great about their jobs.

In a survey carried out by Best Companies Ltd, 85% of employees said they were proud to work there and 80% said their job is an important part of their life. Almost two-thirds of the 367 employees earn more than £35,000 and they can all join the final-salary pension scheme.

Employees say their job is good for their personal growth, as well as stimulating, and they believe they can make a valuable contribution to the success of the organisation. Individual development plans, training and job rotation provide opportunities to develop careers. Top sales performers can win trips to destinations such as South Africa and Dubai. Employees get together at least twice a year for networking and social events.

The survey says that 77% of employees are excited about where the organisation is going and are confident in the leadership skills of senior management. They think their managers talk honestly and openly, are excellent role models and good listeners.

Source: *Best Companies Ltd, www.bestcompanies.co.uk*

1. What is job rotation?
2. Explain how job rotation provides opportunities for employees at Medtronic to develop their careers.
3. What evidence is there to suggest that employees at Medtronic are motivated?
4. Discuss the theories of motivation that you think may have been used by senior managers at Medtronic.

Make the grade

P4 Remember this for P4. You need to be able to examine how employees can be motivated in the workplace.

The benefits of team working

Elton Mayo concluded that working as part of a team is motivational and Maslow identified that people have social needs and that these needs could be met at work through teamwork. Team working can therefore offer many benefits for businesses and employees that include:

- making a contribution to departmental and organisational success
- employees wanting to be part of a team
- attainment of team objectives
- empowerment
- **innovation**
- a way of implementing change
- **multi-skilling**
- taking ownership of decision making
- knowledge sharing
- **synergy** (working together is more productive than working as individuals).

Contribution to departmental and organisational success

In many businesses, employees are expected to work as a team, and teamwork within a department is expected to contribute to the success of that department. This success should then contribute to the success of the organisation as a whole.

Teams of employees are often put together to solve problems and make improvements because teamwork encourages employees to be creative, share ideas and support one another. This approach contributes to the success of an organisation because it:

- Makes use of the different strengths and skills of team members so that a greater variety of tasks may be tackled.
- Brings people together who need to be involved in a project (either from within a department or from different departments).
- Allows the team to decide how tasks are completed, based on the views and requirements of all team members.

Teamwork can then improve productivity because employees are brought together to work on a project and can discuss potential problems at an early stage rather than passing work to each other that it may not be possible to complete. For example, if a team of employees from all the different areas of car production meet to discuss a new design, engineering will be able to discuss which design features can be produced and which cannot, so that ideas and drawings can be changed at an early stage. If teamwork did not take place, it is possible that a design team could implement a design and later find that a part of the car cannot be built as it cannot be engineered.

Research and investigate

For employees to be able to work well in teams, they must make use of each other's strengths and skills. Carry out research into the work of Meredith Belbin and find out what he considered the nine team roles to be. Complete Belbin's Self-Perception Inventory and find out which role you would take when working as a member of a team.

Wanting to be part of a team

Many employees want to be part of a team as it improves their working lives, meets their social needs and helps them to do a good job. For example, many employees in manufacturing have been used to working on small, repetitive tasks that did not require skills and provided little job satisfaction. In modern manufacturing businesses, such as Toyota, organising employees into teams has enabled them to become multi-skilled (through job rotation) and empowered to make their own decisions. This has led to employees being more motivated to do a good job as they feel accountable to each other and are recognised for their contribution to the team and to the success of the business.

Working as a member of a team also improves employees' working lives as they are not working in isolation; team working provides an opportunity to interact with colleagues, which meets their social needs at work.

Attainment of team objectives

To enable a team to meet its objectives, good communications and consultation must take place and employees must receive training.

Each team needs to have a system for two-way communication with management, who must clearly communicate the aims and objectives of the business to the team, along with the role of the team in contributing to those aims and objectives.

The members of the team also need established methods of communicating with each other in order to decide priorities and allocate tasks. Regular team meetings need to take place to co-ordinate activities, as do team briefings at which the team leader can give the team essential information.

Employees also need training to ensure that they can contribute to meeting the team's objectives. To enable a team to operate effectively, team members need to be able to do each other's jobs and this may require skills training. Training such as team-building skills may also be required in order to help team members communicate effectively with each other and value each other's strengths.

Good communications and training are motivational to employees and therefore should help productivity within the business to improve.

Empowerment

Empowerment is very much a part of team working because employees have a great deal of control over their own work. As a team, employees can often decide how and when tasks are completed; it becomes the role of management to make team working possible and to smooth the way for progress to take place, rather than controlling what employees do.

Managers need to communicate their aims and objectives to the team and encourage team members to share ideas and take the initiative. They should then ensure that team members can take responsibility, and provide training where necessary.

The benefits to the business of empowered teams are that team members can deal with day-to-day problems themselves and the team leader can take over some of the work formerly done by a manager; this can lead to a reduction in the number of managers needed. This, in turn, can reduce the costs of the business.

The benefits to employees are that they have the opportunity to take responsibility and do more meaningful work which, according to Herzberg, is motivational. By taking responsibility, employees can also demonstrate their abilities and suitability for promotion.

Innovation

When employees work in teams, they are motivated to do a good job and are concerned about the quality of the work that they pass on to the next member of the team. Taking more responsibility for the quality of their output leads employees to look for continuous improvement and work together to solve problems. Teams can, therefore, suggest product or process innovations and, as these innovations have been developed by the team, they are more likely to be implemented successfully.

This is beneficial to employees as they will be motivated by their achievement and by receiving recognition for their achievement. It is also of benefit to businesses: process innovations usually have financial rewards, either through cost savings or through improved product quality which customers will pay more for; product innovations can put a business ahead of its competitors, which can also lead to financial gain in the form of improved sales revenue and profits.

Implementing change

Team working can help a business to implement change. This is because giving teams the responsibility for deciding how tasks should be done helps to improve employees' knowledge of the processes used. This encourages them to look at more aspects of the business than they normally would in order to generate ideas and solve problems. Employees then have a greater understanding of the business and the needs of its customers and are therefore more willing to embrace change.

People are also more ready to accept change if the ideas for change have come from them. When employees work in teams, they generate their own ideas for improvements and are therefore more ready to implement any changes that need to be made.

Multi-skilling

In successful teams, team members can undertake a wide range of tasks and are able to do each other's jobs. To be able to do this, each member of the team must receive skills training and, as they gain experience in working as a team and rotating around tasks, they become multi-skilled. This is of benefit to a business as it means that processes are more likely to run smoothly. For example, at Toyota, any member of a team can do another team member's job and this helps to avoid any hold-ups in the production process if a member of a team is absent for any reason.

Taking ownership of decision making

Working as part of a team requires employees to make their own decisions. This is beneficial to employees as it gives them responsibility, making the work they do meaningful, which, for many, will motivate them to do a good job. It is also of benefit to businesses because it encourages employees to be creative and innovative and look for solutions to problems rather than turning to management to find solutions. Another benefit of this is that fewer managers may be needed in businesses that organise workers into teams and this will then save costs.

Team working at Toyota Manufacturing UK

Toyota Manufacturing UK recognises that people are the foundation of the company and that highly competent, motivated and respected employees commit to work towards fulfilling the objectives of the company.

Toyota realises that both short- and long-term success depends on the continuous commitment of employees. Total involvement, training, multi-skilling, job rotation and good communication play a part, as do good terms and conditions, company support for education and an opportunity to discuss work issues with the company through the Toyota Members Advisory Board.

Within departments at Toyota, employees are divided into groups and teams and this team structure is a key element of the company's effectiveness. Maximum flexibility and mobility of employees between work roles are essential to make the most effective use of resources. Training is therefore directed to developing skills to meet job requirements. Through on-the-job training, employees are encouraged to learn many tasks so that movement and rotation within job responsibilities are possible.

Simply training and developing individuals are not enough. Each employee needs to understand how their contribution fits into the whole group and be aware of other employees' skills and knowledge so that they can all work together to achieve objectives. Each team or group, therefore, has a group leader who has a key role in regularly assessing how well each employee works within the team and what their skill and motivation levels are.

One way in which teams improve working methods at Toyota is through the review process. When a team discusses an issue, the conclusions tend to be more considered. Individuals tend to have hidden agendas or prejudices which cloud decisions, but by bouncing ideas off one another, teams are more likely to reach an effective answer. This also means a decision is reached through consensus; so if all support it, no one can complain.

Source: www.toyotauk.com

1. Outline the benefits to employees of working in teams.
2. Explain how Toyota ensures that its employees become multi-skilled.
3. Show how Toyota is benefiting from synergy.
4. To what extent does team working at Toyota contribute to the success of the organisation?

Knowledge sharing

As team members must work together to complete tasks and solve problems, they must also share ideas. If one team member puts forward an idea, other team members have the opportunity to share their knowledge to help improve the idea. This helps to shape ideas into workable solutions that can help to improve the processes within the business or the products. In addition to the business benefiting from the work of the team, individual team members also benefit as they learn from each other and increase and improve their own knowledge.

Synergy

Synergy is like saying that two heads are better than one. It means that employees working as a team will achieve more than they would if they each worked individually. In practice, teams achieve synergy through discussing ideas and problems and sharing knowledge in order to develop ideas and solve problems. Each member of a team will have different strengths and skills to bring to the work of the team and this helps the team as a whole to complete a greater variety of tasks, generate more ideas or produce higher-quality work.

Make the grade

P3 **M2** **D2** Remember this for P3, M2 and D2. You need to be able to explain and analyse the relationship between motivation, teamwork and job satisfaction and how they contribute to the success of a given organisation.

Discussion...

Not everybody goes to work because they want money. Discuss.

Key words

Division of labour – Breaking down a job into small tasks so that each worker can become a specialist in one task.

Empowered – Given the power to make decisions.

Empowerment – Allowing employees to make their own decisions about what they do and how they do it.

Ergonomics – The science of designing the job, equipment and workplace to fit the employee.

Human relations – A management approach that believes in teamwork and communication and consultation with workers.

Innovation – An idea for a new way of doing something or taking a new idea to market (a new product/service).

Job design – Deciding how the tasks required to complete a job should be divided or grouped into job functions.

Job enlargement – Introducing new tasks into a job role to enlarge it.

Job enrichment – Giving employees work on different levels to challenge them and allow them to use their skills and abilities.

Job rotation – Moving employees around different tasks.

Motivation – What causes people to behave in a certain way or to achieve goals.

Multi-skilling – Training employees to be able to complete a range of tasks.

Piece-rate – Paying an employee for the number of items produced.

Productivity – A measure of the efficiency with which a business turns inputs into output. Labour productivity is output per worker.

Scientific management – A systematic method of determining the best way to do a job and specifying the skills needed to perform it.

Synergy – The whole is greater than the sum of the parts: employees working as a team will achieve more than they would if they each worked individually.

Total quality management (TQM) – An approach in which a culture of quality is adopted in the workplace and each employee is responsible for the quality of their output.

Work study – An analysis of a specific job in an effort to find the most efficient method in terms of time and effort.

Assignment

You must show understanding of how employees can be motivated.

You should base this assignment on a business of your choice. A large business may be more suitable than a small business as there would be more employees for you to interview and gather views from.

For this assignment, you should produce a report.

1. a) Begin your report by explaining what job satisfaction is.
   b) Explain why it is important for employees at your chosen business to have job satisfaction.
   c) Explain what team working is.
   d) Explain why it is important for employees at your chosen business to work in teams. **(P3)**
2. Using different motivation theories, explain the different ways in which employees at your chosen business could be motivated to do a good job. **(P4)**
3. Using different motivation theories, explain the relationship between motivation, teamwork and job satisfaction. **(M2)**
4. a) You should explain why job satisfaction increases motivation and why teamwork can improve the motivation of employees at your chosen business.
   b) Explain how teamwork, job satisfaction and motivated employees will contribute to the success of your chosen business. **(D2)**

To achieve a pass grade you need to:	To achieve a merit grade you need to:	To achieve a distinction you need to:
P3 explain the importance of job satisfaction and teamwork in the workplace	**M2** explain the relationship between motivation, teamwork and job satisfaction	**D2** analyse the relationship between motivation, teamwork and job satisfaction and how they contribute to organisational success
P4 examine how employees can be motivated in the workplace		

Chapter 19
The importance of training and review

What are you finding out?

In every business, employees generate ideas and use their knowledge and skills to help the business to meet its aims and objectives and remain competitive. For a business to improve its performance, it must develop its employees, and this means training.

Training is extremely important for employees because they need to be able to carry out their job roles effectively and therefore must be given the opportunity to learn and to update their knowledge and skills.

It is also important for businesses to review their employees' performance. Employees need feedback and need to know how they are performing against their targets and objectives. Regular feedback is motivational for employees and it also helps managers to identify training needs and candidates for promotion.

This chapter will help you to:

- Describe the importance and benefits to an organisation of training its employees.
- Explain the benefits of performance appraisal.

The need for training

Employees need training for a number of reasons. When they first start a job, they need **induction training** so that they know something about the business they work for and the people they will work with. They must also receive health and safety training and employers must consider their obligations towards developing employees and enable them to do their jobs competently. As their employment continues, employees may also need to update their skills and learn new skills in order to be able to complete a range of tasks.

Induction and initial training

Induction training is provided for employees, in their place of work, when they first start working for a business. It is very important that new employees receive induction training because it ensures that they get to know the business and are able to work competently and safely.

Induction training includes:

- An introduction to the business and its aims and objectives.
- Meeting the people the employee will be working with.
- Initial health and safety training.
- Instruction on what to do in case of fire or emergency.
- A tour of the workplace.
- What to do in case of illness.
- An introduction to procedures (for example, disciplinary and grievance procedures).

Initial training is the training new employees need to be able to perform their job roles. Some businesses provide courses away from the workplace so that new employees receive initial training before they begin their role. Some businesses provide initial training on the job. This means that the employee will be in the place of work, either performing the job with a more experienced person supervising them, or watching a more experienced person perform the job. Once employees are considered to be competent in their job roles, they will be left to perform their jobs unaided.

Fieldwork

Arrange to visit two businesses and find out what their induction training for new employees involves.

Business must train employees to handle materials safely

Legal reasons

Employers have a legal responsibility to provide health and safety training for their employees. Under the **Health and Safety at Work Act 1974**, employers have a duty of care towards their employees, which means that they must do all that is reasonable to ensure the health, safety and welfare of their employees while they are at work.

Whatever the size of a business, employers must ensure that employees are trained in:

- Safe working practices, for example how to use a piece of equipment or chemicals properly.

- **Manual handling** (The Manual Handling Operations Regulations 1992) to make sure that all materials are handled, stored and used safely.

Above all, the workplace must be safe, therefore employers must provide all necessary training to ensure that it is safe.

Research and investigate

The Health and Safety (First Aid) Regulations 1981 require employers to provide adequate and appropriate first-aid equipment, facilities and people so that employees can be given immediate help if they are injured or taken ill at work.
Using the internet, find out what the minimum first-aid provision must be on any work site.

Financial implications of training

It is important that a business trains its employees and helps them to develop their careers. If employers do not do this, it is likely that some employees will leave the business so that they can advance their careers elsewhere. This has financial implications for a business as a commitment to training and developing employees requires funding. However, this can be seen as a worthwhile investment for the following reasons:

- It encourages employees to stay with the business, which means that the business is benefiting from their knowledge, skills and experience.
- Trained and experienced employees who stay with the business will become candidates for internal promotion, which saves a business the expense of **external recruitment**.
- As employees will be less likely to leave the business, money will be saved on the recruitment, selection and training costs of new employees.

The prospects of internal promotion are one of the main reasons that employees will stay with the business they work for. Investing in employees who may then take up promoted positions within the business is therefore very worthwhile as it helps a business to retain its experienced staff. Also, it can be cheaper for a business to promote existing employees than recruit new people as it is often the case that to attract employees from other businesses, higher salaries have to be paid.

Ethical implications of training

Employers have a moral obligation to train employees. In addition to being a legal requirement, employers have a moral obligation to train employees in health and safety. The purpose of health and safety training is to reduce the number of accidents and injuries in the workplace, and employers are morally bound to care for their employees.

Once employees begin working for an employer, they should also be assisted to perform their jobs competently. Employers are morally bound to care for their employees and this includes providing them with the training they need to be able to perform their jobs. Employees may be lacking a skill or knowledge, which in turn may increase the time they take to complete a task or even stop them undertaking it in the first place. Offering training will increase employees' confidence in their abilities and will also improve **productivity**.

If employees feel unable to perform their jobs properly, they will become demotivated and leave the business. It is therefore important to train staff to ensure they can do their jobs and to make them feel that they are valued.

To be able to do the job competently

Unless employers recruit very experienced employees, then they will need to provide training to ensure that employees can perform their jobs competently. Initial training will allow employees to be able to start their jobs but, as time goes on, employees may need further training. For example, some employees need to be made aware of new laws and regulations governing businesses and this often means that these employees need to attend training courses to update their knowledge and find out what the implications for the workplace are.

In some businesses, there are new initiatives that may help to improve the way in which the business works and may help it to become more competitive. An example of this would be **ISO** 9001 which is a series of quality-management system standards. If a business wanted to have ISO 9001 accreditation, then it would be necessary to train employees so that they know what is expected of them and how they could meet the quality standards. It would also be necessary to train managers so that they could implement the standards.

To update skills

Training is often needed to help employees update their skills. Most businesses want to expand and this often means entering new markets. For example, if a business wants to

Training and development at Comet

At Comet, all employees receive product training. Virtual classrooms are used along with one-minute knowledge bites and online product modules to introduce new recruits to products and current employees to new products. Because the pace of change in electrical retail is fast, training on new products, product features and benefits needs to be carried out regularly.

Comet considers that having the right approach, right conversation and the right knowledge makes all the difference to their customers, and will always provide employees with the information they need at the time they need it.

Comet is also committed to promoting internally. Employees that join the business as sales associates, call-centre colleagues or engineers all have the chance to apply for the established management development programmes; they just have to show that they have the right attitude and ambition to succeed.

Employees are provided with the skills and knowledge to progress along the career path that's right for them. There are plenty of routes to select from: team leader in one of the contact centres; sales manager in one of the stores; assistant category buyer at head office.

Source: www.cometjobs.co.uk

1. What initial training do employees at Comet receive?
2. Describe the induction training that a new employee in a Comet store might receive.
3. Explain the reasons why you think Comet invests in management development programmes.
4. To what extent does the training provided at Comet help employees to perform their jobs competently?

break into a new foreign market, it may need to update the marketing skills of its employees so that they become familiar with the way that market works and the local customs and ways of operating in that country.

Businesses must also keep changing their work practices to stay ahead of the competition and must ensure that employees have the skills to cope with new technology. Many businesses, for example, are finding that they need to have a website and, although they may not expect employees to create that website, they do need employees to be able to upload appropriate information to it. In manufacturing, new technology frequently becomes available and employees need to be trained to use new machinery as it comes into use. Even in retailing, employees need to be trained so that they are familiar with new technology as it arrives in the shops. Recent innovations such as Blu-Ray and wireless home entertainment systems have created a need for employees working for electrical retailers to receive training so that they can explain the benefits of these systems to customers.

Multi-skilling training

Many businesses now require their employees to work in teams. Working as a member of a team often means that employees need to be able to perform a range of tasks so that they can perform the jobs of any member of the team. This means that employees become multi-skilled. For employees to become multi-skilled, employers need to invest in training.

For employers, this is a worthwhile investment because it improves the efficiency of the business. For example, if one member of a team is absent from work and another member of that team can perform his or her job role, then work can continue and productivity will not suffer. It is also of benefit to employees because they are learning new skills that may help them to progress their careers.

Task

Design and carry out a small survey in which you ask people about the training they have received in their current jobs and what they think the benefits of that training have been.

Make the grade

P5 Remember this for P5. You must be able to describe the importance of training to a given organisation or an organisation of your choice.

Training courses

There is a wide range of training courses available for employers to use to train their employees. These include in-house courses, external courses and vocational and professional courses.

In-house courses

In-house courses are training courses that are tailored to the needs of a business or a particular group of employees within a business. They can be provided by external training providers and usually take place in the workplace. There are many businesses that provide in-house training courses and they specialise in a specific type of training. For example, some provide training in health and safety and employment law, while others provide training that is specific to an industry, such as the health and social care industry.

However, quite often, in-house courses refer to training that has been created by the business itself to meet its own needs and is delivered by people who work for the business; for example, training and development managers. A good example of this is health and safety training in factories that has been developed to help employees whose first language is not English. Some British factories have created their own training videos using warning words (such as 'Watch out') in different languages so that employees can work more safely. The training sessions use situations that may occur in a particular business and are delivered in-house by the factories' own staff.

Fieldwork

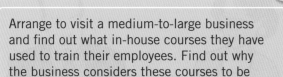

Arrange to visit a medium-to-large business and find out what in-house courses they have used to train their employees. Find out why the business considers these courses to be important.

External courses

External training courses take place away from the workplace, for example at specialist training centres. People can choose to go on a training course at a specialist centre before commencing employment and pay for the course themselves or employers can choose to send employees on external courses.

There is a wide range of external courses available, ranging from cabin crew and pilot training to construction skills. These courses are of benefit to employers because they offer specialist skills training that often cannot be provided in-house. Employers then benefit from having trained employees who can perform their jobs competently, therefore the courses are a worthwhile investment. Employees benefit because they are gaining worthwhile skills. If employees have paid for their own courses, then it is usually because they wish to apply for jobs in a specific industry and the course provides them with the necessary skills they need to be able to apply for the jobs they want.

Vocational and professional courses

Vocational and professional courses usually take place in colleges and universities and enable those taking the courses to attain a recognised qualification. There is a wide range of courses available on different levels and with different types of qualification.

Ryanair

Cabin crew on Europe's largest budget airline struggled to open emergency exits during a fire because of inadequate training, a report by safety investigators says.

Cabin-crew members at both the front and back of the aircraft tried to open the doors on the right side but found them too heavy. Greater force than usual is required to open an aircraft door in an emergency because the act of opening it automatically deploys an inflatable slide. The crew members, both believed to be female, had to call on male staff to help them to open the doors.

An Air Accidents Investigation Branch report, published after a two-year inquiry into the incident, said that most of Ryanair's 'new entrant cabin-crew personnel' were not properly trained in opening exit doors. 'The door-opening forces which they encountered during training were considerably less than those that would be encountered in a real evacuation with an armed evacuation slide.' They had been 'advised' that the doors would be heavier but had not practised opening them in realistic emergency conditions.

Ryanair saves money by using external courses for cabin-crew training at centres across Europe, including Poland and Latvia.

Source: 'Ryanair cabin crew struggles to open doors on burning plane', by Ben Webster, *The Times*, 2 August 2004 ©The Times 2004 / nisyndication.com

1. Explain why external courses need to be used to train cabin crew.
2. Describe the importance of training to Ryanair.
3. Evaluate Ryanair's approach to training its staff.

Colleges offer National Vocational Qualifications (NVQs). These are work-related, competence-based qualifications that employees undertake while working for an employer. They cover all the main aspects of an occupation, including current best practice, the ability to adapt to future requirements, and the knowledge and understanding needed to perform a job competently. NVQs can be taken at five different levels: levels 1 and 2 are equivalent to GCSEs; level 3 is equivalent to A levels; level 4 is equivalent to a university degree; and level 5 is equivalent to a higher degree. NVQs are available in a wide range of work-related areas from playwork to accounting.

Professional courses lead to a recognised professional qualification, for example in accountancy or law. Professional courses are usually provided by universities but are backed by the professional bodies from specific professional areas. For example, a university may offer an accountancy course that is backed by the Association of Chartered Certified Accountants (ACCA) or a marketing course backed by the Chartered Institute of Marketing. Professional courses enable people to become qualified and then apply for jobs in their chosen professions.

Performance appraisal

Performance appraisal is the process of assessing the work performance of employees. Performance appraisals usually take place once a year in the form of an interview or meeting between an employee and his line manager.

In appraisal meetings, the performance of employees is compared with any goals, targets or objectives they have been set. This is called the review process. If an employee's performance has not met expectations, training needs can be identified to help the employee make the progress required. If an employee has met or exceeded expectations, he or she may be considered as a candidate for promotion.

Once the review of performance has taken place in the appraisal meeting, new objectives for the coming year are agreed between the employee and their line manager. If the objectives for the employee relate to new skills or the need for knowledge or skills to be developed or updated, then any training that the employee may need can be identified and agreed.

An appraisal meeting

The benefits of performance appraisal

The performance appraisal has many benefits for both employers and employees. These include the opportunity to:

- identify training needs
- reveal problems
- discover new skills
- improve communication
- provide evidence for promotion or dismissal
- provide evidence for pay rises
- improve efficiency and effectiveness.

Identify training needs

One of the main benefits for both the employer and employee is that training needs can be identified. This is a benefit for the employer because the finance available for training employees needs to be used in the most effective way. By using appraisals, employers can identify the training that employees need to be able to do their jobs competently and effectively. This can prevent high costs arising from sending employees on training courses that are not relevant to their needs. This is also of benefit to employees because they can identify the training that is going to help them develop their knowledge and skills and, therefore, their careers.

Reveal problems

As an appraisal involves comparing the performance of employees with any targets or objectives they have been set, it can reveal any problems that employees may have had in meeting those targets and objectives. If problems are revealed, having a one-to-one meeting enables these problems to be discussed. It may be that some employees need support or retraining to enable them to improve their performance or it may be that some employees need to change their job role and could perform better if given a different role elsewhere in the business. Without the appraisal process, problems with the performance of employees may take longer to be discovered, which can cause productivity to suffer and employees to leave because they are unable to cope with their jobs.

Discover new skills

In addition to an employer being able to evaluate the performance of each employee and assess training needs, the benefits of the appraisal are that it also provides an official meeting that is centred on the employee and gives each employee the opportunity to discuss their abilities and career prospects. The appraisal interview, therefore, often reveals things about an employee which the line manager may have been unaware of, such as new skills that the employee has learned. Many employees undertake learning outside the workplace and gather new knowledge and skills that are relevant to their job roles. An appraisal interview gives employees the opportunity to discuss with their line manager how they could best make use of these.

Improve communication

During the course of busy working days, many employees and line managers do not have the time to meet and discuss performance. Many daily conversations between a line manager and employee are simply instructions or feedback on the progress of the work. Performance appraisals provide the opportunity for an in-depth discussion about the progress of the employee rather than the work itself. The line manager can provide detailed feedback on the employee's performance and this helps to improve communication between line managers and employees.

As the appraisal meeting is centred on the performance of an employee, the communication between the employee and line manager can make the employee feel valued, and this is motivational. It is an opportunity for the employee to receive recognition for achievement and discuss advancement, which, according to Herzberg (see Chapter 18), is motivating for the employee.

Provide evidence for promotion or dismissal

When evaluating the performance of employees against targets and objectives, it is inevitable that a line manager will find that some employees have performed well and others have not. For those who have performed well, the meeting offers an opportunity to discuss career prospects and opportunities within the business for promotion. Performance appraisals provide evidence of employee's achievements that may otherwise have gone unnoticed, and this helps employers to identify employees who can be considered for promoted posts. This is beneficial to an employer because, if employees do not achieve recognition in this way, they may be tempted to look for better jobs with other businesses.

For those employees who have not performed well against targets, it may be that their performance is so poor that they will be considered for dismissal. However, the performance of an employee would have to have been consistently poor and noted on more than one occasion for the employer to be able to begin disciplinary or dismissal procedures. It would be more usual for an employer to offer further training to an employee as a result of poor performance or move the employee into a different job role. This, however, depends on the extent of the poor performance and the abilities of the employee.

Provide evidence for pay rises

In some businesses and organisations, pay is linked to performance (**performance-related pay**) and the performance appraisal is used to evaluate the performance of employees against targets in order to decide whether employees merit a pay increase. If employees meet their targets, they are moved up the pay scale; but if they do not, they have to work to meet targets for a further period of time (usually one year) before they are considered again for a pay rise.

Performance-related pay is considered to be a way of rewarding employees for good performance. In order for performance-related schemes to work, they should be based on clear, measurable targets that must be agreed by both employer and employee.

Improve efficiency and effectiveness

As performance appraisals allow line managers, and therefore employers, to identify any training needs that employees may have, this can result in employees receiving the training they need to become more effective in their job roles. If employees are more effective, then the overall efficiency of the business will improve.

Similarly, performance appraisals are used to identify good performance and the strengths of employees, and this can help managers to make more use of their skills and knowledge to improve the overall efficiency of the business. For example, it may be that, in an appraisal meeting, it is discovered that an employee has good communication and leadership skills and would make an effective team leader. If that employee is then moved into a team leader role, this would be motivational for that employee (increasing their effectiveness) and may also increase the motivation, and therefore productivity, of the team.

Make the grade

P6 Remember this for P6. You must be able to explain the benefits of performance appraisal in a given organisation.

Discussion...

There is no point spending a lot of money training employees because then they will leave to find better jobs. Discuss.

Key words

External recruitment – Identifying the need for new employees and seeking to attract suitable candidates from outside the business.

Health and Safety at Work Act 1974 – The law that requires employers to ensure the health and safety of employees when at work.

Induction training – An introduction to the business, its systems and health and safety requirements. It also includes an introduction to existing employees that the new employee may be working with.

ISO – Stands for the International Standards Organisation. ISO 9000 is a worldwide quality certification procedure. ISO 9001 is part of the quality standards.

Manual handling – A wide range of handling activities performed by people. This includes lifting, lowering, pushing, pulling or carrying. The load may be either inanimate, such as a box, or animate, such as a person.

Performance-related pay – A bonus or salary increase paid when an employee has met targets, goals or objectives.

Productivity – A measure of the efficiency with which a business turns inputs into output. Labour productivity is output per worker.

Assignment

You must show understanding of the importance of training and review.

The business organisation

You should base this assignment on a business of your choice. A large business may be more suitable than a small business as there would be more employees for you to interview and gather views from.

For this assignment, you should produce a presentation that would be suitable for a new human resources manager in your chosen business.

1. The first part of your presentation must describe the importance to your chosen business of training employees. **(P5)**
2. The second part of your presentation must explain the benefits to your chosen business of performance appraisal. **(P6)**

To achieve a pass grade you need to:	To achieve a merit grade you need to:	To achieve a distinction you need to:
P5 describe the importance of training to an organisation		
P6 explain the benefits of performance appraisal		

Unit 10

Personal selling in business

Chapter 20 Understand the role of sales staff

What are you finding out?

Selling is a human characteristic. When we want something, we sell our ideas to somebody else. For example, you might use your ability to sell ideas to persuade a friend to accompany you to a sports event.

Selling involves communication between a seller and a buyer which is designed to convince the consumer to purchase the products or services on offer. The objective of selling is therefore to make a sale. It is in fact the culmination of all of the marketing activities that have taken place beforehand. It involves matching the needs of a customer with the goods and services on offer. The better the match that is created, the more likelihood that there will be a lasting relationship between the seller and the buyer.

If selling did not take place, very little would ever happen. Organisations would not exist and products would not be manufactured. Life would not be product driven and we would live frugal lives. You only have to look around your house or your classroom to realise that almost everything that you have acquired originates in one way or another from a process of selling. In this sense, being able to sell is at the heart of what every organisation does. It is also something on which the organisation will depend.

This chapter will help you to:

- Understand the role that those involved in selling undertake.
- Appreciate how sales staff have to establish customer requirements.
- Identify the knowledge and skills required by those involved in selling.
- Explain the role of sales staff, as well as the sales techniques that they use.

Understand the role of sales staff

It is easy to take sales people for granted. In fact they are all around us. Whenever we walk into a retail environment, we are faced by those involved with selling. In everyday life we seek answers to questions and try in many different ways to influence others. You may find that your teacher is persuading you to attend a particular event or to join a group. Or you may have a friend who wants you to go to a concert at the weekend. At home your brother or sister might be persuading you to change the television channel. And when the channel is switched over, you may hear politicians selling their policies! They are also, in a very different context, employing selling skills. In one way or another everybody uses selling skills. In this sense, selling skills are lifelong skills that help us to survive and succeed.

Task

Think about the nature and type of selling skills used by:

a parents

b teachers

c lawyers

d politicians.

Did you know...

Most buying decisions are based upon emotions!

Selling goods, services and the product surround

The role of those involved in selling is to sell the goods or services on offer. When we think of goods or services, we tend to think of something tangible. At a very simple level a customer thinks about the product as something **tangible** like a book, car or newspaper. Each of these you can feel, touch and see. The service is something that you receive, like a haircut, a ride on public transport or an entry to a museum. In fact, goods are not just goods. Services are not just services. Customers are not just buying these features. They are really purchasing a whole series of benefits when they buy a product or service, and this is known as the **product surround**. It is the knowledge of the product surround that makes selling a more sophisticated and complicated business.

For example, in buying toothpaste, a customer might look for:

- The flavour and appearance of the product.
- A reputable and well-known brand that they can trust.
- The ability of the product to make teeth bright.
- How the product contributes towards decay prevention.
- The price and value for money of the product.
- A nice environment in which to buy the toothpaste.
- Friendly staff and no long checkout queues.
- A store that is convenient for the customer.

One of the first rules of selling is to think about all of the features and benefits that the customer might want. Knowing what these features and benefits are helps the seller to highlight the ability of the product and service to supply these benefits. Within the product surround, for example:

- Tangible features might include shape, design, colour, packaging, size, the ability of the product to perform tasks.
- Intangible features are not so obvious. These might include the reputation of the business, the brand, the location of the business, credit facilities, spare parts, free delivery and guarantees.

Visiting a local restaurant

Peter consumed a wonderful dish today. The food was excellent but the product was a disaster. He went to his local restaurant, which had advertised a vegetarian buffet. When he got to the restaurant, signs on the door indicated 'Buffet now open'. After he went in, the waiter told him that they no longer did the buffet as it was losing money. Peter decided to stay and ordered from the menu. The temperature in the restaurant was cold. He ordered tea but it was warm, not hot, and had a tea bag floating on top. The dish was tasty and really enjoyable, but he had to wait 30 minutes for it to be prepared. The restaurant did not accept credit cards and he had to pay with cash. Staff were friendly, but they were also clumsy. Peter would not return to the restaurant again.

1. Identify elements of the core product and the product surround from what was being offered within the restaurant.
2. Explain why this example illustrates that a product is much more than a core item.

Another way of thinking about a product is to think about what it does. For example, a lawnmower would be expected to cut grass; a car would be expected to travel from A to B; a pair of scissors would be expected to cut. This is the **core product**. Everything else from the product, such as guarantees, reputation and the brand image, is within the product surround.

Did you know...

You can now buy a battery-powered, self-twirling spaghetti fork!

Establishing customer requirements

When we think of sales people we think about them making a **sales pitch**. However, that is not the first thing that a seller should do. If all a sales person does is talk, then clearly they are not listening. It is only through listening and asking questions that a sales person will find out what a customer requires.

One of the important qualities of selling is therefore to listen. As a seller listens they may be listening not just with their ears but also with their eyes. They may look at the **body language** of the customer and the signs that the body language might display. For example, if a customer has bought a product before and has been disappointed with it, they may use hand gestures to show their frustration. On the other hand, if they have liked a product they may smile as they describe it.

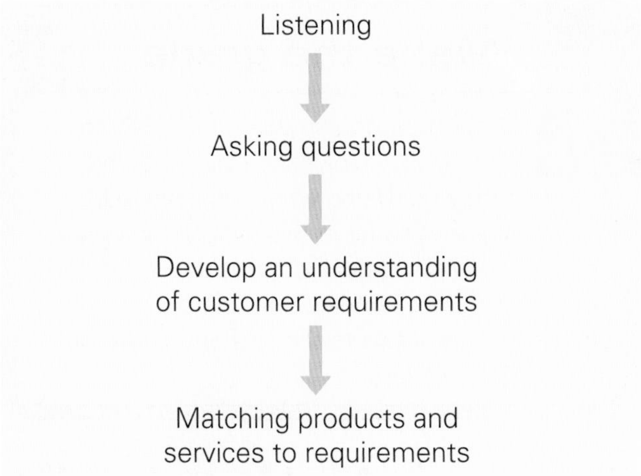

Figure 20.1 Matching products and services to customer requirements

By listening to customers, a sales person is indicating that they are interested in the needs of the customer and want to match their needs with appropriate goods and services. It also indicates that the sales person genuinely is interested in their needs and is not being too pushy. This helps them to build and develop good relationships with their customers.

Matching goods or services to customer requirements

By listening to customers it is possible to find out about the type of product or service they require. For example, a seller may quickly establish that the product or services that they offer are not those required by the customer. That would then save a lot of time and effort spent on persuading a customer to buy a product that they are either not going to buy or, if they do, buy something that they do not really want! It also helps the sales person to tailor their sales pitch precisely to the needs of the customer. This helps to save time. It also makes the process of selling much more efficient.

Did you know...

The UK has a professional association called The Institute of Sales and Marketing Management which describes itself as a 'professional body for sales people'.

Providing information

Those involved in **personal selling** require supporting information that helps the selling process. This may simply be in the form of information in a leaflet pushed through a letterbox. In some markets, advertising supports the selling effort. Adverts may be used to develop **leads** – individuals who show an interest in a product or service. They may see an advertisement within a newspaper or magazine and then follow this up with a phone call. Sometimes organisations provide articles and photographs in magazines. Another way of providing information about products and services is through **direct mail**. This is mail that is addressed and sent to the customer's home. Direct mail may include reply cards that customers can respond to or order forms.

Task

Working in groups, identify a product or service that you might collectively like to purchase. Use the internet to find out as much as you can about that product or service. How might all of the information that you have found support the process of selling?

Developing customer care

Every day of their working lives sales people come into contact with their customers. Where customers buy products or receive services on a regular basis, sales people will get to know them well and will use a range of techniques to build and foster relationships with these regular customers. To do this they need to provide good customer care (see Unit 11). Customer care is important as it helps to ensure that repeat business takes place. It also makes customers feel good about the processes that they have gone through and **adds value** to a transaction so that a customer feels that they are getting more than just a product.

Gathering feedback

By listening to customers, sales people are able to gather feedback. Most organisations will provide their field sales team with documents that help them to collect information that can then be recorded and analysed. For example, they may be able to electronically record information on a notebook or laptop computer. They may simply have record cards for each customer that enable them to record information. This will provide valuable information for the seller. They can then focus much more precisely upon the needs of each individual customer next time a visit is required.

Three key characteristics

When talking to customers there are three key elements to consider. These are that the seller is:

1. The *first point of contact* between an organisation and its customers. The behaviour and professionalism of the seller will influence how the customer judges the organisation.
2. *Representing the organisation* and is, as far as the customer is concerned, the friendly face of the organisation. If the seller misbehaves or says the wrong thing, then that could damage the reputation of the organisation in the eyes of the customer.
3. *Promoting the product* on behalf of the organisation. The seller should, on the one hand, be positive about the products or services on offer; however, they should, on the other hand, be truthful.

Did you know...

Franklin W. Woolworth once said, 'I am the worst salesman. Therefore I must make it easy for people to buy.'

Discussion...

Is everybody capable of becoming a sales person?

Make the grade

P1 Remember to use this for P1. Talk to somebody involved in sales and find out what they do. Using what you have read and learnt about so far in this chapter, as well as your interview, describe the role of sales staff. Try to use examples that relate your understanding of this to the role of the person that you interviewed.

Appreciate the knowledge and skills required by sales staff

Those involved within selling develop a series of tools and techniques that serve them well. For example, having a good positive personality and being able to get on with customers is particularly important. However, it is not just about personality; sales staff also need to be well organised and be able to make a whole series of judgements when dealing with customers. It is not an easy role for anybody, however experienced they may be. Every day selling brings new, interesting and challenging situations. To respond to these, sales staff require many different skills to help them respond appropriately and also build long-term relationships with their customers.

Product knowledge

If you are selling a good you need to show your customer that you have expert knowledge of that product. This is important as those who are selling are in a privileged position. For example, they may be asked for advice by the seller. In some industries where product knowledge is very advanced, it is necessary to employ senior professional people in a sales role. For example, in the pharmaceutical industry, doctors are employed to talk to senior medical professionals within the National Health Service.

What are the features of the product?	• Specifications • Technical details • Product features and benefits	• Allow customer to trial product • Provide a product demonstration
What is the price of the product?	• Negotiate price with customer • Illustrate how price compares with competitors	• Arrange a discount for bulk ordering • Allow credit terms
How long will the product last?	• Technical specifications • Servicing arrangements	• Use feedback from other customers • Illustrate the guarantee arrangements and technical support
Will it be able to undertake these sorts of tasks?	• Brochure • Illustrations	• Show how the product works • Talk about how others have used the product

Figure 20.2 Using product knowledge to answer questions

Product knowledge may be acquired in a variety of ways. Sales staff may go through a series of training programmes. They may be asked to read press reviews of competitor products and read a whole series of literature. This should help them to answer technical questions and also be able to comment with authority upon the benefits that their products have over those of competitors.

Sales motivation

Selling is not an easy thing to do. It is also something that some individuals feel less comfortable doing than others. To be able to sell and to enjoy it, staff need to feel motivated. This means that they must have enthusiasm for the job and the incentive to do it well. When dealing with customers, almost every situation is likely to be different. For example, one customer might be unhappy about their last experience, while another could be returning for repeat business. They may have many questions or issues to settle. Selling involves knowing how to respond appropriately in each instance. The customers may have trust in the actions of the sales person and may be spending considerable amounts of money. So, indirectly the sales person may be taking on quite a big responsibility.

As the sales person completes each sale, they will know that the successful use of their sales skills may also directly impact on their earnings; therefore the more they sell, the more they can earn. A sales person should always be positive. On the one hand, there may be a sense of real excitement as they complete a sale. On the other, they may be earning a **commission**, a bonus to their income, which relates to each sale. Sales staff might also from time to time receive rewards if they exceed their sales targets. They might receive watches, a laptop or even a free holiday. Many organisations will also recognise successful sales staff by promoting them so that they can manage territories and other staff.

SALES ASSISTANT/ RETAIL SALES ADVISOR

We are an established electrical retailer, selling the latest flat panel televisions and home cinema products, as well as a large range of top name domestic home appliances (white goods).

Due to expansion of our business, we are looking to recruit a skilled electrical retail sales assistant/retail sales advisor for our Tring store.

We will provide full training on our systems and products

We are looking for people with the following attributes:

- Sales experience within the consumer electronics/audio visual industry preferred though not essential. (If you really know how to sell we want to hear from you!)
- Highly motivated, personable with a friendly, positive attitude.
- Flexible approach to working and committed to selling.
- Smart dressed and well presented.

You may have worked in the following capacities: audio visual sales, retail assistant, retail manager, store manager, car sales, sales assistant, floor manager, sales supervisor, sales associate, electronic sales.

Example of an advertisement for a sales post

Did you know...

According to Mark Benedict (a writer of books about selling) in 2007, 'If you are not being successful in your sales performance, then you are doing something wrong: and that wrong has something to do with your way of thinking. And that way of thinking has something to do with negative thinking.'

Closing sales

Simply talking to a customer will not lead to a sale. A sales person needs to ask the customer if they want to make an order, in order to close a sale. The major consideration is deciding on when to ask or when to close the sale. The way in which most sales staff do this is to look for **buying signals**. These are often very subtle signals that indicate that the buyer is ready to buy. Sometimes the signal may be verbal. At other times the signal may be non-verbal and expressed through body language. Sales people will always be looking and listening for buying signals that enable them to close the sale. For example, the potential buyer might say:

'How long would it take for my order to be delivered?'

'Is that style available in the wood effect?'

'Am I required to pay a deposit?'

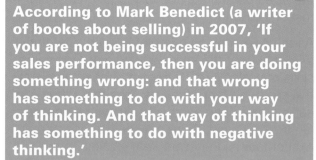

The seller might simply ask if they would like to make an order. Or they could adopt the less direct approach and say, 'We can deliver on Thursday if you order today.' Or even more directly, they might say, 'If you were to order, would you like the red or blue model?' As the seller closes the sale, it is important to be positive, emphasise the key benefits of the product and also summarise the way in which the order is meeting their requirements so that the buyer feels good about the agreement.

Task

In pairs, think about something that you have persuaded somebody to do over the last week. Why were you successful? What skills did you use?

Developing sales techniques

In order to be able to sell, individuals have to be confident about the product, as well as in their own selling skills and techniques. Selling is an opportunity and it is not a foregone conclusion that the **prospect** or buyer will make a purchase. When you meet somebody who might make a purchase, you have the opportunity to talk with somebody who has probably chosen your organisation as one that might be able to satisfy their needs. It is then up to the sales person to find out more about that customer and then, if appropriate, try to match their products and services with the needs of the buyer.

Customers often do not have a long attention span. They will want to know precisely and concisely what is on offer and whether it is what they want. They might want to know about technical specifications or they might want to know about reputation. It is important to understand what their requirements are and for the sales person to get to the point and address their issues and concerns.

Sales staff might be put into a variety of different situations. These might include:

- *Cold calling* – Contacting the prospect, either by phone or by visiting their premises without arranging an appointment beforehand, is called **cold calling**. This sort of selling is undertaken in order to obtain new business. As customers do not know the sales person and may not have heard of the organisation, this is a difficult sales technique to use successfully. As a result the success rate is likely to be low.
- *Face-to-face selling* – This presents the ideal opportunity for a sales person to identify customer needs and attempt to satisfy them. This requires many different people skills. For example, they need to show they are interested in the customer, show empathy, be able to use their product knowledge, be positive and helpful, have knowledge of competitor products and so on.
- *Drop-in visits* – A sales person needs to manage the records of their customers or clients over a period of time. As new products come out or new services are being offered, they need to think about which customers might require such products and services. So if a sales person is working outside the organisation in the **field**, they need to set up appointments and arrange to meet their customers at convenient times.
- *Telemarketing* – This involves selling products by contacting potential customers on the phone. The objective might simply be to identify some leads. Although the success rate of telemarketing tends to be low, it is a cost-effective technique of creating new business. It is much less time consuming than visiting organisations and allows two-way communication using a telephone.

Did you know...

According to the UK's Department for Business, Innovation and Skills, the rise of telemarketing has also led to an increase in telemarketing fraud.

Legislation affecting personal selling

When you are involved in selling, you have responsibilities to your customers. To protect customers, there is **legislation** relating to sales and the relationship of the seller to the buyer. These laws are in the best interests of both the buyers and the sellers.

The key pieces of legislation affecting selling are as follows:

Sale of Goods Act 1979

(This has been amended by the Sale and Supply of Goods to Consumer Regulations 2002.)

The Act and Regulations impose a number of conditions. These are that:

- The seller must have the right to sell the goods (for example, they were not stolen).
- The goods should match any description given when selling them (i.e. goods should fit the description).
- The goods should be of satisfactory quality.
- The goods should be fit for the buyer's purpose (a TV should work and pick up channels).
- Where goods are sold by sample, the bulk delivery should match the sample.

If these conditions are not met there are various remedies open to customers such as a refund or a repair and replacement.

Did you know...

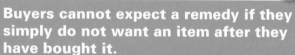

Buyers cannot expect a remedy if they simply do not want an item after they have bought it.

Supply of Goods and Services Act 1982

This implies three terms when goods and services are supplied:

1. The supplier will carry out the service with reasonable care and skill.
2. The service will be performed within a reasonable time.
3. A reasonable price will be charged.

Consumer Credit Act 1974

All organisations offering credit (for example, banks and retailers) must be licensed through the Office of Fair Trading (OFT). It sets out strict requirements for organisations offering and selling credit. This is to protect consumers against lenders charging very high interest rates and making it difficult for customers to amend or cancel agreements.

Did you know...

Moneysupermarket.com provides a service that enables customers to compare interest rates on loans so that they can get the best possible deal.

Consumer Protection Act 1987

This Act provides further protection for consumers. Firstly, it places an onus on the seller to protect consumers from defective products. Secondly, it regulates the safety of consumer products such as flammable items and poisonous items. Thirdly, it makes it a criminal offence for sellers to mislead consumers over prices.

Trades Descriptions Acts 1968 and 1972

These make it a criminal offence to provide a false or misleading description of goods, services, accommodation or facilities. Organisations can be prosecuted for not abiding by this. Under this Act it is a criminal offence to:

- Sell goods that are wrongly described.
- Wrongly describe goods.
- Make false claims for services.

Did you know...

In 2008 the Advertising Standards Authority stated that Tesco, the UK's largest supermarket, exaggerated claims about how much cheaper their products were than Asda's and Morrisons'.

Consumer Protection Distance Selling Regulations 2005

These provide protection to consumers who shop by phone, through mail order, on the internet or through television shopping channels. Protection includes:

- The right to receive information that is clear about goods and services before customers decide to buy.
- Confirmation of the transaction in writing.
- A cooling-off period of seven days during which the consumer can withdraw from the contract.
- Protection from credit card fraud.

Task

Working within groups, think of situations that either you or your family have been in when buying goods or services. Could any of the above examples of legislation have affected your purchase?

Organisational policies

Every organisation will have a slightly different approach when developing policies that influence how it sells to its customers. The policies could influence the relationship that the organisation has with customers and also influence how its sales staff approach their role. These may include the examples in Figure 20.3 below:

Reflective practice

The role of somebody working in sales is not easy. Sometimes things go well and sometimes they do not. It is important that those involved in sales reflect on the processes in which they have been involved. One way of doing this is to use the Gibbs Reflective Cycle. This was developed by Professor Graham Gibbs in 1988 as a way of thinking about learning by doing.

The first thing for a sales person to do is to think about what has happened during the selling process. This is the 'Description' phase. This is followed by a period of reflection as they consider their thoughts and feelings at the time.

Price matching	Some organisations refuse to be beaten on price. They will try and match their prices against the lowest prices in the market. If consumers find a price lower than theirs, they will even reduce prices to match that price.
Discounting	Organisations might offer a number of different types of discounts. Discounts might be provided to regular customers. Trade discounts might be provided for organisations in the same line of business. Cash discounts might be offered for prompt cash payments.
Guarantees and warranties	Guarantees are agreements to provide some benefit for customers if goods prove to be defective. Sometimes consumers are offered the chance to have a warranty, but they might have to pay for this.
After-sales service	Selling should not finish with the sale. Customers might need their products to be regularly serviced and this provides an opportunity to constantly reassess their needs.
Customer care	Different businesses will have different standards of customer care. Customer care helps to keep customers that businesses already have and save money on having to look for new customers to sell to.

Figure 20.3 Examples of organisational policies

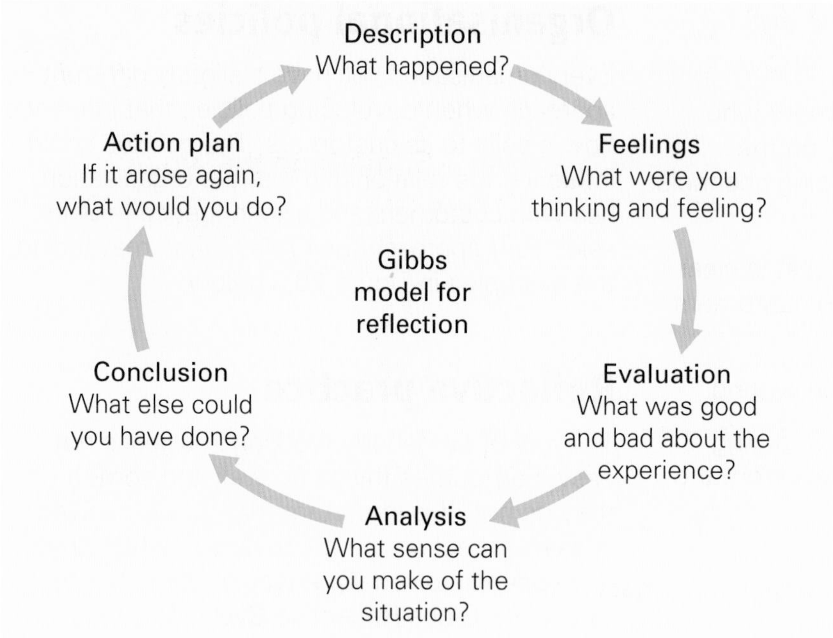

Figure 20.4 Gibbs Reflective Cycle

As they evaluate, they make judgements about what was good and bad about the experience at the time. Then comes the analysis during which the sales person tries to make sense of what happened at the time and considers what it all meant. As they conclude, they then think about what else they could have done and the action plan then identifies what they could do differently. This helps sales people to adapt their practice based on improving their understanding of the situation in which they have been placed.

Make the grade

M1 Remember to use this for M1. Sales techniques vary between different organisations and within different markets. Sales staff are the public face of an organisation. Using the title 'A day in the life of a sales person', explain the different situations that a seller might be placed in during the course of their work. As you do so, explain the role of sales staff and the sales techniques that they might use.

Key words

Adds value – Process through which customers feel that they are getting more from a transaction.

Body language – Gestures, postures and facial expressions.

Buying signals – Signs or indications that are either verbal or non-verbal that a buyer is intending to make a purchase.

Commission – Extra bonus to income that relates to the number of products sold.

Core product – Features of a product that enable it to do what it is intended to do.

Direct mail – Personally addressed sales and promotional materials delivered to the consumer.

Field – Situation where sales staff work away from business premises.

Leads – People who show an interest in a product or service.

Legislation – Laws passed by Parliament.

Personal selling – Face-to-face selling that persuades a buyer to purchase a product.

Product surround – Everything provided by a product or service designed to meet customer needs.

Prospect – Potential customer targeted in the hope that they will make a purchase.

Sales pitch – Presentation used to persuade a customer to purchase a product.

Tangible – Something that you can touch, feel or see.

Assignment

You must understand the role of sales staff.

Supporting a new member of the sales team

You have been asked to support a new member of the sales team who has started work today. You work for a large retailer that has premises in your local town centre. Although your organisation gets really busy, you have many competitors, and it has been said that the reason that your organisation is successful is because of the quality of the sales team.

1. A new member of staff has joined the sales team as a trainee. Send them an email describing what a member of the sales team does. For example, explain how they establish customer requirements and then attempt to satisfy such requirements. **(P1)**
2. You now need to describe the wider role that sales staff undertake. Produce a series of short training activities for the new member of staff. These activities will help that member of staff to learn about the role of sales staff as well as the techniques that they use. For example, this will help the member of staff to understand about their role in representing the organisation, having a motivation to sell, product knowledge and providing customer care. **(M1)**

To achieve a pass grade you need to:	To achieve a merit grade you need to:	To achieve a distinction you need to:
P1 describe the role of sales staff, dealt with in the next chapter	**M1** explain the role of sales staff and the sales techniques they use	
P2 identify the techniques used when making personal sales		
P3 explain the knowledge and skills used when making personal sales		

Chapter 21
Demonstrate personal selling skills and processes

What are you finding out?

The responsibility of those involved in selling is to move goods into the marketplace, from those seeking to sell them through to those wishing to buy them. In selling, this is undertaken by communicating with customers, identifying their needs, presenting products and information and making the sale.

Today we live in an age in which customers have the power to make more choices than ever before. The environment for selling has never been more challenging. To deal with this, a successful sales person needs a whole range of personal selling skills. They also need to be able to operate in an environment in which they manage a sequence of processes that ensure the sale goes through smoothly.

This chapter will help you to:

- Understand the need for and identify the techniques used when making personal sales.
- Look at and compare the selling skills and processes used in different situations.
- Explain the knowledge and skills used when making personal sales.
- Prepare to make personal sales.
- Use selling skills and processes to make sales.
- Evaluate the preparation, skills and processes used in different situations.

Personal selling skills

When you walk into a sales situation, what do you expect? You would hope that you would be greeted by somebody intelligent, friendly, agreeable and smartly dressed and that your questions would be answered and supported with appropriate advice. You would also hope to meet somebody who would understand your needs, arouse your interest, be efficient, would not waste your time and would know about the products. You would also hope that they would not push sales products at you, not invade your personal space and then give you, the customer, time to make a decision. You can probably think of situations where that has happened and where you have come across skilled sales people. You may also think of situations where that has not happened.

Did you know...

In selling it is said that appearance provides the seller with an important competitive edge.

Communicating with customers

Having good communication skills is extremely important for anybody involved in selling. This is because it is through communication that a customer will make a decision about whether to purchase a product. For example, verbal communications enable a sales person to use the spoken word in a precise and supportive manner to communicate a message about the attributes of products or services on offer. Communication helps customers to make sense of all they see so that they can rationalise and take everything into account before they make a decision.

Type of communication	Application
Spoken	Provides precise detail, supports queries, promotes and persuades, answers questions, reassures customer, provides positive support.
Written	Contains product knowledge, informs customer, supports their understanding of product applications.
Non-verbal	Positive body language, showing enthusiasm, interest, listening to the customer, being positive and supportive, exhibiting good manners. This helps to show empathy with the needs of the purchaser.
Face to face	Saying the right thing, listening, smiling, supportive and enthusiastic attitude, being positive and helpful.
Remote	Communicating with customers through electronic media in different locations.
Eye contact	Showing that the seller is genuine, wants to help the customer, is really concerned that they are ready to solve problems for the customer and are more than able to meet their requirements.

Figure 21.1 Key elements of communication within the selling process

Task

One person should act as a seller and one a buyer. The buyer needs to specify a product or service that they would like to purchase. The seller needs time on their own to make notes about what they could offer. The buyer needs time to identify their precise requirements. The seller and buyer should meet and go through a simulated selling process. When the activity is finished the seller and buyer should discuss the skills shown by the seller as well as their strengths and weaknesses.

Did you know...

With increasing internet usage for shopping, home shopping will soon account for 30% of all retail sales in the UK.

Purposes of communication

In a selling situation, communication has many purposes. As the buyer enters the selling environment, communication, often non-verbal, can help to provide them with reassurance. This makes the buyer feel at ease. Listening helps the buyer to feel that their needs are being considered. Communication provides the buyer with information that helps the seller to understand how the buyer's needs can be met. This creates the right environment for the buyer to consider their possible purchase and if the sale is achieved, the buyer will leave feeling that the right decision has been made.

The purposes of communication can be met in a number of ways within the selling environment. These include:

a *Greeting* – When customers are greeted by a sales person, the sales person is making that all-important first impression. The greeting indicates who the sales person is and provides the customer with the opportunity to understand the sort of customer service that they are about to be provided with. The business might have a policy about how to greet customers and the sales person might have been trained to greet customers in a certain way.

b *Introduction* – A sales person should not talk too much when introducing themselves to customers. Instead they should be prepared to listen and also ask probing questions in order to find out more about their needs. It is during this stage that the sales person needs to appear positive and professional. They also need to be honest. If they do not know something, they need to admit it and find out, perhaps by talking to a colleague. It is during the introduction that the sales person needs to find out the customer's priorities. It may be useful to get the name of the customer and their contact details. This will enable the seller to contact the buyer, for example to deal with any queries that they discussed. It also helps the seller to follow up the conversation. The seller must always bear in mind that the customer will have a limited budget and therefore it is in the seller's interest to try to establish what this is in order that the seller can suggest products or services within the correct price range.

c *Attracting customer's attention and interest* – From an early stage in the selling process it is important to take the customer through the selling process in a stimulating way. To help them do this, sellers use a model called AIDA, which stands for:

- **A** A customer's attention is captured and they are made **AWARE** of the product or service on offer. In this situation the seller greets and introduces themselves to the customer in a positive way.
- **I** The products on offer, the environment and the skills of the sales person stimulate their **INTEREST**. There needs to be discussion and interaction in order for this to be achieved.
- **D** Customers will want their needs to be met. They may feel that they are deprived because they do not have the product or service, and this stimulates a **DESIRE** for it.
- **A** **ACTION** involves the decision to purchase the product or service on offer.

d *Identifying and meeting customers' needs* – From the very outset, the sales person wants to make customers feel valued. Customers will probably have approached the organisation selling the product because they may have wanted advice. The role of the sales person is to listen and ask questions. It is important to understand what customers want, when they want it, and how they plan to use the product or service on offer.

e *Presenting products/product information* – AIDA will help with the presentation strategy. As a sales person presents products they need to back up their presentation with product information, used to support the points that they want to make. During the presentation, the sales person must constantly evaluate whether the product or service is appropriate for the needs of the **prospect**. It is unethical to sell something that they may not need. Sometimes the larger the purchase, the more complex the selling process becomes. The buyer might want time and personal space in order to think about their decision. Alongside the presentation, the sales person might use a number of aids. These might include:
- product demonstrations
- allowing the buyer to use a product for a weekend
- samples
- various types of brochure and sales literature
- recommendations from other buyers.

As this process develops, the sales person must try to overcome any misunderstandings. Timing is crucial for the sale. A sales person needs to look for buying signals that indicate that the buyer is close to a decision. For example, the buyer might be very positive and make statements such as 'I like this,' 'It would work well,' 'This is within our budget' or 'It would fit.'

Selling the services of a restaurant

Within each industry there will be different ways of handling sales. For example, selling the services provided by a restaurant will be completely different to selling those of a bank. If a new restuarant opens in to a city, one of the first things the owner might do is to ring all of the local organisations and offer to host meetings or provide them with a discount. They will try to become friends with the right people such as local hotels and businesses who might recommend its services. Those working within the restaurant should be trained to advertise the services of the restaurant outside business hours. They might be provided with business cards and promotional materials to do this. Menus could be sent to local organisations. When customers finish their meal it is important to check that they are satisfied with the food and they should be thanked for coming to the restaurant. Whenever there are local events somebody from the restaurant should go in order to sell its services. What the owner of the restaurant is doing is emphasising its unique selling points (USP).

1. What would the role of selling be in this case-study example?

2. Could you add to the list of selling functions listed above?

Did you know...

One industry that is growing is that of individuals selling products online using websites such as eBay and Amazon.

Task

List ten things that those involved in selling should not do when trying to sell to customers.

Appearance

Sales people represent the organisation for which they are working. For example, if they look untidy that does not say much about their organisation. Working in sales mean that appearance is important. It might mean that staff have to wear a suit. In some circumstances they may have to wear a uniform and it is usual in most situations for them to wear an organisation's name badge. Personal hygiene is particularly important.

Did you know...

Wilkinson's is a large retail group selling affordable products in stores throughout the UK. The colour of the staff uniform in Wilkinson's stores is red.

Task

Working in groups, describe the uniform for five different retail outlets known to you. Rate each of the staff uniforms out of five, with five as the highest and zero as the lowest.

Attitude

When thinking of buying a product, the last thing the purchaser wants to be faced with is sales staff who are not interested in meeting their needs. If staff are lazy, biased, pushy, unkempt, negative and difficult to talk to, this will simply encourage the prospect to go elsewhere. Those working within sales need to think about the following points:

- *Positive* – It is easy to tell whether somebody is positive. Those who are positive smile, say the right thing, are supportive and are constantly looking to provide help. Being positive is also a way of thinking. It is a way of looking at the world from the bright side of life, being optimistic and always believing that there are solutions to problems.
- *Manners* – These are all about how individuals treat each other. If somebody asks another person to do something, they would use the word 'please'. After they have done it, they would then say 'Thank you'. Simple things like holding doors open for others or helping them if they are carrying things are all about manners. Manners are an important element, determining whether selling relationships could develop. They show that individuals are considerate.
- *Language* – It is easy to take how we talk for granted. In a selling situation it may be necessary to talk differently, for example using full sentences and being polite and formal at all times. The sales person should avoid using local **colloquialisms** that might confuse the buyer. These might be local expressions or street language which the buyer would not understand as they might not come from that culture. As a result, the sales person needs to speak more formally. Customers might not understand technical terms. The sales person should not confuse a buyer in order to win a sale.

- *Courtesy* – A famous expression is 'Treat others as you would like to be treated.' Being courteous means that the sales person respects the buyer. A courteous person helps and supports others.
- *Consideration* – This is a word usually associated with courtesy. It means carefully taking into account the views, thoughts and interests of others. It also means going the extra mile to support the needs of customers.

Discussion...

It has been said that 'the customer is always right'. Should this influence how a sales person carries out their activities? Use examples to support your thoughts.

Did you know...

There are two ways to increase sales. A business can either get more customers or sell more to existing customers.

Preparing the sales area

A customer will have certain expectations when entering premises. They will expect the premises to be clean. The sales area should represent the image that is being portrayed by the organisation. For example, the furniture might be the same colour as the colour on the organisation's stationery, packaging and logos. Information for the customer should be displayed in places that are convenient for the eye. There might be **point-of-sale displays**. These are usually near the point of sale and draw the attention of the customer towards products. There should be logic about how the sales area has been organised. This is sometimes known as **merchandising**. Products within the sales area should be positioned through merchandising around the expected movements of each customer. Nobody likes a sales area to look untidy. Products need to be stacked neatly and clearly labelled and priced. Those involved within sales have a clear responsibility to manage the work environment in which they operate.

Task

Think about how outsiders to your school or college might form judgements about your organisation when they enter the reception area. How is this area organised? In what way does it attempt to provide a positive image of your school or college?

Personal space

Personal space is the distance around someone's body, or their territory, which they feel uncomfortable about if it is invaded by somebody else. For example, many individuals are not very happy if others stand too close to them when they communicate. A customer's personal space is generally something to respect. It becomes invaded when a sales person listens to their conversation on a mobile, looks at their bags to see what they have purchased or listens to a private conversation they may be having with a partner.

Task

Discuss instances where you feel that your personal space has been invaded. Why did you feel that it had been invaded?

Did you know...

According to psychologists, one way in which individuals deal with personal-space issues such as crowding on trains and buses is through dehumanisation. This is where individuals imagine that those invading their territory are objects, not other human beings.

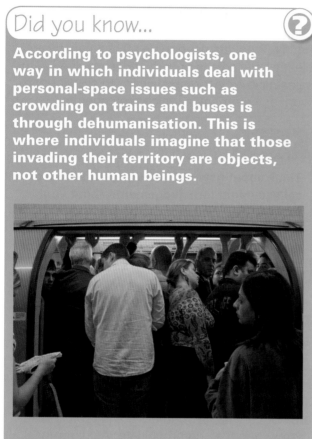

Make the grade

P2 P3 P4 M2

Remember to use this for P2, P3, P4 and M2. This activity should involve you in preparing to make sales. Both this and the previous chapter should be used in meeting these grading criteria. Look at two very different environments in which selling takes place. For example, one could be a retail environment where physical products are sold and one could be where services are sold through telemarketing. Identify the different techniques that should be used to make sales in each of these different environments. Describe the differences between the different environments. Comment on the knowledge and skills required in each context. Also comment on the constraints such as legislation. Describe how in each different environment those involved in sales would prepare to make personal sales. Make comparisons between both of the environments for each of these situations.

Personal selling processes

Selling in a highly competitive world means that preparation and planning are very important. Knowledge as well as skills help those involved within sales to be successful. Sales staff will undoubtedly have sales targets that they want to achieve. In order to achieve those targets they must understand all of the processes so that the needs of their customers are achieved.

Did you know...

It has been said that sales people are born and not made.

Making sales

The mnemonic used to describe how to make sales and the sequence of events that it creates is known as the five Ps.

Figure 21.2 The five Ps of selling

To initiate sales a sales person needs preparation. Good product knowledge is vital as it enables them to take questions from prospective customers. It also enables them to get to know the product and service on offer. Sometimes as part of preparation, it is possible to go through a customer's records so that the sales person can respond to the individual needs of each customer. Knowledge of competitors and their products enables sellers to respond to queries about the relative merits of each product. Good preparation improves the chance of closing a sale.

The next stage in selling is prospecting. Sometimes the prospect might come into a retail environment. In other situations they may be located using customer records. **Direct mail** might have been used to stimulate enquiries for staff to follow up.

The pre-approach phase involves trying to learn about the customer.

The presentation is the stage in which the selling process begins and the sale begins its process to being made. The acronym AIDA (see page 240) helps to describe what is necessary during the selling process

After a sale has been made, the customer may require post-sale support. This stage involves following up the sale. It is important to ensure that the customer feels that their needs have been met and are happy with the product or service that they have purchased.

Task

Using the internet, find out the after-sales customer service policy for one organisation

After-sales service

After-sales service is part of the product surround. Customers expect a whole range of after-sales services as part of their product purchase. In many ways, the purchase of a product is the start of the partnership between the customer and the supplier.

After-sales support might include:

- *Delivery* – Delivery of goods to customers at the right address at the right time and to the right place. Agreement may have been made to fit the goods at the time of delivery or to take old products away and dispose of them.
- *Warranty* – An agreement between the buyer and seller. It identifies situations where the seller of the product will deal with any problems or issues associated with the product without any cost.
- *Customer care* – Selling is one part of the relationship with the customer. After the sale, the seller might phone the customer to ensure that they are happy with the purchasing processes that they went through. They would try to ensure that the customer felt that they had made the right decision.
- *Satisfaction* – Alongside customer care, it might be possible to find out if the customer is satisfied with the products.
- *Follow up* – As part of a follow-up process, the seller may offer other or complementary goods or services that the buyer might require. Following up helps to build relationships with the purchaser through what is known as **relationship marketing**. This helps the buyer to feel confident in the services provided by the seller.
- *Feedback* – After-sales service enables the seller to gain valuable feedback that can be used to inform and possibly change or improve services in the future.

Did you know...

An after-sales service policy for Developments, a building firm, is simply to 'Call us'.

Handling complaints

Customers are an important source of ideas and information that can lead to product improvement. Complaints help businesses to find solutions. Complaints need to be handled sensitively and quickly. This might mean replacing products or advising customers with any difficulties that they may have when using products. The worst thing to happen for a company is for customers not to bother to complain and then simply to switch to other products or companies. By complaining, customers can get customer satisfaction.

Task

Working in a group, try to think of products or services that you repeatedly purchase. List ten rules for sellers that would help them to develop patterns of repeat purchase among their customers.

Repeat sales

This is a sign of customer loyalty. It is also a sign that customers are happy with the products and services on offer, as well as the processes that they have been through when purchasing products and services. If the selling process is geared towards developing long-term relationships with customers, then repeat sales will be generated. It will mean that they trust the organisation, like the communication with them and that their complaints, if any have been made, have been dealt with efficiently.

Up-selling

Individuals and organisations constantly want to experience better-quality products and services. Up-selling involves going back to customers who have already made a purchase. The sales people then try to encourage the purchaser to buy similar but more expensive items. These are usually upgrades or add-ons and help the seller to make the most of the selling opportunities to the buyer. For example, when a customer buys a car, the showroom will attempt to sell them a range of extras such as mats, winter packages and other accessories. They may also through the selling process encourage them to buy a model with a higher specification.

Recording information

To support the selling function, a **database** is usually kept. Much of this information will have been obtained from the transaction. Information from customers will be at the centre of the database. This might include details such as customer name, address, date of sale, details of items ordered, prices and discounts, and terms and conditions for the transaction. Information will have been recorded from:

- Sales, when and where they have taken place.
- Payments by customers.
- Customer information submitted by customers.

Liaison with other departments

As and where selling takes place, a whole series of functions across a business organisation need to work together. Although selling is the part of the organisation that meets the customer, the whole of an organisation should be geared towards serving their many needs. For example, the products may go to a department that takes the products out of the warehouse for customer collection. Products might have to be despatched to the customer. The accounts department may have to set up arrangements for a customer to be provided with credit facilities. A service department may need to set up a whole series of dates for service or for installation.

Make the grade

D2 Remember to use this for D2. Perhaps the best way to do this is to look at the skills that you have observed in two contrasting situations. Remember that in evaluating you are using judgements. Looking at all of the skills and processes necessary for sales to take place, identify where, how and in what circumstances skills and processes have been effective in meeting customer needs. Remember that to evaluate work you must give a judgement that is supported by additional facts or research data.

Key words

Colloquialisms – A casual form of local expression not found in formal conversation.

Database – A collection of data that are organised so that they can be easily accessed and updated.

Direct mail – Mail posted directly to prospective customers, designed to promote goods or services.

Merchandising – The organisation of displays and products in a way that is convenient for the consumer and most likely to prompt them to make a purchase.

Point-of-sale displays – Specialist displays, usually close to the point of sale, that identify other products that a customer may want to purchase.

Probing questions – Questions that are designed to explore in order to find out more about the needs of customers.

Prospect – Potential buyer.

Relationship marketing – Activities designed to build trust and develop long-term relationships between the buyer and the seller.

Unique selling points (USPs) – Very specific features of a product or service that make it different from those of their competitors.

Assignment

You must be able to demonstrate personal selling skills and processes.

Working in a sales environment

This activity should be undertaken as a simulated retail-based training exercise. Put yourself in a position in which you are working within a professional sales environment.

1. Imagine that you are advising a new member of staff on the different techniques required to make personal sales. Write a list itemising five important things that they must remember to do when trying to make personal sales. **(P2)**
2. Selling involves having some specialised knowledge, particularly about the product and also about the legislation relevant to the selling process. Create a poster that you would put up on the wall of an office that would help to explain what knowledge and skills are required to be used when making personal sales. **(P3)**
3. Prepare the following to send in an email. If you were to construct a professional training environment, explain what it would be like and what you would include within it. Describe how you would expect staff to be dressed and explain what you would expect them to do in order to prepare to make sales. **(P4)**
4. Work in groups of two for this activity. The activity needs some preparation. One person should act as a seller and one a buyer. The buyer wants to buy some jewellery for their partner. In front of the class, the seller and buyer

▶

should meet and go through a simulated selling process. If necessary, it may be possible to video record this so that when it is played back the strengths and weaknesses of the seller's skills could be discussed. Having made a sale to one learner this activity should then be repeated in different groups. **(P5)**

5. Make a list of the skills and processes required for selling in the following situations:
   - a bookshop
   - a jewellery store
   - over the phone from a call centre
   - at a car showroom
   - at an estate agent's
   - in a pharmacy. **(M2)**
6. Create a short report. Undertake a reflective evaluation of your own sales skills. Identify where you think your selling skills are strong and where they are weak. In situations where you feel that they might be weak, identify how you would try to improve those skills. Having worked upon these skills, undertake another sales simulation to see if your skills have improved. **(D1)**
7. Make a list. Undertake an audit that enables you to evaluate what are good sales skills and processes and what are poor sales skills and processes. Think about your experiences as a customer. Describe situations where you feel that the sales skills of a sales person have been weak. You must identify at least two situations. Finally, construct a form that would enable customers to provide feedback on your selling skills. **(D2)**

To achieve a pass grade you need to:	To achieve a merit grade you need to:	To achieve a distinction you need to:
P2 identify the techniques used when making personal sales	**M2** compare the selling skills and processes used in different situations	**D1** demonstrate the confident use of personal selling skills when making sales
P3 explain the knowledge and skills used when making personal sales		**D2** evaluate the preparation, skills and processes used in different situations
P4 prepare to make personal sales		
P5 use selling skills and processes to make sales		

Unit 11

Customer relations in business

Chapter 22
Customer service provided in business

What are you finding out?

Businesses serve their customers every day but do they provide good customer service; in other words, do they meet the needs and expectations of their customers? Customers can be internal or external and each has individual needs and expectations; for example, some customers need information and advice, others simply want a transaction to be processed quickly and efficiently. Meeting the needs of customers is essential to the survival of a business; meeting and exceeding customer expectations is essential to the long-term success of a business and to increasing profits.

This chapter will help you to:

- Define customer service and customer satisfaction.
- Describe different types of customers and their needs and expectations.
- Explain how different customers' needs and expectations can differ.
- Outline the benefits of good customer service.

Customer service

Customer service takes place every time a business comes into contact with its customers, for example when a sale takes place, when information, advice and assistance are given, and when a complaint is handled. Customer service can take place face to face, over the telephone, via email or the internet or in writing. Good customer service means putting the needs of the customer first and ensuring that their experience of the business is a good one. If customers receive good customer service, then they will return and the business will have loyal customers. However, if customers experience poor customer service, they will take their custom elsewhere.

Task

Think of a time when you experienced poor customer service. Make notes on what made the customer service you received poor and how you felt about the business/organisation.

Customer satisfaction

Customer satisfaction measures how well a business or organisation has met the expectations of its customers. Individual customers have many different needs and expectations and will judge how well their expectations have been met using different criteria. For example, customers purchasing from Amazon.com may be concerned about the price and the speed of delivery of their goods, whereas customer satisfaction for customers shopping in Waterstone's shops may be centred on the layout of the store and the information available from staff.

Different types of customers

The customers of a business or organisation can be internal or external customers. **Internal customers** are people within the organisation; for example, within a school, teachers will be internal customers of the reprographics team when they make a request for photocopying. **External customers** are people outside the organisation; for example, parents are external customers of a school.

Did you know...

In 2009, Play.com came top of a customer-satisfaction index for retailers. The online retailer scored 87 out of 100 in a national customer-satisfaction index for the retail sector, closely followed by Amazon.co.uk with a score of 85 and iTunes with 82.

Source: Brand Republic

Internal customers

The diagram below shows the different internal customers a receptionist at a large doctors' practice would have to deal with. In a large practice, nurses, health visitors and midwives all see patients and rely on the receptionists to pass on notes and messages. Even community nurses who work from the practice must work with the receptionists to organise their visits and take messages.

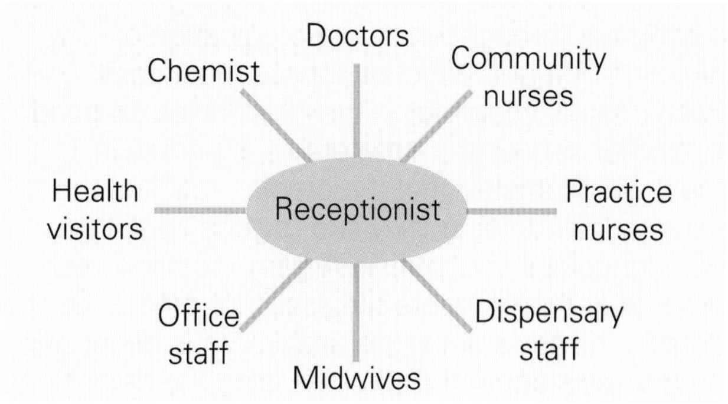

Figure 22.1 A receptionist's internal customers

The main external customers for the receptionist would be the patients but receptionists also deal with suppliers and representatives from drugs companies who call in to see the doctors.

Task

Copy and complete the table below to show the internal and external customers for the headteacher at your school:

Internal customers	External customers
Teachers	Students

Within a business, internal customers may work alongside one another, for example the chefs and front-of-house staff in a restaurant; or they may be on different levels, for example the store manager and assistants in a large supermarket. Whether people are colleagues or managers and **subordinates**, they are all dependent on each other, and for the organisation to run smoothly they must provide good customer service to one another.

For a product or service to be provided to an external customer, there is often a chain of internal customers through which the preparation or handling of that product or service must pass. Each internal customer in the chain relies on good customer service from the previous person in the chain to ensure that the product reaches the external customer quickly and in good condition. For example, if you shop in Argos, you hand your order in at the till where the assistant processes the details, the assistant in the storeroom is dependent on the assistant at the till processing the details correctly in order to find the correct goods, and the assistant at the counter is dependent upon the assistant in the storeroom to bring the goods out quickly and in good condition so that they can be passed to you – the external customer.

The Devonshire Arms

The Devonshire Arms is a 17th-century village pub and tea room serving good-quality, home-cooked food and fine ales. It is situated in the beautiful Derbyshire village of Hartington which is very popular with tourists, especially walkers. The landlord and landlady, David and Dale, enjoy a brisk trade serving tourists and local customers.

On a normal weekend, there are two bar staff plus the head chef, two people preparing snacks, two waitresses and one person washing dishes working in/from the kitchen; this includes David and Dale. At the Devonshire Arms, it is essential that the staff work as a team to ensure that the food and drinks that the customers order arrive at their tables in a timely and appropriate way. Communication between staff members, therefore, is extremely important and David and Dale insist that orders for food are clearly communicated to the kitchen staff.

1. Who are the internal customers of the head chef at the Devonshire Arms?
2. Draw the chain of internal customers who would be involved in serving a meal to an external customer.
3. To what extent is good customer service between internal customers important to the Devonshire Arms in meeting the needs of its external customers?

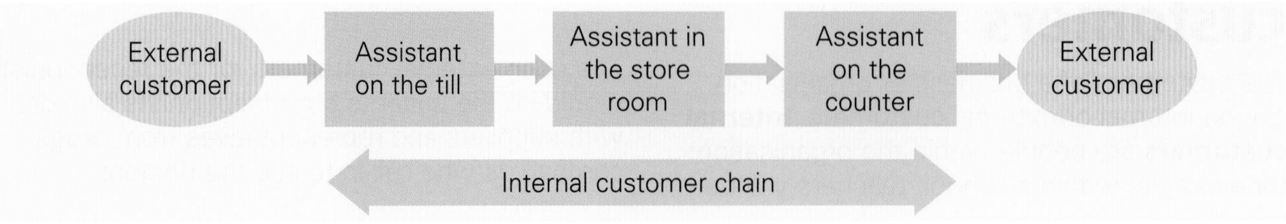

Figure 22.2 The internal customer chain in an Argos store

Fieldwork

Arrange to visit a local business to interview a member of staff. At the interview, you need to find out who the member of staff regards as their internal customers and what customer service to the internal customers involves. Make sure that you prepare your questions before you go so that you get the most out of your visit.

External customers

External customers may be members of the public, other businesses or both. For example, a business selling double glazing would sell products to householders and to businesses.

There are also many different types of external customers, each with different needs. These include:

- existing customers
- new customers
- individuals
- groups
- families
- business people
- different age groups
- different cultures
- customers with special needs, such as non-English-speaking customers and customers with visual, hearing or mobility impairments.

Existing customers

Existing customers know the business and expect the products/services they purchase to continue to be available with a good standard of customer service. Many businesses have loyal customers, but even loyal customers will take their custom elsewhere if they experience poor customer service. Businesses will often make sure that their existing customers are looked after very well as they rely on them for **repeat business** and, if existing customers are happy with the business, they will recommend it to new customers, which will then help the business to expand.

New customers

All businesses need new customers. Many businesses spend a great deal on marketing and promotion to attract new customers but, if the customers then experience poor customer service, they will not return. New customers need to be made to feel welcome by a business and the product/service provided must meet their expectations.

Did you know...

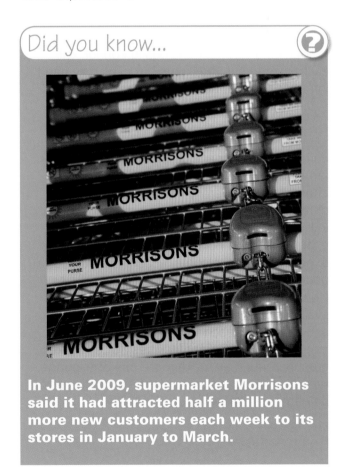

In June 2009, supermarket Morrisons said it had attracted half a million more new customers each week to its stores in January to March.

Individuals

Many businesses deal with customers on a one-to-one basis. For some businesses, this means that they can give these customers their full attention and ensure that their needs are met. For example, a business that supplies computers to order would be able to find out the customer's exact requirements and create a machine to meet their needs.

Groups

A group is a number of people who want to make the same or similar purchase. It is more difficult to meet the needs of groups as the needs of each individual must be met while dealing with the group as a whole. For example, a group of friends dining out in a restaurant will each order different food, but the food for the whole group must be served at the same time. Similarly, a group of tourists on an open-top bus in London will each want to see the sights but each may need information in a different language.

Families

Families can be made up of a range of different family members from babies to grandparents. Therefore, each family member will have different needs, but as a family group they will expect a consistent service. For example, a family taking a holiday abroad in a hotel all expect a warm welcome, accommodation of a good standard, good food and good facilities. However, different food would need to be available to meet the needs of young children and adults and each family member would expect to use different facilities; for example, grandparents may make more use of a lounge, whereas young children might expect there to be games and a play area available.

Business people

Business people have similar expectations to any other customers in terms of the quality of customer service they receive. However, they have additional needs; for example, most mainline train services have recognised that many of their customers are business people who like to work during their journey and have provided plug sockets for mobile phones and laptops. Similarly, many hotels now provide free Wi-Fi internet access in all rooms, allowing business people to keep in touch with the office and home.

Different age groups

Many businesses and organisations provide products and services for people of all ages. Different age groups can be:

- under fives
- young children
- teenagers (13–19)
- young adults (18–21)
- adults
- middle aged
- senior citizens.

People in different age groups have different needs and usually require different types of services. A leisure centre, for example, would offer a variety of activities to suit different age groups such as a crèche for the under fives, activity days for young children, holiday clubs for teenagers, coaching sessions for adults and gentle exercise classes for senior citizens.

Different cultures

Culture relates to the traditions, values, opinions and behaviours that people from different regions or countries have as a group; it refers to a way of life. For example, part of the British culture is to have a roast Sunday lunch, to drink tea and to eat fish and chips. People from different cultures have widely differing needs, especially for food. As Britain is now a multicultural society, many new businesses have emerged to meet the needs of people from different cultures, such as halal and kosher butchers.

Did you know...

In Portugal, you should never yawn or stretch in public – it's considered extremely rude. Meetings in China should begin with a handshake and a subtle nod of the head; not too vigorous, though, as this is considered aggressive. You should not stand with your hands in your pockets in Poland; it's considered disrespectful.

Source: Condé Nast Traveller

Thomson

Thomson aims to meet the needs of many different types of external customers. It has a wide range of holidays available tailored to meet the needs of specific market segments (groups of people with similar characteristics or who share similar interests) and each has its own brochure. Some of those currently available are:

- Thomson Family Collection – for families
- Thomson Platinum – for those who want luxury holidays in 4- and 5-star hotels
- Thomson Gold – for couples
- Thomson A La Carte – for those who require high standards of service, excellent facilities and fine food
- Thomson Villas with Pools – for families or groups who want their own space
- Thomson Faraway Shores – for those who want to travel further afield.

The hotels in each brochure (except the Villas brochure) are carefully selected to ensure they meet the needs of the customers. For example, those featured in the Thomson Family Collection brochure each have facilities and activities for children and crèches, whilst those in the A La Carte brochure are all 4- or 5-star offering the finest cuisine.

Source: www.thomson.co.uk/

1. State three different types of external customer that Thomson aims to provide services for.
2. Describe the needs that each of these types of customer might have when on holiday.
3. Discuss the reasons why Thomson offers such a wide range of holidays.

Make the grade

P1 **M1** Remember this for P1 and M1. For a given business or a business of your choice, you must describe three different types of customers, their needs and expectations and how those needs and expectations can differ.

Customers with special needs

All customers have individual needs but some customers have very specific needs that businesses and organisations need to meet. By law, under the Disability Discrimination Act (DDA) 1995, businesses and organisations must make 'reasonable adjustments' to allow disabled people to have access to goods, facilities and services, education and public transport. For example, many retailers have adapted their premises to ensure that there is access for wheelchair users and have installed induction-loop systems for customers with hearing impairments. Government departments have led the way in providing information leaflets in a number of different languages and in formats for the visually impaired such as large print and audio.

Customers' needs and expectations

All customers share the need to be listened to and made to feel welcome and want to be considered of importance to the business. However, customers have different needs at different times and therefore a variety of customer service situations can arise. These include:

- providing information
- giving advice
- providing assistance
- dealing with problems
- dealing with special needs
- ensuring health and safety and security
- meeting organisational targets.

Providing information

Customers often require a wide range of information, therefore employees need to be very knowledgeable about the business or organisation and its products and services. If employees cannot provide this information, then a sale and a valuable customer may be lost.

Employees may be asked to provide information to customers (for example, a rail passenger asking for times of trains), or to colleagues (for example, a marketing assistant needing to know times when a conference room would be available). In each situation, it is important to ensure that the information given is accurate and reliable. In addition, customers expect that information will be given to them in a courteous manner and that the person giving the information will provide all essential information.

Giving advice

There are many occasions when customers want advice. They may want help in making a decision, for example, to choose a bottle of wine to complement their meal or to select software to perform a certain function; or they may seek guidance, for example asking a resort representative about the best sights to see or the best route to walk into the city centre. It is essential that employees can speak knowledgeably about their products and services as poor advice can lead to dissatisfied customers. As with giving information, customers expect that advice will be given to them in a courteous manner.

Providing assistance

This is the most common form of customer-service situation. All employees provide assistance, whether it is to their colleagues within the business or to external customers. Most employees do this as a matter of routine, others because it is their job. For example, in the workplace, you would expect somebody to hold the door open for a colleague carrying a heavy load – that is routine – whereas a receptionist in a business would be called upon to give assistance as part of their job.

In retailing, part of a shop assistant's job is to help customers make a purchase. Although this includes offering information and advice to the customer, it also involves providing assistance to process the transaction and provide packaging for the goods purchased.

Customers may need more assistance in some situations than in others. For example, a family going on holiday abroad may need assistance with pushchairs at an airport, with warming baby food on an aeroplane and with their luggage at their destination.

The way in which assistance is given is very important. Customers must not be made to feel a nuisance. The best customer service is provided when customers' needs for assistance are anticipated and customers' expectations are exceeded; for example, staff at the Rainforest Café in London immediately provide high chairs at tables when they see a family with young children are about to be seated.

Dealing with problems

Rarely does everything run smoothly. Problems can arise that are beyond the control of the business, for example a problem on a railway line that prevents the trains from moving. But often problems are within the control of the business, for example dirty facilities at a roadside services. Sometimes problems can be of a customer's own making, for example a passenger at an airport losing their passport. In each situation, the way in which the problem is dealt with is all-important. Customers may be worried, upset or angry and need the person dealing with the problem to be calm, able to listen and able to provide information and advice in a reassuring manner.

Customers expect problems to be dealt with and not ignored. If problems are ignored, customers do not feel valued and are unlikely to continue to use the business in the future. Above all, if the problem is within the control of the business, customers expect a sincere apology and, in many cases, some form of compensation. If a customer purchased a food item that was later found to have deteriorated but was within its use-by date, for example, that customer would expect a replacement but may also receive additional goods as compensation for the inconvenience.

Did you know...

70% of complaining customers will use a business again if the complaint is resolved to their satisfaction.
95% of complaining customers will use a business again if the complaint is resolved instantly.

Source: Lee Resource Ltd

Dealing with special needs

Some customers have very specific needs and businesses need to make sure that they can meet these needs if they want to keep valued customers. The Disability Discrimination Act requires organisations supplying goods or services to make 'reasonable adjustments' to ensure that a person with a disability can gain access to the service or provision, but businesses can often do more to make people with disabilities feel more welcome. For example, some hotels have rooms on the ground floor especially fitted out for wheelchair users which include wheel-in showers, handrails and light switches and sockets at an appropriate level; and the hotel may provide additional assistance at reception.

All customers expect to be able to communicate with a business, therefore businesses need to provide extra services to those with visual and hearing impairment and to non-English-speaking customers. Marks & Spencer have taken steps to ensure that their website is accessible to the disabled, the visually impaired and those with motor deficiencies and cognitive disabilities. Some of the things they have done include the use of clear, simple language that is easy to understand, avoiding the use of blinking or flickering elements, careful use of text and background colours, the use of clear, legible fonts and non-text alternatives to ensure those using screen-readers can access the website.

Ensuring health, safety and security

Customers expect to be safe when using a business and its services and, by law, businesses must ensure that customers on their premises are safe. However, there are some businesses and organisations that need to provide extra services to ensure the health and safety of their customers. If you went swimming, for example, you would expect the swimming pool to have a lifeguard. PGL, which runs activity holidays for children, must ensure that their instructors are properly trained so that they can ensure the safety of children taking part in activities such as rock climbing and archery.

Internal customers must also feel safe and secure. The Health and Safety at Work Act 1974 states that an employer has a duty to ensure that the workplace is safe and that there are no risks to health.

Some businesses also need to pay particular attention to the security of their customers. For example, at airports all baggage is checked and labelled and body scanners are used to ensure that passengers are not carrying anything that may cause harm. Customers expect to feel secure when they travel.

Meeting organisational targets

Employees often have targets to meet that are given to them by the managers of the organisation. Therefore, as internal customers, employees will make requests of their colleagues to help them fulfil these targets and they expect cooperation, as all employees should be working towards the same objectives and goals. If one internal customer in the chain fails to meet expectations, then other members of the internal customer chain may be unable to complete tasks and meet their own targets.

Make the grade

P1 **M1** Remember this for P1 and M1. For a given business or a business of your choice, you must describe three different types of customers, their needs and expectations and how those needs and expectations can differ.

Fieldwork

Arrange to visit a local business and find out:

1. How many different types of customers they have (don't forget internal customers).
2. What the business considers to be the needs and expectations of its different customers.

The benefits of good customer service

There are a great many benefits in providing good customer service, not only to the customer but to the organisation and its employees as well.

Benefits to the customer

If a business is providing good customer service, then it is meeting the needs and expectations of its customers and providing them with a good experience. This will result in satisfied customers who will feel confident in dealing with the business in the future, as they will feel that they are able to rely on the service provided. Many people use businesses whose name they recognise because they know exactly what to expect when they use that business and, as businesses know this, they spend a lot of money creating and maintaining a brand image. McDonald's is a good example, as customers of McDonald's know the type of food they will be served, the layout and standards to expect in the restaurant and the speed of service they can expect.

Benefits to the organisation

The main benefits to the organisation of good customer service are shown in the diagram below but, ultimately, the very survival of the business depends on its level of customer service. If customers experience poor customer service, rather than complain, many will choose not to use that business again. Only a small percentage of customers complain about poor service so, very often, a business does not have the opportunity to put things right.

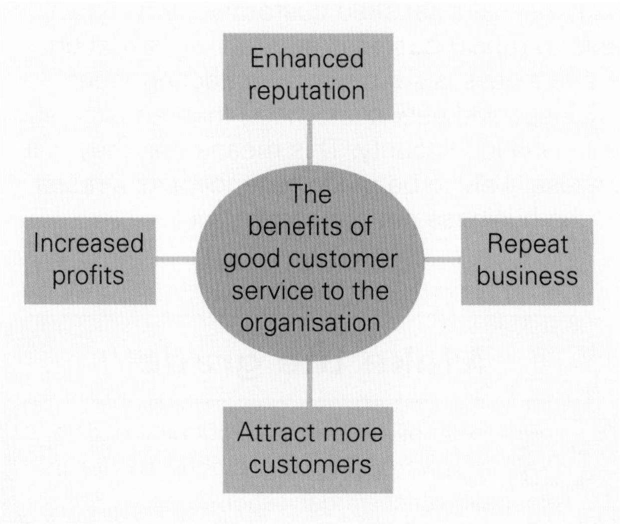

Figure 22.3 Benefits of good customer service

Businesses can become well known for their level of customer service, whether it is good or bad. If a business consistently offers good or excellent customer service, then this enhances its reputation. For example, Marks & Spencer has a reputation for providing excellent customer service and its enhanced reputation attracts customers to its stores. The more customers a business can attract, the more sales it will make, resulting in higher profits.

It can take a business a number of years to build a good reputation for its level of customer service, and the main part of this process depends on the customers themselves. If customers experience good customer service, they will use the business again and provide repeat business. This in itself can ensure the survival of the business, but each satisfied customer is worth a great deal to a business because satisfied customers recommend businesses to their friends, who then become new customers. This is known as word-of-mouth promotion.

Unfortunately, if a business provides poor customer service, then word of mouth can be very damaging as dissatisfied customers will also tell others about their poor experience.

Repeat business is very important. If customers use a business regularly they become loyal to that business and stop considering alternatives. A business therefore builds its customer base and can target its loyal customers with special deals and promotions and additional products. Loyal customers are also the best form of advertising as they recommend the business to others. High levels of recommendations lead to the business growing and making more sales, which in turn lead to higher profits.

All businesses want to attract more customers, and many spend millions of pounds on promotional activities to do just that. However, providing good customer service can be far more effective in attracting new customers. If existing customers are happy with the service provided, they become loyal customers and recommend the business to others. This is also far more cost effective to a business than 'buying' new customers through advertising and promotion.

The aim of many businesses is to increase profits. Good customer service leads to an enhanced reputation, loyal customers and the growth of the business through attracting new customers via word of mouth. This leads to increased sales, which in turn lead to increased profits. To many businesses, the high standard of their customer service has become a **competitive advantage:** in other words, something that attracts customers to that business and away from its competitors.

Task

The chart below shows the reasons why businesses lose their customers:

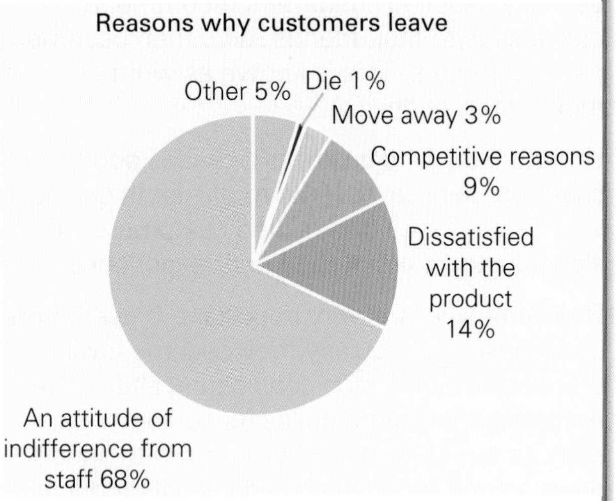

Figure 22.4 Why businesses lose their customers

Source: Michael Leboeuf, *How To Keep Customers for Life* (2000)

Arrange to interview 20 teachers in your school to find out if there are businesses that they will not use any more and, using the same categories as in the chart, the reasons why they have left those businesses. Graph your results and find out if the percentages in each category closely match those above.

Benefits to the employee

Employees benefit greatly from providing good customer service to external customers as they then feel that they are doing a good job and experience job satisfaction. This means that employees enjoy their work and all that it involves and will do their jobs well. It is also very motivational for employees to receive positive feedback from customers.

However, providing good customer service to internal customers is as important to a business as providing good customer service to external customers. If good customer service exists internally, employees will benefit from a pleasant working environment and will be happier in their jobs. This, in turn, has benefits for the business because if employees are happy at work, they will be less likely to leave. This means that the business does not need to keep recruiting and training staff, which is a costly process.

If colleagues are friendly and supportive to one another, carrying out the job becomes more enjoyable. This leads to happy staff and if staff are happy, external customers notice this and feel more comfortable in their dealings with a business. This again can benefit the business as it will have satisfied customers, which can lead to repeat business and recommendations. If a business is successfully attracting repeat business and new customers, then employees will have job security. This means that they will be less likely to be made redundant as a result of the business not performing well.

Make the grade

P2 Remember this for P2. You must outline the benefits of good customer service in a selected business/organisation.

Research and investigate

Use the internet to find the annual reports for companies that are well known to you. What indication is there in the reports that the business makes customer service a priority?

Discussion...

If a business does not meet the expectations of its customers, it will not be successful. To what extent do you think this is true?

John Lewis

The John Lewis Partnership is one of the UK's top-ten retail businesses, with 27 John Lewis department stores and 201 Waitrose supermarkets. It is also the country's largest employee cooperative, with 69,000 employees. At John Lewis, employees (partners) share the ownership of the business and the profits and share in the decision making. The business believes that the commitment of its staff is a unique source of competitive advantage which has contributed to 80 years of profitable growth and a reputation among customers that is second to none in the UK retail industry. It was the vision of its founder, John Spedan Lewis, to create a company dedicated to the happiness of the staff through their worthwhile, secure and satisfying employment in a successful business.

Source: John Lewis Partnership Annual Report 2009

1. John Lewis prides itself in providing good customer service. Explain the benefits of John Lewis's approach to:
   a its internal customers
   b its external customers
   c the business itself.

Key words

Competitive advantage – A position that a business aims to achieve over its competitors, through the quality or range of its products, promotion or higher standards of customer service.

Customer service – All aspects of contact between a business and its customers.

Customer satisfaction – Measures how well a business or organisation has met the expectations of its customers.

Internal customers – People within the organisation who work together and supply each other with goods and services.

External customers – People outside the organisation who buy goods or services or who use the services of the organisation.

Repeat business – Sales to existing and loyal customers of a business.

Subordinates – The workers that a line manager is responsible for.

Assignment

You must demonstrate that you are knowledgeable about customer service.

Customer relations in business

You have been invited to attend an interview for the position of Customer Service Assistant at Fantastic Land (a theme park). As part of the interview, you must make a presentation to the panel to demonstrate that you know the different types of customer that you might encounter and their needs and that you are aware of the importance of good customer service.

Produce a presentation for your interview that includes:

1. A description of at least three different types of customer that you might encounter at Fantastic Land (you must include internal and external customers). **(P1)**
2. A description of the needs and expectations of the different types of customer you have described in 1. **(P1)**
3. An explanation of how the needs and expectations of these customers will differ. **(M1)**
4. An outline of the benefits of good customer service to: a) the customers of Fantastic Land b) Fantastic Land as an organisation c) yourself, as an employee of Fantastic Land. **(P2)**

To achieve a pass grade you need to:	To achieve a merit grade you need to:	To achieve a distinction you need to:
P1 describe three different types of customers and their needs and expectations	**M1** explain how different customers' needs and expectations can differ	
P2 benefits of good customer service in a selected organisation		

Chapter 23 Developing skills in customer service

What are you finding out?

Providing good customer service requires you to have good customer service skills. You need to know how to present yourself, what interpersonal skills you will need and how to communicate clearly and confidently with customers. Different types of customers have different needs and expectations and you need to know how to demonstrate good customer service in a range of situations with different types of customers. You will find out what is required to provide good customer service in different situations, for example dealing with a complaint or providing assistance.

This chapter will help you to:

- Understand the requirements for good presentation, communication and interpersonal skills in different customer service situations.
- Display confident presentation, communication and interpersonal skills when demonstrating customer service in a range of customer service situations.
- Anticipate and meet the needs of different customers.

Skills in customer service

When at work, all employees represent the business or organisation they work for and so must ensure that they present themselves to customers in an appropriate manner. This means that care must be taken over personal presentation and the way in which interactions with customers take place, and this requires good interpersonal and communication skills. As much care and attention to detail should be taken when dealing with internal customers as is taken when dealing with external customers.

Workers in different jobs are expected to dress differently

Presentation skills

The way you present yourself and your work area affects how the customer views you and the business or organisation you work for. If you look as if you don't care about your appearance or the equipment you use in your job, then customers will think that you do not care about the service you are providing and do not value them. They will not feel secure and may think that you cannot do your job properly as you do not have an air of efficiency about you.

Personal presentation

First impressions count and customers will judge you and the business you work for by your appearance. The way you look will vary according to the industry you work in. For example, you would not expect a pilot and a construction worker to wear the same clothes or pay the same amount of attention to the neatness of their clothing, but the way you look and present yourself must be appropriate to the environment you work in.

In many businesses, employees are part of the product/service. For example, in a restaurant the service is as important as the food; in a hotel the service from the hotel staff is as important as the quality of the accommodation. Therefore, for employees in these industries, good personal presentation skills are essential.

The key areas of personal presentation that you must pay attention to are:

- personal hygiene
- uniform/dress
- hair
- make-up
- jewellery.

Customers can be put off by staff with poor personal hygiene, especially in service industries. Imagine being served a cup of tea in a café by an assistant with poor personal hygiene – you probably would not bother to order a piece of cake! If you work in a situation in which you are in close contact with customers, you need to ensure that you shower regularly, keep your nails clean and neat and your hands clean. Even if you are not in close contact with external customers, you will probably work closely with colleagues (internal customers) and therefore great care must still be taken over personal hygiene.

The way in which you dress must be appropriate to the business you work for and your role in that business. If you work with external customers every day, then you will be expected to wear clean, neatly pressed clothes with clean and polished shoes that are in a good state of repair, and generally be of smart appearance. Many businesses will provide you with guidelines on the standards that they expect; for example, some businesses may require men to wear ties and women to wear skirts rather than trousers.

Many businesses and organisations provide a uniform, which has a number of benefits to the organisation itself and to the individuals wearing the uniform. These include:

- Presenting a professional image.
- Allowing staff to be easily recognised.
- Providing a sense of belonging (being part of a team).
- Being functional and providing protection.
- Providing staff with clothes for work.

In some organisations, wearing a uniform is essential. You would not expect nurses, for example, to all be wearing different clothing as this would make patients feel insecure and doubt their professionalism.

If you are provided with a uniform, you still have the responsibility of looking after it, ensuring that it is washed and pressed regularly, and wearing it correctly so that you look smart. The box below shows the dress standard guidelines for staff working at The Trafford Centre in Manchester.

Your clothing forms only part of your personal presentation; you also need to ensure that your hair is clean and tidy and, if appropriate, tied back. Staff working at The Trafford Centre must have their hair tied back, with either plain hair accessories or the scrunchies provided, at all times if it is below shoulder length, and their hair should be of a natural colour and style in keeping with The Trafford Centre dress standards.

You must also ensure that you follow your employer's guidelines on the amount of jewellery you may wear. Some businesses or organisations will allow you to wear only a wedding ring for reasons of hygiene or safety. For example, staff

Dress standards at The Trafford Centre

Your appearance is an essential part of the customer service that every team member at The Trafford Centre will be expected to deliver. First impressions are the lasting impressions that our customers will remember.

You have been provided with a uniform that is your responsibility, and you should follow these dress standard guidelines at all times. Only the uniform provided should be worn and in the correct manner as follows:

- Jackets – These should be worn buttoned up at all times when you are working in public areas.
- Waistcoats – These should be worn buttoned up at all times.
- Footwear – Only the footwear provided, or suitable authorised alternatives, should be worn. Shoes should be clean and polished at all times.

Ladies

- Blouses – The cowl neck feature should be fastened at all times.
- Tights/stockings – Flesh-coloured tights or stockings should be worn with a skirt, and plain black socks with trousers.
- Skirts – The length of skirts may not be altered.

Gentlemen

- Shirts – Shirts should be buttoned up fully at all times. Sleeves should not be rolled up.
- Socks – Socks should be worn at all times and be plain and black in colour.
- Ties – Should be worn at all times.

Source: www.traffordcentre.co.uk

working for the NHS in Scotland should not wear hand or wrist jewellery (other than a plain wedding ring or one other plain band) when providing patient care, and employees of the Hampshire Police must not wear jewellery if it is likely to place the wearer or any other person at risk of harm (for example, necklaces or hoop earrings could be pulled by an assailant; large rings could scratch another person).

Make-up is another part of your personal presentation that you must take great care over. Again, many businesses set their own guidelines but, if they do not, you must make sure that make-up is natural-looking and that you do not wear too much.

Fieldwork

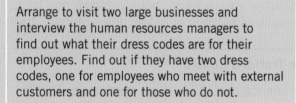

Arrange to visit two large businesses and interview the human resources managers to find out what their dress codes are for their employees. Find out if they have two dress codes, one for employees who meet with external customers and one for those who do not.

The impression you give to customers and colleagues in the workplace is not only formed from your appearance, it is also affected by your **body language**. Body language describes how we communicate with others using our posture, facial expressions and gestures. Customers can be easily offended if you do not greet them with a smile or you turn your back on them, so it is important to understand the types of posture, gestures and facial expressions that are appropriate in customer-service situations.

There are two kinds of body language – open and closed. Open body language is when your posture, gestures and expressions show that you are friendly and interested in what a customer has to say. This includes smiling and making eye contact, facing the customer and using open palm gestures. Closed body language is when your posture, gestures and expressions show that you are unfriendly and uninterested – for example, having your arms folded and not making eye contact.

Using open body language will make customers feel valued, listened to and understood. Smiling and greeting customers confidently are essential in putting them at their ease. Closed body language, however, can make customers feel as though they are an inconvenience. How have you felt when a shop assistant at a cash desk has looked unfriendly and failed to make eye contact?

Presentation of your work area

Have you ever been into a hotel or café to find it very cluttered and dusty? This can be very off-putting and does not give customers confidence that the staff are interested in what they are doing or in them. The presentation of your work area and the equipment you use is therefore very important. There is a saying in retail that 'retail is detail' and this refers to the general cleanliness, housekeeping and attention to detail of the merchandise in a store. If you walk into a shop that is well lit, tidy and clean, and has the merchandise displayed in an orderly and attractive way, you are far more likely to make a purchase than if the store is dull, untidy and dusty. The presentation of your work area therefore says a great deal about your attitude to customer service.

The same thing applies to any equipment you use. Suppose you served tea and scones to a family in a café and the tray you used had not been wiped clean. This would suggest that you did not care about your job or the customers and this might result in the business losing those customers.

Interpersonal skills

You will need a wide range of **interpersonal skills** to be able to provide good customer service. You have to ensure that your behaviour and attitude are appropriate to the customer service situation, that you create a good first impression and are courteous, concerned, interested and thoughtful as the situation demands. All types of customers in all types of situations will expect you to show them respect and be efficient in carrying out your duties.

Behaviour and attitude

Your behaviour and attitude towards customers matter a great deal. You represent the business you work for and if you behave inappropriately, customers will form a poor opinion of you and the business you work for.

If you walked up to the counter in a shop and the staff all stood talking to one another rather than serving you, you would have every right to feel annoyed. Similarly, if staff who served you in a café were chewing gum rather than talking to you, you might also feel that you were not a valued customer. Both of these examples show inappropriate behaviour by staff and yet many of us have experienced similar situations. It is therefore important that you show customers that you are interested in them and want to serve them. You can do this by:

- Greeting a customer confidently, with a smile, as soon as they present themselves.
- Listening carefully and asking appropriate questions.
- Responding immediately to their requests.
- Ignoring distractions such as the telephone or the actions of colleagues.
- Being friendly.

In all your dealings with customers, maintaining a positive attitude is essential. Customers will sense if you are just 'going through the motions' and are not really interested in them. You need to be polite at all times and show enthusiasm. A positive attitude and a smile are almost always rewarded with a happy and grateful customer.

Task

When you next go shopping for clothes, make a mental note of all the instances when you experienced positive behaviour and attitude from the staff who served you and all the instances when you experienced inappropriate behaviour and attitude from those who served you. When you return home, note down your experiences and what you have learned from them.

First impressions and greeting customers

First impressions are lasting impressions, so you do not want a customer's first impression of you to be a negative one. If it is, you may not get a second chance as many customers will go to a competing business the next time around, and so a customer will be lost to the business you work for. If you greet a customer confidently, with a smile on your face, and you have taken care with your personal presentation, then you will make a good first impression.

At the Devonshire Arms in Hartington, an essential part of training new staff is to show them how to greet customers. The landlord and landlady insist that their staff say a confident 'Hello' to customers as they approach the bar. This makes customers feel welcome and comfortable.

Did you know...

It takes 12 positive service incidents to make up for one negative incident.

Source: Lee Resource Inc

Courtesy and confidence

It is true to say that 'good manners cost nothing' but being **courteous** also has rewards. If you remember to be polite when you speak to customers and always say please and thank you, then, very often, customers will be courteous to you and will be pleased with the level of customer service they have received.

You must also speak confidently when you communicate with customers. Greet customers in a clear and confident manner as this makes them feel welcome and lets them know that you are available to assist them. You will develop the confidence to provide good customer service as you develop your customer-service skills and your knowledge of the business and its products or services.

Concern, interest and thoughtfulness

There are many different customer-service situations, from giving advice to dealing with problems, and in each situation you will need to be courteous, confident and careful to listen. However, each situation will require you to react in a slightly different way. For example, if a customer has a problem, you may show concern; if a customer wishes to describe their ideal holiday to you, then you should show interest; and if a customer has a particular need, then you should demonstrate thoughtfulness. It is the way in which you communicate with customers that will be remembered more than what you actually say, and so you must ensure that you convey the appropriate emotion.

Respect for customers

Customers are the people who pay your wages, as without them a business would not earn revenue (money from sales) and therefore would not be able to employ you. You must therefore show respect to each and every customer regardless of their attitude towards you. You can demonstrate respect for customers by making them feel valued. To do this, you must:

- Ensure that customers have your immediate and full attention.
- Greet customers and, if possible, use their names.
- Listen carefully to what customers have to say and react accordingly.
- Pay close attention to the way in which you present yourself and the area you work in.
- Ensure that, as far as is possible, you meet customers' needs and expectations.

Responding to different customer behaviours

Not every customer will be pleasant and polite or communicate their needs clearly and in an appropriate manner, so you need to be prepared for this. It is easy to deal with very pleasant customers as it is not difficult to respond in a polite manner yourself and make the customer feel valued. However, if customers are abrupt, then you must also remember to show those customers respect and try to meet their needs in a polite and courteous manner. You will often find that, by doing this, customers will respond in the same way, as you have made them feel valued.

Sometimes customers want to complain and can sometimes raise their voices. In situations such as these, you need to remain calm and listen to what the customer has to say. Quite often, a customer just wants somebody to listen and will then calm down. You just need to ensure that you are polite and courteous so that you do not make the situation worse or give the customer more cause for complaint. There will be occasions, though, when you are unable to deal with a customer complaint yourself and, on these occasions, you need to calmly explain that you will get another member of staff to deal with the complaint.

Some customers, especially senior citizens, want to talk to you for a long period of time, which may cause problems for other customers who may be waiting to be served. On these occasions, you need to be very polite but also very confident in bringing the conversation to a close with phrases such as, 'It has been lovely to meet you, enjoy the rest of your day,' or 'Thank you, I hope that we will see you again soon.'

Tact

In all customer service situations, you need to be **tactful**. This means that you must consider the feelings of your customers and try not to say anything that might offend or upset them. This is particularly important if a customer is returning goods that are defective or faulty, as you must not say anything to suggest that the customer may be at fault.

Being tactful also means that you need to pass on unwelcome news in a way that will cause the least amount of distress to a customer. For example, garage employees often need to inform customers that their cars need a lot of work

Legoland

Read the job advertisement for an Admissions and Guest Services Assistant at Legoland in Windsor and answer the questions that follow.

Admissions & Guest Services Assistant

The Admissions department are responsible for welcoming our guests and providing them with the highest standard of service to ensure a fantastic start to their day. It is the team's responsibility to offer information and guidance to allow our guests to get the most out of their day and to have the most memorable experience possible. The Admissions department consists of four areas – Car Parks, Ticket Selling, Ticket Monitoring and Annual Pass sales.

The Guest Services department is a fast paced and exciting environment where no day is the same. The Guest Services team provides help; advice and assistance to ensure a memorable visit for our guests and by doing so take pride in surpassing their expectations.

Salary: £5.80 per hour plus benefits

The Person

We aim to provide the highest standards of service and enjoyment for our guests, so the following attributes are essential to be part of the LEGOLAND Windsor team:
- A passion for serving others
- Well groomed personal appearance
- Friendly, outgoing personality
- Confidence and a real desire to interact with children
- Ability to work as part of a team
- A willingness to work hard and have fun at the same time

Source: www.legoland.co.uk

1. What aspects of personal presentation skills would you need to pay close attention to if you were successful in being selected to work as an Admissions and Guest Services Assistant at Legoland?
2. Which interpersonal skills do you think you need to fulfil this role and why would you need them?
3. Describe two different customer service situations that might arise at Legoland and explain how you would deal with them.
4. To what extent do you think it is important to Legoland to recruit people with good personal presentation and interpersonal skills?

doing to them to make them roadworthy and that this will cost a lot of money. In situations like these, you have to make sure the customer is fully informed, but you need to provide the information in a sensitive and positive manner.

Efficiency

If you demonstrate **efficiency**, it means that you are doing your job well and in a competent manner; you are being effective. If you are efficient in your dealings with customers, you will immediately inspire confidence and customers will feel secure in the knowledge that you know what you are doing and can meet their needs and expectations. For example, if you go into a travel agency with a list of requirements for your perfect holiday and within a matter of minutes, the member of staff dealing with you is able to show you two or three holidays that meet your requirements, then you will feel encouraged to make a booking because you feel that the member of staff is competent and able to process your transaction correctly.

You can develop your level of efficiency as you become more familiar with your role in the business you work for and the way the business works and you become more knowledgeable about the goods or services that the business provides. However, you also need to be committed to providing good customer service and enthusiastic about the business and what it has to offer.

Research and investigate

Use the internet to find job advertisements for jobs in other leisure, travel and tourism businesses. (Tip: look at the websites of organisations that you know such as Alton Towers.) Make a list of the personal presentation and interpersonal skills that are required for these jobs.

Communication skills

Communication is the process by which information is exchanged, in this case between you and your customer. Communication is not just about talking to a customer or delivering a message; it is also about how that message is received and understood, and you will need good communication skills in order to ensure that you not only communicate clearly but also communicate in an appropriate manner.

In order to communicate effectively with customers, you will need to use appropriate:

- pitch and tone of voice
- language
- pace
- listening skills
- body language.

You must also learn to vary the way in which you communicate, in order to suit the customer service situation. For example, the way in which you communicate with a child would be different from the way in which you would communicate with an adult.

Pitch and tone of voice

Appropriate communication is not just about what you say; it is also about the way you say it. For example, we would all agree that saying 'Can I help you?' is better than saying, 'What do you want?' But if you say 'Can I help you?' in a bored, uninterested or tired way, then the effect on the customer may be just the same as if you had said, 'What do you want?' You need to speak to customers in a clear and confident manner, using a positive tone of voice that shows that you are genuinely interested in their needs and their response.

If you need to communicate information to a customer, you need to ensure that you vary the pitch of your voice a little and try not to speak in a monotonous tone as this may cause the customer to switch off after a while and miss what you have said to them. If you have ever flown, think of the cabin crew communicating the safety information to you (even if that is by video); hopefully you will have noticed that when delivering this important information, cabin crew vary the pitch and tone of their voices to ensure that they communicate clearly and emphasise the most important details.

Did you know...

Frequent flyers take little notice of cabin crews' safety talk, so Air New Zealand found a novel way of ensuring that passengers listen to this essential communication – three cabin crew and a pilot applied full body paint to look like their uniforms to film a video to talk passengers through the aircraft's safety procedures!

Language

The language you use when communicating with customers should be straightforward and easy to understand. It is especially important not to use technical terms or jargon that are specific to your business. For example, in the card and gift industry, there are terms such as cop (roll of curling ribbon), IBC (individual boxed card) and plush (cuddly toys).

You must do your best to be polite and courteous at all times and must therefore avoid the use of slang (local terms) and colloquialisms (words/phrases appropriate to familiar conversations) such as 'innit' instead of 'isn't it' and 'ta' instead of 'thank you'.

Pace

Everybody has their own particular way of speaking. Some people, by their nature, speak very quickly and others very slowly. However, you need to be able to communicate clearly with customers and therefore need to speak at an appropriate pace according to the needs of the customer. You need to remember that customers can absorb only so much information at one time and you must therefore pause occasionally and clarify the main points with your customer. It is also important to pause and maintain a silence long enough for your customer to respond to you or ask questions.

Listening skills

Listening skills are central to effective communication. You have to make sure that you listen closely to what customers say to you and avoid interrupting them so that you can find out exactly what they want and meet their needs.

To be an effective communicator, you need to engage in active listening. This means that you have to concentrate fully on what a customer is saying rather than just 'hearing' what is being said, so you must avoid distractions and interruptions. You must also show that you have understood what the customer has said and **empathise** with them, using phrases such as, 'I understand how you feel' or 'I see what you mean.' It is then important to check that you have fully understood a customer's requests; you can do this by repeating some of the main points of what they have said back to them and giving them the opportunity to confirm the issues. Finally, if you need to ask the customer questions, try and make sure that you ask **open questions** so that customers have the opportunity to give you more detail.

Task

In small groups, take it in turns to read the air cabin crew safety talk below. You must deliver the talk in a suitably serious manner but also ensure that you maintain the attention of your audience. Take a vote on which member of your group was most effective in communicating this message.

Air cabin crew safety talk

All carry-on items should now be stowed securely, either in the overhead lockers or under the seat in front of you. Your mobile phones and all other electronic devices should be turned off. Make sure your seat belt is fastened; to fasten, insert the metal tip into the buckle and adjust the strap so that it is tight across your lap; to release the belt, just lift the top of the buckle. Please remain seated with your seat belt fastened any time the seat-belt light is on, and even if the light is off, you should keep your seat belt fastened while you are in your seat. Smoking is not permitted anywhere aboard the aircraft including the toilets.

Emergency exits are located at the front and rear of the aircraft and are clearly marked with an exit sign; however, if there is a loss of power, emergency lighting on the floor of the cabin will lead you to an emergency exit. If the cabin pressure changes, oxygen masks will drop down from above your head. To use these, you should pull the mask towards you, fit it over your nose and mouth and place the elastic around your head to secure the mask and breathe normally. Be sure to fit your own mask before helping somebody else to fit theirs. Life jackets can be found under your seat. To use the life jacket, pull the tab to release the jacket from its container and then slip it over your head. Fasten the two straps at the front of the vest and adjust them to fit your waist. To inflate the jacket when leaving the plane, pull down on the red tabs at the bottom of the jacket or manually inflate it by blowing into the tubes.

Before take-off, make sure that your seat is in the upright position and your tray is folded away. Please read through the safety-information card, which is in the seat pocket in front of you. Enjoy your flight.

Task

Work in groups of three. One person should be the customer, one the customer service assistant and one an observer (who should take notes). Role play some customer service situations in which the customer has to provide a great deal of information about his or her needs, for example a customer in a travel agency describing their ideal holiday. At the end of the role play, the observer should test the assistant's memory on what was requested and provide feedback on how well the assistant listened. Swap roles and try the role play again.

Body language

The correct use of open body language will help you to communicate effectively. Your facial expressions must show that you are interested in what the customer has to say and that you have understood what has been said; this means that you must display appropriate emotions. Use open palm gestures and lean forward slightly to show that you are actively listening to the customer, and remember to make eye contact.

Make the grade

P3 **M2** Remember each of the skills outlined above for P3 and M2 as you must demonstrate confident presentation, communication and interpersonal skills in different customer service situations.

Customer-service situations

You will need to demonstrate good customer service skills in a range of customer service situations, which include face to face, on the telephone, in writing, via email and also in urgent and non-urgent situations and routine and difficult situations. In each of these situations, good communication and interpersonal skills are very important.

Face to face

Providing good customer service face to face can be easier because you can see the customer's reaction and you can have a two-way conversation. This will help you to understand the customer's needs and be better able to meet those needs. However, you will need to ensure that you have excellent personal presentation skills.

On the telephone

Even though a customer cannot see you when you are providing customer service using the telephone, you should still smile as you will then sound more friendly and welcoming. First impressions still count and, for this reason, many businesses provide a script for those employees who answer the phone. This is to ensure that a professional image is given to the customer and the right tone is set from the beginning. A typical greeting might be, 'Good morning, MyBusiness, Katrina speaking. How may I help you?'

To provide good customer service on the telephone, you should:

- Answer promptly (within four rings).
- Greet customers politely (using the script if one is provided).
- Smile when speaking and use a cheerful tone.
- Provide information clearly.
- Engage in active listening.
- Avoid interrupting the customer by putting them through to an extension too quickly.
- Make notes/take messages accurately.
- Take a contact name and number in case you need to call the customer back.

In writing

There are many circumstances in which customer service is provided in writing, for example confirmation of a booking, a response to a complaint or an invitation to an event. On each occasion, the communication must be of a high standard because badly set-out documents with spelling and grammatical errors will give customers a poor impression of the business.

Written communication should therefore be:

- Properly set out.
- Free from spelling and grammatical errors.
- Easy to understand and jargon free.
- Addressed correctly.
- Written in a polite and courteous manner.

When writing to customers, it is important to include all the necessary information to respond to the customer's needs, but you also need to make the main points very clear to avoid any confusion.

Email

Many businesses now use email to communicate with their customers as it is quick, easy, and inexpensive. However, because it is so easy to send an email, this can result in a lack of attention to detail and, as with any written message, an email does not come with facial expressions or gestures that you would get in a face-to-face meeting, and there's no tone of voice to interpret as you could over the telephone. Therefore, great care needs to be taken over the wording of email messages to ensure that they are polite and courteous and do not unintentionally cause offence to customers.

When emailing customers:

- Remember who you are emailing and address the recipient in the correct way.
- Take your time so that you avoid errors and always check what you have written before you click Send.

- Be polite, as being too brief can cause your message to be misinterpreted.
- Use humour sparingly, as you may cause offence.
- Make sure that you have a meaningful 'Subject' line.
- Make sure that you sign your email messages so that recipients know who they are from.
- Tell your customer if you forward a message to somebody else to deal with, so they know who to expect a reply from.
- Don't type messages in CAPITALS as this is considered to be shouting and is rude.
- Don't overuse punctuation such as exclamation marks ('!').

Urgent/non-urgent

When dealing with customers, you will sometimes be faced with situations that appear to need your urgent attention. You need to be able to assess whether a customer service situation is urgent or non-urgent, and you cannot always rely on a customer to help you determine this, as many customers will regard their situation as urgent even if it is not.

In any situation, you need to remain calm, listen carefully and then make sure that you ask the right people to assist you such as a qualified first-aider, if somebody has been taken ill or had an accident, or a supervisor or manager.

Difficult/routine

The longer you work for a business, the better you get to know the way in which the managers of that business expect you to deal with routine customer service situations, and you will develop good customer service skills. However, difficult customer service situations will arise and you need to be prepared.

When faced with a difficult situation, such as unacceptable behaviour or an angry customer, you need to:

- React calmly and in a positive manner.
- Distance yourself from personal remarks.
- Identify the cause of the problem.
- Acknowledge the customer's feelings and involve them in solving the problem.
- Get assistance from a supervisor or manager if you are unable to resolve the situation yourself.

Customers

Working with customers can be a very enjoyable and rewarding experience but occasionally you will be challenged by people with particular needs that may be difficult for you to meet. Some customers may be difficult or abusive because they are not satisfied with the product they have purchased or the service they have received; others may have particular needs due to being disabled; and others may need technical information.

Difficult/abusive customers

More often than not, customers become difficult to deal with or abusive because they feel that they have cause for complaint. Customers complain because the quality of goods or the quality of service does not meet expectations. However, handling a complaint efficiently can mean that a customer will continue to use your business. Therefore, in addition to the guidelines for handling difficult customers above, you also need to:

- Make sure that you listen carefully to everything the customer has to say.
- Show that you understand the customer's point of view.
- Apologise but make sure that you do not blame others.
- Try and reach an agreement that will satisfy the customer and take action to ensure that what has been agreed will be carried out.

If a customer is very abusive even after you have remained calm and courteous, then you must call on a supervisor or manager to assist you.

Disabled customers

All businesses must do what is reasonable to ensure that disabled customers have access to their services, for example having wheelchair access to their premises or hearing loops at customer-service points. However, you may be called on to provide extra assistance to disabled people, for example selecting a product for a blind person or finding a chair for somebody who has difficulty in walking. In these situations you should aim to meet the needs of the customer as efficiently as you can but remember to communicate clearly with the customer so that you know their exact requirements.

If you are faced with a situation that you cannot deal with, for example communicating in sign language with a deaf person, then you should make sure that you know what systems the business you work for has in place to meet the needs of customers and who you should call on for assistance.

Discussion...

All businesses should provide training for their staff in customer-service skills. Discuss.

Customers who need technical information

There are many customers who like to make informed decisions before they make a purchase and these customers may require detailed technical information that you do not have at your fingertips. Imagine you work for a retailer of electrical items and a customer wishes to know the specification of different washing machines! It would not be appropriate to refer this customer to the manufacturer's information booklet for each machine and expect them to read through them, as the customer would expect you to be able to help. Over time, you would gain the knowledge and experience you need, but even the most experienced assistant can sometimes be asked for technical information that they do not know; therefore, in these situations, you must explain that you will find out. You must then fulfil your promise and find the information for the customer, or find somebody who can help them. Customers will appreciate your efforts if you have done everything you can to obtain the information they require.

Make the grade

D1 Remember the information above for dealing with customers in different situations as, for D1, you must anticipate and meet the needs of different customers in three contrasting situations.

Shopping in London

Paula and Claire travelled to London for a day out shopping on Oxford Street. They arrived bright and early and as they walked along Oxford Street, they saw the staff in the Japanese clothes store, UNIQLO, having their team talk for the day ahead. They walked past and entered one of the many well-known women's fashion stores and looked around. The store was not busy and Claire soon found a shirt she was looking for. She tried it on and then took it to the cash desk. She was pleased to see that there was no queue and that there were two staff behind the desk. However, it was a good few minutes before Claire was served, as the staff were talking to one another, putting away coat hangers and then, to Claire's annoyance, one walked away and the other made a phone call! When she was eventually served, the young man who served her did not greet her or make eye contact. Claire was relieved to leave the store.

Paula and Claire then entered a department store to look at some luggage. Claire selected a small suitcase and took it to the cash desk. The lady on the desk greeted her with a very cheerful good morning and complimented her on her choice. She quickly processed the transaction and asked Claire how she would like the item wrapped and then asked her about her day. Claire was very pleased with her purchase and she and Paula sat and had a cup of coffee in the in-store café.

1. Outline the interpersonal skills that the young man in the women's fashion store should have demonstrated.
2. Explain why Claire felt a more valued customer in the department store than she did in the women's fashion store.
3. Discuss the importance of good communication skills when working in a retail store.
4. To what extent do you think that a staff team talk at the beginning of each day might improve customer service in an organisation?

Key words

Body language – Describes how we communicate with others using our posture, facial expressions and gestures.

Communication – The process by which information is exchanged.

Courteous – Polite, well-mannered and considerate.

Efficiency – Good organisation and the ability to do the job well.

Empathise – To identify with customers and show understanding for their point of view.

Interpersonal skills – The skills needed to communicate and interact with and to relate well to other people.

Open questions – Questions that allow respondents to answer in their own words. These questions often begin with How, What, When, Where, and Why.

Tactful – Polite, considerate and sensitive to the feelings of others.

Assignment

You must be able to apply appropriate presentation and interpersonal skills in customer service situations.

Customer Relations in Business

This assignment must be completed when you are on work placement or when you have arranged to spend a period of time working for a business of your choice.

You must prepare a log book that you can use to record evidence for this assignment (or use one that has been prepared for you). Your log book must be signed by the person observing and supervising you in your workplace.

1. Record evidence in your log book to show that you have demonstrated presentation, communication and interpersonal skills in different customer service situations. Different customer service situations include:
   - face-to-face
   - on the telephone
   - in writing
   - via email
   - urgent and non-urgent situations
   - routine and difficult situations. **(P3)**
2. To meet the criteria for a Merit, you must present evidence that you have displayed confident presentation, communication and interpersonal skills when demonstrating customer service in a range of customer service situations (this can be the same customer service situations used for task 1). **(M2)**
3. To meet the criteria for a Distinction, you must present evidence that you have **anticipated** and met the needs of different customers in three contrasting situations (this can be the same customer service situations used for task 1). **(D1)**

To achieve a pass grade you need to:	To achieve a merit grade you need to:	To achieve a distinction you need to:
P3 demonstrate presentation, communication and interpersonal skills in different customer service situations	M2 display confident presentation, communication and interpersonal skills when demonstrating customer service in a range of customer service situations	D1 anticipate and meet the needs of different customers in three contrasting situations

Chapter 24
Providing consistent and reliable customer service to create customer satisfaction

What are you finding out?

In a modern business environment it is sometimes difficult to find widespread differences between some products. In these situations customers might be satisfied despite the product or brand. However, it is in these situations that good customer service enables one organisation to distinguish itself from another. For example, most airlines provide a consistent and reliable product enabling travellers to reach their destinations. What distinguishes airlines is not necessarily the product itself, but the quality of service that customers receive and the way that this contributes towards their satisfaction.

Customer service is not something that just happens. Providing customers with good customer service and satisfaction takes place over time.

This chapter will help you to:

- Describe what contributes to consistent and reliable customer service.
- Understand the importance for business organisations of satisfying their customers.
- Appreciate the need for codes of practice.
- Analyse the importance of customer service for different business organisations.

Providing consistent and reliable customer service

It could be argued that providing customer service is a cyclical process. This is because everything an organisation does starts with customers and then later finishes with customers.

Having anticipated customer needs, it is then important to provide customers with **consistent and reliable customer service**. Happy customers are those who will return again and again to the same company and even recommend products and services to friends. Providing high quality, consistent and reliable customer service enables an organisation to meet the needs of its customers better than its competitors. In this way, an organisation can use the service it provides to create a **competitive advantage**. In competitive markets, it may not be the products that determine whether a business succeeds or fails. Instead it may be the quality of customer care that makes the difference.

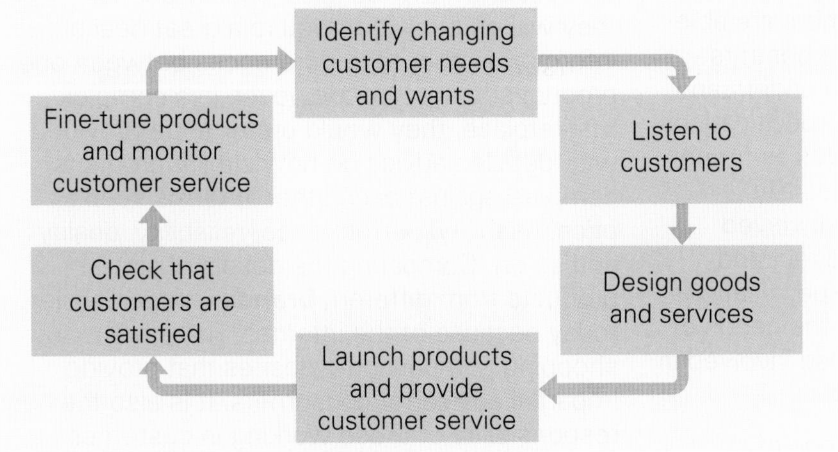

Figure 24.1 Providing customers with products and services

Scope of job role

The quality of customer service depends largely on an organisation's employees. Staff who are appointed should be interested and committed to providing the highest possible levels of customer care. To ensure that employees provide the highest possible customer service, they need to be trained so that they can learn how to deliver

Problems with a mobile phone

A customer purchased a mobile phone from a reputable company, but a few months later the phone began to malfunction. The customer sent the mobile phone back to the company to be repaired. The customer wanted a replacement but the company said that the phone showed signs of corrosion around the battery. Corrosion occurred because of normal exposure to air, but the company still refused to replace it.

1. What role would a person working in customer service have in trying to resolve this issue?
2. What would have been the best way to satisfy the customer in this instance?

services in a consistent and reliable way. For example, training will help them to learn about the needs of customers, how to provide them with service in different situations and how to deal with their specific needs.

Knowledge of products and/or services

When individuals buy products or receive services they have expectations. They look for a whole series of benefits and product or service features. It is, therefore, important that those who are dealing with customers are able to translate the product and service benefits into a language that customers can understand. There may be a range of technical specifications that they need to understand, as well as fitting or installation details and instructions. By understanding the products, those involved in customer service are providing direct and focused support that enables the specifications of the product or service to match the needs of each consumer. It is helpful for those involved in customer service to:

- Understand the qualities of a range of competing products.
- Attend product launches.
- Be trained in the benefits of different products.
- Read press reviews of different products.
- Discuss the relative benefits of products with colleagues.

Did you know...

1080p and 1080i are the numbers that refer to the horizontal lines that make up a digital television image. The 'p' and 'i' refer to the method the television uses to interpret the lines. The i refreshes every 1/60 of a second, whereas a 'p' refreshes either every 1/60 or 1/30, which means that the best sets have a high number of 'p' for the best pictures.

Task

Working in a group, discuss how a member of staff working for a large electrical retailer would acquire and use the product knowledge necessary to provide good customer service for its customers.

Type and quality of products/ service

If a consumer buys a relatively straightforward product with few technical specifications, they will probably not require a great deal of information about the differences between one product and another. However, in a complex marketplace, they would prefer to be provided with detailed advice on how similar products compare against each other in terms such as price, usability, performance, reliability, quality and so on. Comparing the details of similar products from different **brands** is much easier today because of the internet. There are many shopping comparison websites that provide impartial advice for consumers. It is also the responsibility of those working in customer service to offer informed and helpful advice. As well as showing customers the different details of each product, they should be able to talk about feedback from previous customers so that customers can make informed decisions.

Did you know...

Kelkoo (www.kelkoo.co.uk/) has been voted the favourite shopping comparison website for the last four years.

Staff attitude and behaviour

Those involved in customer service are there to resolve problems. Nobody will want problems to become bitter or be dealt with badly. Employees need to show that they understand the needs of their customers. They should be positive and create empathy with their customers. In some circumstances they might also need to show sympathy, particularly if products are faulty. It is important for staff to be easy to deal with and to set high standards when dealing with customers. Staff should:

- Be honest in what they say to customers.
- Talk to customers in a way that they understand.
- Be enthusiastic to help their customers, no matter what the problem or the issue.
- Make sure that the expectations of the customer are met and that any problems are properly resolved.
- Use the way in which they deal with customers to create positive customer relationships with the organisation.
- Deal with customers in a way that encourages them to use the products and services of the organisation again.

Did you know...

If a member of staff works well with customers and suppliers in a way that builds relationships and their confidence, they are usually said to have good 'people skills'.

Timing

When dealing with customer service issues, timing is always likely to be a key issue.

When working with customers you do not want to keep them waiting for a long period of time. If you are not able to deal with them immediately, then it might be necessary to apologise to them. If you are dealing with somebody else and are conscious of somebody waiting for your attention, then it is useful to indicate to that person that you will be with them as soon as you can. Sometimes timing issues can be dealt with by:

- Making appointments to see customers at designated times.
- Providing customers with detailed written information, such as that within a brochure, while they are waiting.
- Offering refreshments to customers while they are waiting.

Timing is a key personal skill. It is usually possible to recognise signals from customers, particularly **buying signals**. This would indicate that a customer would want to buy a product.

Sometimes queries might have been taken on the telephone and cannot be immediately answered. When this occurs it may be necessary to call customers back. To do this it might be useful to ask customers when the best time is to return the call.

Task

Work within groups to think about and then discuss some of the timing issues within your school or college. For example, how convenient is your timetable? Are there times within the week when you have too much time on your hands or are there particular days when there is too much on? What do you think about the period of time over which you are asked to complete assessments? Do you have tutorials with your tutors? Is it possible at certain times during the week to see your tutors and receive feedback advice?

Accessibility/availability

There may be situations when products run out of stock. This could be because of an unexpected demand for them. Potential new customers may then come along with high expectations of getting their needs met, only to find that you are unable to supply the goods. In this circumstance, it is useful to check with the supplier to find out when new stock is expected to arrive. The customer should then be told how long it is likely to be before they arrive. If necessary they may be put on a waiting list that ensures that they receive the products that they want when they arrive. In this circumstance it may be necessary to sympathise with the customer while at the same time making sure that they feel that their needs are going to be met soon.

Did you know...

During 2008 the average UK absence rate from work was 8.1 days per employee. The highest levels of absence were within the public sector.

Meeting specific customer needs

Each customer should be treated differently and provided with the sort of service that matches their expectations. They may simply be making an enquiry and wanting information that would help them to come to a decision. In this instance, supplying them with a brochure might meet their needs or allowing them to use, see or test a product. Customers may want advice and to find out more about a product or they may wish to place an order. It is up to the person involved in providing the service to find out what these needs are. For example:

- A query may be made about the physical size of the product.
- They may want to know about the cost of running it.
- The technical specifications may be queried.
- It may be necessary to change the address on an order.
- They may want to know about how long a product might run before it needs to be serviced.

Individuals working in customer service should be able to find out the answers to such questions.

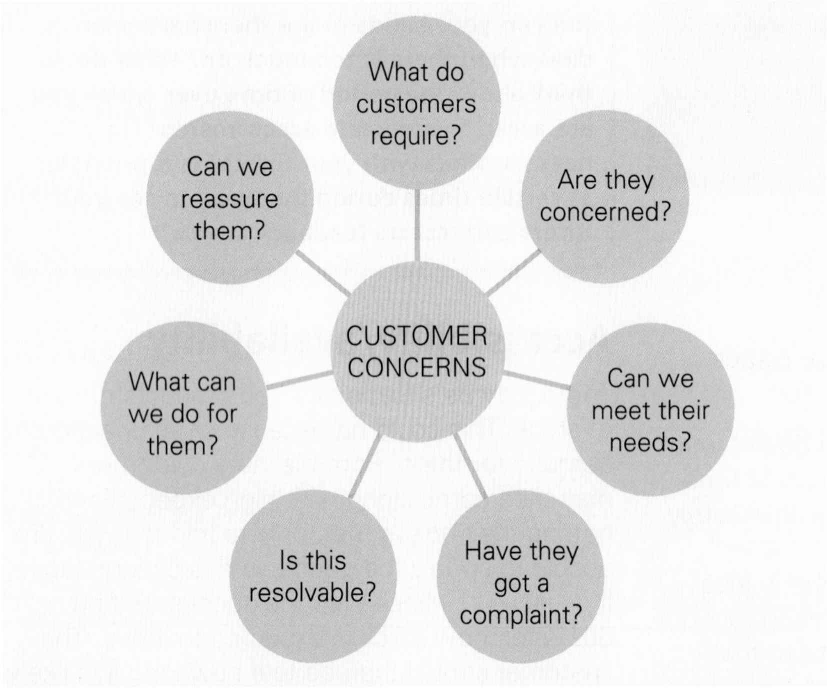

Figure 24.2 Questions to think about when meeting customer needs

Working under pressure

Working within a customer service environment is not likely to be easy. Sometimes there may be a number of serious issues that need to be resolved quickly. For example, there may be faults with a number of products that have just been sold and several customers have contacted you asking you about how to deal with this. At the same time, another customer might phone to ask why their product has not been delivered. You may be trying to calm people down, but you are feeling stressed as there are so many problems to deal with and you are struggling to find the time to do so. In these situations it may be more difficult to feel positive. In resolving problems yourself, you are also dealing with the problem that you are under pressure.

In these circumstances, it is important to remain calm. Take deep breaths. You might be able to ask for help from others. Work out your priorities. Perhaps it may be best to list them, then deal with each in turn. Try to remain positive as you do so. Sometimes there are situations where you just have to go that extra mile. You might feel that by working through your lunch hour that you may be able to catch up, or you may need to ask your team leader for some overtime.

Did you know...

Many employees say that they are not suffering from pressure simply because they do not want to let others know that they are struggling to cope.

Confirming that a service meets needs and expectations

Maintaining records about customer transactions enables an organisation to understand the customer experience more closely. To confirm that a service has met needs and expectations an organisation might use post-sale surveys. These help to record levels of satisfaction experienced by customers. They may be sent to purchasers' homes shortly after completing a purchase. Alternatively, a simple phone call can be used to ask a customer a few questions. The survey may try to find out:

- Whether the product or service has met expectations.
- If the product literature was suitable and informative.
- Whether the customer was offered a demonstration.
- If the appearance of the staff and showroom lived up to expectations.
- Whether any explanations were clear.
- Whether the delivery took place on time.

Task

Think about the last major purchase that you made. Design a series of questions that could be used in a post-sale survey. Think about the sort of actions that might be taken if a negative response is provided by customers.

Dealing with problems

Working with customers is not likely to be easy. But it can be rewarding when their needs are met and they feel satisfied with the product that they have bought or with the service they have received. However, there are many different types of problems that may crop up. For example:

- A delivery is late.
- The product is damaged.
- A faulty product has to be returned.
- The wrong information has been supplied with the product.
- The product does not fit.
- The customer cannot get the product to work.

Task

Briefly discuss what you might be able to do in each of these different circumstances.

Customer complaints are sometimes inevitable. It is important that in each instance the facts are accurately recorded. Then it is important to think about how good customer service can be used to help and support the customer. If necessary, the team leader might need to be involved, particularly if a cost is incurred.

Make the grade

P4 Remember to use this for P4. Think about the examples that you have experienced of good or bad customer service. You may want to interview another student. Find out about the key requirements for consistent and reliable customer service. As you find out key requirements, cite examples of what makes customer service consistent and reliable. Also cite examples of when individuals have been provided with poor, inconsistent or unreliable customer service.

Customer satisfaction

Customer care programmes should be designed to provide customers with **customer satisfaction**. Remember that customers are created when they are involved in some form of transaction. This means that something of value is being exchanged or provided. Customers want good value. They want to feel that they have been rewarded through their transaction. When a customer feels pleased with a transaction they:

a Become an **advocate**. This means that they are so pleased with the product and the service they have received that they recommend them to others.
b They experience 'customer delight'. This is when customers are fully satisfied because the product and service that they have received have exceeded their requirements.

Task

Identify situations in which you have been more than satisfied with the product and service you have received. This may be a shop or a small manufacturer that you visit. Think about what makes you satisfied with all that you have received. Is it the quality of the products? Have the staff been friendly? Has help been provided for you? Is there post-sales service?

Confidence in the service

Customers need to be confident in the service that has been provided for them. When they approach an organisation they will have certain expectations about what they are likely to receive. Think about this in terms of the restaurant. You will want to know that you can go there and get a table. You might have seen the menu before and know what sort of dishes are on offer. Given the reputation of the restaurant, you know that you will not have to wait too long for the food. You may then be really pleased with the service that you receive as well as the meal. The restaurant might keep you on an email list and then regularly ask you for feedback and provide you with details of a whole series of special offers. What has happened in this particular instance is that the expectations that the customer has have been met by the product and service. This means that next time the customer goes out for a meal, this restaurant is probably likely to be top of their list.

Discussion...

What is it about famous brand names that provides customers with confidence in the service that they are about to receive, and do expectations differ between famous brands and local organisations? Discuss what your expectations about customer service would be if you were to visit:

a McDonald's
b Frankie and Benny's
c T.G.I. Friday's
d Your local fish and chip shop
e Your nearest Starbucks.

Value for money

When making a decision about a purchase a consumer is not simply buying the product. In fact they are buying a whole range of benefits. These benefits might include the location of the business, the customer service they are offered, the credit terms they might be supplied with, the after-sales service on offer, the choice of products they have to view, the help they are given, the friendliness of the staff, the environment in which they shop and the catalogues with which they are supplied. The list is almost endless. In fact, it makes you realise that a product is not simply a product. It is something that provides a whole series of benefits for the customer to make the customer feel that they are purchasing something of value. It is this that the customer looks for. They will want value for money. They will also want to know that there are lots of positives from the transaction that they have made.

Did you know...

According to a number of websites, nearly-new cars offer much more value for money than new cars.

Task

Think of all of the products or services that you repeatedly use over and over again. Identify five reasons why you come back to these products and services.

Word-of-mouth reputation

As we saw earlier, when somebody is so happy with the product or the experience that they have received, they then recommend it to others. This is because their levels of customer satisfaction have been more than met. The customer is then actively talking to others who might want to use the service. This is clearly a cycle of success for a company, as it reduces the costs of their promotion and increases their **revenue**. It is a well-known fact that keeping customers and valuing them, rather than going out to get new customers, is far easier and costs much less money.

Internal customer satisfaction

Internal customers are individuals at any level working within an organisation. When employees deal with each other, they expect to be treated in the same way as an organisation deals with its customers outside the business. If customers are repeatedly satisfied with the products they are getting or the services that are being provided for them, then internal customers such as employees within an organisation are happy that the work they are putting in is being appreciated. Delighting customers makes their jobs easier. It also makes their jobs more rewarding. This can provide **job satisfaction**. In a busy, focused work environment individuals enjoy working in teams. When everybody pulls together to meet the same objectives, it can make the work much more meaningful. In a positive and focused work environment, good communication helps individuals to work with each other as part of a team. In contrast, poor communication makes it more difficult to satisfy customers. See Chapter 18 on teamwork.

Codes of practice

To ensure that customers are satisfied, organisations often agree to abide by a series of rules. In fact, they are influenced by **codes of practice**. These are a voluntary or legally enforced code comprising a set of regulations and guidelines that organisations follow. These regulations then influence how employees behave.

Codes of practice are good both for customers and for organisations. Employees can use the guidelines in a whole series of situations to ensure that customer needs are met. The guidelines themselves are focused on satisfying customers. On the one hand, codes of practice set out guidelines and responsibilities. On the other hand, they give expectations to customers and set out what they can expect to receive.

There are different types of codes of practice. These are:

An industry code of practice

These provide a series of guidelines that are constructed by employees, employers and professional bodies within an industry. They create codes of practice for dealing with customers in that particular industry. For example, the Motor Industry Code of Practice for Service and Repair commits garages to a whole series of rules that ensure that they do business fairly and maintain high standards. Standards relate to pricing and to completing the agreed work.

Her Majesty's Revenue and Customs (HMRC)

HMRC has its own Code of Practice. The aim is to help taxpayers to understand their rights. It also helps them to understand their obligations, particularly when it comes to paying tax. The Code of Practice sets out ways in which staff at HMRC:

- provide advice for customers
- publish information
- deal with confidential information
- provide interpretations of tax law.

The Code emphasises that staff at HMRC will be as helpful as they can for all taxpayers.

1. Why has HMRC got its own Code of Practice?

2. How might this Code help both employees of HMRC and taxpayers?

An organisational code of practice

Written within organisations, these occur when organisations create their own standards and guidelines designed to meet customer needs.

A professional code of practice

Some industries have professional bodies. One of the functions of these professional bodies is to monitor standards. These bodies might represent doctors, dentists, accountants, nurses, as well as teachers. For example, the General Teaching Council for England has a Code of Conduct and Practice for registered teachers. These codes set out minimum acceptable standards.

Ethical standards

Ethics are moral principles or rules of conduct which are generally accepted by most members of society. They involve what individuals and groups believe to be right and what is considered to be wrong. An ethic is therefore a guide as to what should be done or what should not be done.

From an early age, parents, schools, religious teachings and society in general provide us with moral guidelines to help us to learn and form our ethical beliefs. Many ethics are reinforced in our legal system and thus provide a constraint on business activities, while others are not. In areas not covered by the law, there may well be social pressure to conform to a particular standard.

Through the media we hear about questionable business practices. Issues might include insider trading, animal-rights protestors involved in disputes with organisations producing cosmetic and pharmaceutical products tested on animals, protests about tobacco sponsorships, and trading links with unfriendly or hostile nations.

Today consumers are more aware than ever of the ethical and moral values underlying business decisions. They may be concerned about what an organisation stands for, who it trades with, what it does, whether it supports any political party, whether it is an equal-opportunity employer and how it behaves in the community in general.

Make the grade

M3 Remember to use this for M3. Find out how a range of different types of business organisation deliver customer service. As a customer you will also experience customer service from different organisations. Compare levels and quality of customer service in the different organisations and start to think about how effective customer service benefits the customer, the organisation and the employee.

Assignment

You must be able to understand how consistent and reliable service contributes to customer satisfaction.

Investigating customer service

For this assignment you need to undertake an investigation into the nature and type of customer service provided by organisations.

1. As a class or in groups, arrange a visit to a local organisation that has a reputation for providing good and consistent customer service. You may do this by writing to the organisation or it could be an organisation for which a friend, colleague or member of your family works. Before going, construct a questionnaire. The purpose of your questionnaire will be to ask questions that help you to know and understand about the customer service provided by the organisation. For example, find out about how they meet customer needs. To do this you need to look at your notes or the text to find out what makes good and consistent customer service. Have a mechanism for recording your answers. For example, this may include spaces within your questionnaire that enable you to do so. When you are back at school or college, display all that you have found out on a poster. **(P4)**
2. For this activity you will need to find out how customer service benefits customers, an organisation itself and employees. Think about all of the different benefits that organisations get from good customer service such as repeat custom, value for money, and how individuals benefit by receiving job satisfaction. Interview at least two individuals who work for different businesses. Find out what they feel about how customer service affects their organisation and how they measure whether the customer service they provide meets customer expectations. **(M3)**

Key words

Advocate – A happy and pleased customer who recommends the product and service they have received to others.

Body language – Non-verbal gestures, facial expressions and postures that indicate how a customer feels in a particular situation.

Brands – Name, symbol or distinctive element of products that distinguishes them from each of their competitors.

Buying signals – Verbal and non-verbal signs that mean a customer wants to close a sale.

Codes of practice – Voluntary or legally enforced guidelines or regulations.

Competitive advantage – An element that enables an organisation to compete more effectively than its rivals.

Consistent – Uniform pattern of behaviour that takes place time after time.

Customer satisfaction – Felt by customers when products and services have met their needs.

Internal customers – Employees, teams and managers who work within an organisation.

Job satisfaction – The pleasure that an employee gets from their work.

Revenue – Income from sales.

To achieve a pass grade you need to:	To achieve a merit grade you need to:	To achieve a distinction you need to:
P4 explain what contributes to consistent and reliable customer service	**M3** analyse the importance of customer service to different businesses	

Chapter 25 Monitoring and evaluating customer service

What are you finding out?

Monitoring and evaluating the quality of customer service provided by an organisation should be an ongoing process. To do this, a whole series of data from across the organisation should be looked at and constantly monitored. By monitoring customer service, it is possible to **evaluate** feedback from customers. By evaluating customer service, it is possible to make judgements based on real facts about the company, obtained from customers. For example, it may be possible to identify situations where an organisation has provided poor customer service, as well as situations where an organisation has provided good instances of customer service. What an organisation will want to do is to provide consistently good customer service so that it keeps its customers, and those customers will tell other people about the company. Providing good customer service is a continual process of monitoring and review and making improvements where possible.

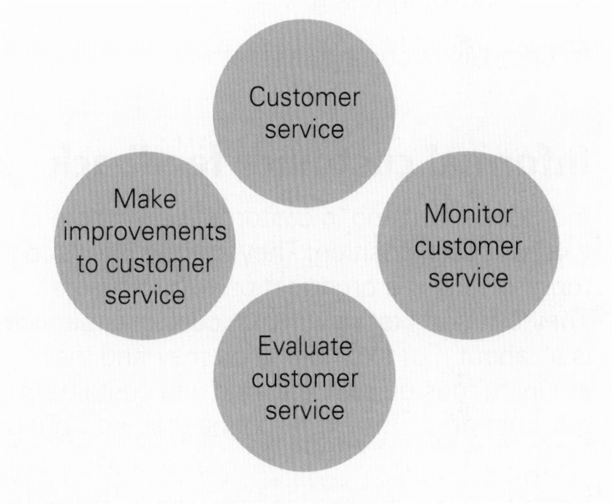

Figure 25.1 The ongoing process of evaluating the quality of customer service

This chapter will help you to:

- Understand and describe how customer service can be monitored and evaluated.
- Explain how monitoring and evaluating improves customer service for the customer, the organisation and the employee.
- Analyse how monitoring and evaluating can improve customer service for the customer, the organisation and the employee.
- Outline how improvements to customer service within an organisation could be made.

Monitoring customer service provided by an organisation

The purpose of monitoring customer service within an organisation is to get accurate customer feedback. There are a number of different ways in which customer service may be monitored by an organisation. For example, these might include:

- informal customer feedback
- customer questionnaire/comment cards
- staff feedback
- mystery customers
- complaints/compliment letters.

Informal customer feedback

Individuals working in customer service are in a very special position. They are the interface representing the organisation to customers. They can see first hand what customer service is all about. For example, they may find that at lunchtimes queues are long and customers get frustrated. They may notice that individuals have difficulty filling in forms. They may find that certain customers are unhappy about a particular service and often mention this in their conversation. By watching customers, they may notice that some customers are not happy with services that are being offered. This sort of information is informal feedback about customers and is one of the ways companies learn about what their customers' needs and expectations are.

Did you know...

Sometimes weekly meetings of customer service staff are know as 'post-mortems'. These provide an opportunity to discuss any examples of customer service issues.

Customer questionnaire/ comment cards

If an organisation keeps records of the names and addresses of all of its customers, customer questionnaires can be used to find out how satisfied they are with the product or service that they have received.

Marley's Delivery Pizza Palace

Score on a scale where 1 is not very good and 5 is excellent.

1 2 3 4 5

Delivery

1. Did the pizza arrive at the time promised?
2. How satisfied are you with the speed of delivery?
3. Was the product damaged when it arrived?

Communication

4. Was it easy to find out about our service?
5. Did you have to wait long for your call to be answered?
6. Were you happy with the telephone response?

Product

7. Are you happy with the variety of pizzas on offer?
8. Did the quality and taste of the pizza meet your expectations?

Figure 25.2 Specimen customer feedback form

As with any questionnaire, it is important to think about its design in order to collect appropriate information. In the questionnaire shown, a scale is used to rate a customer's response. Note – a space is often left on a questionnaire to allow for more detailed comments to be added if the customer does not feel they have given enough information when answering the questions asked.

Questionnaires can be collected during face-to-face meetings or electronically via email or pop-ups.

Choose the answer which best explains your preference and tick the box next to it. **Please tick more than one** if a single answer does not match your perception. Leave blank any question that does not apply.

You are planning a holiday for a group. You want some feedback from them about the plan. You would:

- ☐ use a map or show them the place.
- ☐ phone, text or email them.
- ☐ give them a copy of the printed itinerary.
- ☐ describe some of the highlights.

You are not sure whether a word should be spelled 'dependent' or 'dependant'. You would:

- ☐ find it in a dictionary.
- ☐ think about how each word sounds and choose one.
- ☐ see the words in your mind and choose the way they look.
- ☐ write both words on paper and choose one.

You are going to choose food at a restaurant or café. You would:

- ☐ choose something that you have had there before.
- ☐ look at what others are eating or look at pictures of each dish.
- ☐ listen to the waiter or ask friends to recommend choices.
- ☐ choose from the descriptions in the menu.

Figure 25.3 Example of an internet questionnaire

As part of **customer assurance** schemes, many organisations use comment cards. Comment cards are usually short forms designed to find out what you think about a particular service such as the service in a hotel, restaurant or fast-food chain. They ask only a few questions. This type of data collection is cheap to produce and easy to collect, as well as taking only a small amount of time for the customer to complete.

Staff feedback

When staff work closely with customers they are in a good position to find out what the customer really thinks about the organisation. A member of staff can observe and listen to their customers and find out what sort of issues they are concerned about. Some of the relationships between members of staff and customers might have built up over a long period of time. The staff may be trusted by customers and so, when something goes wrong, customers are happy to confide in them.

Visit rating Benny's Bakery

Outstanding Poor

Quality of our product:
☐1 ☐2 ☐3 ☐4 ☐5

Freshness of our product:
☐1 ☐2 ☐3 ☐4 ☐5

Cleanliness of our premises:
☐1 ☐2 ☐3 ☐4 ☐5

Value and price of our product:
☐1 ☐2 ☐3 ☐4 ☐5

Friendliness of our team:
☐1 ☐2 ☐3 ☐4 ☐5

Promptness of our team:
☐1 ☐2 ☐3 ☐4 ☐5

Experience overall:
☐1 ☐2 ☐3 ☐4 ☐5

Figure 25.4 Example of a comment card

Did you know...

According to Deborah Meaden, one of the Dragons from the BBC's Dragon's Den, 'In the UK, I've experienced some of the best customer service in the world. I've also experienced some of the worst. People are much more aware of the importance of good service to their customers. The customer is absolutely king, customer care is the most important thing you will ever, ever get in the business.'

Did you know...

When an employer takes into account the opinions and feelings of staff, this creates a sense of fairness and trust that improves the way in which employees engage with their work.

Mystery customers

This involves somebody posing as a shopper. They will then go into a retail outlet in order to find out and be able to comment upon the level of service provided. For example, they might comment upon:

- How they are greeted by staff.
- How promptly they are dealt with.
- How knowledgeable the staff were when helping them.
- What questions they were asked.
- The selling and customer service skills of the staff.
- The appearance of the branch.
- The quality of facilities such as toilets.
- Hygiene standards.
- Whether they were provided with the correct advice.

Shopping as a mystery customer enables customer service to be evaluated. Sometimes this process enables the mystery shopper to find out about the motivation of staff and whether staff require training. Mystery shopping is a useful way of identifying where potential improvements are required in customer service, as well as identifying ineffective and inefficient practices. By going to various locations, mystery shoppers are able to compare their experiences across a range of branches.

Task

Working in groups, think about your experiences as customers. Compare the best experiences that you have had as a shopper with the worst experiences. Comment on why some experiences were very good and make a list of all of the reasons that made the experiences good for each person. Do the same for those experiences that were very bad. Use this task to comment upon what makes a) good and b) bad customer service.

Did you know...

In the Leisure and Tourism category of the National Customer Services Awards in 2008, the winner was Wycombe Wanderers Football Club.

Complaints/compliment letters

Customer complaints can provide valuable information. This is because they help to identify where weaknesses in customer service might lie. For example, if a number of complaints are received about the same service, then this indicates that there may be a problem or an issue that needs to be resolved. Complaints might be received personally, through the post, electronically through email and also through telephone calls.

Feedback slips or questionnaires are one way to deal with customer issues. Some organisations have a free customer-service telephone number. Complaints help an organisation to act quickly in evaluating the complaint and seeing if changes need to be made.

Occasionally customers might send letters that compliment the customer service they have received. Again, this helps an organisation to monitor its customer service. By finding out what customers really like about a particular service they have received, it might be possible to **benchmark** that practice and allow other branches to learn about it. A benchmark is a standard of excellence that others might want to follow.

Did you know...

When Jack Taylor founded Enterprise Rent-A-Car, his motto was 'Take care of your customers and employees first, and profit will take care of itself.'

Portakabin's customer satisfaction interviews

Over recent years, Portakabin has carried out customer satisfaction interviews with the vast majority of its clients. These ask questions on all aspects of customer service and record scores on a scale of 1 to 10 (where 1 is very poor and 10 is excellent).

Questions have been asked in four categories:

- Customer experience with sales and administration – the company's response to an enquiry, the level of service received, the speed of a response and how clearly information was presented.
- Delivery and installation – the service provided by the installation team and the haulier.
- The building itself – whether it was clean and fault free on delivery and, if not, what steps were taken to put things right.
- The client's overall impression of the service – the courtesy and technical knowledge of Portakabin staff, value for money and whether they received 'peace of mind'.

1. Why would Portakabin have undertaken this research?
2. How might they have used the findings from this process?

Evaluate customer service provided by an organisation

By collecting information, an organisation can find out about the standards of service that it is offering. It is an important way of acquiring valuable intelligence. This is because it helps those working within customer service to know the way in which their customers measure their performance. If an organisation wants to set higher standards of performance in customer service than their competitors and the customers do not think that standards are high, then clearly there is a problem or issue that needs to be sorted out. There are many different areas that might be of concern for customers. For example, these might include:

- Appearance and cleanliness.
- The time they have to wait before service is offered.
- Levels of support and understanding from staff.
- Courtesy and politeness of staff.
- How happy customers are with the service.
- Whether certain products or services fail on a regular basis.
- Changes in levels of customer satisfaction.

Monitoring all of these areas and more helps to provide the raw data from which those involved in customer service can then evaluate the overall customer experience.

Did you know...

Researchers from Harvard Business School recently surveyed 362 businesses; 80% of them felt that they delivered superior customer service. The researchers then surveyed their customers. Only 8% of customers felt that they were delivering a superior experience!

Level of sales

One of the first indicators that level of customer service might not be up to expectations might be when sales or **turnover** start to fall. Sales might be falling for one type of product or service, or at one branch of an organisation. There may be some very specific reasons for this. By monitoring customers' feedback, it may be possible to find what is happening. It will also help to identify what the problems are so that the necessary action can be taken.

Repeat customers

If customers are satisfied with the products and services they are receiving, they will come back for more products and services. This is a clear indication that these customers are satisfied. Their expectations have been met. However, if very few customers are coming back, then the opposite is true. It will mean that many are not happy with the products and services on offer. This is why it is important to monitor repeat business. It is also very useful to find out why some customers are not coming back.

Did you know...

According to a Watchdog poll in 2009, the UK's favourite supermarket was Waitrose.

New customers

The lifeblood for many organisations is their ability to win new customers. Not all customers have the same characteristics. An organisation may provide goods and services for teenage boys. They may also provide different goods and services for young women in their 20s. For example, Boots make-up brand No 7 is focused on a completely different market from their No 17 brand. By knowing precisely about the nature of their groups of customers, it may then be possible to **target** groups in order to win new customers.

If an organisation is not attracting new customers, it is important to know why. For example, competitors might offer more attractive prices. They may also be providing better customer service. By evaluating what it is that competitors are doing, it may be possible to think about decisions that need to be made.

Discussion...

Think about the ways in which customer service might be used to attract new customers in a) a hairdressing business, b) a newsagent, c) a supermarket and d) a mobile phone shop.

Levels of complaints/ compliments

The number of complaints received as well as the number of compliments received are a useful and simple guide to how well an organisation is performing. If customer service is improving, the number of complaints should be falling and the number of compliments should be increasing. If the opposite is happening, then there are some issues that require consideration.

Staff turnover

When a member of staff leaves an organisation, the organisation may be losing a valuable resource, particularly when that member is popular with customers. If a number of staff leave, losing all of this collective experience may cause real problems for the business. Recruiting new staff may be expensive. They would then need to be trained and it may take time for new staff to develop the appropriate skills and settle in.

It may be possible to find out why staff are leaving and deal with issues that concern them. This can help improve staff turnover in the future. For example, if the staff felt they did not know how to do their job properly, then they might leave the company because they felt uncomfortable dealing with customers. This would be a failure of management. But if the company ran a good staff customer-service training programme, then staff would feel confident and eager to please the customers. They would feel satisfied with their job role and the customer would feel satisfied with the company. Both the customer and the organisation would 'win'.

Make the grade

P5 Remember to use this for P5. Interview a manager or owner of a local business organisation. Before you do so, construct a questionnaire that helps you to find out how it monitors and evaluates customer service. Use your notes and experience of how to monitor and evaluate customer service to construct a series of questions to ask them.

Improvements to customer service within an organisation

Every organisation has to make a decision about the levels of customer service it supplies for its customers.

Improving customer service helps to motivate staff and also ensure customers are satisfied with the company. However, it is not just a matter of improving customer service. This might cost the company a lot of money. For example, if a takeaway employed more staff to reduce queues, they might need to put up their prices to pay the wages of the extra staff. If they put up the prices, then the customers might not be able to afford the cost of the food or might look at alternative takeaways. Careful consideration has to be made when making any changes.

Did you know...

The quality of customer service cannot exceed the quality of the people who provide it!

Improvements to quality of service

Monitoring and evaluating customer service provides data that can help with decisions that have to be made. The data from all around the business is invaluable. It means that problems and issues can be addressed and that customer service can be targeted and improved over time. Organisations should constantly seek to improve the quality of their customer service.

Improving the quality of service will make customers feel happy and valued. There are many ways in which this might happen. It may simply involve improving the décor of the organisation, reducing the time before the service is delivered, emphasising the courtesy and politeness of staff, or setting up a customer-care programme. In the short term, the purpose of improving quality is to improve customer satisfaction and make customers happy. In the longer term, it will help to create a difference in the minds of customers between a business and its competitors, so that customers think twice before using competitors, and use the business with better customer service instead. If customers are happy they will recommend the company to their friends and family and thus bring more business to the company.

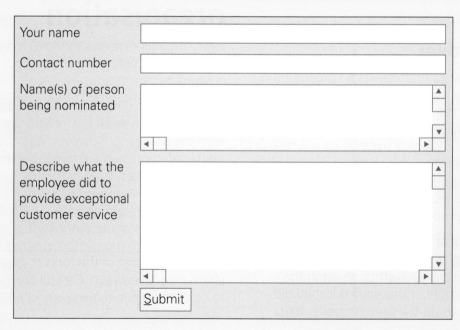

Customer Service Awards 2009

Has an employee done something special or impressed you this year? Have they carried out their duties well and gone the extra mile? Reward their efforts by completing this form.

Please make your Customer Services Award nominations by 1 October 2010.

Thank you for taking the time to give us the opportunity to reward our staff.

Your name	
Contact number	
Name(s) of person being nominated	
Describe what the employee did to provide exceptional customer service	
	Submit

Our Customer Services Awards event takes place every year. We use it to raise awareness of customer-care issues. It also helps to ensure that you, the customer, get the best possible service that we can provide.

1. What would be the purpose of customer services awards within a business?

2. How might this motivate staff?

Reliability

Reliability involves providing the same dependable customer service in every instance. It involves being consistent. This then becomes something that consumers can look forward to because they know exactly what they are going to get. For example, if a mail order company guarantees to deliver goods within seven days and does so, then it will have lived up to its promise and will be providing a reliable service for its customers. However, if a customer orders goods only to be told that they are not in stock or that the company does not have their size, then it will be thought of as unreliable.

As customers depend on those they buy from, they expect reliability. Imagine the frustration of waiting for the last train at night and it not turning up. Think about the disappointment caused to people if a music festival had to cancel the headline act at late notice because the lead singer was ill.

There are many ways in which reliability can be improved. Initially, it may involve simply improving the reliability of the raw materials for the products or services. Training may also help staff to cope with unexpected events and improve the reliability of their service. Reliability is closely linked to customer expectations.

Did you know...

There is a professional body called the Institute of Customer Service (ICS) whose mission is to 'lead customer service performance and professionalism and we aim to be the authoritative voice of customer service – the touchstone for those whose focus is on the delivery of world-class experiences'.

Improvements to the organisation

Birmingham City Council currently describes itself as a city in transformation. The council has taken a radical route to improving its **operational efficiency** and this is raising job satisfaction for staff. Their programme recognises that customer satisfaction depends on how staff handle their customers. The council aims to recognise the importance of customer service and develop staff to the highest standards possible. What Birmingham City Council is doing is not unusual. Good customer service has increasingly become focused at the heart of many business strategies. This is because the quality of customer service is what customers recognise as something of real value that they receive when they deal with an organisation.

Improving services

There are many ways in which services can be improved. For example, like Birmingham City Council, an organisation may focus on improving the training for its staff so that both their efficiency and the way they deal with customers improve. The use of technology to support front-line services may be improved. For example, ICT may enable customer-service operatives to access information more quickly and efficiently. This may save the customer time and also ensures that their query may be acted upon precisely.

Task

Think about the customer service facilities within your school or college. Working in groups, suggest ways in which customer services could be improved.

Did you know...

According to PC World, only 5% of returned products are faulty.

Keeping staff

Customers get to know staff over the period of time that they use organisations, so much so that many might identify the organisation with the helpful levels of service from staff that they know. They might also come to depend upon staff. If staff turnover is high, then the service might become less reliable. It is also expensive to train and develop new staff.

Did you know...

During 2007 the toymaker Mattel recalled more than 18 million Chinese-made toys worldwide.

Attracting new customers

When services are improved, this will help an organisation to attract new customers. In the past customers may have felt that a rival offered better customer service. When they perceive that changes have been made, and the customer service is now better than that offered by their rival, they may start using the business again. One of the business objectives for improving customer service may be to attract new customers.

Increase turnover

Investing in customer service may increase the turnover or sales of an organisation. The improvements in customer service may be launched alongside a whole host of promotions designed to increase sales. For example, there could be a publicity campaign promoting all of the new services and informing potential customers about all of the changes that have taken place.

Compliance with legal obligations

All organisations have to obey the law. There are many different legal requirements that organisations have to abide by, ranging from health and safety legislation through to paying their taxes. Customers will want to know that they are dealing with an honest and reputable company. In fact, many would prefer to buy from a supplier with a good image than one that has been in the press for breaching its legal obligations. For example, who would want to deal with an organisation that has been prosecuted for breaching data security?

Improvements for employees

As an organisation focuses upon developing its customer service, the improvements it undertakes will make life easier for employees. This is because they will take pride in their work and feel proud that they are working for an organisation that is serving the needs of its customers well.

Job satisfaction

This is the sense of pleasure that employees feel when they undertake a job well. For example, Tesco uses training to improve the customer service skills of their employees, which improves their job satisfaction. Employees are more satisfied at work when:

- The work is interesting.
- Customers are happy with what they are providing.
- They are challenged but not stressed.
- They are praised for the work they undertake.
- They are learning and developing at the same time.

Task

Think about and then list all of the skills that you would like to develop while at school and college.

The working environment

Employees prefer to work in a physical environment that is attractive and provides them with good working conditions. For example, this might include the lighting, heating, air conditioning, furniture and fittings and also noise levels.

Make the grade

P6 **M4** **D2**

Remember to use this for P6, M4 and D2. Using all that you discovered when undertaking P5, identify how monitoring and evaluating the customer service for a business organisation could potentially improve service for the customer, the organisation and the employee. As you do so, and in order to gain D2, provide a detailed analysis that, in each instance, provides examples that help you to explain why. Once you have done this, identify a whole range of potential ways in which improvements to customer service could be made and introduced for this organisation.

Key words

Audit – Analysis of the current situation facing an organisation.

Benchmark – High or excellent standard or practice that can be used across a business organisation.

Customer assurance – A series of procedures designed to measure customer satisfaction.

Evaluate – To make a judgement on the worth or value of something.

Morale – A sense of optimism and happiness.

Operational efficiency – All of the activities that an organisation engages in that help it to meet the needs of its customers.

Target – Identifying a specific group of customers to supply goods and services to.

Turnover – Word often used to describe sales within a business organisation.

Assignment

You must know how to monitor and evaluate customer service within an organisation.

Investigating customer service

You work for an organisation that is concerned about the quality of customer experience that it is providing for its customers. The organisation is a small but exclusive restaurant in the centre of a large town. Where the restaurant is situated, there are many similar types of businesses, but trade has been declining for the last few months. You have been entrusted to find out what is happening to the provision of customer service and also to identify what could be done to improve what is being provided.

1. Construct an email to the restaurant manager that itemises all of the different ways that levels of customer service could be monitored and evaluated within the business. If you suggest any form of data collection, construct the forms to do this. **(P5)**
2. Make a list of the sort of improvements that a restaurant could introduce in order to improve its customer service. Refer to how the quality of service could be improved, as well as improvements in reliability, improvements to the organisation and improvements for employees. **(P6)**
3. Construct a poster that shows how monitoring and evaluating customer service can provide benefits for the restaurant. Indicate how the benefits affect the customer, the organisation and the employee. **(M4)**
4. Write a plan indicating how customer service could improve for an organisation over a five-year period. Set out a series of customer service objectives, follow this with suggested actions to improve customer service and then list the benefits for the customer, the organisation and the employee. **(D1)**

To achieve a pass grade you need to:	To achieve a merit grade you need to:	To achieve a distinction you need to:
P5 describe how customer service can be monitored and evaluated	**M4** explain how monitoring and evaluating can improve customer service for the customer, the organisation and the employee	**D1** analyse how monitoring and evaluating can improve customer service for the customer, the organisation and the employee
P6 outline how the improvements to the customer service in an organisation can be made		

Unit 12

Business online

Chapter 26 Understanding online business activities

What are you finding out?

By 2010, the internet – or more accurately the world wide web – has become such a central part of business life it is hard to find businesses, or organisations of any size or substance, that do not have a website. In most cases, the website represents the 'personality' of the business.

This chapter will introduce you to the vast range of activities that are capable of being carried out online. You will learn how different sectors can make use of the internet, whether they are selling things or delivering important services. You will find out how different kinds of organisation make use of the internet.

You will investigate and learn how different websites serve different types of business purposes. Some simply present a site visitor with information; with other websites, you can make purchases, and in many cases this adds to an offline, physical store. Increasingly, websites offer customers the chance to 'customise' products online and allow interaction with the content. Web technology allows a business to get to know who their customers are, where they are from and what they have looked at on its site.

Put like this, can you imagine your own existence today *without* the internet?

This chapter will help you to:

- Understand different types of online activity.
- Explain how businesses operate online.
- Explain the issues a business needs to consider before going online.
- Explain the operational risks of going online.
- Create web pages to meet user needs.
- Outline the impact of online business on society as a whole.
- Compare businesses working online.
- Explain how websites help achieve aims and objectives.
- Evaluate benefits and drawbacks to society of increasing online business.

Understand different online business activities

Someone once said there are now more web pages online than there are stars in the sky. So any attempt to capture the *full* range of online activities is bound to fall short. Let's just say the internet can help many kinds of organisation to achieve their aims and objectives.

The range of online organisational activities

Organisations that can successfully use the internet could be illustrated from a very broad range of markets and sectors. These include:

- businesses selling to consumers (B2C), such as tesco.com
- businesses selling to other businesses (B2B), such as rs-online.com
- local councils, e.g. newcastle.gov.uk
- central government departments, e.g. dwp.gov.uk (Department for Work and Pensions)
- charities and voluntary organisations, e.g. oxfam.org.uk
- pressure groups, e.g. foe.co.uk.

All these kinds of organisation (and others) can achieve many different sorts of aims and objectives by having a 'presence' (i.e. you can find their website) online.

Before we go on, how can we separate an 'aim' from an 'objective'?

An 'aim' tends to be a fairly general thing. For example, the 'aim' of your school or college could be to offer a first-rate education to all of its learners. The 'aim' of a local council might be to improve services to the people; the 'aim' of a private commercial business could be to 'be the leading manufacturer' or 'the UK's top retailer'. Aims point the organisation in a general direction. Objectives are narrower and more specific. For example, an aim to be 'the leading manufacturer' will generate many more specific objectives. Objectives could be 'to reduce manufacturing faults by 75% (three-quarters) within six months'; to 'increase sales by 50% (half) by March'. Taken together, successfully achieving your objectives adds up to achieving your aim.

Fieldwork

In a group, arrange to investigate online organisations falling within the categories identified above. Create a table headed B2B, B2C, etc. and, for each organisation, list as many aims and objectives from an online presence as you can.

Let's look at some specific types of activity that can be carried out online.

Direct online selling of services

The internet is increasingly being used as a vehicle for directly selling services to the consumer. Whereas a new 50-inch plasma-screen TV can be purchased via a website, it must be physically moved and transported. However, a service is an unseen thing and there are many kinds of service that can be delivered online. The following examples illustrate this.

Car insurance

There are now many online motor insurers offering a quick, easy and cost-effective way to insure a vehicle. Examples include:

- Elephant.co.uk
- Swiftcover.com
- Morethan.com
- Swinton.co.uk
- Directline.com
- Sainsburysbank.co.uk.

And remember there are *many* others, in fact so many that there are now several online

intermediary services allowing consumers to compare insurance quotes. One of these is ComparetheMarket.com.

Comparethemarket.com

These services are quick, convenient and cost effective. An online insurance business does not have the overheads (e.g. buildings and offices in every location) that a physical business has. This enables them to pass on savings to the consumer.

Banking

Most major banks offer their full range of services online. Users can track their finances by accessing accounts and maintain full financial control from their home or business 24 hours a day. Examples include:

- Barclays.co.uk
- Co-operativebank.co.uk
- Halifax.co.uk.

Again, there are intermediary sites offering comparison services. An example is Moneysupermarket.com. The internet has also allowed for specialist online banks.

Government services

At some time in our lives all of us need the help, advice or support of central (or national) government services ('from the cradle to the grave', as they say). Many services that are funded by government – so-called 'public services' – are needed by everyone; this includes hospitals, schools and colleges, job centres, careers advice, taxes, GP practices, pensions, business advice, and social and family support.

Central government services can be accessed from www.direct.gov.uk. This is a 'portal' site. This means that it acts as a single point of access that can be used for all government information or services.

Other public services are available at the local level. These 'local authorities' or councils represent a local area. In the UK all local councils have their own websites. These give citizens access to local information about the range of services available.

Fieldwork

Access the website of your own local authority (council). Prepare a presentation outlining the purposes of the website and conclude by summarising how local citizens benefit.

Did you know...

A survey of 16- to 24-year-olds has found that 75% of them feel they 'couldn't live' without the internet. The report, published by online charity YouthNet, also found that four out of five young people used the web to look for advice. About one-third added that they felt no need to talk to a person face to face about their problems because of the resources available online.

Information

On the web there is an entire industry *just* devoted to giving information. We can check the weather, trace our ancestry, look up bus and train timetables, flight times and costs, GP and hospital casualty times. If we need information on just about any topic under the sun, we can use a search engine. Today, we even have a commonplace reference in our language – 'just Google it'.

We saw earlier that many specialist sites are now available giving consumers' or professional buyers' comparisons of providers. For whole industries, we can access so called 'portal sites' where we can research industry-specific information. For most people now, the web would be the first option for quick and easy access to information.

Internet services

To make good use of the world wide web, many businesses need the services of specialist 'internet service providers'. An internet service provider (ISP) is a company that collects a monthly or yearly fee in exchange for providing a subscriber with internet access.

When looking for an ISP, the first consideration is the type of access needed. Some ISPs offer dial-up access, which is the slowest type of connection, as well as high-speed broadband. For cable service, a business would need to check with local cable TV providers to see if cable access is offered. For a DSL service, there may be multiple choices.

ISP services range in price according to the package offered and type of service. Dial-up is the least expensive and extra services differ between providers. Some offer multiple email accounts, others vast amounts of web space, and still others discounts for paying in advance. DSL and cable companies will also differ, so businesses need to think carefully about the terms before deciding on an ISP.

Some companies offer the full range of internet services, from designing a website, registering the domain name (i.e. the web address), to hosting the site. The website content can be kept up-to-date using a 'content management system' (CMS).

For any business considering transferring business activity to the internet, careful consideration needs to be given to the type and quality of ongoing support that is on offer.

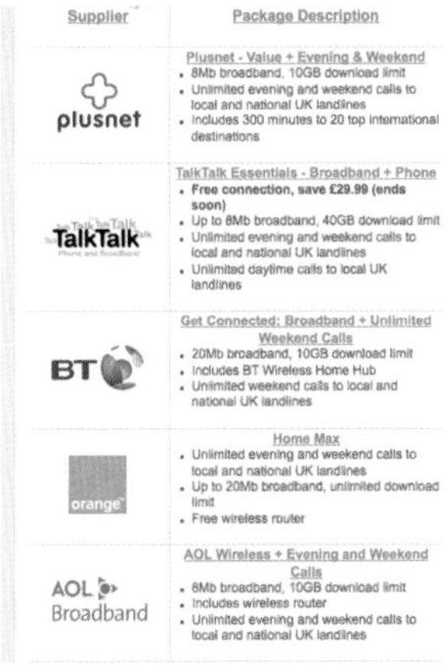

Supplier	Package Description
plusnet	Plusnet - Value + Evening & Weekend • 8Mb broadband, 10GB download limit • Unlimited evening and weekend calls to local and national UK landlines • Includes 300 minutes to 20 top international destinations
TalkTalk	TalkTalk Essentials - Broadband + Phone • **Free connection, save £29.99 (ends soon)** • Up to 8Mb broadband, 40GB download limit • Unlimited evening and weekend calls to local and national UK landlines • Unlimited daytime calls to local UK landlines
BT	Get Connected: Broadband + Unlimited Weekend Calls • 20Mb broadband, 10GB download limit • Includes BT Wireless Home Hub • Unlimited weekend calls to local and national UK landlines
orange	Home Max • Unlimited evening and weekend calls to local and national UK landlines • Up to 20Mb broadband, unlimited download limit • Free wireless router
AOL Broadband	AOL Wireless + Evening and Weekend Calls • 8Mb broadband, 10GB download limit • Includes wireless router • Unlimited evening and weekend calls to local and national UK landlines

Internet service providers

Advertising and marketing

The internet offers businesses fantastic opportunities to market their products or services. After all, it is '*world*wide'!

Marketing online

The basic idea of marketing is to find out who customers are, where they are and what they want. No business starts up and succeeds unless there is a '**market**' for what it offers. The internet helps business to find out.

> **Fieldwork**
>
> Get together in a group of four classmates. Design a short survey to find out if there is a 'market' for a car-washing service at your school or college. You will find that people want to know things like the price, when, where, etc. Assuming that there is a market, discuss the possible ways in which the internet could help such a business.

Marketing identifies facts about the 'market' and then sets about making sure that the business organisation serving the market fully meets customer needs. This is at the heart of marketing – *satisfying customers*.

The internet can help business marketing in many ways.

Identifying the market

When you were invited to find out whether people at your school or college would use a car-washing service, you were doing *primary* 'market research'. Primary research discovers new information to be used only by you. By using the internet, a business can carry out a lot of 'secondary research' too. How many people live in an area? How many car owners are there? How many people use the internet? What age groups? Secondary research means using information that has been gathered elsewhere.

Businesses can research trends nationally and internationally. They can do this by investigating market trends within particular industries.

Analysing the business situation

The internet lets a business see who its competitors are, where they are and where possible threats may come from. The business can also identify potential opportunities.

Targeting a market

'Markets' for products can be broken down into parts known as 'segments'. So for cars the market can be segmented by:

- large or small vehicles
- price
- family size
- driver age
- driver sex.

When a **market segment** is identified, marketers can 'target' that segment through advertising or promotion, price, product features or product placement (the so-called 4 Ps).

Advertising

Online advertising is a big industry today.

Online advertising 'overtakes TV'

A report in September 2009 said that online advertising spending in the UK had overtaken spending on television advertising for the first time.

Online advertising grew by 4.6% to £1.752bn in the first half of 2009 despite economic decline and there was a fall in overall advertising spending of 16% compared to the same period in 2008. Spending on television advertising fell by 16.1% to a total of £1.639bn.

The study was by the Internet Advertising Bureau, who are the trade organisation for digital marketing, and PricewaterhouseCoopers.

Online advertising includes different types as advertising such as email campaigns, classified adverts, display ads and search marketing.

According to the authors of the report, the recession had caused more businesses to shift advertising spending from traditional media outlets such as print, radio and television to online.

Source: BBC news

The case study refers to four different kind of online advertising:

1. Email campaigns
2. Classified ads
3. Display ads
4. Search engine marketing.

Investigate and find out what each of these methods involves and create a poster display to show each method.

Fieldwork

Select one of the following industries and carry out a UK-based web search.

1. Motor retail
2. Chemicals
3. Electrical
4. Food and beverages
5. Information technology.

List the sites you have found giving information about that industry. Select one of these and summarise the sort of information available on the site.

Education

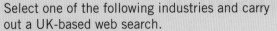

Because the world wide web is an information-giving medium, it can be an ideal way of delivering educational or training materials. Many training courses are now available online. Educational providers can use the web to put together online courses supported by a 'virtual learning environment' (VLE).

Sector

A 'sector' in this context refers to a section or part of our 'economy'.

When people refer to our 'economy', this refers to the ways in which we use our resources (i.e. money, buildings, land, people and machinery) to produce what we need. (Ever heard someone say they need to 'economise'?) Our economy can be divided up and classified into different parts or 'sectors'. This is because different organisations operate for completely different purposes. Examples are:

- Hospitals/clinics/GP surgeries/schools, etc. – these organisations exist to offer vital services and are paid for by the government.
- Commercial businesses – exist to make private profit for individuals.
- Voluntary sector – to support or promote good causes.

The way in which we can make sense of different parts of our economy is like this:

Public sector

These organisations are funded by government, which raises the money from public taxation, e.g. income tax, VAT. These organisations work for all of us – 'the public'. Public sector organisations exist because we all agree that we need these services, they work in the 'public interest'. The two most obvious ones are health and education but there are many more.

Examples of public sector organisations:

- The local council
- A central government department
- A primary care trust
- A college of further education
- A secondary school
- A primary school

Note: never confuse the 'public sector' with a 'public limited company' (plc); they are completely different things.

Fieldwork

Working with another classmate, investigate your local area and make a list of at least six different public sector organisations. Create a simple table listing the name of the organisation and a summary of the service it provides. List the web addresses of each organisation.

Private sector

Whereas the public sector works for the public as a whole, the private sector works for private profit. Your local hospital exists because we all might need its services, but the local supermarket exists because business executives have decided that this is a good place to sell goods in order to make profit for shareholders.

Private sector businesses are called 'private' because they base their activities on success (profit) for themselves. There is a huge range of activities covered within the private sector.

Among *very many other things*, private sector business covers:

- manufacturing
- retail
- insurance services
- financial services
- chemicals
- publishing
- broadcasting
- media
- web design.

Fieldwork

Investigate and find out the general kinds of local businesses that exist in your area. Does one large private organisation tend to be the major employer? Carry out an online search to see how many local businesses have a web presence.

Voluntary/not-for-profit sector

This sector is sometimes referred to as 'the third sector'. As the description suggests, this sector works in support of a wide variety of causes and issues. The sector relies almost entirely on individuals getting involved on a voluntary, non-payment basis. Many of these are 'single-issue' organisations. If these voluntary bodies did not exist, these issues would still be around but with fewer funds.

Make the grade

M1 **D1** When you are investigating the ways in which voluntary bodies use the internet and considering how they can make use of it, you can use this information to help you achieve M1 and D1.

Types of online presence

The internet 'carries' the world wide web. The internet could be described as the 'tracks' that carry the web 'train' all over the world.

Did you know...

The internet has been around since about 1957 but it has only become *really* useful for everybody since the creation of the 'world wide web' in the early 1990s.

Surprisingly, internet technology, i.e. the ability to get computers to be able to connect to each other, has been available since the 1950s, when the USA became frightened of the USSR's ability to send spacecraft orbiting the Earth. However, it is 'web technology' that makes the internet so important. The world wide web allows documents (pages) to 'hyperlink' to each other using HTML (hypertext mark-up language).

In many ways, how businesses make use of web technology depends on their needs. Some business organisations exist entirely online and they depend on the internet. Others don't have such a need for online work. However, the days are gone when it is a rarity to have a website.

There is now a wide variety of types of online presence. These are listed below.

'Passive' brochure-ware

As web technology has improved over the years, the capabilities available to a business online have also improved. A business can simply display the goods it has available for sale. This is something like a paper brochure, where the reader simply looks at the pictures of the product and comes to some kind of a decision about whether they wish to investigate further.

Volunteering levels almost unchanged in England

Government's citizenship survey finds percentages of adults participating are similar to last year

Volunteering levels have remained almost static over the past year in England, according to the Communities and Local Government Department's latest citizenship survey.

Forty-three per cent of adults questioned between April and June said they had volunteered formally at least once in the previous 12 months, compared with 41 per cent in 2008/09.

Figures for informal volunteering at least once in the previous year fell from 62 per cent in 2008/09 to 57 per cent.

Formal volunteering is defined as giving unpaid help through groups, clubs or organisations to benefit other people or the environment. Informal volunteering is defined as giving unpaid help to people who are not relatives.

People aged under 25 were most likely to volunteer informally, while 64- to 75-year-olds were the most likely to volunteer formally. Levels of formal volunteering were highest in the south-east.

Mike Locke, director of public affairs at Volunteering England, said he was happy to see levels of formal volunteering back up to 43 per cent. He also noted that the percentage of 16- to 25-year-olds who had volunteered at least once in the previous year had increased from 38 to 44 per cent.

Bill Garland, deputy executive director of CSV, said the challenge was to shape opportunities to match people's availability. He said better volunteer management would help.

'We would also want to examine the possibility of citizens being given the right to participate in the delivery of local authority services such as parks, schools, libraries, children's centres and care homes,' he said.

Source: Paul Jump, Third Sector Online, 29 October 2009

1. Investigate the online activities of the so called 'third sector'. In what ways does the web help these organisations?
2. Compare two of the third-sector organisations with a presence on the internet. What similarities can you find between the ways they use the world wide web?
3. Choose a voluntary or not-for-profit organisation, investigate and make simple recommendations as to how they might make use of the web.

Think about the internet for a moment. What is *actually* happening when a consumer looks to shop online? Usually, there is the consumer sitting alone looking at the web page. This is a *one-to-one* interaction. Each web page displays with this fact in mind; there is one individual *potential* customer viewing the page. A '**passive**' web page simply looks back. The display is the same whether the person looking is in Outer Mongolia or Swindon. The goods on show never change. The viewer sees what they see, whoever or wherever they may be. That passive web page will never change until someone looking after the website decides to change the content.

Many web design services and many web marketing specialists try to offer businesses far more than just passive content, as we shall see.

Fieldwork

Investigate the web and see how many examples of 'passive' brochure-ware you can find.

Complementing offline services

Many businesses with an online presence use their website to add to what they already do from a physical store. A physical store exists to display and sell goods. A website can encourage people to buy, 24 hours a day. These complementary websites offer customers the chance to make purchases via the website. These sites are therefore called 'transactional' sites. This means that people can 'transact' via the site (i.e. pay for something). This is a real 'step up' from a passive site.

Examples of these types of online activities might be easier to find these days than passive online brochures. There are now many examples, some of which are listed below.

B&Q (www.diy.com)

The B&Q hardware and DIY stores are nationwide with an HQ in Southampton. Since around 2001, B&Q has also operated an online outlet available via diy.com.

B&Q sell directly from the web

Tesco (www.tesco.com)

Tesco, of course, operates physical stores everywhere, but it also operates a website at tesco.com. Having an online presence for Tesco allows the company to give information about all kind of services that are not easily accessible in a physical store.

Fieldwork

Investigate at least three websites made available by businesses that also have physical outlets. Make a list of the various services and features that can be accessed on the website. Summarise why you think these businesses benefit from a web presence.

Next (www.next.co.uk)

Next is another business with very successful and popular physical outlets in most major towns and cities. However, the business also offers a website. Customers can view products across all ranges and, of course, shop online if they wish.

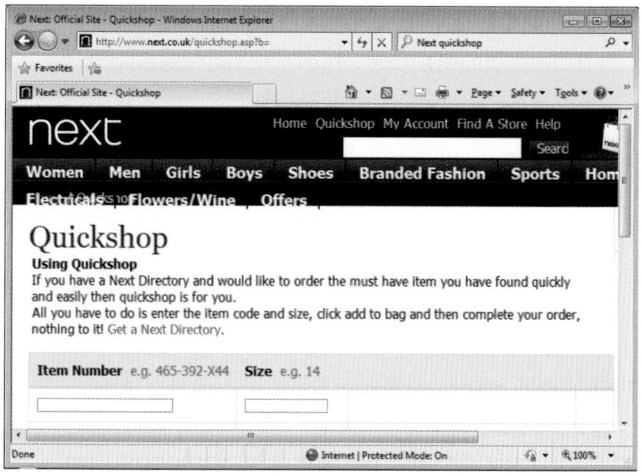

Quickshop feature on the Next website

Fieldwork

The UK-based DVD and video-rental outlet Blockbuster is a business that operates both physically on the high street as well as online. This kind of complementary online offer is designed to support the main business.

In contrast there is a US-based business doing a similar thing but operating entirely online. This is Netflix, which can be found at www.netflix.com.

Investigate these two businesses and create a poster display summarising the similarities and differences between the two. Why do you feel that Blockbuster still operates in the high street?

Offering interactive customisation

When we looked earlier at the idea of a 'passive' website, we saw that to be 'passive' means the site just sits there looking back at you. If you went out with a new girlfriend or boyfriend and they were just passive *all of the time*, they would soon start to get on your nerves! People like a response. The technology available on the internet now enables web designers to create web pages that respond to a visitor.

What is 'interactivity'?

When something is **interactive**, it offers some form of response to a user's actions. In website terms this can mean different things. You may have used an interactive website when doing your course. Online testing can be interactive.

For example, say you were given an online test that asked you, 'In the following sentence, what is the missing word?'

'This summer I am hoping to go to Barbados for my ________'

1. laziness
2. Dad
3. overcoat
4. holidays

An incorrect selection might respond with 'No, try again'.

This is 'interacting' with you.

Online gaming offers obvious interaction. For business websites, interactivity can allow the business to create the feeling of a relationship with the visitor. However, websites can only do this if they capture your own details first. This is why so many sites ask you to 'register' with the site. There is usually nothing more sinister in this. The web designers simply want the site to know who you are on a future visit and to be able to respond to you personally.

Customisation

'Customisation' is slightly different. To '**customise**' something means that a product has been changed to suit your own personal tastes. The web can allow customers to change images shown on screen so that they can see how a product might look. This goes some way to bridging the gap between actually being *physically* in the store and sitting at your PC.

Fieldwork

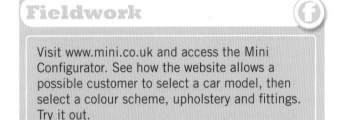

Visit www.mini.co.uk and access the Mini Configurator. See how the website allows a possible customer to select a car model, then select a colour scheme, upholstery and fittings. Try it out.

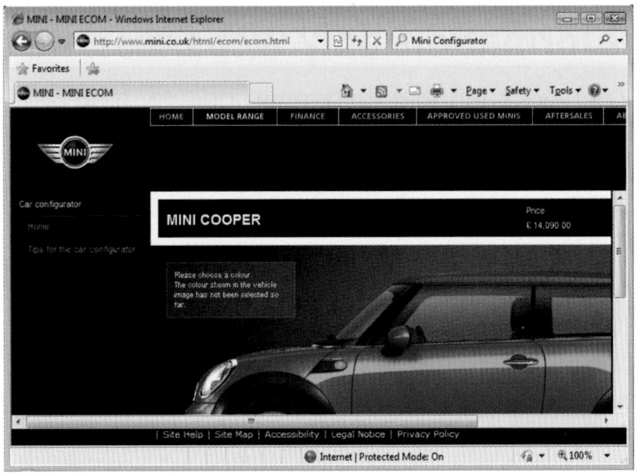

Card Corp

Founded in 1988 by Ivor Jacobs, Card Corp aims to plug a market gap by producing short-run print items such as business stationery. It focuses on providing a cost-effective, high-quality online service. This avoids many of the costs and delays associated with communication and the transfer of information.

This integrated approach to technology has given the company a single system that offers:

- online ordering, design, approval, despatch and order tracking
- automatic data capture
- the conversion of designs from low resolution (on the website) to high resolution (in print)
- the rendering of material into a press-ready format
- digital printing
- automated guillotining and finishing.

Having built its own system, the company is also well placed to amend its processes in response to customer requests.

'Whenever a customer or supplier comes to us and says they'd like a certain feature to be added, we go back and write it in. They're the people who are using it, so we have to take their suggestions on board,' says Ivor.

Because it has integrated technology from the start, many of the traditional measures of business success, such as cost savings or increased sales, do not apply to Card Corp. The benefits are more straightforward – technology made the company possible. It enabled the company to meet an unanswered demand and to do so very profitably. Card Corp has very few direct competitors and, with sales snowballing, turnover is increasing at an annual rate of 80–90%.

1. Investigate www.cardcorp.co.uk and with a classmate, list the main features of the website.

2. In what ways do you feel customers benefit from this online service?

3. What do you think was 'the unanswered demand' referred to in the case study?

Information-only websites

We have seen that the web is ideal for many business purposes. People can access services from both public and private sector organisations and they can view, choose and purchase physical goods.

Many websites simply offer information. This can be intended for business (e.g.www.businesslink.gov.uk) or for consumers (e.g. www.kelkoo.co.uk).

Fieldwork

Under the following categories, investigate online and summarise information services available for:

- maps
- phone numbers
- the local council
- a primary care trust.

Key words

Customise – Where a website uses information to change what is displayed in order to suit a particular customer.

Passive – A website that merely presents information.

Market – An online 'space' where businesses and people can come together to buy and sell.

Interactive – Where the website invites the visitor to engage with the content.

Intermediary – An organisation that operates between buyers and sellers.

Market segment – A part of an overall market (e.g. young mums).

Target market – The group within a market that a marketing effort hopes to attract.

Assignment

You are working for a consultancy firm and you have been asked to do some research on business organisations operating online. The purpose is to be in a strong position to advise business managers. Your own line manager needs material that she can use in presentations to clients.

Task 1

Investigate and describe three different business organisations that operate online. (This can include businesses which also have a physical presence on the high street.) You should select at least one organisation from the public sector.

Task 2

Explain how each of these business organisations operates their activities online. (Do they sell directly? Do they email clients? Do they offer online services?)

Task 3

Describe the benefits to one of the organisations of marketing its product or service online. (Market size and scope; customer service; availability; personalisation or customisation?)

Task 4

Compare the main features of the three business organisations operating online.

Consider:

- Product – is it a service or physical goods?
- Website features
- Market – local, national or global?
- Private or public sector?
- Profit or not for profit?

To achieve a pass grade you need to:	To achieve a merit grade you need to:	To achieve a distinction you need to:
P1 describe three different business organisations that operate online	**M1** compare the features of three business organisations operating online	**D1** make recommendations for a business organisation considering going online
P2 explain how they operate their activities online		
P6 describe the benefits to a business organisation of marketing a product or service online		

Chapter 27
Issues related to doing business online

What are you finding out?

The internet is a worldwide resource and it continues to grow and spread. It would be easy for a private sector business looking for more profits to think this is the answer to all of their prayers. There would be more customers, a bigger market to attract, 24-hour availability – it all sounds fantastic. However, there are many issues and concerns that should be considered before adopting an online strategy.

To place a business online needs a good deal of careful planning. The planning involves many different aspects of an organisation, whether this is a private business or a public sector body.

This chapter will help you to:

- Understand the planning needed before going online.
- Understand the ways in which an online presence is successfully achieved.
- Understand the risks involved in going online.
- Understand the staffing issues involved in operating online.
- Understand financial concerns involved in going online.
- Understand the distribution concerns involved in running an online business.

Planning issues

The first thing to consider should be fairly obvious – is the business suitable for online operation? Think for a moment about the various business activities you personally know of. These might include:

- bars
- nightclubs
- youth clubs
- football club
- fish and chip shops
- Indian or Chinese or Asian takeaways
- bus companies
- taxi firms
- garages
- wine stores
- others.

Which of these would you say were *unsuitable* for online business? The answer to this might be, 'It depends on what you expect.' Could an online visitor to a website gain any benefit from the website of a nightclub?

Would a garage be a suitable business to work online?

Fieldwork

Investigate whether any local nightclubs, bars, restaurants or pubs have their own website. Visit the site and write a short statement summarising what the site is seeking to do. How do customers benefit? What might the business be achieving?

Did you know...

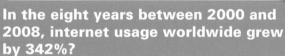

In the eight years between 2000 and 2008, internet usage worldwide grew by 342%?

Bells Online

One local fish and chip shop business with an online presence is Bells of Durham City. The website at www.bellsfishshop.co.uk is a purely passive site offering information only. However, much of the information is crucial to customers (prices, opening hours and menu). The proprietor of Bells is sole trader Graham Kennedy, who says, 'I like the website. How many fish shops have their own website? I want Bells to be better, different, up-to-date and something for the local community to be proud of.'

Mr Kennedy uses the website to promote the business and in doing so, offers useful information to customers from anywhere.

'We are up there – online, with our business personality available for all to see. It is 2009 and I believe this industry needs to promote what it does and how it does it. For example, how many people realise that people like us need to think about sustainability! I bet not many; but we do. I asked around and got a relation of mine to ask a local web designer if he could help. The designer came to see me, listened to what I wanted and then produced about six alternative "looks" for a Bells website. Together, we agreed on the look; I wanted a silver/grey appearance and I wanted a system whereby I could alter the content to keep it up-to-date. This is called a "content management system" (CMS). The designer also arranged the hosting of the site and the domain name registration. I wouldn't be without the website now.'

1. In your own words, summarise the advantages for Mr Kennedy, the owner of Bells, in having his business represented online.
2. What problems might Bells have experienced when the website went live?
3. Investigate Bells Online and create a short summary of what the site offers. Could you suggest any improvements?

Other planning issues relate to:

- the domain name
- setting up the website.

Website domain names

Computers only really understand numbers. However, the 12-digit number that represents a web address would be 'gobbledegook' to humans. This is why we have 'human-readable' domain names. In the case study above, Graham Kennedy of Bells was given the option by his web designer of a number of domain names. He chose 'bellsfishshop' because that seemed to him to be the closest way of linking the name to the business. He then could have had .com, .org, .eu, if he had wished. It is important for any business to choose a domain name that will effectively 'announce' the business.

Domain names can be purchased and registered at very reasonable cost.

Website set-up issues

Setting up a website can be a very simple process but this depends largely on the kind of activities that are required from the site. We have already seen that websites can be offered simply as flat, passive, information providers, or they can be fully interactive and personalised with customisable features.

If a business needs a website that is to be fully 'transactional' (where you can sell from) and there are a lot of business systems needing to connect to it, then there will be a need for expert advice and support.

For large businesses offering an online selling service, the website needs to connect to a number of internal databases. These may contain product details, images, reference or catalogue numbers, stock availability, location, prices, delivery times and so on. The website must be a well informed, up-to-date and dynamic aspect of an integrated e-business. This cannot merely be done by an in-house web design 'amateur'. In these cases, the web design task will be 'outsourced' and completed following detailed investigation by designers and ICT staff.

A big consideration for any organisation going online is 'Do we have the resources to cope?' By 'resources' we must include:

- staff
- storage
- delivery procedures

- ICT or call centre facility for orders
- stock
- customer service.

Legal disaster?

In the USA several years ago, a young lawyer saw what he thought was a fantastic opportunity to take advantage of the web. He decided to offer a range of legal documents online. These documents would include contracts, deeds and other regular legal papers. In the lawyer's mind this would be easy. Create standard documents according to people's instructions then let them check aspects of the documents online. Agree the fee, send the documents digitally, then via mail. What a way to increase business!

When this US-based lawyer received an enquiry from Bulgaria he was puzzled as to what to do. Others from Japan, China and Germany caused more worries.

It was soon obvious that this online venture could not possibly succeed.

1. In what ways would better planning have helped the lawyer?
2. What 'resources' was he missing that might have helped?
3. In your opinion, is this sort of legal service possible online?

Implementation issues

To implement a successful website means to actually place the site online and make it work successfully for the organisation. We have already seen that careful planning is required to do this. There are several reasons for this.

Availability of technical and design skills

The website requirements of the organisation determine the level of technical or design skills that are going to be needed. Bells Fish Shop did not need great technical skills because the website has very simple demands; i.e. to update the textual content as needed. However, the tesco.com website has considerable technical support needs. This is because the site has to integrate with many other business systems used by Tesco. A large database of products is one of these systems.

These are important management considerations for any business that intends to mount an online operation. What staff skills does the business possess? Do we have people who can maintain the website? Do we have people with the technical ICT skills to support the processes that feed the site?

Customisation

We saw earlier that customisation is an important feature of web technology. An online customer is in a one-to-one interaction with a web page. The messages that are displayed can therefore be 'customised' (or 'personalised') to suit that particular person. One online business that has led the way in customisation is amazon.com. A customer needs only to register and make an online purchase. At the next visit, the website will recognise who you are and make recommendations according to what you previously bought. Obviously, to design this kind of feature into a website requires higher-level skills.

Extent of online operations

We know that websites can range from passive information presenters to fully interactive, customisable and personalised offers. The range of online activity is vast. We can consider the needs of Bells Online and compare to B&Q online. In one case, there is no need for interactivity (unless someone thinks it is a good idea to look at a virtual fish and chip meal); in the other case, perhaps there is a need for interactive bedroom or kitchen design.

Fieldwork

Investigate www.diy.com and look for interactive room-design features. What implementation issues do you think this might have for B&Q? (Think: customer expectations?)

Relationship with partners

A business that has taken a decision to go online must always remember that this might cause a big change to the way the business works. These changes could have an effect on existing partner businesses. An example of this might be where a business decides that it can successfully sell from a website and deliver *directly* to an online customer. The effect might be to put another business, e.g. a delivery or courier firm, in trouble.

Operational risks

When a business decides to go online, we could say they have decided on a new 'strategy' to do business. The aims remain the same but the organisation has decided that there can be a new way to help achieve them.

Any 'strategy' must be put into practice. It is managers and staff who do this, at the so-called 'operational' level. So what are the risks for the running of a business organisation, if the business is online?

There are several risks, which are discussed below.

Payment security

Millions of internet-based business 'transactions' (i.e. payments made in return for goods or services) take place every minute. The internet is an open and sometimes insecure network. It is vital for any business that when a payment system is adopted it is secure. This is not only important for the business, it is important for the online customer. One of the biggest fears for customers is theft of bank account or credit card details. Online businesses therefore often take care to reassure customers that their online ordering and payment processes will be secure.

Fieldwork

Visit www.diy.com and under 'Support Centre' > 'Website Policies', find the section describing the company's 'ordering securely' advice to customers. Summarise why you feel B&Q offers this advice.

Unfamiliar trading conditions

A business that has been used to operating within a particular market needs to consider the changed conditions that could apply online. The internet is an open medium. When a business makes an online 'offer', this could be taken up by potential customers from anywhere.

One business that has become a very successful online operation is electrical wholesaler RS Components. This website is at http://uk.rs-online.com. RS Components discovered that whereas their traditional customers were electrical trades people, increasingly private consumers were visiting the site and attempting to make purchases. The business had, by going online, discovered an entirely new market.

Errors in ordering

The online business must have systems in place that ensure orders are correctly processed. Online customers, particularly private consumers in B2C (Business to Consumer) markets are very easily put off an online service if they find it unreliable. Customers expect their orders to be correctly and quickly dealt with. It is important for business managers to set up ordering processes that are accurate and efficient.

Potential misuse of personal information

Just as private online customers have fears about theft of bank details or card details, they also have fears about loss of private and personal information, even theft of identity (so-called 'spoofing').

Online customers should be advised never to buy as a result of 'unsolicited' emails. These are emails that have not been requested and just arrive unannounced, so-called 'junk' emails. If recipients do wish to look further, they can always look at the website linked to the mail, without opening the email, and look at the 'contact us' link. Alternatively, they might use a search engine to look into a business.

Vulnerability to hostile attack

A business working online has the risk of opening up many sorts of data to outside attack from so-called hackers. Illegal hackers can break into insecure data systems and steal data on employees, customers, sales, products, finance or anything else. It is important that data are protected and a number of measures can be taken. These measures include:

- firewall software
- anti-virus software
- 'encryption' of data (i.e. scrambling the content)
- password protection
- user authentication.

All of these measures will help to protect a business's confidential data and many of them can be written up in an ICT security policy.

Fieldwork

Find out if your school or college has an ICT security policy that you can read. List at least three of its main points and summarise why these things are important.

Website updating

We saw earlier that updating the content of a website is essential. Hardly anything is more destructive to a website's appeal than the knowledge that its content is completely out-of-date. This is why a CMS system, such as the one used by Bells (see case study), is useful.

Language problems with global customer base

The language question has caused even the most mature online businesses to have some embarrassing moments:

Examples

Kentucky Fried Chicken's advertising slogan, 'Finger Lickin' Good' was translated into Chinese as 'Eat Your Fingers Off.'

The Pepsi slogan, 'Come Alive with the Pepsi Generation', translated for Taiwan, read as 'Pepsi will bring your ancestors back from the dead.'

Hardware and software failure

For the business thinking about transferring activities online (selling, informing, delivering a service), the prospect of ICT failure, either in hardware (individual computers or entire network system) or software (the application programs in use) is a potential nightmare. This is why it is so important to plan ahead and consult with advisors about the level of ongoing specialist ICT technical support that will be needed. The collapse of an ICT network could spell complete failure for a business that is dependent on consistent online availability.

Global business regulations

A major question for any business operating globally via the web is, 'Whose rules apply?' If a business buys from a supplier in Canada but does not get what it ordered, what do they do?

The UK government issued revised guidance for businesses on the 'Distance Selling Regulations' in September 2006. The then Minister, Mr Ian McCartney, said:

'Consumers deserve protection, whether they are buying from their local shop or online. But businesses need to have a clear idea of where the law stands. That's why this guidance will support businesses in their efforts to operate distance sales and give consumers the protection they deserve.'

In the EU, the 2002 E-commerce Regulations put e-commerce rules for the whole of Europe into UK law. Among other things, member states have to ensure that contracts can be concluded electronically.

Other questions that need to be considered relate to product features such as labelling and safety. In the UK there are rules about the information contained on labels on products. Products placed on sale in the UK must also meet certain health and safety rules. In other countries, the same standards of safety often do not apply. Any business conducting purchases across international borders needs to carry out very careful research and negotiations.

Staffing issues

People are central to a successful online operation, even if the business is fully trading via the web. Customers or clients need advice, support and information. Often customers need further explanation or reassurance about products. In addition, what if something goes wrong with a product? Even in an online operation, it could be people (staff) who make the difference between success and failure. This means employing staff with the right skills, in the right context. Staff concerns are therefore another important consideration for a newly online business.

Using a call centre

Having a web presence immediately places a business on a global scale. Customers could make enquiries, try to place orders, complain, cancel orders from anywhere in the world. The question is, does the business have the staff on hand to respond? One increasingly common option for many organisations is the use of a 'call centre'. This is a centralised team that permanently staffs a computerised telephonic system.

When B&Q first began online operations, a call centre team was hired to respond to customers. Today, many banks and insurance services use call centres.

Make the grade

M2 When you are analysing the benefits to businesses and customers of conducting business online for M2, you could look into the features of websites that are designed to respond quickly to customer needs.

Lack of personal contact with customers

The web offers great potential to gain new customers. However, online customers demand high standards of customer care. Not only must orders be despatched, be accurate and as expected, if there are any queries or problems, they need to be dealt with in a friendly and sympathetic way. This is a vital aspect of online marketing.

Any business moving online needs to think about ways in which the lack of direct face-to-face contact with a customer can be overcome.

Make the grade

M2 When working towards M2, you could mention the importance of well-trained staff to deal with online enquiries.

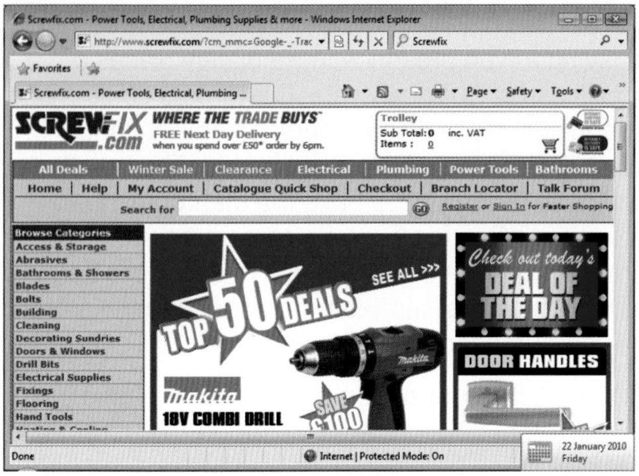

The Screwfix website is an award-winning site that offers a number of features that are designed to benefit customers

For staff, handling communications with distant, remote customers requires particular skills. If staff feel far from human contact with the outside world, this could be a problem.

Task

Imagine you are advising a local medium-sized company. The firm is about to go 'live' on the internet with a 'transactional' website and *will not* be using a call centre. What would be the most important set of skills you would require from office staff?

Unfamiliarity with the technology

Any organisation introducing new processes relating to the internet must have the internal staff skills to cope. No serious online business can hope to succeed if the staff know nothing about the internet or the web, or are unable to use a PC.

Breakdowns in service

It is important for an online business to be aware that, in the event of a breakdown in internet service, the business could be badly affected. Sales could be lost and customers could be put off. It is important, therefore, that staff have the proper training to handle enquiries by telephone if necessary. Staff should also be ready to offer support and advice to customers who may feel frustrated during a period of loss of service.

Financial issues

The initial investment costs of operating online have to be considered. Web design costs can be modest. However, as in most things, the more that is invested in this, the better the product is likely to be. For a business intending to make the web a core aspect of its operation, web design will be a major undertaking. This will be costly. For a business needing only the most basic web presence, this will not be the case.

For a newly online business, there will be several areas needing initial investment:

- web design
- hosting and domain-name registration
- hardware and networking
- software
- ongoing website maintenance
- ICT support
- training
- distribution and storage.

Ability to cope with increased market interest

When a business starts to operate online, the visibility of the business is much greater than before. A small operation on an industrial estate can appear just as big as a multinational business when seen online. If the website is well-constructed and carries the right information, new customers should come along.

This is exactly what a business will hope for – new customers, more revenue and hopefully more profit. This is success in private sector terms. However, as we have seen earlier, the background systems must support the website. No business can afford to make false promises online. An online business must fulfil customer expectations. The customer gets what they want, at the right time, in the right place, in the right condition – *as expected.*

In the USA a purely online business was set up called Kozmo.com. The business was a so-called 'e-tailer' (an online retailer). Via the Kozmo website, an irresistible offer was made, *'delivery within one hour at anytime'*. The problem was that the business paid as much for the products and to store and deliver them as it was getting for them.

The Wine Store

Mr Smith had run his wine store in a small town for a number of years with some success. Always keen to try new things, Mr Smith had invested quite a lot in home-brew wine kits but with a twist. Customers could select their kit and the wine store would do the brewing to the highest standards. The wine was quite cheap and the quality high.

The internet seemed a great idea.

'I got a cousin of mine to design a website for me. He was quite good if not quite a professional. I bought a great domain name – I couldn't believe it was still available. It cost me about 30 quid altogether and my site was ready to go online.'

The Wine Store website did go live but Mr Smith thought it should do better.

'I hadn't paid for a transactional site. People had to order by email. On the Monday after launch I only had one email. I contacted the local press and they did an article by the end of the week. I started to get a few more emails from the region. We looked at these orders and started responding to them.'

Mr Smith then took a call. 'The *Mail on Sunday* wanted to do a piece. This was published a week or two later. On the Monday after the *Mail's* article I got 2,000-plus emails. Within a day I had another 1,000 or so. It was obvious we couldn't cope with this. I decided that selling wine kits online should be left to someone else.'

1. What in your view did the Wine Store do wrong?

2. What were the main issues the business should have considered?

3. Suggest ways in which Mr Smith might have handled the online business venture more successfully.

Tax liabilities

When goods are bought and sold across international boundaries, there are questions of tax liabilities to be considered. Value-added tax (VAT) is liable, for example, on goods sold within the European Union. These liabilities are described in EU VAT rules. If a UK business sells to private consumers or non-VAT registered business *within* the EU, then the current standard rate of VAT (from 17.5% from January 2010) must be charged.

Goods that are imported into the UK must be declared for 'Import Duty'.

Fieldwork

Investigate www.businesslink.org.uk and create a short summary on paying taxes for imports and exports within and beyond the EU.

Make the grade

D4 When you are evaluating the benefits and drawbacks to society of increasing business online, for D4, you could discuss possible loss (or gain) of tax revenues.

Distribution issues

As we have already seen, a business starting to trade on the internet immediately has the potential to draw customers from far and wide. While this may at first appear to be a good thing, there are some big questions to be answered about the physical distribution of the goods. Of course, for digital products, or those that are capable of digital transfer (e.g. music, video or film material or games) this does not apply.

Many goods capable of being promoted and sold online are fragile. The appointment of appropriate distributors (couriers, transport companies), who can safely and securely handle such items, is important. A business seeking to distribute such products also needs to have insurance in place, together with good customer information and guarantees.

Many services available online have no such distribution problems. Insurance, banking, flight bookings, hotels or holidays are easily dealt with online. This is simply because these services can be digitally delivered.

Key words

Domain name – The human-readable part of a web address (e.g. amazon.co.uk).

Transactional – Where buying and selling (transactions) can take place.

Network – Where computers are connected within or beyond an organisation.

Operational – The actual running of an organisation or part of it (e.g. selling).

Digital – Consisting of numbers (0's and 1's in computer language).

Liability – Responsible for.

Call centre – An organisation specifically set up to make or receive telephonic communications.

Assignment

Operational issues in the online business

You continue to work for the consultancy referred to in Chapter 26's Assignment and you have been invited to put together some materials for a business seminar to be held in two weeks. This seminar is intended to make business leaders in your area more aware of the potential of online business, but also to be more realistic in terms of possible problems.

Your manager, Jasmin Podacjeki, advises, '*Try to keep your information simple but clear. Perhaps you could do slides and notes for each of the following.*'

1. In a structured series of notes, carefully explain the issues a business organisation would need to consider before it goes online. Cover planning concerns (e.g. domain name) and implementation factors involved in online operations (e.g. what will the website offer customers?). **(P3)**
2. Explain the various operational risks for a business organisation operating online (e.g. security, content updates, global visability). **(P4)**
3. Analyse the benefits to businesses and customers of conducting business online (e.g. for customers – always available; speed, convienience; for the organisation – cash flow, speed of service delivery, public relations). **(M2)**
4. Suggest ways in which a business could deal with the various operational risks associated with an online presence (e.g. firewall software, staff training). **(D2)**

To achieve a pass grade you need to:	To achieve a merit grade you need to:	To achieve a distinction you need to:
P3 explain the issues a business organisation would need to consider to go online	**M2** analyse the benefits to businesses and customers of conducting business online	**D2** suggest ways in which a business could deal with the operational risks associated with an online presence
P4 explain the operational risks for a business organisation operating online		

Chapter 28
Creating a web presence for a stated business need

What are you finding out?

It is quite possible today that large numbers of young people from the age of 14 – perhaps younger – have already created web pages or even websites of their own. What follows is simply a *basic* introduction to the fundamentals of web-page design.

It is quite a simple process to create a website and there are several ways of doing it. On the internet there are a number of software tools available to help. Before designing a website for a business, there are one or two things to consider.

This chapter will help you to:

- Understand the different ways in which web pages can be created.
- Create elementary web pages.
- Understand the different methods used for formatting and editing.
- Understand ways in which information from different sources can be used on a website.
- Understand the need for thorough review and checking of a website in order to meet a business need.
- Understand the ways in which website content can be managed.

A new website will need a 'web host' to publish the web pages to. A web host is usually a business with computers that are permanently connected to the internet. After the website is designed, the files will need to be transferred to the web host's computer (called a web server), so that the rest of the world can see the site.

There are other things involved in getting a first website up and running. As we saw earlier, a domain name is needed, and the website should be as 'search engine friendly' as possible. This means carefully choosing keywords and language for each page to make sure that people find your site near the top of any search results. Then work needs to be done to promote the new website.

Now, how will you design the new site?

There are a number of ways of creating web pages. We will look in simple terms at two:

- Using 'web development software' such as Dreamweaver or MS FrontPage.
- Directly coding the web pages in HTML; this is the 'language of the web' and is described below.

Web development software

It is possible to use software that automatically creates the HTML code for you. This software uses a WYSIWYG interface, meaning 'What You See Is What You Get.' This means it is possible to create whole websites without knowing any HTML at all. A number of alternatives are available and professionals and keen amateur web developers have their favourites.

Adobe Dreamweaver is a commercial web editor that allows you to create web pages and build complex websites. This tool is one of the most widely used and offers a range of features that allow developers to manage whole websites. The current version is Dreamweaver CS4.

Microsoft also produced their own web-editing software called MS FrontPage. This was discontinued in 2007.

What is HTML?

HTML is the language (code) that computers understand. HTML tells the computer the layout, style and content of web pages. HTML means 'Hypertext Mark-up Language' and it is a relatively simple code, devised in the early 1990s by an Englishman, Tim Berners-Lee, for use in the CERN laboratories in Switzerland.

Task

Create a simple web page using HTML.

Open a text editor such as Notepad.

Type the following, *exactly* as it is shown here. These are called 'tags' and each tag is enclosed in angled brackets <>:

<HTML>

<HEAD>

<TITLE>This is my first web page today</TITLE>

</HEAD>

All tags should be closed using 'closing tags'. These are tags preceded by a forward slash /.

Save the file as First.html (In your BTEC Folder? Remember where it is!) (This is important: If you do not add .html, Notepad saves as a .txt file and this will not work.)

Open First.html in your browser (double click on the file name). Look at the bar along the top of the page and you should see 'This is my first web page today' along the top of the page. The page has a title but no content.

Add content by reopening the file (First.html)

Underneath the </HEAD> tag, type:

<BODY>

This is the bit that shows on the web page in the browser window.

</BODY>

</HTML>

Save as First.html in Notepad and reopen in your browser. The text should now appear at the top of your new web page.

'Hypertext' simply means that you can link from one digital piece of text to another. 'Hyperlinks' are the essence of what makes the web work and you use them almost constantly on useful websites to navigate around the site and across the web.

It is useful to know a little HTML. HTML can be written in any text editor. Typically, Notepad is used to write out the code and then it should be saved with the file extension .HTML.

There are many tags to learn in HTML. Professional web designers usually do not directly code in HTML. Instead they use web development software.

Formatting and editing

Web design involves carefully thinking about the way a web page appears to a visitor to the site. Two basic processes take place in creating a page: these common processes are formatting and editing.

The **format** of a web page refers to how the page looks. Does it contain a lot of text? Which parts of the text 'link' elsewhere on the site or beyond it? What is the colour of the background to the page? Does the page use images? Does the page use tables?

There are of course many more features than these basics. Web technology is developing very quickly and many large businesses use very sophisticated websites.

The following Task asks you to do some very basic formatting.

Adding HTML links

It is hypertext that makes the web work. In HTML, links are added using the <a> tag.

Task

In Notepad, open up the First.html file for the simple web page you created earlier. See if you can 'format' some of the text on the page.

1. **Immediately below the <BODY> tag, type a new tag <h3>A Heading for My Page</h3>**

   Remember to save the file (First.html).

   Open the file in your web browser.

   You should see that you have added a heading. HTML headings are defined by the tags <h1> to <h6>.
2. **Around the first line of text you did before, add <p> before and </p> at the end.**
3. **Enter a short paragraph of text about yourself. Adding <p> at the start and </p> at the end of the paragraph.**

Using the <p> tags you have now defined paragraphs for the text on the page.

Example

<a href="http://www.Google.co.uk">This is a link</a>

Try inserting this link into your HTML by placing the above line after the final paragraph on your page.

(Note: in HTML, all of your web page content must be placed between the <body> and </body> tags.)

The tag <a href> means 'anchor hyperlink reference'. This in itself is not important to you but you should be aware that what you are doing is embedding a reference to another web page from your own text. In the above case, you have taken the person reading your web page away from your site to the external site offered by Google.

Task

Suppose you created another web page. This page will be your second piece of web design, so logically should be saved as 'Second.html'.

1. **Create the web page in the same way you did earlier with the title. <title>'This is my second web page today'</title>**
2. **Add some body text to the page. <body>My Second Page</body>**
3. **Save the file as Second.html in the same folder.**
4. **Go back to First.html file and change the <a href> tag to read <a href ="Second. html">Link to my Second Page</a>**
5. **Open up First.html and you should have a link that takes the viewer to your second page.**

See if you can add a link into Second.html back to First.html.

Using graphics

Of course, a web page that just includes row after row of text is quite uninteresting. The use of digital graphics in web pages means that still images, streaming video, animations and other forms of presentation can all be used.

Adding an image to a web page

Using HTML, you can tell the web page which image you want to display and where it is. The tag for adding an image is:

<img src="Image.jpg" width="104" height="142" />

In this case, the file 'Image.jpg' is the file name of the photograph to be shown on the page. The width and height are 'attributes' for the size of the image as it shows on the page.

Task

See if you can add your own image into your own web pages.

Tag	Description
<b>	Defines bold text
<big>	Defines big text
<em>	Defines emphasised text
<i>	Defines italic text
<small>	Defines small text
<strong>	Defines strong text
<ins>	Defines inserted text
<del>	Defines deleted text

Other HTML formatting tags

Combining information

Web pages display images, animations and video as a matter of course. What we have learned from the basics of HTML is that all the web page HTML source code needs is to know the location of the file and the file extension. The availability of digital information from many different sources gives the web a great deal of variety in what it can display.

Typically a business will want to show images of products or services. For display on a computer screen, images have to be in digital form (i.e. numbers).

Digital image capture (or 'digitisation') is the process of creating a digital image file directly, using either a digital camera or scanner. An original work can also be digitised indirectly using a photograph of the original work, using a scanner or digital camera.

Commonly used digital capture devices fall into two general types: **scanners** and **cameras**:

- Scanners are available in several forms including drum, flatbed and film. Traditionally drum scanners provide the highest quality, but are expensive to use and hard to operate.

Recently, flatbed scanner technology has become a viable, easy-to-use and high quality alternative at a reasonable price.

- Digital cameras are increasingly being used for image capture – especially where flatbed scanning is impractical or might cause damage to the original material (for example, a sculpture or a fragile manuscript). Today, affordable consumer cameras are capable of delivering images of high quality for print or web use.

Software applications often provide digital images that can be saved and used for the web. These packages include highly sophisticated image-editing facilities (e.g. Photoshop) or animation (e.g. Macromedia Flash).

Original artwork can be used on the web once the work has been digitised using a scanner or digital camera as described above.

Clip Art is available from many sources and these images are easily available.

Task

Create a short presentation on the various image-capturing devices available. Which would you recommend for a small business and why?

Checking the web page

Once a web page has been designed and created, it is essential to check the way that the page displays on the screen, as well as its content. The look and feel of the site are crucial because they say a lot about the organisation. There are several things to look for:

- Image resolution – the resolution of an image is the factor that determines whether the image is sufficiently clear and crisp. It could be a real problem for a business if images of products were not clear enough for potential customers to see.
- Colours – does the colour scheme on the site look good on the eye? It is possible in digital imaging and presentation to be very specific about tones and shades on a website.
- Links – the links should work and this is an absolute essential. Nothing can guarantee a visitor leaves a website more quickly than finding that links (both internal and external) do not work.
- Inappropriate content – people visit a website because they hope to find what they want. What the site contains needs very careful thought. The idea is that the site should keep people interested. This is called it's 'stickiness' because visitors want to 'stick around' on the site. Content should be well laid out, clearly written and up-to-date. Offensive text or images, irrelevant materials or just plain boring repetition should be cut out.

Task

With a classmate, investigate at least two websites from businesses that you find interesting. Using the site, list the main features that you like.

Reviewing the website

At the end of the web-design process, it is essential to review the end product. Usually this (like the planning at the start) is done in close consultation with the business requiring the website. Several questions are asked:

1. **Does the site deliver the intended purpose?**
   - Is it persuasive?
   - Is it 'sticky', therefore encouraging visitors to stay?
   - Does it offer a unique benefit to the consumer?
   - Does it convey the correct look and feel for the organisation? (colour and design)
   - Does it give useful information?

2. **Does the website target the right audience? Check that:**
   - Correct balance of text and images.
   - Does it use appropriate images? (For example, a website intended for young clubbers should contain images suggesting youth, fashion, glamour, enjoyment.)
   - Offers something that appeals to the age range.
   - It is accessible? (There is a legal requirement to provide website accessibility for people with eyesight problems – e.g. audio or large font.)
   - Does it use the right language (e.g. non-technical or technical)?
   - Are there any cultural issues?

Publishing the website

A website, as we have seen, consists of files that must be saved to a suitable host server, either on the organisation's own internal 'intranet' or to an external host. Once the website is published it goes live on the world wide web. From this point, the business organisation becomes 'visible' on the internet. The business now has a presence on the web.

From this point, depending very much on the nature and purpose of the website, content must be managed carefully.

Bells Fish & Chips

We met Graham Kennedy earlier. Graham is a sole trader and runs Bells Fish & Chips near Durham. Graham commissioned his website from a young professional designer and he knew that because his was to be a passive, promotional site, he was unlikely to have a great deal of site maintenance to do.

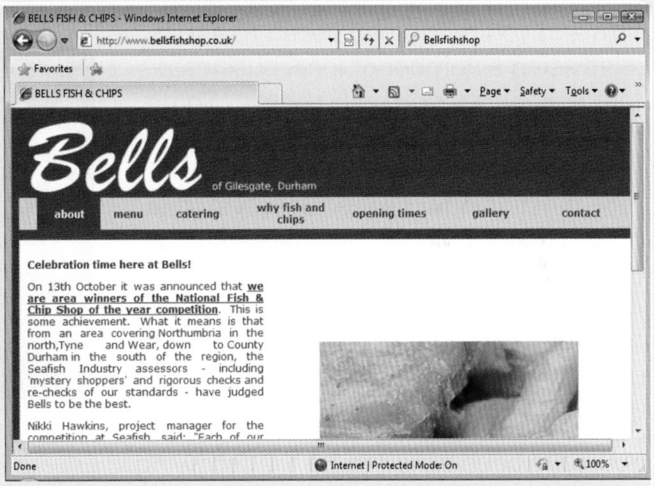

Bells can manage their website content any time

'I spoke to my designer at the start of the process and straight away he suggested a CMS (content management system). This would mean that the website style and layout were fixed and all I had to do was update the text as I needed to. This was important to me because of prices and menu changes. I also knew that fish sustainability was important and I felt I needed a way of saying something about the kinds of fish we would be selling in the shop.'

All Graham has to do is to access the CMS system using his own password and username and he sees the facility shown above.

1. Why is a CMS so important for a small business like Bells?
2. What in your opinion are the main objectives for Bells in having an online presence?
3. Evaluate the notion of a website for businesses (like Bells) delivering physical services at the local level? Justify your views.

Key words

Hypertext – Text containing links (via 'hyperlinks') to other web pages.

Hyperlink – A word or words that link to another web page.

HTML – Hypertext Mark-up Language; the code that is understood by web browsers in order to display a web page in the intended way.

Formatting – Setting the correct layout of the content in a page.

Editing – Amending the content of a page.

Tag – Within HTML, 'tags' are the instructions contained within angled brackets <> that tell a browser what to do.

Assignment
Jack Lumley Garden Furniture

Introduction

You are working for a web consultancy firm and you have been asked to assist in advising a number of local businesses that are considering going online. Some of these businesses are well on the way to successful implementation of a fully functioning website. However, one or two need more encouragement and persuasion. One of these businesses is run by the Lumley family, headed by the 'old man' and founder of the business, Jack Lumley. Lumley's wishes to generate more sales revenue.

You have been asked to do the following:

1. Jack needs to see the basics of how a website for his business would look and how it might work. You have been asked to create at least four web pages for Lumley's, just giving them the outline framework for a useful promotional site. Include:
   - Home Page
   - Products
   - About Us
   - Contact Us.

   The pages should link together and be clearly laid out. **(P5)**

2. In a short report to Jack Lumley, explain how the website will assist in achieving the business's aims and objectives (i.e. increase sales). **(M3)**
3. As an appendix to the report completed for Task 2, justify the use of the different construction features you would suggest in the design of a website for Lumley's. **(D3)**

To achieve a pass grade you need to:	To achieve a merit grade you need to:	To achieve a distinction you need to:
P5 create web pages to meet a user need	M3 explain how the website assists in achieving the aims and objectives of the business user	D3 justify the use of different construction features in the design of a website

Chapter 29
Understand the impact of an online presence

What are you finding out?

At the start of this unit we looked at various kinds of business organisation that might go online. Any kind of organisation could choose to have an online presence. Your own school or college may well have a website. If so, what is the purpose of the site? Ask, does it help to sell courses? In the case of an FE college, the answer is probably yes, it does. In the case of a school, the answer may well be 'to a limited extent'.

This chapter will help you to:

- Understand the ways in which a web presence can help a business within its market.
- Understand the ways in which a web presence can help a business in its marketing effort.
- Understand how a web presence helps a business offer better service.
- Understand how a web presence offers financial advantages.
- Analyse how a website assists in achieving business aims and objectives.
- Understand the impact of increased online business on society.
- Analyse the consequences of increased online business on society.
- Evaluate the benefits and the drawbacks to society of increased online business.

Many government services have websites. In some cases, e.g. the DVLA, these services are usefully delivered online and save considerable time. Similarly, services like Job Centres can give information online.

What we know is that the range of internet use from organisations in many different sectors is growing. The reasons are:

- better service
- better public knowledge
- increased awareness of government services locally and nationally
- increased awareness of local democracy
- better contact points.

But for private business, the main aim in adopting an online strategy is to drive customers to the business, encourage them to buy and, if the experience is successful, to encourage them to return and buy again, hopefully leading towards the business making more profit.

The web offers a range of opportunities to help achieve this aim.

Market presence

We all know that in a traditional market we have people displaying items for sale and people with money to purchase the things they want. There is an exchange taking place. The concept of the market applies in all private business, everywhere. This is why businesses are concerned to gain 'market share'. Market share means what proportion of the total market sales a business gets. The word 'market' also features heavily in other ways when speaking of private business. The word 'marketing' means to make sure your business's goods or service meet the needs of the market.

How does the adoption of an online strategy help a business in its marketplace?

In the market, say, for vacuum cleaners, a particular manufacturer might have no visibility at all until people become aware of the existence of the product or the firm. When James Dyson first invented the bagless cleaner, he had real difficulty in letting people know that his business existed.

The online market is just as competitive as a traditional marketplace

Markets are competitive places. A business must compete if it is to survive and be a success. Having a market presence is very important. It means that a business is known to customers, as well as competitors. The significance of the web is that a business can, by going online, immediately make a statement to everyone that it is here, that it is making an offer to the market and that it is a competitive force. Here is how the web helps to grow a better market presence:

1. **Global presence** – it is a worldwide thing. Having an internet presence extends the 'reach' of the online message (or offer) all over the world.
2. **24/7 visibility**.
3. **Equality of presence** – even the smallest operation can, using an impressive and carefully designed website, appear on an equal footing with far bigger competition. Customers need value and reliable service. Building relationships is important too, especially in B2B (business to business) markets. This is a real opportunity to grow a customer base, sell more and gain more revenue.
4. **Speed of response to customer interest** – the web can offer immediate response. Automated email responders can be instantaneous. However, these must be followed by direct contact. Where an online ordering system is built into a website,

customers can receive order confirmation very quickly. Online payment can be immediate too. The speed of transactions allows for far better business efficiency.

5. **Analysis of online competition** – the web offers a great research tool for an online business. It is possible to gather information about competitors from all over the world. Changes in market conditions can be checked. For example, the business could find out about trends in sales much more quickly in specific parts of the world. Because other online businesses are so visible, their online offer can be analysed. A business can look out for threats and opportunities much more easily online.

There are specialist web analysis firms offering services to measure traffic in business websites. This is called 'web analytics'.

Amazon 1-Click

Amazon 1-Click has done the ultimate in reducing barriers for customers. Set up a 1-Click account, and with literally *one* click, the product the customer is looking at is on its way. But Amazon has also done a good job of knowing that shipping (delivery) can often be a big deterrent, so it has rolled out offerings like Amazon Prime, which comes with an annual fee, but includes free one-day shipping on any products ordered through Amazon.

1. Why do you feel Amazon has made this online offer?
2. What potential problems might this cause the business?
3. To what extent do you feel that the process involved in making an online purchase could put customers off?

Did you know...

In research by Econsultancy, nearly a quarter of organisations said they used Google Analytics and no other web analytics tool.

Before a business can be really competitive, it needs to know things about the market it is in. This is called 'market intelligence'. Think about how you would feel if you wanted to start a new business selling designer knitwear. The first thing to consider is who else is doing this. Where are they? What are their prices?

The web provides a great opportunity to gather information about:

- competitor activities (the web is so visible)
- customer preferences and feelings
- market trends.

Fieldwork

Visit www.clickz.com and create an information sheet giving details of the general kinds of intelligence this website could offer a business.

Marketing benefits

Online research

Marketing is the process of satisfying customer needs profitably. Successful businesses make this activity their number-one priority (even if they don't have a specialist marketing function). They are always asking, 'How can we meet customer expectations?' 'How can we do this better?' 'Are our products (or services) really what customers want?' This reinforces the point made in the previous section: a business *must* know its market.

When a business begins to operate online, there are a number ways that the business can find out about its customers. One of the best ways is to make sure that its website captures data about customers as they make a purchase.

Screwfix is a part of the Kingfisher Group and is the UK's largest direct and online supplier of trade tools, accessories and hardware products, despatching thousands of parcels every week for next-day and weekend delivery to tradesmen, handymen and DIY enthusiasts all

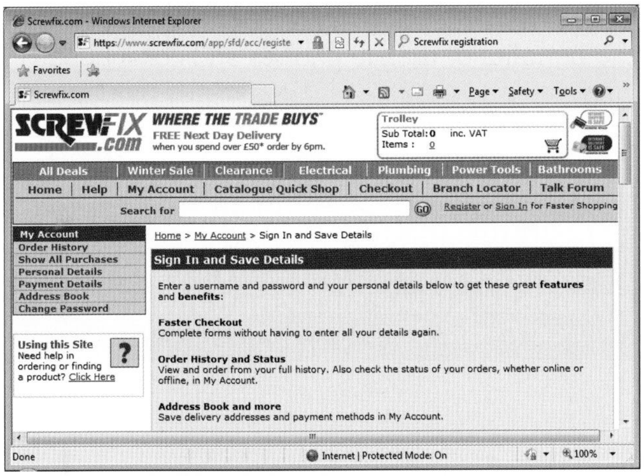

The registration process with Screwfix

over the UK. Screwfix also operates a growing number of Trade Counters across the UK which have over 13,000 items in stock, available for immediate collection.

Screwfix's website invites customers to register on the site with their own user name and password. In doing so, customers pass over personal information to Screwfix that allows the business to understand who they are and offer a better service in future. If they wish, online customers can navigate to find the following information on the Screwfix site under the Privacy link:

Access to new markets

The web offers a global 'market reach'. In other words, potential customers anywhere have the chance to browse through products or service information and place an order. The website should encourage them to stay on the site and hopefully become a regular customer. (It is far cheaper to keep existing customers than attract new ones.) This will have the effect of attracting more and more customers, because a good reputation spreads. This effect is called 'viral' marketing. An online business based near you may now be delivering products to Eastern Europe because of an online presence. In the past, this breakthrough would only have come through a travelling sales force, paper brochures or networking.

Accessing different markets

One of the other effects of a good online presence is that it can open up completely *new* markets. A good example of this is RS Components at http://uk.rs-online.com. This company has made innovative use of the web for a number of years. Originally selling electrical components to the electrical trade only, the business soon realised online that a lot of customers were private individuals. This new market, the home DIY market, had previously not been the focus of the business (i.e. their target market).

Information We Collect & How We Use It

When you place an order, or use any online form on our website we need to know your name and other information such as your postal address, email address, telephone number and your credit card number and expiry date or bank account details, etc. By submitting this information you consent to use of the information in accordance with this Privacy Policy as amended from time to time.

We gather this information to allow us to process your request. The relevant information is then used by us, our agents and sub-contractors to provide you with the service you have requested and to communicate with you on any matter relating to the provision of the service in general.

We may also use aggregate information and statistics for the purposes of monitoring website usage in order to help us develop the website and our service and may provide such aggregate information to third parties. These statistics will not include information that can be used to identify any individual.

Source: www.Screwfix.com

Access from a range of devices

It is now possible to connect computers without the use of wires – a wireless connection. Wi-Fi (**wi**reless **fi**delity) uses radio frequencies to send and receive data. More and more wireless laptops are being used. These devices have to be connected and enabled to work with Wi-Fi.

> Did you know...
>
> **There are now over four billion mobile subscribers worldwide. Mobile subscriptions have grown an average 24% each year between 2000 and 2008.**
> **Source: ClickZ Stats**

Many mobile phones now use WAP (wireless application protocol) technology to offer 'always-on' connection to data services, as well as a range of other features. These phones can send and receive data by connecting to the internet.

A PDA

A personal digital assistant (PDA) is a hand-held device that runs a reduced version of standard software. A PDA comes with personal information management software and can be used as an organiser or a diary planner that is portable and capable of connecting, using Bluetooth or Wi-Fi, to a PC. It is capable of connecting to the internet; it can act as a global positioning system (GPS) and run multimedia software. A so-called 'smartphone' combines the benefits of mobile phones and computing.

> Did you know...
>
> **Brazil, Russia, India and China are the leading countries in terms of growth in mobile phone subscriptions.**
> **Source: ClickZ Stats**

Level of customer response

When a business moves to an online strategy, there are certain basic things that they must get right. Customers who purchase online have very high expectations. When they are using a site, they expect the information contained on the site to be up-to-date, accurate and easy to understand. From the business's point of view, these things must be priorities and built into the whole management of the website.

It is also important that the offer that is made from the website is attractive to visitors. Here we are not just talking about an offer of '10% off' or 'buy one, get one free'; we are speaking about the entire reason for buying online.

> **Task**
>
> **With a classmate, think of three products that can be bought both online and offline, and write a list of reasons why someone might purchase any of these products online, rather than go into a physical store.**

The offer made online is known as the 'online value proposition' (OVP). This is the equivalent to the unique selling proposition (USP) of physical products. It looks at the question of, 'Why buy product X rather than product Y?' Marketing specialists try to design features into products that make them more appealing than alternatives.

Now, think of two websites offering similar things; think of a website and a physical shop in town. What is it that might persuade someone to buy online?

There are a number of ways in which the online business might try to make a better offer.

Door-to-door delivery

The web allows direct contact between a customer and a product manufacturer or supplier. This means that there are lots of cost savings that potentially could be passed on to the customer. One of these is to cut out 'intermediaries', who may, in the past, have bought and resold products. Today, the direct and immediate contact permitted by the web means that goods can be shipped directly and quickly to the customer. This is called direct distribution.

So, with very little personal inconvenience, a customer views, selects, orders and pays online. The online business is set up for speedy distribution anywhere and products are shipped immediately. This 'product fulfilment' aspect is central to online business success.

Access 24/7

Very few physical businesses are capable of offering 24-hour service, seven days each week. By using automated responses or, in the case of large-scale operations, call centres that can be located anywhere, customers can place orders and receive their goods at any time.

Web technology is evolving constantly and there is even software available now that can automate the entire customer relationship function (CRM software). Remember, customer relations are central to success – especially in B2B (business to business) markets. Using a CRM package, a business can have a database of clients, suppliers and customers and ensure that communications between the business and its important stakeholders are slick and efficient. This should have the effect of giving the business a 'good name'.

Online order tracking

Offering customers the option to track exactly where their order is in the delivery process as part of an online shop can improve both the efficiency of a business and customer satisfaction.

The benefits of online order tracking are:

- Knowing in advance when an item of stock is likely to run out makes ordering easier and reduces stock-holding levels. The business can be confident it knows stock levels accurately and can re-order just at the right time.
- Being aware of an order's position in the delivery process can help efficient trouble-shooting and improve staff productivity because less time is spent chasing a shipment.
- Allowing customers to check for themselves (online) what stage their order has reached will reduce the time spent by staff responding to and solving client queries and problems.
- A greater level of customer service is achieved, as both buyer and seller can access information regarding delivery status and specifications at the click of a button.
- Customer frustrations and potential complaints can be reduced by the availability of a proactive method by which they can see their order status.

Financial advantages of operating online

There are a number of financial advantages of operating online. These advantages can mean that cost savings can be passed on to customers, who often get a better deal.

Improved cash flow

Cash flow is vital to a business. Every business needs enough cash and other resources to keep the organisation running.

This is the way cash flow works:

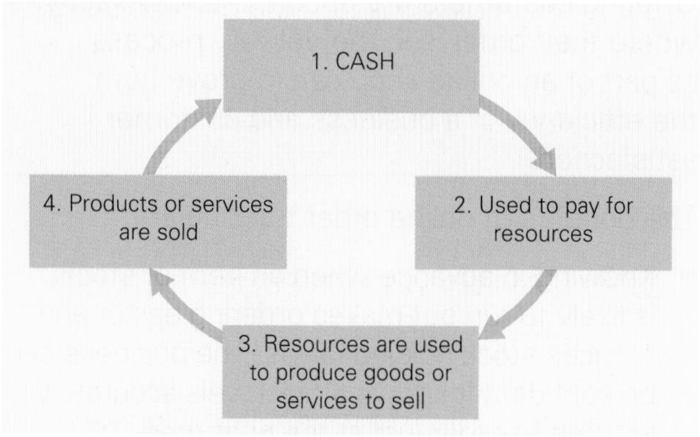

Figure 29.1 The cash-flow process

Cash comes into the business through sales. If there are interruptions to this flow of cash, there could be trouble. Cash-flow problems and lack of capital to operate (pay wages, etc.) can lead to failure.

Being online, especially with a good website that allows for rapid online payments, can really help to speed up the cash flow into the business. More cash comes in and, as we saw earlier, there is less need to carry large quantities of stock.

Low-cost location

In the online world, location is less important than in the physical world. A suitable business could choose to locate anywhere and have the advantage of cost savings, yet still be able to deliver its products or services via the web.

Low-cost labour

Being able to locate the business anywhere means that the business could employ staff in an offshore location where wages are much lower than they would be in the UK.

Lower overheads

Overheads are costs that a business must pay, no matter how much they are selling. These are costs to do with rent or lease of equipment, buildings or land. There are costs to do with fuel and power, with telephone bills or internet connection. After initial start-up costs have been paid, the business can possibly start to take advantage of the lower costs of being online. These savings, depending on the business, could include less office space or fewer staff required, or less need to advertise.

Effects on customers

The availability of an online shopping opportunity has a number of effects on customers. Remember that a 'customer' could be a business organisation as well as a private person. As we have seen earlier, there are many different markets with B2C and B2B sales. If we were to add in other web opportunities such as auction sites such as eBay, we also have C2C markets to consider.

Positive effects for customers include the following:

Convenience

The first major benefit of shopping online is that a customer doesn't even have to leave home to buy items. This is an advantage at holiday time when shopping centres and other shops get incredibly crowded. People don't have to spend time circling car parks for a space, walking up and down aisles, or standing in long lines at the checkout.

Wider choice

Online customers often find they have more choices online. This is because, unlike a physical store, online companies have access to more product storage space. In a physical store, the goods on display are usually display only; customers might often find that the product is not in stock. Online, large quantities of stocks are held in distribution warehouses. Customers get an instantaneous message to say that an item is available. You'll find a number of different colours or designs available online. You may also find a wider array of products, including more obscure finds.

diy.com offers a wide choice of garden tools

Flexibility

Customers have complete flexibility in choosing an online supplier. The speed and availability of access to online offers really broaden the range of options. Shopping comparison sites allow customers to compare prices and terms.

Other benefits

An online offer has to be attractive to customers. Otherwise, why would they buy online? One of the ways in which online businesses achieve this is by 'extending' products online. This is done by offering additional information, warranties, guarantees, extra back-up service, expert advice or product endorsements (i.e. recommending something) from previous customers.

Fieldwork

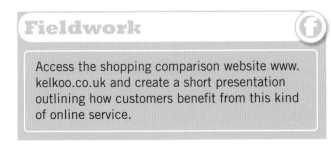

Access the shopping comparison website www.kelkoo.co.uk and create a short presentation outlining how customers benefit from this kind of online service.

Drawbacks

There are one or two ways in which online shopping might *not* offer advantages:

- There is a lack of direct contact with products and the company. One of the important elements in selling is missing from an online process. This is *direct* contact with sales staff. In business, selling is often about creating a relationship with customers and clients. When companies involved in B2B selling are remote and only interacting online, there can be a problem because it is then very easy for a buyer to switch to another supplier.
- In consumer markets there is the problem of being remote from a physical product. Consumers often need to touch and feel a product before they will buy.
- No goodwill element – goodwill arises when a customer and a business engage regularly with each other and are able to reach understanding and accommodate each other, often in terms of price discount or other terms involved in buying and selling. A distant online relationship may not allow this to develop.

Impact on society

In your class at school or college, would you consider yourself a 'group' or just (say) 20 individual people? What things do you – as a class – have *in common*? Let's list a few possibilities:

- room
- timetable
- courses
- teachers
- building
- assessments
- hopes
- worries.

It would be possible to go on for a while. The point is that the things you share in common with your classmates creates a group.

Now broaden that out to your town, your region and the country as a whole. We all have things in common. It is these common factors taken together that make people a social group, and therefore creates a 'society'.

Does online business have any impact on society – i.e. all of us; and if so, in what ways?

Did you know...

In November 2009, visits to Facebook had increased by 86.1% over the previous year, according to Experian Hitwise. While more *individuals* visited Google, the number of page views received by Facebook made it the most-viewed website in the UK.
Source: Guardian Online

Social isolation

Does online business, or the internet in general, cause social isolation? If someone is socially isolated it means that they feel lonely and in some cases they *are* alone. They do not have people to meet or interact with any more. As human beings we are 'social' creatures. We prefer being with other people and the more we have in common, the better we feel.

In pre-internet days people left their houses and went out to the shops to do their shopping. Of course, most people still do this. Further back in time, people would walk around to the very local corner shop. There they would meet other neighbours who were also doing their shopping. In other words, people got together to share a common set of experiences. The growth of supermarkets in the 1960s started to break down this kind of social interaction. However, people were still meeting other people. Today a visit to the shops often means a trip out to a shopping centre in the car.

Shopping online is a solitary thing. The web is a one-to-one interaction between the web page and the consumer. It is not a 'social' experience.

Social networking

The online social-networking boom shows no signs of falling away, with almost twice as many British internet users having an online profile than two years ago, helping to make Facebook the most viewed website in the UK, according to new research.

As more people, especially older people, are getting online, they are experimenting with social networking and blogging, according to regulator Ofcom. More people are using the internet to create their own content than ever before, with 38% of online users having a social-networking profile, compared with 22% in 2007.

There has, however, been a drop-off in the number of people who regularly use the web to find information for their work or study – from 48% two years ago to 35% – while the economic downturn has also led to a drop in the number of British consumers who go online to buy goods.

Source: 'Social networking booming with doubling of online profiles' by Richard Wray, *Guardian* 16 October 2009. Copyright Guardian News & Media Ltd 2009

1. What do you understand by 'social networking'? Do you think it helps to reduce social isolation?
2. Investigate the advantages or disadvantages of social networking for your local community. Is it a good thing?
3. What are the drawbacks for society in a drop in the number of British consumers going online to buy goods?

Visiting the shops can be a social activity

So online shopping – in fact doing anything online – *can* keep people indoors. However, more and more people are using mobile technology. They can access the web from many different kinds of device. This means that people need not be socially isolated to go online and shop.

Doing business online in a business-to-business context could also cause a lack of social interaction. Online business is done with the click of a mouse button. Buyers trawl the web for prices and deals. There is no contact between people (i.e. sales staff). What sales contact that exists is done via email or telephone.

Task

Create a poster display to illustrate the impact that increased online business might be having upon society as a whole.

Make the grade

M4 **D4** When you are investigating social networking and the drop in numbers buying online, you can use this information to help you to achieve M4 and D4.

Breakdown of communities

A 'community' is where a group of people share many common concerns. There is a feeling of being together. Communities frequently developed because, in the past, people often

Is computer use bad for you?

Lady Greenfield, director of the Royal Institution, said consistent computer use could be 'infantilising' the brain. While a child who falls out of a tree will quickly learn not to repeat the mistake, someone who goes wrong on a computer game will just keep playing.

As a result, people will eat too much, or eat the wrong foods, without thinking about the consequences. She said this had led to the cutting of attention spans, and had stifled empathy and imagination, according to the *Daily Mail*.

Source: 'Computers could be fuelling obesity', by Ben Leach, *Daily Telegraph*, 13 May 2009

1. In your own words, explain what you understand by 'infantilising the brain' mentioned in the first sentence of the extract above.
2. What are your views on the effects of computer games on people? Do you agree that people are more inclined to take unhealthy risks?
3. In your opinion, would an increase in online shopping have similar health effects to the growth in online gaming? Justify your answer.

moved to certain parts of the country where there were lots of jobs. These jobs tended to be based on large-scale industries such as coal mines, steel, engineering, car manufacturing, shipbuilding and textiles. Whole towns, villages and regions used to identify with particular occupations. A young person starting work when they left school would do that job for life. The effect of this was that people in an area had lots of things in common.

Today, few people can expect to start a job at 16 or 18 and to still be doing the same job when they are 60. People will change jobs or careers regularly.

Task

See if you can design a survey to find out if there is a 'generation gap' between your parents, your grandparents and your friends and classmates in terms of their online shopping. Compare your findings. See how the different age groups compare.

Think about the area where you live. Do you feel part of a community? Does the internet make you feel part of a *real* community?

As more and more businesses operate online – in the virtual world – there is a danger that fewer and fewer people will feel they want to leave their homes and visit the local community shops. Large supermarkets now deliver groceries to the home.

Make the grade

M4 When you ask your friends and family about their use of online shopping, you can use this data to analyse the consequences of increased online business for M4.

There is no doubt that the UK has to compete in a global marketplace by increasingly working online. Businesses gain many benefits. However, for individuals who are not able to use the web, either because of a lack of understanding or appreciation (caused by age?), lack of accessibility (disability?) or lack of interest, there is a possibility of a growing disadvantage. For those who are willing to use web technology to the full, there could be increased opportunity, better jobs, better prospects and more awareness of the wider world.

Make the grade

D4 To fully evaluate, for D4, the benefits and drawbacks to society of increasing business online, look back to the benefits to business and consider factors like job security and business growth.

Key words

Automated – Happens without human intervention, using digital technology.

Community – A sub-group within society, e.g. a neighbourhood, street, estate.

Market presence – The extent to which a business is known within a particular market (e.g. cars).

Market reach – The global spread of a business's presence.

Online strategy – The aims and objectives that relate to being online.

Society – The whole community of people sharing common interests and concerns.

Social networking – Online communities sharing things (e.g. workplace, school, city or college).

Assignment

Social impact of online business

You continue to be employed by a consultancy firm that is advising business managers about online business. There is a meeting in two weeks' time and your manager wants you to help her with research. You have been given the following tasks:

1. Prepare a set of presentation slides that outline the general impact of online business on society. **(P7)**
2. Prepare additional notes with extra slides to analyse the consequences on society of an increase in online business. **(M4)**
3. Add to the slides and notes you prepare for Task 2 by evaluating the benefits and drawbacks to society of increasing business online. **(D4)**

To achieve a pass grade you need to:	To achieve a merit grade you need to:	To achieve a distinction you need to:
P7 outline the impact of online business on society	**M4** analyse the consequences on society of an increase in online business	**D4** evaluate the benefits and drawbacks to society of increasing business online

Unit 16

Exploring business enterprise

Chapter 30
Preparing for business

What are you finding out?

This unit will help you to understand the skills needed to set up and run a business. It will also provide you with an overview of the regulations that have to be met by new businesses and the importance of creating a detailed business plan.

This chapter helps you to understand your own strengths and weaknesses. It is important to be aware of these because setting up and running a business is not suitable for everyone. You already need to have some of the right attitudes and qualities as well as the willingness to develop new skills.

This chapter will help you to:

- Understand how to prepare for business.

Did you know...

The best website for supporting those wishing to set up a business of their own is provided by Business Link. Business Link is an organisation that specialises in supporting anyone thinking of starting up and running a business of their own. (www.businesslink.gov.uk)

Your own strengths and weaknesses

Setting up and running a business are not tasks that should be taken on lightly. They require special skills and a willingness to work very hard, particularly in the early days when the business is being planned and set up.

It is essential to carry out a personal audit to see whether you have the skills and qualities required. The chart on the next page enables

Anita Roddick, founder of The Body Shop

Anita Roddick, the founder of The Body Shop, died in 2007 at the age of 64. She set up The Body Shop when she was 30. She was a fearless campaigner on a number of issues, including protecting the environment, and the use of natural ingredients in cosmetics. She set up her first shop in 1977 using a loan of £4,000. At the time she was a single mother with two small children. Roddick was able to see that people in Britain and elsewhere were looking for alternative forms of cosmetics using natural ingredients. The Body Shop started off on a very small scale producing shampoos, lotions and body creams, which were sold in small plastic bottles that were recyclable. It was a struggle setting up the business and Anita and a small number of employees had to work very long hours to make a success of her business.

Anita Roddick set up The Body Shop when she was 30

From the start Roddick had a belief that her ideas would be a success and would take off on a large scale. The Body Shop immediately set out to operate in a different way from traditional cosmetic firms that relied on heavy advertising and the use of extensive packaging to sell products. The Body Shop in contrast used minimum packaging and made sure that its products were not derived from testing on animals. Anita Roddick campaigned on a range of issues including saving the Amazon rainforests and making sure that, when ingredients were sourced from poor countries, people in these countries received a fair price. Anita Roddick was an extremely determined individual, with a good head for business and knew how to create positive publicity for her company. She was a tireless worker, not only involved in making the business a success but also campaigning on a number of issues.

1. What particular attitudes and qualities did Anita Roddick have that enabled her to set up her business?
2. Are there any of these qualities that you believe are essential – that is, without them a new business venture would fail?
3. Do you think that you are like Anita Roddick? What are the main similarities and differences between the way that you tackle important new tasks and those described in the case study?
4. Does the case study indicate that a new entrepreneur needs support or is it possible to 'make it' entirely on your own?

(Put a tick in the column)

1	2	3	4	5
I am willing to work hard to achieve important targets that I set for myself				I tend to give up easily if the going gets tough
I like to see things through from start to finish				I am not very good at finishing things off
I am good at making things happen				I prefer to be led by others
I find it easy to build a picture of what needs to be achieved				I am often uncertain about the future direction I am heading in
I am good at persuading other people				I am not very good at convincing others
I pay attention to the details required to get tasks done well				I tend to muddle along and sometimes miss out key steps

Figure 30.1 Personal audit

you to carry out an audit of your strengths and weaknesses. This chart focuses on general attitudes and abilities.

In each case rank yourself from 1 to 5 depending on whether you are closer to the statement on the left-hand side or the right-hand side. The statements relate to organising and carrying out important tasks.

If your answers are mainly in the 1s and 2s you are likely to have important attributes for setting up an enterprise.

Without exception, people who make a success of working for themselves and running their own business have to work hard. In order to do this they need to have good health. Most of them will get up early in the morning, and be prepared to work evenings and weekends when the pressure of work builds up. They have to make sure that tasks are finished off to a good standard. The term 'mover and shaker' is often applied to someone who gets things done. To get things done they have to make sure that the small things are done, as well as the big things. In addition, they need to be able to persuade others that their ideas are sound. They need to build a picture or vision of what they are going to achieve that is believable.

The activities outlined above will have made it clear that your strengths and weaknesses depend on:

- Your personal circumstances. Do you have time available to set up a business? Are you a confident person who is willing and able to work hard?
- Your experience, skills, knowledge and abilities. Do you have the right sorts of qualities required to set up a business?
- Having the knowledge and skill to do or produce things, e.g. to look after small children (nursery), carpentry skills (furniture business), etc. However, it should become clear that in addition to these job-specific skills, you also need to have general business skills that will enable you to turn a good idea into a successful business.

If you don't already have the experience, knowledge and skills, then you may be able to work on them. That is why this unit is particularly helpful because it provides you with insights into the practical business skills that are required to develop a business enterprise.

Task

Identify the knowledge, skills and abilities that you would particularly like to develop to enable you to run a successful business.

The *Dragons' Den*

The *Dragons' Den* television series featured a number of 'Dragons' – investors willing to put some of their own money into start-up businesses in return for a share in the profits. The Dragons were all successful entrepreneurs who became household names – Deborah Meaden, Theo Paphitis, James Caan, Duncan Ballantyne and Peter Jones. Budding entrepreneurs were given a short time to present their ideas before being asked key questions. Most of those who requested an investment were turned down – because:

- They were not able to convince the Dragons that they had a good business idea.
- They did not appear to have the drive and determination to make the business work.
- They did not seem to be able to follow their ideas through from start to finish.
- They had a poor understanding of business basics such as how much profit they were making or how big their market was.

1. If you were being interviewed for *Dragons' Den* (regardless of your product), what messages would you be seeking to put across about yourself?
2. How would you be able to convince the Dragons that you can make things happen?
3. How would you convince the Dragons that you have good powers of persuasion?
4. What weaknesses do you have that you would need to work hard to overcome before making a 'pitch' on *Dragon's Den*?

Did you know...

A number of business commentators suggest that businesses are most likely to succeed when:

- **The business owner has a passion for what they are doing.**
- **The business owner is physically fit, with strong powers of concentration.**
- **They have a positive attitude to work.**
- **They are not easily deterred by failures.**
- **They like to be independent.**
- **They are good at interacting with other people.**

Do you have the qualities listed above?

Contributing to a business

Your own contribution

Running a business involves a lot of personal commitment. It will take up a lot of your time.

This case study illustrates how the responsibility of running a business eats into your personal time. In addition, you will need to contribute some of your own money to the business. Other people will be reluctant to invest unless the owner shows their belief in the business by risking some of their own money. Typically, at least 50% of the money required to set up and run a business in the first year will need to come from the owner. In addition, the owner may ask family and friends to contribute and this presents a fresh burden of responsibility.

The Sunshine Nursery

In 2006 trained nursery nurse Meenum Mandal set up her own nursery after renovating the basement of a large building close to the centre of Birmingham. To get the Sunshine Nursery up and running, Meenum needed to pay careful attention to many regulations – including those governing child protection, health and safety on the premises, fire regulations, and even rules about on-street parking when parents dropped the children off at the nursery. Meenum describes how she spends a typical working day in the following extract from her diary:

6.a.m Alarm goes off. Have a quick shower and get ready for work

6.30 Breakfast

6.45 Drive to work

7.00 Arrive at work and make sure that everything is tidy for the first arrivals

7.30 Other staff arrive – have a quick staff meeting and go through the routines for the day

8.00 First children arrive at nursery – help to take coats off and store belongings

8.00–10.00 Supervising children and staff

10.00–11.00 Meeting new parents looking for places for their children at the nursery

11.00–12.30 Answering the phone and doing paperwork – writing reports on each of the children

12.30–1.15 Supervising children while they have their lunch

1.15–2.45 Interviewing for a new nursery nurse position – three applicants

2.45–3.00 Time for a quick coffee with the successful applicant

3.00–4.00 Talking to parents who come to pick up their children

4.00–4.30 Meeting with staff to organise arrangements for the next day

4.30–6.30 Doing the paperwork and accounts for the business

1. How much time does Meenum spend working on this typical day?
2. How is her work more demanding than if she was working for someone else?
3. Would you be prepared to put in the same sort of commitment as illustrated by Meenum?
4. Meenum also frequently works part of the weekend. What additional work do you think that she might do related to running the nursery at the weekend?

You may also have to contribute some of your own space. Often when people set up a small shop they live over the shop. Many other self-employed people like plumbers, decorators and builders will have to convert part of their own home to office space. They may receive phone calls 24 hours a day (for example, for emergency plumbing work). Other self-employed people such as web-page designers and those selling direct from home work from their own houses.

Activity

Use the following table as a template to add additional ideas of your own:

Business idea	Examples	Additional examples
Copying an existing good idea	Flower selling at a railway station	
A gap in the market	A specialist mobile disco	
Turning a skill or hobby into a business	Making pottery, breeding rare snakes	
Another source for business idea		

Ability to contribute to and run a small business

Most people at some time or another come up with an idea for a business enterprise. This may simply involve copying a good idea that you have seen somewhere else – e.g. selling flowers at a busy railway station. You may spot a gap in the market – for example, there may be a number of mobile discos in your home town, but there might not be one that plays the kind of music that you and your friends like. There might be an opportunity for you to turn a particular skill or hobby that you have into a business venture, e.g. making and selling pottery or breeding rare snakes for resale.

Another way of thinking about the sort of contribution that you can make to a business is to carry out an audit of your existing skills. Having listed your skills, you could then work with a small group of other students to see if together you can suggest how they can be converted into business ideas.

My existing skills

Can they be converted into business ideas? See the chart on the next page.

Can your skills be converted into business ideas?

Personal savings

Your ability to run a business will also depend on having personal savings.

Unless you are the favourite niece or nephew of a rich childless aunt, the chances are that you will have to save up some money before setting up in business. Some businesses can be set up with very little capital. For example, the founder of Marks & Spencer, Michael Marks, simply bought a tray full of small items like needles and thread, which he took from door to door. However, most small businesses will require

Type of skill	Brief description of the skills that you have:
Using information technology, e.g. web-page design, word processing, design and layout skills	
Research skills – finding things out	
Planning skills – being able to create well-focused plans	
Working with others – e.g. working with young children, working to help others, etc.	
Specific skills – e.g. sporting skills, cooking, making textiles, plumbing, construction, etc.	
Communication skills – e.g. explaining things well, talking to people, making presentations	
Other skills that might be helpful in starting and running a business	

Figure 30.2 Can your skills help you to run a business

several hundreds if not thousands of pounds of capital. So before you set up in business you must be prepared to save up.

Availability of time

Some people have a full- or part-time job while they are setting up their business. For example, Mark Shaw, described in the case study on page 356, worked as a lecturer while he set up his business.

The impact on personal and social life

It is very important that you should have a good work/life balance. Work/life balance refers to combining social and family commitments with time spent at work. In addition, it is also important for you to save some part of the day for yourself to do the things that you want to do. Unfortunately for some entrepreneurs, business activity can become an obsession – so that they live, sleep, eat and breathe the business. It is important to be aware of this. If you have important family and social commitments that you value, you should make sure that you give these due priority. For example, you could make sure that each day you set aside what you consider to be a suitable amount of time for yourself, your family and friends.

Barriers to starting/ running a business

There are many barriers to creating and running a successful business. These include:

- Lack of management experience.
- Not having sufficient capital to set up and run the business – businesses can quickly run out of funds in the early days before sales pick up.
- Choosing a poor location – the danger of choosing a low-cost location is that people may not know about you.
- Lack of planning – success depends on a lot of detailed and careful planning.
- Trying to expand too quickly – don't be too ambitious at the start. Early success often leads entrepreneurs to expand too rapidly and then run out of cash.
- Having a poorly designed website (or no website at all). Today many customers and suppliers look for businesses on the internet. If they can't find them they will be tempted to go elsewhere.

Make the grade

P1 To show evidence that you can meet the criteria for P1 you need to demonstrate ways in which your strengths and weaknesses can be applied to preparing for and contributing to a business. In the section above we have encouraged you to use a number of auditing tools to identify your strengths and weaknesses. You should include your copies of any of these audits that you have carried out in your business folder. Now make a summary list of your strengths and weaknesses. For each strength, explain how this strength would help you to set up an effective business. For your list of weaknesses you will need to explain how you would address each of these weaknesses if you were going to set up a business of your choice.

Professional help

Everyone that sets up in business needs support and help from others. One of the best sources of help is Business Link. Business Link is a government-funded service that provides the information, advice and support needed to start, maintain and grow a business. Business Link helps its customers get expert advice and provides advisors for business on a local basis.

As well as Business Link, enterprise agencies and chambers of commerce also offer support. For those between the ages of 18 and 30, additional help is provided by The Prince's Trust.

An accountant will help a business to sort out financial details and to pay tax. Organisations such as Business Link will also help a new business owner to find a mentor, an experienced and successful business person who will help you to organise your own business.

Having the support of your family and friends is vital – they can act as a great source of advice and inspiration – particularly in the early days.

Benefits of running a business

Most young people at one time or another consider setting up a business. The main attraction of doing so is that they are able to pursue an activity that they enjoy while at the same time having the independence of working for themselves.

Task

Working with other members of your class, brainstorm ideas for a local business that you could set up together. The purpose of a 'brainstorm' is simply to generate ideas – they don't have to be thought out in detail or be too serious at this stage. Everyone in the group should generate at least one idea. Next go through the ideas one by one, identifying whether they would be feasible and whether other members of the group would want to contribute to them. Try to refine your ideas down to two or three that have the most support and are felt to be achievable. Finally, consider what the benefits would be to individuals and group members of setting up one of these businesses.

It is likely that the business you have chosen to set up as a result of doing the Task above is one that is reasonably interesting to do. This is a major reason why people set up in business: the interest factor. Another important reason for setting up a business is so that you have more independence. Rather than having a 'boss' or 'supervisor' telling you what to do you will be able to make important decisions for yourself – e.g. how long to work, how much to pay yourself, who to employ, what to produce, etc.

Every year thousands of young people in Britain set up small businesses in:

- fashion
- retailing

- website design
- hairdressing and other personal services
- catering and restaurants.

They do so because this is their passion. For them, work is not just a job that they do to earn money – it is something that they live for most of their waking hours.

Personal objectives

You can see therefore that running a business helps many young people to achieve their personal objectives.

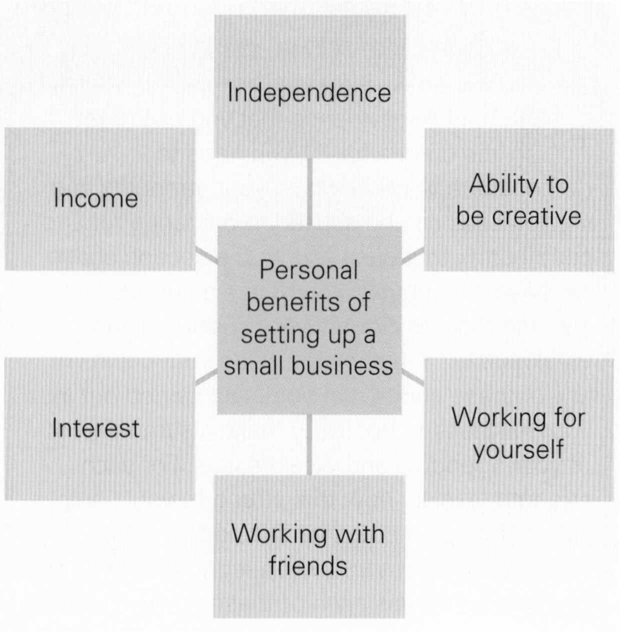

Figure 30.3 Some of the main benefits of starting your own enterprise

Mark Shaw – Transition Sport

Mark Shaw is a good example of an entrepreneur who has been able to turn a passion for sport into a successful business. After school Mark went on to study Sports Science at Nottingham Trent University. While studying for his degree he was actively involved in Triathlons – a tough sport requiring participants to swim, cycle and run long distances. During the 1990s the sport was becoming established in a big way in this country and Mark started organising events. This involved a lot of commitment – hiring venues, advertising the events to triathletes, preparing the courses, informing people about the events, organising the marshalling and supervision of events, including health and safety issues, providing prizes and publishing results. As with any outdoor sport, the weather is a key factor to be considered, so meticulous planning is required. Mark set up his own company, Transition Sport, to manage the events and was soon running some of the biggest Triathlon competitions in the UK. In the first decade of the 21st century Mark decided to extend his operations to France and bought a large country house, lake and park to act as a base for outdoor sports and triathlon events. He had to carry out much of the work of restoring the property on his own, working with friends – and today the venture has paid off.

1. What personal objectives do you think that Mark was able to achieve by setting up Transition Sport?
2. What sorts of risks has Mark taken in getting his business off the ground?
3. What personal attributes does Mark appear to possess that have made the business so successful?
4. What benefits will there be to Mark from running his business?

Personal objectives are very important and help to explain why many small businesses are set up. Particularly important among these is the desire to work for yourself without being told what to do by someone else. Coupled with this is a desire to benefit from the fruits of your own labour rather than having someone else take all the credit (and a lot of the profit) for your activity. Another personal objective is to be able to shape your own future and to shape your own business – to take it in a direction that you see fit. And, of courses, running a business should provide an income for the entrepreneur, although the size of this will depend on the success of the business.

Business objectives

Personal objectives are closely associated with business objectives but it is helpful to identify some of the specifically business-related objectives.

Foremost among these is the desire to make a profit. Without profit the business will go under and not be able to do all of the things that the business owner wishes.

The profit a business makes is what is left over after all of the costs of running the business are subtracted from the sales revenues. Most businesses actually make a loss in their first year of trading. This is because it takes a little time for the business to become established and for start-up costs to be covered.

Other business objectives will relate to:

- Increasing sales year by year.
- Increasing the share of the market that the business accounts for.
- Building the reputation of the product or business.

Impact on personal and social life

Before starting up and running a business, a prospective entrepreneur should be aware of the possible impact on personal and social life.

There is a clear trade-off between time available for personal and social life and time spent on the business.

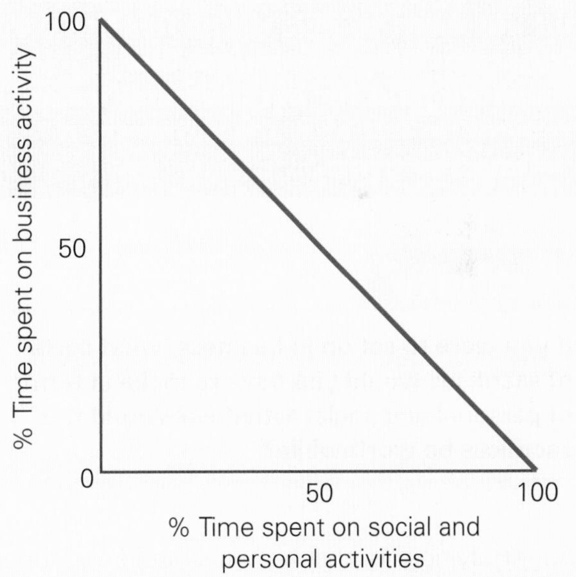

Figure 30.4 Trade-off between business and social activity

You can see from the diagram above that the more time the business person spends working at their business, the less time they have for personal and social activities.

The American writer Tamara Monosoff wrote a book called *Secrets of Millionaire Moms* in which she looked at the problems of running a business and a family at the same time.

In the book she suggested that women tend to be successful at running businesses because they are very good at juggling their day-to-day lives to fit around a variety of tasks, including bringing up children. She interviewed 17 successful businesswomen. She found that many women go into business to work for themselves but typically this does not lead to more free time because there are so many important deadlines to be met. Fortunately many women run their business from home or after hours, so they can be near their children when they work. The research showed that typically to be successful at business, some aspect of personal or social life has to be sacrificed, such as housework, getting together with friends, or having some time for themselves.

Did you know...

Teri Gault, a successful businesswoman in the United States, did not want to give up on her fitness as her business expanded. She therefore paid for her personal trainer to come to her at work rather than visiting the gym.

Activity

If you were to set up in business, what sorts of sacrifices would you have to make in terms of personal and social activities? Would the sacrifices be worthwhile?

After studying this chapter you should now be in a position to:

- Identify possible types of business that you might like to start up.
- Evaluate your own strengths and weaknesses to see if you have the qualities and skills required to set up a business.
- Identify the skills and abilities that you would need to acquire if you were to set up in business.
- Identify the contributions that you would need to make to set up in business, e.g. time, space and money.
- Assess what the benefits to you would be in starting up a business – including personal benefits and business benefits.
- Assess whether the time spent on running a business would be worth it, given the sacrifices to personal and social life.

Make the grade

M1 To achieve a merit M1 requires that you should explain, using examples, the benefits of starting a business. Base your work on a specific business that you could set up. Identify the personal objectives that you could meet if you were going to set up this enterprise. Then look at the business objectives that the business would achieve. Set these out in a brief report with the title – 'The benefit of setting up my chosen business idea'.

Key terms

Audit – Record or list. A skills audit is a list of skills that someone has.

Objectives – Goals that are aimed for. Personal objectives are things that you want to achieve yourself. Business objectives are goals that you want your business to achieve.

Prince's Trust – Organisation whose chair is the Prince of Wales, and that runs programmes to encourage young people to take responsibility for themselves. The Business Programme provides money and support to help young people set up in business.

Template – Outline of a document for you to fill in

Assignment

You need to identify your own strengths and weaknesses for setting up a business and then give examples of the benefits of setting up in business.

Most young people at one time or another consider setting up an enterprise of their own. However, it is necessary to consider first whether you have the right skills. Using some of the auditing tools set out in this chapter, set out a profile of yourself, which you can use to judge whether you have the right skills to set up in business, setting out your strengths and weaknesses. **(P1)**

In addition, set out and explain the benefits of setting up in business in order to attract a potential partner to set up in business with you. **(M1)**

In your assessment you will need to do the following:

To achieve a pass grade you need to:	To achieve a merit grade you need to:	To achieve a distinction you need to:
P1 explain how knowledge of personal strengths and weaknesses can be applied to preparing for and contributing to a business	**M1** explain, using examples, the benefits of starting a business	

Chapter 31
Influences on preparation for business

What are you finding out?

This chapter introduces you to a range of important aspects that you need to consider in setting up a new business. These aspects are:

- The rules governing the setting up and organisation of a new business.
- Marketing the business and organising sales activities.
- Organising the financial aspects of the business.

This chapter will help you to:

- Understand how different aspects affect preparation for business.

Regulations and laws governing small businesses

The starting point for setting up a small business is to make sure that you carry out the proper legal formalities and make sure that the business complies with regulations.

In this section we look at:

- The rules involving setting up the business.
- The licences required.
- The records that must be filled in, including tax returns.
- Complying with health and safety regulations.

Rules

There are a number of rules (regulations) that small business owners need to be familiar with.

Legal status

A small business typically takes one of four possible forms:

- sole trader
- partnerships
- private company
- public company.

Anyone can set up to run a business enterprise. The simplest forms of enterprise are the one-owner business (sole trader) and a partnership made up of two or more partners.

The fastest way to get into business is to become a self-employed sole trader. A sole trader needs to formally register and let Her Majesty's Revenue and Customs know within three months of becoming self-employed. This is so that income tax can be levied on income.

A sole-trader business requires no formal paperwork to set up. A partnership can be set up by word of mouth agreement between the partners. However, most likely the partners will want to create a legally binding 'partnership agreement', which a solicitor will help them to draw up.

In law both sole traders and partnerships are the same as the person/people that set them up. So, for example, if Joe the Plumber owes money to a supplier, it is Joe that the supplier will take to court.

If you run out of money, you may end up in court

Companies are different. They are more complex to set up and involve more paperwork. Companies are owned by shareholders. Shareholders are people who have put money into a business in return for a share of the profits. They can purchase one or several shares in the business. It is essential that detailed rules and guidelines are set up covering the relationship between the business with its shareholders and with people outside the business. When you set up a company you must register it with the Registrar of Companies. Two main documents need to be filled in:

1. **A Memorandum of Association** sets out the internal working of the business, e.g. the rights of shareholders to vote and to receive profits, how directors will be appointed to direct the business, etc.
2. **Articles of Association** set out the relationship between the business and

Documents that must be filled in:	Certificates created by the Registrar of Companies:	Enabling a business to:
Memorandum of Association	Certificate of Incorporation	Be recognised as a legal body in law
Articles of Association	Certificate of Trading	Start to trade

external stakeholders – for example, the name and address of the company, whether it is a plc (public limited company) or Ltd (private limited company).

Once the Registrar of Companies is happy with the paperwork they will fill in a Certificate of Incorporation and a Certificate of Trading.

Task

Decide on a small business that you would like to start up. What would be the most suitable form for the business to take? What paperwork and registration activity would you need to produce to set up your chosen business?

Regulations

Business activity is highly regulated. In simple terms this means that there are lots of rules created by government and other bodies to make sure that business is being conducted properly. The rules are designed to protect the various individuals and groups that businesses have dealings with, including other businesses. For example, there are regulations about how many hours employees can be expected to work in a week, rules about employing younger workers, rules about health and safety, and rules that protect consumers.

Licences

A licence is a document setting out that an organisation is permitted to carry out certain activities or to make use of something. Different types of business require different licences to operate. For example, some shops, petrol stations and pubs are licensed to sell alcoholic drinks. Usually the licence sets out who they can sell to and at what times, as well as other conditions.

Did you know...

Some businesses require licences from a local authority, e.g. taxi companies, nightclubs, pet shops and scrap-metal dealers. Local authority environmental health departments issue licences for hotels, restaurants, abattoirs, hairdressers and those who work with asbestos, as well as mobile shops and premises selling food, massage and skin-piercing services.

The licence described above is an example of a trading licence. Shops and market stalls may require a trading licence setting out the days they can operate and under what conditions.

Other licences relate to the use of certain resources. For example, a software licence sets out the arrangements through which a business can use software, e.g. on how many machines it can be installed and who can use it. Businesses must be very careful to keep within the licensing arrangements or be subject to the resulting penalties.

Formal records

Businesses are required to keep a number of records to show that they are complying with regulations. For some people this is regarded as one of the biggest problems for a small business. They argue that the excessive paperwork makes it very difficult to run a business smoothly.

Records that need to be kept include:

Tax records

This includes records of income earned by the business and costs paid out. Businesses are expected to pay income tax calculated as a percentage of the income earned by employees, as well as value-added tax (VAT) on the price of goods sold. VAT is collected by businesses on the government's behalf. All businesses pay VAT on most purchases.

Self-employed people are taxed on their business profits. The profit is calculated by taking costs from sales revenues. There are also some allowances that are not taxed. Her Majesty's Customs and Revenue (HMRC) tax year runs from 6 April to 5 April the following year. Tax has to be paid in two instalments, the first on 31 January and the second on 31 July. Tax paid at these times is based on the amount owing in the previous tax year.

If you set up as a limited company, you will pay tax on your income each time you are paid. This is called PAYE (Pay As You Earn).

In addition, HMRC collects national insurance contributions. These are payments that a company collects from employee wages which eventually help to pay for their pension, as well as covering sickness and unemployment pay.

Health and safety records

Businesses with employees who work in an office, shop, warehouse, catering or leisure facility need to register with their local authority (usually its environmental health department). New businesses must notify the Health and Safety Executive or a local authority inspector. Businesses must display a Health and Safety notice if they have employees. If a business has five or more employees it has to produce a Health and Safety Policy. Businesses are expected to record all serious incidents involving the Health and Safety of employees and customers. It is very important to record these because they can be the subject of legal prosecution in the law courts. The COSHH (Control of Substances Harmful to Health) regulations require employers to identify work tasks that are likely to be harmful and take steps to minimise the risks.

All businesses are also required to show they have carried out a fire-risk assessment.

Leasing and hire-purchase agreements

Businesses also keep records covering the leasing and hiring of vehicles, equipment (such as photocopiers) and sometimes premises. A lease is an arrangement whereby one business grants the right to use an item to another business in return for regular payments. Part of the lease may involve the regular servicing of equipment such as office computers or a motor vehicle. It is essential that clear and accurate records are kept of payments made and amounts owing on such a lease.

The records need to be kept carefully and accurately and be open to public scrutiny.

Fieldwork

Interview the owner of a local business to find out what sorts of records it has to keep. What are the main areas of business activity that it keeps records about? Who is responsible for keeping and updating these records? For what purposes are the records used?

Did you know...

***The no-nonsense guide to government rules and regulations for setting up your business* available from Business Link is a really useful source of information.**

Make the grade

P2 P2 asks you to identify ways in which regulations and laws for small businesses can affect preparation for business. One way of carrying out this task would be to talk to a local small-business owner to find out about the regulations that affect their business. Set out the list into various headings, e.g. environmental regulations, health and safety, fire safety regulations, etc. In each case find out who is responsible for making sure that the regulations are kept – e.g. local health and safety inspectors. Find out what the business needs to do to keep within the regulations. Alternatively, investigate the regulations that a business of your choice would have to bear in mind using the *no-nonsense guide to government rules and regulations* mentioned above.

Marketing and sales

In this section we examine the very important part played by marketing and sales in preparing for business. Marketing helps a business to find out what customers want and then to provide an appropriate mix of suitable products, promoted in an effective way at attractive prices and sold in the best-possible locations. Selling involves providing the buyer with a worthwhile benefit. A good business takes endless trouble to supply products that meet the needs of customers in every way. The art of successful selling is to make sure that at the point when customers are in a position to buy, every advantage offered by the product is crystal clear in their minds.

Reaching and retaining customers

One of the first steps in setting up a business is to plan the marketing of the product or service. Marketing boils down to creating, producing, promoting and delivering a product or service that meets customers' needs.

Before setting up in business, you must either:

- make sure that people want to buy what you want to make

or

- find out first what people want to buy in the product category in which you are interested, and then plan to make it.

For any type and size of business, four of the most important questions are:

1. Who are you selling to?
2. What do they want?
3. When and where do they want it?
4. What price are they prepared to pay?

Important questions for any business

The questions are all interlinking. You can't really answer the first question until you have an idea of your answer to the second, and you can't answer 3 and 4 unless you have already answered the first two.

In practice, a company will know that its expertise and experience lie within a certain category of products and that there is a wide range of different people who are potential customers for different products in that category. It is the matching of a particular product with a particular customer segment that creates a good business.

For instance, a car manufacturer might have built up a very strong business selling saloon cars to middle-aged people, but want to extend its business into the younger end of the market by manufacturing sports cars. It cannot properly answer the question 'Who are you selling to?' until it has decided that 'what they want' is something it can make – i.e. sports cars.

Customer care

It is very important to keep customers happy. There are many ways of making customers' lives easier. A good starting point is to sort out those things that are likely to make them irritated. For example, this might involve making sure that you have in stock the products that they want, or that you reduce or eliminate queuing time.

A business owner should identify ways in which they can improve their product for customers. This might involve providing better after-sales support, e.g. help with any problems customers have in making the product work. It is very important that everyone who works for the company understands how important it is to build excellent relationships with customers – so that they keep coming back and pass the word on about how good you are to their friends.

Task

Choose a product idea that you think could be a successful idea for selling across the UK. What consumer segments do you think that the product would particularly appeal to? How would you go about selling the product? Through which distribution outlets would you sell it? What product benefits would you seek to communicate to customers? What sort of customer care activities would be most suitable to support ongoing consumer confidence in the product?

Marketing information

Successful businesses are armed with lots of information about the markets in which they operate. In particular this information is about the customers and the competition.

It is relatively easy to come up with an idea for a new business. However, it is essential to find out whether customers will buy from you. Market research is therefore required to find out about customer habits and what they need. Armed with this information, you can then adjust your product to meet the requirements of customers. It is also important to find out about the competition. What do they offer, where and when? How much do they charge?

There are some simple methods of carrying out market research. For example, if you want to open up a new shop, then you must find out how many customers pass by per hour – this is called measuring the 'footfall'.

If you want to launch a new product, first try it out on friends and family. You could then give out free samples to see what people think. If you want to find out about local competitors, then walk around the area in which you want to set up and have a look directly at the competition. Alternatively, look in a local trade directory or newspaper to find out about competitors.

Marketing should involve identifying representative samples of consumers and then asking them questions. A representative sample is one that is typical of your market. Make sure that you don't stop carrying out market research until you have enough information to help you make a decision about whether to set up or not or what to produce.

Your customers can be broken down into segments, i.e. groups of customers who are broadly similar. For example, in the tea market you might find segments of regular tea drinkers or ones who just drink one cup of tea a day; alternatively you might segment them according to whether they use tea bags, or drink specialist tea such as fruit-flavoured teas, green tea or Earl Grey tea.

Each segment of the market has different habits and needs, so you should target your marketing at the specific segment. The important thing is to identify promising segments – i.e. ones that are most likely to be attracted by your product or business.

Analysing and meeting customer needs

Market research information is either primary or secondary. Primary information is information you gather yourself; secondary information is information that someone else has already gathered and published.

Speaking to members of the public is primary reseach

Primary information is usually obtained by interviewing a sample of the target market. The questions should be clear and simple and wherever possible should be pre-tested in a pilot survey, which can be tried out on a few people. It is often easier to analyse the results of a questionnaire if you give the interviewees alternative answers to the questions. These are called 'closed questions', for example:

How often do you shop here?

a Every day
b Once a week
c Once a fortnight
d Hardly ever

The questions can be asked either in person (often the best way), or through the post (this can be slow and produce a poor response), or by telephone (which is quick and easy, but perhaps not so reliable – people sometimes don't take a telephone questioner as seriously as someone they actually meet).

Sampling might be 'random', which in effect means that you simply ask the first people you see, or 'structured', which means that you only interview people who are representative of your target market. For instance, if you are interested in selling to male teenagers, you don't ask old ladies to answer your questions.

Data must then be sorted out and organised into an easily understood form. In this way you can identify patterns of buying behaviour. For instance, if you are selling high-quality chocolates, you might learn that your target market only buys products like yours on Fridays and Saturdays. If you repeat the survey several times over a period, you might be able to identify trends – perhaps you will learn that people are gradually starting to buy expensive chocolates on Thursdays too.

This information can be represented in graphs, 'pie' charts, bar charts and pictures. When the information has been studied and digested, the business then will be able to initiate a plan of action, or adapt an existing one.

Activity

Market research for a coffee shop

In all towns and cities you find a range of tea and coffee shops. Some of these are part of a chain such as Starbucks or Costa Coffee. Some are one-off businesses. Carry out some market research to see if there is a market for a new independent coffee shop in your nearest town. First of all check out the competition to find out about the range of products and services offered and the prices charged. Then produce a questionnaire for customers. Find out about the market – what age groups and gender groups are the most frequent users? What are they looking for? Is it possible to come up with an attractive coffee shop proposition that will create a successful new business?

Competition

In what ways do rival coffee chains compete with each other?

Every business must be aware of its competitors. Direct competition exists when businesses produce similar products and appeal to the same group of people, e.g. competition between Starbucks and Costa Coffee.

Even when a business produces a unique product with no direct competition, it must still consider indirect competition. Consumers can choose to spend their money on one product rather than another quite different product – for instance, if it is too expensive to go to a coffee shop for a coffee and a pastry you might decide to go out for a pizza instead.

Firms compete with each other in many ways. Generally, competition is over product quality and performance. There can also be price competition and in some product categories, such as mobile phones, bonus gifts are important (e.g. so many free minutes).

For shops, the sharpest competitive edges are created by 'location', opening hours and the friendliness and efficiency of service. Companies also compete on the effectiveness of their advertising. If it were possible to have two identical but competitive products, the one whose benefits were more powerfully projected in the advertising would outsell the other.

Activity

Identify the main ways in which two competing coffee shop chains in your local town compete with each other. How do they compete in terms of:

- **product quality**
- **price**
- **free gifts**
- **location**
- **opening hours**
- **friendliness of staff**
- **efficiency of service**
- **effectiveness of advertising?**

Building customer relationships

Research shows that customers often stop buying from a company when they feel that they have had a bad experience with the company or that the company is not interested in their problems. One survey showed that two out of three customers would stop buying from a company if they had just one bad customer-service experience.

Customers want to feel that they have a relationship with a firm. They want to feel important. This is particularly important in dealing with complaints. The customer wants to feel that they are being listened to rather than simply being told about company policies and procedures.

Businesses should view the relationships they build with customers as lasting over a lifetime. This means that a lot of time and effort should go into each occasion company employees interact with customers – being polite, helpful and listening well.

This is where online businesses can sometimes lose out to traditional businesses. Online businesses often simply involve making sales to customers. If this isn't supported by a helpline and customer service lines to deal with returns and customer complaints, the online business may quickly find that customer relationships have been irreparably damaged.

Cost and price of products or services

In choosing a suitable price for your product or service you need to carry out some research. The price you set needs to be attractive to customers.

The two main methods of pricing are:

1. Cost-based pricing, and
2. Value-based pricing.

Cost-based pricing involves setting a target profit over and above your costs. For example, you could aim to make a profit of 20% on top of your costs.

The break-even point of a business is the point at which it just covers its costs. For example, a coffee shop might calculate that it needs to serve 200 customers a day to cover its costs. After this it will make profit.

So with cost-based pricing you need to decide how much mark-up you want to add to the break-even to make your desired profit. The mark-up is how much you charge on top of the sum required to break even, e.g. a mark-up of 20% per item.

It is a balancing act to maximise your mark-up while at the same time not scaring customers off because your prices are too high.

For example, if you chose to mark up your coffees and pastries by 20% and found that customers were going elsewhere, you would either have to reduce the mark-up you charge or to work out ways of lowering costs.

Other methods of pricing a product include:

- Skimming – i.e. initially charging a high price to attract customers with a 'must have' attitude to your product. Then when they are satisfied, lower the price to attract another group of customers who are also keen but not quite as well off as the first group. Later you can reduce prices still further to appeal to a broader market looking for 'affordability'. The idea of skimming comes from taking the cream off the milk first.
- Penetration pricing involves charging a relatively low price when you first launch your product to get into the market. Once customers know about your product and like it, then you can start to raise your prices.
- Psychological pricing involves charging a price at a point such as 99p or £19.99 to make consumers think that the product is cheaper than it actually is (rather than £1.00 and £20).
- Competitor pricing involves charging a price a little below that of competing businesses.

Value-based pricing is determined by the value that customers attach to products. For example, top-quality restaurants are able to charge high prices because customers attach a high value to the food served there. By creating high-value products, restaurants are able to make high profit margins. By finding out what customers want and delivering it to them, a business is able to maximise the returns from value-based pricing.

Jane's Bakery

Jane produces bread and sandwiches, which she sells from a small bakery outlet close to a busy road. Her bakery is close to several offices, shops and a small factory. She marks up her bread by 20% and her sandwiches by 30%.

She faces quite a lot of competition from high-street outlets such as M&S, as well as a Pret-â-Manger store, which sell sandwiches. There is also a Greggs bakery. She has found that while these outlets offer a range of good-quality sandwiches, it is possible to beat the competition by providing a greater variety of to-order sandwiches. She stocks a range of ingredients that she fills the sandwiches with. Recently she has found that the number of customers buying from her has been falling and this leads to a waste of stock – bread and ingredients that have gone past their 'sell by' dates.

1. Why do you think that Jane has been able to mark up her sandwiches by a higher percentage than her bread?
2. Why might Jane's sales have fallen?
3. What actions can Jane take to win back custom?
4. What are the implications of the actions you have suggested for Jane's policy of cost-based pricing?

Promoting products or services

Sales promotion is all about convincing the people who form your target market that your product is the one that they should buy, convincing them in such a way that they remember your product name and qualities, even when competitors start trying to promote their own product.

You should time your promotion campaign to 'break' when customers are most likely to buy and you are ready to supply. Posters, press advertisements, radio commercials, even TV commercials are all important media. They can be expensive.

Producing simple leaflets and handing them out yourself or putting them through letterboxes are cheaper and still effective methods (don't forget to put your name, address and phone number on the leaflet).

You could try persuading the local media to give you editorial coverage for nothing. This might involve inviting journalists to see your work or inspect your premises. Sometimes newspapers are keen to publicise the result of local market research.

The best publicity is 'word of mouth', personal recommendation. 'Word of mouth' publicity is free in one sense, but it has to be earned. You must look upon every customer as a potential sales representative. This keeps you on your toes. A satisfied customer can bring you in many more customers. A dissatisfied customer can do you a great deal of damage.

Activity

Some friends of yours are setting up a new nursery in your town. The name of the nursery is Smarties – for Smart Kids. What methods would you use to promote the nursery? Outline the advantages and drawbacks of each of the methods you have suggested.

Unique selling points

Unique selling points (USPs) are distinct reasons why customers should buy your product rather than someone else's. It is helpful to have more than one USP.

Your USP may be that you provide a new product, but it is more likely to be the fact that you provide a better-quality service, a faster service, a friendlier service, a more reliable service, a more convenient service, that you are nearer to customers, etc.

Small businesses often gain an advantage over larger ones in that they are able to provide a more flexible and personal service.

Activity

Working as a group, brainstorm a list of 20 local businesses that individual students feel to be good businesses. In each case identify the USP of each of these businesses. How does the USP encourage customer loyalty?

Selling

Most days of your life you are involved in some form of selling activity. It might be persuading a friend to come with you to a concert or asking a relative to buy something for your birthday. What you are doing is using your relationship to sell your ideas to someone else.

Selling is particularly important in setting up an enterprise. Initially very few customers will know about you. You have to go and find your customers and persuade them to buy from you. You may want to post leaflets door to door to alert people to the existence of your business. You may advertise in the local press. However, in addition you are likely to have to meet customers face to face to persuade them that your business idea is a good one. Persuasion and communication skills are thus highly important.

Personal selling involves interaction between individuals or groups of individuals. The object of personal selling is to make a sale, and it is the end product of all the marketing activities that have taken place beforehand. It involves matching a customer's requirements with the goods or services on offer. The better the match, the more lasting the relationship between the buyer and the seller.

The main benefit of personal selling is the ability to communicate with and focus on customers individually and with precision. For example, if you go into a travel agency and ask for details about a holiday, the sales assistant may explain and point out the features of the various packages and any discounts or promotions they might offer.

Selling involves special skills. Sales staff represent an organisation and so need to give a positive image. It is important that they do not offend customers by their appearance. Your mode of dress should reflect the products being offered. For example, if you create a fashion business you should dress in a fashionable way.

When selling to your target customers, make sure that you focus on the benefits that they are looking for. For example, if customers are looking for a cheap holiday in the sun, then price and the likelihood of it being sunny are the key features that you should focus on rather than other benefits such as historic sites, local food, etc.

Did you know...

There are a few useful hints about good selling. First of all get your customer talking to find out about what they want. Then start to stress the benefits of your offer. Make sure that you illustrate ways in which your offer matches the benefits that they are looking for. Find out the objections that customers have to your offer and then combat each of these objections with persuasive arguments. A free sample of your product is a good way of showing how you compare with the competition. Price may be a sticking point, so try to negotiate on price. When the point arrives when you come to make a deal – close it. Once the deal is closed don't continue trying to persuade because this may have the reverse effect.

Activity

Working as a small group, identify products and services that you are hoping to buy in the near future. Then act out the role of sales person and customer. The sales person should seek to find out what benefits the customer is looking for and focus their sales pitch accordingly.

Make the grade

P3 To provide evidence for P3 you need to describe how small businesses prepare to market and sell products or services. You could investigate how a small local business markets and sells its products. If you have set up a mini-enterprise, you could outline the marketing and selling steps taken in setting up your enterprise. Alternatively you could outline the marketing and selling methods that you would employ for a business idea of your choice.

Environmental issues

Today environmental issues are very important in setting up a new business. Your business is responsible for any environmental damage it causes and there are no limits to financial penalties.

If your business is going to create waste, then you need to check out what is acceptable with the Department for Environment, Food and Rural Affairs (DEFRA).

There are special rules about how waste must be stored. For example, non-hazardous waste can be stored and disposed of in non-hazardous containers. Special wastes are more dangerous and toxic wastes need to be held in a special waste container. If any special waste is mixed with non-hazardous waste, then all of the waste is immediately classified as special waste.

Businesses have to pay a landfill tax on wastes sent to landfill.

Emissions of waste that go into waste-water systems or into the air must be checked with the local authority and the Environment Agency.

There are special regulations covering the disposal of electrical waste products. There are also regulations covering solvents, refrigeration, air conditioning and fire-fighting equipment that must be disposed of through special procedures.

Financial issues

There are a number of important financial issues that you will need to consider:

- Where will the finance come from?
- What are going to be the main costs when setting up?
- What are going to be the main costs of running the business?
- How can the cash-flow position of the business be monitored?
- Which external organisations need to be paid, e.g. the payment of tax?

- How to measure the financial success of the business?
- What should be the main financial priorities of the business?

Sources of finance

Where will you get the money from for your business? To start off with you will most likely put some money in yourself that you have saved up.

However, this is unlikely to be enough. You may be able to persuade family and friends to invest in the business. If you are setting up a private limited company you could invite them to become shareholders, taking a share of the profits.

Another important source of finance is a bank loan. Banks will sometimes be prepared to match the finance provided by the owners of a business provided they can see that the idea is a good one and that it is backed up by a sound business plan. Another source of finance provided by a bank is an overdraft. With an overdraft you can take out more money than you have in your account up to an agreed limit. Interest is worked out on a daily basis. Many small businesses also fund part of their business activity using a credit card. The credit card enables the holder to make purchases and then pay back at the end of the month or in agreed instalments over a period of time.

A bank may help with finance if you have a good business plan

Another source of finance is leasing. Here the business leases an item such as an office computer. They make payments at regular intervals and do not own the item. Hire purchase is a similar arrangement for motor vehicles and other items of capital. With hire purchase the purchaser will become the owner once a final payment has been made after an agreed term (e.g. two or three years).

Jonathan Ross

Jonathan Ross has set up a small independent coffee shop in a student district. The coffee shop sells a range of coffee drinks, hot chocolate and teas. In addition it sells cakes and pastries. Jonathan needed £10,000 to set up the business, including decorating the premises, installing the equipment and the furniture. He hires two staff. The coffee shop is open long hours and his staff costs are £1,000 a month. Other costs of running the coffee shop including the costs of supplies come to £1,200 a month. The money that the coffee shop takes varies from month to month. In a good month sales can amount to £7,000, while in a poor month they can be as low as £2,000. Jonathan was lucky to be given a gift of £5,000 from his parents to set up the business.

1. What other sources of finance could Jonathan have used to set up the coffee shop?
2. What sources of finance would help Jonathan to manage the day-to-day running of the business?
3. Why might Jonathan need to borrow money during the course of the year?
4. Outline how two of the sources of finance that you have mentioned would be particularly helpful to Jonathan.

Start-up costs

Setting-up a business involves considerable expenditure. Equipment and stationery have to be bought, premises need to be made fit for the start-up, legal fees need to be covered and there are high initial promotion and advertising costs to make people aware of the business. Careful thought needs to be given to the expenditure involved in setting up. The image a business starts with is likely to remain for a long time. However, it is also important not to squander scarce resources on needless items.

If you are turning something you already do into a business, then you might already possess some of the tools. However, if you want to expand on a more professional basis you will probably want to invest in machinery and equipment.

Make sure that you take into account all of the start-up costs. For example, if you rent out business premises you will additionally usually have to pay rates (a local business tax) to the local council. When you rent out premises the landlord will normally want at least one month's rent in advance as well as a deposit to cover damages.

Operating expenses and income

Once you are up and running there will be a regular stream of costs that you have to pay. For example, there will be telephone, gas, electricity and water bills, as well as tax, insurance and business rates. Don't forget interest payments on bank loans and other sources of finance.

Additionally you will have wages to pay, as well as a salary for yourself.

The items you produce or sell also incur costs to you. For example, if you are buying items to resell, then the cost of the items is classified as a 'cost of sales', along with other items such as travelling to meet your customers.

Fortunately you should have income coming into your business to meet some of your costs. The main source of income should be the sales that you make. In the long term your income needs to exceed your operating expenses if you are going to make a profit.

Being successful in business involves:

- increasing your income steadily; and
- controlling your costs.

You therefore need to constantly review your income to find ways of increasing your sales.

You need to constantly review your costs to identify ways of making cost savings.

Cash-flow forecasting

Many small businesses collapse because they do not pay enough attention to the prices and the quantities of goods they need to sell to make a profit.

Before setting up in business, you must estimate your cash flow for several months ahead. If you calculate that your costs will consistently exceed takings, there is no point in setting up.

The term 'forecast' is used because estimates of cash inflows and outflows are made prior to trading taking place. In future periods you can then refer back to the forecast to check that everything is going to plan.

Fashion style

Pritesh has set up a small fashion clothes shop and has made a forecast of his income (money coming into the business) and expenses (payments) for the first three months of the year.

	January £	February £	March £
Balance B/F	1,000	1,500	2,300
Income			
Sales	3,000	3,600	4,000
Total receipts	3,000	3,600	4,000
Total cash available	4,000	5,100	6,300
Expenses			
Purchases	2,000	2,300	2,500
Wages	500	500	500
Total payments	2,500	2,800	3,000
Balance C/F	1,500	2,300	3,300

The first thing to note is that Balance B/F refers to the end balance at the end of the previous month. (So for example in January the business had cash available from the end of the previous month of £1,000.)

Balance C/F is the balance at the end of the month which is carried forward into the next month.

The major heading 'Income' refers to money coming into the business each month. In this example, this comes from sales. Total receipts consists of all of the types of income added together.

Cash available is calculated by adding the balance brought forward to the income.

Next we deduct the expenses. There are two main expenses – purchases of clothing items and wages. Add these together to get a figure for total payments.

When total payments are deducted from the total cash available to the business each month we have the figure for the balance, which we can carry forward at the end of the month.

1. What is the value of total income (receipts) for the first three months of the year?
2. What is the value of total payments for the first three months of the year?
3. Explain why the balance, carried forward is increasing month by month.
4. Copy out the cash-flow forecast illustrated. Add on an extra three months. Assume that wages are the same at £500 a month; sales increase to £4,500 in April, £5,000 in May and £5,500 in June; purchases increase to £2,800 in April, £3,100 in May and £3,300 in June. Now calculate the balances for April, May and June.

The cash-flow forecast is very important because it shows whether the business has enough cash to meet pressing demands (e.g. from Her Majesty's Revenue and Customs) at any moment in time.

It is very important to look at the figure for closing balances at the end of each month.

For example, if a business suddenly finds itself with a negative closing balance this would indicate that it will have to finance this by using an overdraft or its credit card. If the negative figure is caused by something major such as purchasing machinery, then this may need to come from a loan or some other way of financing a large expenditure.

Cash-flow problems

Wendy James and Louise Ward didn't have much idea about setting up a business when they first started out. The business they set up was called House-to-House. It provides a service for estate agents and letting agencies by:

- Making out inventories (lists of furniture and other household items) and checking them.
- Helping people to move into and out of accommodation.
- Spring-cleaning properties.
- Providing other related services.

Wendy and Louise previously worked in a letting agency and know that it is very difficult to get tenants to do all these important but fairly routine tasks. They were attracted by the idea of setting up their own business and realised that House-to-House would be relatively cheap to set up.

The two women rang round a few letting agencies to tell them what they could offer and soon had plenty of work coming in.

However, their problem was cash flow – paying out expenses ahead of receipts – a common problem in small firms. After two months it became serious. Wendy and Louise were paying wages to a full-time employee and they had to cover all the overheads. Soon they were in a position where they couldn't even afford to put petrol in the car or buy stamps.

1. What is a cash-flow problem?
2. How had the cash-flow problem arisen for Wendy and Louise?
3. What suggestions would you make to deal with the cash-flow problem?
4. If you were to set up a new business how could you avoid cash-flow problems?

Measuring the financial success of the business

In Chapter 1 we saw that a major business objective is to make a profit. But how do we measure that profit?

At the start of a trading period, a business works out its sales forecast – how much it expects to sell each month.

It is then possible to calculate the direct costs of making each sale. For example, if a business makes sandwiches it is possible to calculate the cost of bread, other materials, packaging and wages that go into each sandwich.

For example, if a business has direct costs per sandwich of £1.50 and sells each sandwich for £3.00, then it makes a gross profit of £1.50 on each sale:

Selling price – direct cost = gross profit
i.e. £3.00 – £1.50 = £1.50

In business it is helpful to convert this figure into a profit margin.

The gross profit margin is calculated by dividing the gross profit by the selling price and multiplying by 100. In this example, the gross profit margin is 50% (£1.50 divided by £3.00 multiplied by 100%).

What this means is that for every sandwich sold, 50% of its value can go to meeting the overhead costs such as rent, rates and administration costs of running the business.

Measuring profit

It is important to know how to measure the profit of a business. This is calculated from the profit and loss account.

A profit and loss account shows:

1. The value of sales made by a business.
2. The cost of making those sales.
3. The gross profit (i.e. sales minus the cost of sales).
4. The expenses of the business. These should be deducted from the gross profit.
5. The net profit of the business. This is the profit after all costs have been deducted.

The account below shows how the profit is arrived at for The Honey Shop, a specialist retailer of honey in a major city. It shows how much was spent on buying honey (purchases) and the total revenue received from selling that honey (sales). It also shows the expenses of running the business.

P&L account for The Honey Shop for the year ended 31/12/10

	£	**£**
Sales		30,000
Cost of sales (purchases)		(15,000)
Gross profit		15,000
Less expenses		
Electricity	500	
Insurance	300	
Wages	4,200	5,000
Net profit		10,000

Summarising the account we can see that:

Sales = £30,000

Gross profit = £15,000

Net profit = £10,000

From these figures we can make some very important calculations that tell us something about how well the business is being run. It is important to find out how much profit the company is making for every £1 of sales.

The gross profit margin shows how much gross profit is made for each £1 of sales.

The net profit margin shows how much net profit the business makes for every £1 of sales.

The calculation is easy:

$$\text{Gross profit margin} = \frac{\text{gross profit}}{\text{sales}}$$

$$\text{Net profit margin} = \frac{\text{net profit}}{\text{sales}}$$

For example, for The Honey Shop:

$$\text{Gross profit margin} = \frac{15{,}000}{30{,}000} = \frac{1}{2}\ \text{50 pence for}$$
every £1 of sales

$$\text{Net profit margin}\ \frac{10{,}000}{30{,}000} = \frac{1}{3} = \text{33.3 pence for}$$
every £1 of sales

For The Honey Shop to calculate gross profit margin we need to show the gross profit as a proportion of sales.

Sales amount to £30,000 of which gross profit is one half i.e. £15,000. This shows that for every £1 of sales made there are 50 pence of gross profit. The gross profit is expressed as a % i.e. 50%.

To calculate the net profit margin we need to show the net sales as a proportion of sales.

Sales amount to £30,000 of which gross profit is one third i.e. £10,000. This shows that for every £1 of sales made there are 33 pence of net profit. The net profit is expressed as a % i.e. 33.3%.

When gross profit margins for a business fall, this tends to indicate that:

- The firm has got its prices wrong. Prices are either too high or too low; or:
- The firm has been paying too much for the items that it is buying for resale; or:
- Some of the items the firm is selling are being damaged or stolen.

When net profit margins fall this tends to indicate that:

- The cost of one or more of the overhead costs has risen.

The firm will need to look at ways of cutting these costs or raising its prices.

In preparing to set up a business it is important to be able to forecast the likely profit and loss account for the business at the end of the first six months of trading and possibly at the end of the first year of trading. To do this you should set out the likely sales revenue for the first six months (and year), the cost of sales for the first six months (and year), and the expenses that will need to be paid during these time periods.

Activity

You and a group of friends have decided to set up a car-washing business for a four-week period, cleaning cars at your local school or college. Estimate how many cars the business would clean each week and how much you would charge per car. This will give you a figure for revenue. Next find out the costs of the various items you would need for your car-washing business and the wages that you would pay the 'car washers'. Using this information set out a forecast profit and loss account for the four weeks that you would be trading for.

The assets of a business

The assets of a business are the things that it owns at a particular moment in time.

The assets of a business are shown in a company balance sheet. Also set out in the balance sheet will be the liabilities, that is, what the business owes at a particular moment in time.

The following illustration shows the assets of a small bicycle shop at the end of December. The chart also shows the liabilities of the business.

Super Cycles

Assets and liabilities as at 31 December

	£
Fixed assets	
Shop premises	60,000
Fixtures and fittings	10,000
	70,000
Current assets	
Stock	12,000
Cash	3,000
Less liabilities	20,000
Assets – liabilities	65,000

You can see in this simplified balance sheet that fixed assets amount to £70,000. The fixed assets are the things the business owns that stay in the business – they are not sold – e.g. the building and the cycle repair equipment.

The current assets consist of those things that the shop owns for the purpose of trading, the cycles for sale and cash that will be used to buy new cycles and settle any pressing debts. The current assets amount to £15,000.

The total value of assets is therefore £85,000 (the fixed assets + the current assets).

The business owes (has liabilities of) £20,000. This might consist of a loan and money owed to cycle suppliers.

When we deduct the liabilities from the assets we can see that the business is worth £65,000.

Assets – liabilities = value of the business
i.e. 85,000 - 20,000 = 65,000

A business can grow by increasing the value of its assets.

The business needs to have enough assets to cover its liabilities.

Activity

For the car-wash business described in the previous Activity, identify what the fixed assets and the current assets of the business would be. How would the business be able to afford to buy additional fixed assets?

Financial priorities

As we have seen, financial issues are very important to a business. For example, it is essential to have enough cash to meet pressing payments that a business has to make.

In addition, a business needs to make a profit so that it can invest in fixed assets to grow the business.

A business also needs to have enough short-term (current) assets to meet any pressing short-term liabilities.

Running a business is risky. Risks include not being able to sell enough of your product to make a profit. Another risk is that people who owe you money are slow in paying, while people you owe money to may be demanding payment straight away.

It is quite easy to lose money in business. Losses arise from not being able to sell your products or your stock going out of date before you can sell it.

The ideal of having a secure income is rarely met. This is why marketing, selling and careful financial planning are so important in reducing risks. Marketing and selling enable a business to secure a steady income. Careful financial management enables a business to reduce costs.

Make the grade

P4 To achieve P4 you will need to describe the financial issues that can affect preparation for a business. If you are starting up a mini-enterprise within your school or college you could outline:

- The sources of finance and start-up costs for your business.
- The operating expenses and income that will result from your business.
- Create a projected cash-flow forecast for the first few months of trading.
- Set out and explain a projected profit and loss account for the first year of trading (or for the length of time the enterprise operates for).
- Set out a simple balance sheet for the business at the end of the first period of activity.

Alternatively carry out the same activities for a fictional business of your choice. If you do this you will need to carry out detailed research to find accurate costs and revenues for your business. Market research will identify the prices you can charge and the numbers you are likely to sell. You will need to estimate costs based on research. For example, if you are renting property, what are local rental charges per square metre? How much does it cost to place advertisements in suitable media, etc.?

Make the grade

M2 **D1** To achieve M2 and go on to achieve D1, you will need to analyse (merit level) and evaluate (distinction level) the issues involved in setting up your business. You will therefore need to examine in depth the various elements involved in setting up a business – complying with regulations, marketing and financial aspects. You need to provide a detailed picture of how these elements affect your chosen business and the sort of preparation and planning that must be done to successfully get the business off the ground. Your evaluation will identify why the business will or will not be successful and make recommendations about ways of turning the business into a successful enterprise.

Key terms

Cash flow forecast – A prediction of the incomings and outgoings of cash into a business over a future period of time. Predictions need to be based on accurate forecasts of headings such as Sales and Expenses.

Customer relations – The aspect or function of a business that seeks to develop positive images of a business in the eyes of customers, e.g. by dealing carefully with complaints.

Footfall – The number of people passing by a particular point, e.g. a commercial premise. This is measured by counting numbers passing between certain hours.

Her Majesty's Revenue and Customs – The government department responsible for collecting taxes such as income tax and value-added tax.

Licence – Permission to carry out certain activities set out in a written document.

Assignment

The assignment requires you to identify, describe and analyse some of the key processes that someone would need to carry out before starting a new business venture.

A friend is thinking of setting up a mobile discotheque in your home town or area. Another is considering setting up a hairdressing business. Choose one of these businesses as the basis for the assessment that follows. You can prepare your work in the form of an oral presentation using PowerPoint slides, a series of posters, a guide book or a mixture of the three elements.

- What regulations and laws would a hairdresser or mobile discotheque owner have to research and comply with if they are to set up in your area? Explain how each of these regulations would impact on their business. For example, noise regulations would affect the amount of noise being made by the discotheque and the hours which it could operate. **(P2)**
- What marketing and selling activities would they need to do? Create a marketing and selling plan explaining activities that need to be carried out and at what points of time they would be used and why? **(P3)**
- What financial issues would affect their preparation to set up in business? Identify the main start-up costs for the business and create a cash-flow forecast for the first six months of trading, a projected profit and loss account for the first year of trading and a projected profit and loss account for the first year of trading and a projected balance sheet at the end of the first year of trading. **(P4)**

To achieve a pass grade you need to:	To achieve a merit grade you need to:	To achieve a distinction you need to:
P2 identify how regulations and laws for small businesses can affect preparation for business	**M2** analyse the different aspects that will affect preparation for business	**D1** evaluate the issues that need to be considered when starting a business
P3 describe how small businesses prepare to market and sell products or services		
P4 describe the financial issues that can affect preparation for business		

Chapter 32
Starting a business

What are you finding out?

Having studied how to prepare yourself for business, you are now well placed to find out about the final touches involved in starting up and running a business. Now you must learn how to create a business plan and then identify the key steps in starting up. You should also be familiar with the key sources of advice and support that you can turn to.

This chapter will help you to:

- Understand how to start a business.

The business plan

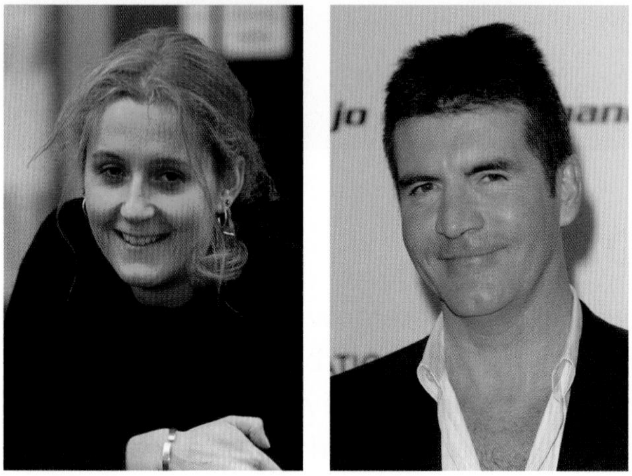

Martha Lane Fox, one of the founders of lastminute.com, and Simon Cowell, the entrepreneur behind *The X Factor*, were both successful because they turned good ideas into successful businesses through careful planning.

> **Did you know...**
>
> **Livewire is an organisation that has been created to help young people set up their own businesses in this country (see www.shell-livewire.org).**
>
> **Livewire has defined a business plan as:**
>
> **'A complete description of a business and its plans for the next one to three years. It explains what the business does (or will do if it's a new business); it suggests who will buy the product or service and why; and it provides financial forecasts demonstrating overall viability, indicates the finance available and explains financial requirements.'**

In the UK we are said to have an 'enterprise culture'. An enterprise culture is one in which people are prepared to take risks. A recent survey carried out by NatWest bank showed that 70% of sixth-formers would consider setting up a business when they have finished full-time education. In this country we do not have to go far to think of enterprising people. Modern-day examples include Martha Lane Fox (co-founder of lastminute.com). There is the inventor James Dyson who developed the bagless vacuum cleaner and Tim Berners-Lee who did much of the early work behind the internet. There are pop impresarios like Simon Cowell who came up with ideas such as *Britain's Got Talent* and *The X Factor*.

Having a great business idea is only the start of developing a great business. What is then required is a lot of hard work and planning to make the business a success.

For most businesses, the business plan will be the main method of convincing prospective fund providers that the business proposal will succeed. The business plan also shows that the proprietor has the commitment and determination to succeed. The business plan should be presented in a form that can be quickly and easily understood. The main part of a business plan normally needs no more than eight to ten pages, supported, if necessary, with more detailed appendices. The plan will then be manageable.

On the next page is a suitable outline for a business plan. It shows the headings that you might like to use and suggests contents under each heading.

Using the template, you should be suitably placed to provide a well-structured business plan that will be taken seriously.

Keep your plan nice and simple so that it doesn't confuse the reader with too much detail.

You can see that the business plan enables forward planning. It provides a route map for the business to follow – guiding key activities such as promotion and pricing, and setting out expected cash flow and profit. Once the business is up and running, it is possible to make comparisons between what actually happens and what was planned.

Heading	Suggested contents
1. Contents page	List of contents
2. Executive summary	An-at-a glance summary of the main points including the objectives of the business
3. The business and the business idea	Write down the name of the business and the address, before going on to describe your product or service. Explain how long you have been developing the business and the steps taken so far.
4. The legal status of the business	Is it a sole trader, partnership or company?
5. The market and the competitors	How big is the market and who are the main competitors? Provide broad details of your customers, e.g. age, gender and income. Briefly outline key findings of any market research you have carried out.
6. Promotional strategies	Explain much you are going to make customers aware of your product, e.g. through advertising.
7. Other marketing aspects	This could include details of pricing and where the product will be sold or made available.
8. Sales targets	How much of your product or service do you expect to be able to sell? What is the basis for making these claims?
9. Resources required	Set out the: • physical resources required, e.g. equipment, supplies • human resources required, i.e. people and their skills.
10. Sources of finance	What are the main types of finance required and who will provide the finance?
11. Cash flow and break-even	Expected cash flow in the first year of running the business and a calculation of sales needed to break even.
12. Profit and loss account	What will the profit and loss account look like at the end of the first year? This is a forecast.
13. Likely balance sheet at the end of the first year	What are the main assets and liabilities that the business expects to have at the end of the first year?

Figure 32.1 Outline for a business plan

Make the grade

P5 Providing a clear outline business plan to start up and run your business will enable you to achieve P5. Use the outline shown above. Make sure that you set out clearly what your business idea is. Are you producing a product or service? What is it? Who do you expect your customers to be – i.e. your target customers? Make sure you demonstrate that you have researched their needs through market research. Outline where and when they want your products or services in your marketing section. Outline where you will sell your product or service from and set out your sales targets.

Starting and running a business

Once you have created an outline business plan, you should be well placed to set up the business. There are a number of important steps still to consider:

The needs of the business

Make sure that you are clear about the resources that you require and the steps involved in doing this. A good idea is to set out a resources action plan. The plan would look something like the following:

Resources required to start up	When they need to be acquired by	Who will take responsibility for acquiring them

The key resources will be:

1. Business premises – to work from.
2. Machinery and equipment, e.g. computer, photocopier, phone, etc.
3. Raw materials or stock.
4. Staff.
5. Any other items, e.g. packaging, carrier bags, etc.

Task

Set out a short action plan for getting the resources to start up a selected business. Use the rows-and-column approach outlined above.

Detailed research will get your business plan off to a good start

Research techniques

To set up in the right way you need to engage in detailed research. You have already seen that you need to research the market and the various regulations associated with starting up a particular type of business.

The research techniques that you need to engage in include:

Primary research

Primary research involves finding out information directly, first hand. Talking to people and interviewing them are essential. This is referred to as getting close to the data. To find out about your market, talk to prospective customers. To find out about regulations, talk to those responsible for implementing the regulations – e.g. fire safety and health and safety officers. To find out about rental charges to hire premises, talk to an estate agent who can quote actual prices. To find out about competition, put in the legwork to look at what the competition is doing. Primary research involves hard work and being prepared to ask questions. But remember that at the start of this chapter we made it clear that business requires hard work and enterprise.

Secondary research

Your primary research should be backed up by your reading. Find out information from newspapers, trade journals and any form of advertising or promotional material provided by competitors. See if there is any published research about your market or regulations that are relevant to your business.

An important part of secondary research today is online investigation. The important thing is to use appropriate search terms. For example, you can find out about setting up small businesses by using the search 'Small business start-up' or something similar. You can find out about the market for toothpaste by using searches such as 'Market research data toothpaste' or simply 'The market for toothpaste in Britain'.

Planning techniques

Planning techniques for your new business do not have to be complex. Useful techniques include:

1. A wall-chart planner, setting out key dates.
2. A visual planning chart. This is another form of visual planning setting out in bars the number of days required to perform start-up operations in sequence. Some of these activities may need to be done in sequence, while others can be carried out simultaneously.

See for example the chart in Figure 32.2.

Figure 32.2 Planning techniques

Controllable and uncontrollable aspects

There are some things that you can plan for and there are some things that are outside your control.

A simple rule for setting up a new business venture is to seek to make as many aspects of the plan controllable as possible.

For example, you cannot control whether your customers will like your product. However, by carrying out detailed market research into what they like and test-marketing new ideas with them, you can make accurate predictions about how your product will sell.

You cannot control new regulations that your local council introduces. However, by researching existing regulations and proposed new regulations, you can make sure that your business is ready to meet these regulations now and in the future.

Activity

Make a list of all of the operations required to set up your business. For each of the activities, set them out on a piece of card. The card should be cut to the scale of the number of days required to set up the business. For example, 12 days = 12 centimetres. On each piece of card write the name of the activity to be completed and the time, e.g. 'Order stock 15 days'. Once you have created a set of cards to represent setting up your business, lay them out on a table and then stick them onto a chart showing the sequence of activities required to complete the project.

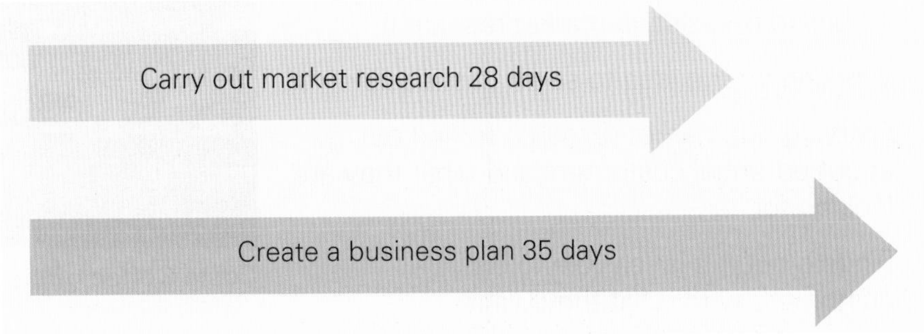

Good business planning therefore involves identifying things that are likely to change that can affect your business. Build potential changes into your plans so that you will not be surprised or suffer when they occur.

Think of all the things that might change that could affect your business, e.g.

- Changes in the price of supplies.
- Changes in interest rates.
- New products introduced by competitors.
- Changing rates and taxes.
- What else can you think of?

Activity

Look at your business plan heading by heading. What are the major changes that could take place under each of the headings that might affect your business? How can you make sure that you are prepared for possible changes?

Timing

Planning a timeline is particularly important. Most businesses set a particular date on which they plan to start trading. It is essential therefore to identify a suitable date and then decide how long it will take to prepare for the launch date. It makes sense to be a little generous with your timing.

The following timeline provides a rough guide to a typical sequence of activities that need to be carried out:

1. Coming up with the business idea (this may be based on existing market research)
2. Working on the idea to see if it is feasible
3. Carrying out market research to find out about potential customers and what they are looking for
4. Finding out if it is feasible to provide customers with what they want
5. Creating a business plan
6. Seeking finance for the business
7. Acquiring the resources for the business
8. Promoting and advertising the business
9. Preparing the goods or service and the sales activities
10. Launching the product/service or business

Looking at the list, it immediately becomes obvious that there is a lot of hard work that must be carried out even before a plan can be created. Then there are a number of other steps required before the product can be launched.

What needs to be done to start and run a business?

Costa Coffee is a good example of a well-run business. The business has been expanding extensively in Britain. New Costa outlets are opening up every week – at railway stations, airports, student unions and city centres. Costa Coffee is successful because it has researched the products that consumers want to buy. It is a highly efficient operation producing speciality drinks, pastries and sandwiches.

Costa Coffee offers a wide range of products

When you examine the range of products displayed by Costa Coffee, you can see why the business is so successful. The toasted sandwiches, sandwiches, drinks and pastries are designed to meet the requirements of a variety of consumers in the coffee shop environment, whether waiting for a train, chatting with friends or breaking up a motorway journey. Every time a new outlet opens, a lot of work goes on behind the scenes:

- Seeing if there is enough potential custom at the outlet (e.g. how many passengers are likely to be waiting at that railway station and for how long).
- Seeing how easy it would be to attract a suitable workforce.
- Identifying the nature of the local competition.
- Working out the financial projections of sales, costs, break-even and profit margins.
- Checking on the local regulations covering health and safety, fire safety and other issues.

These activities illustrate the type of activities that you will need to engage in before you start and run your business.

Activity

Prepare a chart to illustrate the steps required to set up a business of your choice in a locality of your choice. Identify all the steps required.

Materials and supplies

Once a business is set up it will need a steady flow of materials and supplies. For example, Costa Coffee needs fresh supplies of coffee, sugar, tea and cocoa powder. If you visit a Costa Coffee you will see that they need vast quantities of fresh milk every day. So they need to have a regular supplier. The sandwiches and other stock need to be replaced every day. It would be a disaster if their coffee or drinks machines went out of action, even for a day – so these need to be regularly maintained and replaced at frequent intervals.

Sourcing of materials and supplies is a crucial activity. Business owners need to arrange contracts with reliable suppliers. Also you will need storage space on site to have appropriate stock levels.

Activity

What materials and supplies would you require for your business? How would you go about acquiring these?

Advice and support

People

What sort of people would make the best advisors when you want to start up in business? Your best advice will be from people with extensive business experience, particularly in running a business that is similar to your own.

A 'business buddy' is someone who is willing to mentor and give advice to a new entrepreneur. There is a range of organisations such as The Prince's Trust that provide volunteers who are willing to do this free of charge for young people.

Agencies and organisations

There is a range of specialist agencies and organisations that provide advice and support.

Business Link

This is a very effective government-sponsored organisation, which provides a detailed website of supporting materials. The website is available at www.businesslink.gov.uk. If you enter your postcode into this site, it will direct you to local support and advice. Business Link will point you to appropriate agencies that will give you help and guidance.

The Prince's Business Trust

The Prince's Business Trust, whose patron is Prince Charles, seeks to provide help, support, and in some cases, grants to young people, particularly in areas of disadvantage.

Commercial banks

The commercial banks provide small business advisors. The advisor would first need to examine a business plan and would advise about ways of improving the plan. The bank will provide a loan, credit card or overdraft for suitable ideas, provided the borrower is able to put something of worth up as collateral against the money borrowed.

The local council

The local council often offers start-up support and advice for new business.

Online sites

Many online sites provide information for small business owners, including www.startups.co.uk and www.timesonline.co.uk/enterprise.

Funding and financial support

Perhaps the most crucial hurdle in setting up a business is to get the required funding and financial support. Without finance no business can get off the ground.

We have already seen that the starting point is to use your own savings or money from another source, e.g. redundancy money or a gift from a relative.

Next you can turn to family and friends. You may want to set up a private company so that your friends are protected by limited liability.

Next you can turn to banks for help – for an overdraft, credit card or loan.

Another source of funding comes from business angels – or venture capitalists. These are people like the Dragons on *Dragons' Den* who will provide capital in exchange for a share of your business.

Technical support

You may need specialist support to manage a particular technical problem such as how to set up a website and arranging to have it hosted. Alternatively you may have specific technical problems associated with the nature of your product. Typically you will have to pay a specialist to provide you with this help – but it may well be worth doing so. However, first you must look at what they have done for others and how much they are charging for their services.

Education and training

Rather than blindly rushing into running your business, you may want to take a business course for new entrepreneurs. This might be run by your local college or university. Business Link will be able to put you into contact with an appropriate training provider.

Particularly helpful will be sessions on issues such as carrying out market research, creating a business plan and complying with regulations.

Make the grade

P6 To provide evidence for P6 you will need to explain the sources of advice and support available when preparing for a business. A good idea is to include this as a separate section in your business plan. Outline the sources of advice and support that you will turn to in order to help you plan your business idea. Mention websites that give good advice about business start-up. Also identify local contacts that provide help and support, through Business Link. Identify sources of specialist support that would help your business to get off the ground.

Make the grade

D2 To achieve a Distinction (D2) you will need to provide evidence that you can make and justify recommendations for starting a business. You will need to make a strong case in your Business plan. Your business plan should demonstrate that:

- You have a sound business idea.
- That your product or service is carefully planned and designed.
- The you have identified the market and found out what customers are looking for.
- That you have investigated relevant regulations affecting your business and plan to take account of these e.g. health and safety, fire safety and environmental regulations.
- That you have carefully selected an appropriate location.
- That you have worked out the likely costs and revenues from operating your business.
- That you have created financial projections covering at least the first year of trading.
- That you have identified appropriate sources of advice and support to set up the business.

Key terms

Balance sheet – Financial statement setting out what a business owes (liabilities) and what it owns (assets) at a particular moment in time.

Business Link – A government-sponsored organisation that provides advice and support for new businesses.

Business plan – A forward plan used when seeking funding to set up a new business. It also provides a forward plan or guide to work to.

Controllable elements – Those parts of a plan that the business owner has direct control over because they are predictable.

Enterprise culture – A general 'can do' attitude, coupled with a willingness to take risks.

Profit and loss account – A financial statement setting out the revenues and costs of a business from which the profit or loss can be calculated.

Research techniques – Methods used to find out information that will help to create a business plan.

Sales targets – The number (or value) of sales that a business plans to make within a given time period.

Uncontrollable elements – Elements of a business plan that are unpredictable and typically result from events or are instigated by people (e.g. competitors) outside the business.

Assignment

In this chapter we have outlined the various pieces of evidence that you need to create for the purposes of the assessment for this unit. The assignment focused on preparing to set up in business. In this Unit we have been giving you step-by-step guidance to the processes of setting up a business. The various components of the assessment are summarised below:

- On page 383 we showed you how to create a business plan and provided you with an outline template for doing so. Create the plan in a professional way using a word processing package. The plan should be professionally presented to show to a business advisor, bank or someone providing the business with finance to set up. **(P5)**
- On page 388 we asked you to explain the sources of advice that you would use in setting up a business. We suggested that this could be a separate section of your business plan. **(P6)**
- On page 389 we showed you how to provide evidence that you can make and justify recommendations for starting a business. Check carefully through the bullet points to make sure that you cover each of the areas outlined. **(D2)**

Creating a plan for a business venture is a highly rewarding activity. If you follow our step-by-step guide you will be able to produce a professional business plan that will help you to justify and win support for your propsed business venture.

To achieve a pass grade you need to:	To achieve a merit grade you need to:	To achieve a distinction you need to:
P5 outline the contents of a business plan when starting and running a business		**D2** make and justify recommendations for starting a business
P6 explain the sources of advice and support available when preparing for business		

Unit 19

The marketing plan

Chapter 33
Marketing concepts used by business

What are you finding out?

If you set up a business of your own, one of the most important tasks will be to create a marketing plan. This unit helps you to create a marketing plan for a micro start-up business or a social enterprise.

A micro-start up business is a very small business. A social enterprise is an organisation whose prime purpose is to do something socially useful, e.g. engage in not-for-profit recycling activity or working with the elderly.

The unit therefore consists of two key elements. The first element introduces you to a range of marketing concepts that you will need to master. You will then go on to create a marketing plan. You will define the target market that you are targeting your marketing campaign at. You also need to define the benefits of your product or service to customers. The unit requires you to carry out some market research and to use the research to develop marketing tactics and a marketing mix

This chapter will help you to:

- Understand the marketing concepts used by business.

Marketing concepts

Marketing involves finding out about customers and their requirements, as well as other aspects of the market such as what competitors are doing. Armed with this information, it is then possible to provide products and services with the customer in mind. This section on marketing concepts is designed to help you to develop a clearer idea of who your customers might be and what they are looking for.

There are a number of marketing concepts that you need to understand before you can start to create a marketing and promotional plan.

How buyers make decisions (the buyer decision-making process)

How do buyers make a decision whether to purchase a good or not? Marketers know that consumer decision making usually follows a series of stages. These are set out in the flow chart below.

Knowledge of this decision-making process is very helpful to marketers. It suggests ways that you can win customers and encourage them to decide to buy your product again and again.

Attention – Bring the product to the attention of your likely customers. Advertise in places where they are likely to spot it. Give away free samples. Get people talking on the internet about your product.

Information – Provide them with lots of information about your product, where they can buy it, when it is becoming available, what features it has – the more information the better.

Decision – Encourage them to think about the positive aspects of buying your product, find out what sort of offer they are looking for that will encourage them to buy.

Action – Make it easy for them to purchase your product – have enough in stock, have your phone lines open, make delivery easy.

Satisfaction – All of the effort that you have put into marketing your product will be wasted unless customers are satisfied, tell their friends and want to buy more. So make sure that you provide the type of product that customers will continue to buy. Make sure that you listen to what customers tell you about the aspects of your product that satisfy them.

A – **Attention.** Consumers become aware of a particular product or brand. Perhaps they are told about it about by a friend, they see an advert on the television or read about it in a magazine.

↓

I – **Information.** The customer becomes interested in the product and starts to seek further information about it.

↓

D – **Decision.** The customer has to make a decision whether to purchase the product or not.

↓

A – **Action.** Either the customer purchases or puts off the purchase.

↓

S – **Satisfaction.** The customer uses the product and gets satisfaction from doing so.

Figure 33.1 The AIDAS decision-making process

Activity

Some of your female friends are frustrated that there doesn't appear to be a suitable magazine available targeted specifically at young females with a general interest in a wide variety of sports that young females engage in, e.g. running, netball, football, rugby, etc. You have carried out some research and come up with a good concept for a magazine that will come out once a month, sold from national chains of newsagents and be priced similarly to existing sports titles. What do you then need to do to make customers aware of the new title, using the AIDAS model?

Did you know...

Some useful advice about providing consumers with information:

1. **Provide the information when they are most likely to use it – e.g. give information about products for flu and colds in the winter.**
2. **Focus on the difference between your products and those of rivals.**
3. **Keep the information simple so that it is easy to understand.**

Unique selling proposition (USP)

In marketing a product it is important to establish a unique selling proposition which sets your business, brand or product ahead of the competition. Your product may be unique – for example, a cereal bar may have a special recipe and taste and come in distinctive wrapping. However, in addition, there are other aspects – USPs that can set it apart from rivals – e.g. it contains fewer calories, it is endorsed by a well-known health expert, and other unique aspects.

Creating a unique selling proposition is particularly important in providing services. For example, the insurance your company offers may be similar to other insurance offers, but your staff might be friendlier and deal with customer problems more quickly.

Unique selling propositions are usually set out in advertising. The advertisement needs to say to the person seeing or hearing the advert – 'Buy this product and you will get this specific benefit.' The benefit should be one that the competition does not offer.

Activity

In each of the following instances identify the unique selling proposition that encourages you to buy a particular product or service. Identify the USP:

- **for your favourite hairdresser**
- **the cinema that you visit most frequently**
- **a particular website that you use regularly.**

Did you know...

The unique selling proposition of Head and Shoulders shampoo is that it will get rid of dandruff.

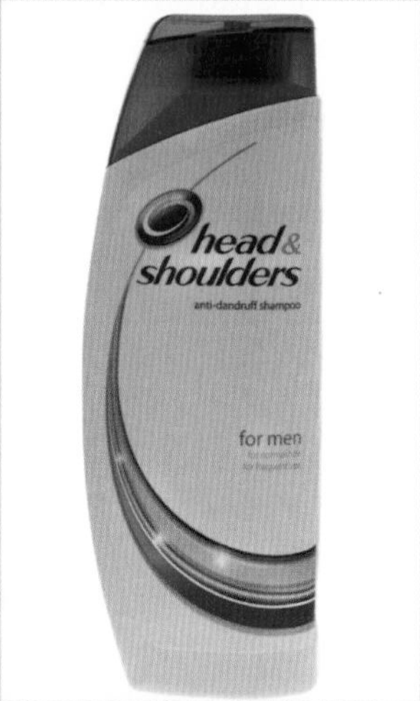

Segmentation and targeting

Segmentation is an important feature of marketing. It involves identifying groups of customers who are broadly similar. They thus form a distinct segment of the total market for a product or service. For example, in the daily-newspaper market there are readers whose primary concern is to read sports stories; there are others looking for current affairs and politics; others may be more interested in fashion; others with an interest in gossip.

National newspapers therefore target particular groups or readers. For example, the *Daily Mail* is targeted more at women readers. It therefore has larger sections dedicated to fashion and gossip about celebrities than most other newspapers. In contrast, the *Sun* is targeted more at male readers with an interest in sport – particularly football. In contrast, the *Financial Times* is targeted more at business readers – it has a lot of stories, features and information about business and the economy, and relatively small sections focusing on football and fashion.

The *Daily Mail* is targeted more at a female readership than other newspapers

Primary segmentation

The most obvious type of segmentation is between customers who buy entirely different products. For example, a firm like Unilever makes toothpaste and soap to meet quite different customer needs. There are not many people who clean their teeth with soap!

Segmentation by demographics and psychographics

Further segmentation can be based on demographic and psychographic factors.

Demographics segment people according to facts about them as members of the population, e.g. their sex, age, size of their family, income, where they live, the type of work they do, etc.

Psychographics segment people according to their lifestyle. A person's lifestyle is their individual pattern of behaviour, made up of their attitudes, beliefs, interests and habits.

Benefits and features of products

When marketing products it is important to be able to distinguish between the features and benefits of a product.

For example, the features of this book include the facts that it is in colour, has lots of pages of content and is priced at £19.99.

However, if it is going to sell well, marketers need to identify the benefits that customers are going to look for when they choose to buy the book. Benefits that customers (teachers and students) are looking for include:

- Detailed coverage of units, enabling them to cover all of the content required by the qualification.
- Help and advice with regard to carrying out assessments.
- Ease of navigation through the various sections of the book.
- Support materials.

Benefits are the advantages gained by buyers from the goods and services that they buy. For example, a cool drink will provide you with the benefit of refreshment on a hot day. An iPhone will provide you with the benefits of instant internet access, being able to text and send pictures to friends, and ease of use.

The benefits offered by a product or service can include:

- Convenience and accessibility.
- Good after-sales technical support and advice.
- Comfort and ease of use.
- Accountability – the knowledge that if things go wrong, the manufacturer will put them right.
- Courtesy and helpfulness of staff.
- Attractive, appropriate and efficient design and packaging.
- Peace of mind – the knowledge that you can trust the company, that your needs are understood and the good or service you have purchased will not let you down.

The more benefits that you can provide for customers, the more likely you are to be able to sell your product and get a 'good price' for it.

Activity

The features of the car I currently own are that it is blue, it is a Peugeot 107 and that it does 40 miles to a gallon of petrol. The benefits I was looking for in purchasing the car were that it should be inexpensive, easy to maintain, safe and economical to run. Think of five products that you buy regularly. In each case, list three features of the product and three benefits that you look for when choosing this product.

Did you know...

In selling a range of hair-care products, L'Oréal uses the strapline, 'Because you're worth it'. Here the advertising is promoting a benefit – that the product helps you to look after yourself – rather than a specific feature of the product.

The marketing mix

When marketing their products, firms need to create a successful mix of:

- The right product
- Sold at the right price
- In the right place
- Using the most suitable promotion.

The ingredients of the marketing mix are often referred to as the four Ps: product, price, place and promotion.

A mix is made of ingredients that are blended together to meet a common purpose. As with a cake, no ingredient is enough on its own: it has to be blended together to produce something special.

To create the right marketing mix, businesses have to meet the following conditions:

- The product has to have the right features – for example, it must look good and work well.
- The price must be right. Consumers will need to buy in large numbers to produce a healthy profit.
- The goods must be made available in the right place at the right time. Making sure that the goods arrive when and where they are wanted is an important operation.
- The target group needs to be made aware of the existence and availability of the product through promotion. Successful promotion helps a firm to spread costs over a larger output.

Fieldwork

Think of a product that you buy regularly such as an item of confectionery or a magazine. How effective is the marketing mix for this product?

Before you start, make sure you know who the product is supposed to sell to (the target market). Is the product aimed at teenagers? Male or female?

Now choose a sample of 30 people to interview from the appropriate group, e.g. females in the age range 13–18. Ask your sample to compare your selected product with three or four rival products. Draw up a table similar to the one below and then compare the brand you use with its competitors.

Now suggest how the marketing mix could be improved for the product you buy.

Product A	Very good	Good	Average	Poor	Very Poor	Comment
Place						
Promotion						
Price						
Product						

Designing the marketing mix

It is important to coordinate the various aspects of the marketing mix. This is where a marketing plan comes in handy. The plan should be designed to integrate the various aspects of the marketing mix.

The product

The product lies at the heart of the marketing mix. There needs to be a demand for the product. One of the first questions to ask is, 'Who will buy the product?'

If you cannot identify who is likely to buy the product and why they might want it, then you are doomed to failure right from the start.

Think of new products that you have recently bought. When you first saw the product being demonstrated or heard about it, you will have thought to yourself, 'That's a really good idea – I could do with one of those!'

Activity

Think of a new product that you have recently bought. What led you to buy the product?

New products tend to result from moments of inspiration, chance inventions, or copying similar ideas that have worked elsewhere. However, this is only the starting point. Two types of research then need to be carried out:

1. Product research	2. Market research
To identify ways of improving the original product idea	To identify whether there is a market for the product and how large it is
Modification	Modification
Marketable products	

Bringing a new product to market

Cadbury regularly introduces new chocolate products to the market. New ideas are developed by product designers. Product developers are encouraged to play with bags of ingredients to develop new ideas. At the same time, market researchers are continually talking to consumers. For example, the Creme Egg Twisted Bar was developed after hearing consumers say that they would like the Creme Egg experience all year round. Sometimes new ideas come from developing state-of-the-art technology such as the newest chocolate-making machinery. At other times ideas are identified by marketers who spot a gap in the market. A lot of time is spent on developing popular brands like Cadbury Dairy Milk and identifying new products that can be introduced to the Cadbury's Dairy Milk range.

The Cadbury Creme Egg Twisted Bar was developed after listening to consumers stating that they would like to be able to eat the product all year round

What are:

1. a) Product development
   b) Market research?
2. Why are these two functional areas important in developing new products?
3. What is more important – product development or market research?
4. For every idea that Cadbury develops, it rejects about 20. Why do you think this is the case?

The price

Pricing needs to be closely tied to product research. There are two main methods that you can choose from to price your product.

Cost-based pricing

The simplest way is to work out the cost of producing the product and then add a percentage for profit. For example, a sign writer might calculate that to cover the cost of materials and the wages they want to pay themselves would come to £20 an hour. They might also decide that they want to make a profit of 50%. They would simply add £10 an hour (50% of £20) when they make quotes for jobs to prospective clients. So, for example, to carry out a ten-hour job, they would make a quote to the client of £300 (10 hours at £20 = £200 + 50% profit = £300.

Market-based pricing

Perhaps a more intelligent way to price the job is to consider what the customer is willing to pay. This can be found out by market research. What the customer is willing to pay will depend on what they see as being a fair price for the job and also the price charged by competitors. For example, customers may only be willing to pay £25 per hour for a sign-writing job that takes ten hours.

Using the same example outlined above:

10 hours at £25 = £250, i.e. a profit of 25% for the sign writer.

While profits may be lower when a business uses market-based pricing, at least it will be able to win contracts.

The price charged needs to be closely tied to the product in the marketing mix. For high-quality products that are highly valued by customers, you can charge higher prices. For low-quality products where there is a lot of competition in the market, it is only possible to charge a much lower price.

The place

Place is concerned with how you get goods to the consumer and where. Traditionally, place usually involved a physical place, e.g. a market or a shop where the supplier would provide the product and meet potential buyers. For many products there would be several stages in getting products to the end consumer. A manufacturer, e.g. a food factory, might make the products and then sell them to a wholesaler, which stored the products. Products would then be sold to a retailer, such as a shop, which sold goods in smaller quantities to the end consumer.

Today the place is just as likely to be through the internet or by mail order. The internet provides a great distribution channel for micro-businesses. Armed with a website, a micro-business is able to reach a very large target audience.

Place and product are closely related. For example, if you are selling clothes via the internet, it is essential to give customers a lot of detail in the form of descriptions and pictures of the items and sizes. Without this detailed information a lot of clothes might be returned and spoiled by customers.

The promotion

Sales promotion refers to a set of methods used to encourage customers to buy a product, usually at point of sale.

Sales promotion is used along with advertising and publicity. It can include the use of point-of-sale materials (e.g. leaflets and brochures), competitions, offers, product demonstrations and exhibitions.

Promotion is closely tied to product, place and price. For example, considerable sums of money may be used on promotional activity for expensive products, using expensive materials.

Types of promotion

In creating a marketing plan, it is important to be aware of the wide range of promotional methods that you can choose from. In this section we focus on two main types of promotion:

- advertising
- promotional activities.

Advertising

Advertisements are messages sent through the media that are intended to inform or persuade (influence) the people that receive them.

Advertising can be defined as a paid-for type of marketing communication that is non-personal but aimed at a specific target audience through a media channel.

Think carefully about the purposes for which you use advertising, e.g.

- To provide information to a target audience.
- Encourage purchases.
- Change views.
- Develop support from the community.

There are many different ways of advertising.

Newspapers

There are several different types of newspapers:

- National and local newspapers
- Paid-for and free newspapers
- Newspapers aimed at a broad audience, and more targeted newspapers.

The cost of advertising in a national newspaper can be very expensive – several thousand pounds for a large display advertisement.

Activity

Either ring up or visit your local newspaper to find out the cost of placing an advertisement. Before you do so have a look at advertisements in the newspaper. What size of advert would you want to use to promote your new start-up business?

Remember that it may be just as effective to get free advertising in your local newspaper by making the paper aware of something interesting about your business that they can base a report on.

Radio

Local radio is a particularly effective way of advertising information about a local business. The radio is listened to by people sitting in their cars or doing the ironing at home, and even by students sitting in their rooms.

Television

Television is the most powerful medium, reaching 98% of households, and viewing figures for some programmes can exceed 20 million. However, with the development of digital and satellite television there are far more channels and viewers can switch between channels during the advertising break. This is a very expensive way of advertising and therefore unlikely to be suitable for a small business.

Cinema

Most cinemas today have a multiplex structure. Advertisers will therefore buy advertising space with the cinema, covering each of the various screens. The main cost in cinema advertising is in creating a film clip to be screened.

Magazines

Magazine advertising enables targeted advertising. Particular magazines appeal to particular segments of the market. For example, *Runner's World* is a very good way of reaching runners to advertise races, running gear, injury clinics and other specific running-related products. To reach wider audiences, adverts can be placed in mass-circulation magazines such as *Hello!* and *OK!*.

Outdoor

Outdoor advertisements can be placed in bus shelters, on the side of buses, and other locations.

Online advertising

Advertising on websites has rapidly grown to become a major source of advertising revenue. Internet advertising is very good at reaching specific targeted populations who are searching for a particular site. However, pop-up advertisements are often seen as a nuisance by web users and so may not be read. There are many different examples of online advertising, including adverts on search engine results pages, banner advertisements and social-networking advertisements such as those you see on Facebook. A great advantage of online advertising is that it can reach a global audience. There are many different types of advertisement formats including floating advertisements that float above the content on the user's screen. A pop-up is a new window which opens in front of the current one being used to display the advertisement. Placing adverts online can be quite a cost-effective way of reaching a large audience; for example, using a cost per click model (CPC) where the advertiser pays only when a user clicks on their advertisement. A cost per view (CPV) model is one where advertisers pay when a targeted visitor goes on to the advertiser's website.

Personal selling

In many markets selling through a team of sales representative is the main promotional tool. Sales teams are expected to inform customers about products being offered and to demonstrate how they can be used. The sales team may also provide training in the use of products.

Which method of advertising would be most suitable for a small business?

Promotional activities

In addition to advertising there is a range of promotional activities that can be used:

Competitions

Many businesses use competitions to promote sales. For example, newspapers often run a bingo or scratch-card competition to encourage buyers to buy their paper and to find out more about the paper. Often when people enter a competition they are asked to provide further information about themselves, which the company running the campaign can then use for further targeted marketing activities.

Money-off coupons

You will often receive money-off coupons through the post or when they are given out free with your shopping. These are designed to encourage you to try out a particular product, often when the product is new or when some of its features have been changed.

Activity

Which of the methods of advertising described above would be suitable for carrying out marketing activities for a small business or social enterprise of your choice? You can see a list of likely costs of different types of advertising in the table below:

Type of media	Cost of advertising
Television	£50,000+ depending on the length of the campaign
Magazines and newspapers	£10,000+ for full-page colour advertisements. Much less for display adverts in newspapers. This is usually charged by SCM or single column centimetres. Find out from your local paper what the charge is.
Radio advertising	Slots of 25 seconds can be around £250–£1,000 per week, depending on the frequency of the advert.
Outdoor advertising	£2,000 for mobile billboard on a vehicle; £7,000 to £8,000 for large billboards
Online advertising	5p per click on many sites
Cinema	£2,000 per month for 15-second commercials before films. It depends on the number of screenings and whether the commercials are to be shown locally or nationally (where the cost will be much higher).

Free gifts with purchase

Free gifts are designed to make a product more appealing, e.g. a magazine with a free nail varnish or hair clip. Often the free gift is designed to promote both the free gift and the product that it is sold with.

Tasting sessions

These are frequently used to promote food and drink. They attract new customers who may not have tried a product before or may remind previous customers of a product they have enjoyed in the past.

Demonstrations

Demonstrations are used to provide more details about how a product works. A good example of a demonstration is when a prospective car buyer is taken out for a trial ride from a motor showroom to demonstrate the features of a new car.

Fundraising

For social enterprises, fundraising is a major way of promoting the enterprise. Charities and voluntary organisations raise money through a range of methods, including sponsored runs and cycle rides, as well as balloon trips, parachute jumps and other means of raising money. These events not only raise money for the social enterprise, but also raise the profile of the enterprise.

Direct marketing

Direct marketing involves sending messages direct to consumers without the use of media provided by third parties. For example, a business can contact customers through direct mail (e.g. leaflets through the post) and email. An important aspect of direct marketing is the recording of response rates. A direct-mail communication will ask the receiver to do something, e.g. make a phone call to a freephone number. The direct marketer can then check the response rate – e.g. how many people receiving the mail responded.

Did you know...

Consumers sometimes have a negative view of direct mail. Letters received promoting products are sometimes termed 'junk mail'. Marketing messages sent by email are termed 'spam'.

Direct mail

Marketers like the quantifiable nature of direct mail. For example, if they send out 10,000 letters and get 1,000 responses, they can quantify this as a 10% return.

Examples of direct mail include advertising literature, catalogues, free trial CDs, pre-approved credit card applications, etc.

Direct mail is very popular for businesses in the financial services sector (e.g. offering loans), and for travel companies. Advertisers are able to negotiate bulk delivery discounts with Royal Mail and other carriers.

Catalogue shopping

Catalogue shopping is a common form of direct mail. Customers are sent catalogues because they have filled in an application form or because they fit the target market that a particular company focuses on. Areas of the UK are divided up according to postcodes, depending on the value and type of houses in that area. Housing is seen as an indicator of income. Catalogues come with order forms and easy means of payment. Today, most catalogue companies also operate online.

Internet shopping

Internet shopping has become increasingly popular in the UK and elsewhere. Online shops provide consumers with information about and the ability to buy goods online. Shoppers have almost unlimited access to any goods that they want to purchase.

Did you know...

Shopsafe is an online site that checks out the safety of online shops, providing guidance so that shoppers can shop safely. It lists the most popular online shops on its site as Amazon, Argos, B&Q, Boden, Boots, Bunches, Carphone Warehouse, Comet, Currys, Debenhams, Dial-a-phone, Dixons, Dorothy Perkins, Empire Stores, Figleaves, House of Fraser, IWOOT, JD Sports, John Lewis, M&S, New Look, Next, Nike Store, Play.com, Prezzybox, Sainsbury's, Tesco, The Body Shop, Toys 'R' Us, and Very.

Sponsorship

Sponsorship is a good way to promote a business, e.g. by sponsoring the shirts of a local football team or a sporting or charity dinner.

Public relations

Public relations refers to activities designed to create a positive image of an organisation. They are designed to be long term rather than short term, as with many other promotional activities. Businesses engage in a number of public relations activities including:

- Press releases. Here a business creates written copy, which they release to newspapers and journalists. The press release enables the journalist to quickly write a story about the business, using the key facts and information set out in the press release.
- Press conferences. These are usually coupled with press releases. A company will invite journalists to a press conference. The press conference will involve a talk often coupled with PowerPoint presentations. The press reporters are encouraged to ask questions to find out more about the company's activities.
- Networking. Businesses additionally promote the company through networking activity. These are informal contacts between members of the company and the wider public, e.g. at conferences and simply through the development of social relations, e.g. informal dinners where company members project a positive image and give out information about the business.

Activity

What public relations activities could you engage in to develop a positive image of a social enterprise or micro-business that you were setting up?

Assignment for Unit 19 – part 1

Chapter 33 provides you with the underpinning marketing principles that will enable you to create your own marketing plan. After reading through Chapter 33 you should start to think about an idea for a small business that you want to create a marketing plan for. Start thinking about some of the marketing concepts that can be applied when you create the marketing plan – e.g. the Unique Selling Proposition, the target market, the components of the marketing mix and a suitable promotional plan.

1. Identify the business idea that you want to develop. Set out on paper a list of the marketing concepts that you will employ in creating a marketing plan for this business. Briefly explain how you will apply each of these concepts in your marketing plan, e.g. what is the USP, will you carry out primary or secondary market research or both, what elements of the marketing mix you will particularly focus on, what will be the key elements of your promotional plan. **(P1)**
2. List the various promotional methods that you could use. Carry out some research using sources such as your local newspaper office (to find out press advertising rates), local cinema (cinema advertising rates), etc to find out the relative costs of different promotional methods. Justify the use of alternative promotional techniques that you could employ. **(P2)**

The following grid shows you what you will need to do to achieve pass, merit and distinction grades.

To achieve a pass grade you need to:	To achieve a merit grade you need to:	To achieve a distinction you need to:
P1 assess own business proposition using marketing concepts	**M1** explain how marketing principles have been used to develop a marketing mix for a micro start-up business	**D1** develop a cost-effective coordinated marketing mix and promotion plan to meet the needs of a defined target market
P2 justify types of promotion for a micro start-up business drawing on evidence of success or failure in the marketplace	**M2** produce a cost-effective promotion plan that communicates consistent messages to prospective customers	
P3 plan marketing for a micro start-up business that is relevant to customer needs		
P4 plan costed promotional activity for a micro start-up business that is appropriate for customer groups		

Chapter 34
Marketing plan and promotional plan

What are you finding out?

This chapter outlines the stages in creating a marketing plan and a promotional plan. It provides you with an outline of the sections of these plans.

This chapter will help you to:

- Plan marketing and promotion.

The sections in a marketing plan

This part of the chapter outlines the sections that you will need to create in your marketing plan.

From the outset it will be helpful to have an overview of what your marketing plan should look like. Figure 34.1 provides a useful template for you. It relates to Sally's Sandwiches. Sally hopes to set up a sandwich business in her local town. She will prepare sandwiches from her own state-of-the-art kitchen unit and deliver them on demand to local businesses in the area.

Market definition and opportunity

A crucial starting point for the marketing plan of a micro-business is to identify what market it is selling to. For example, are you selling to a local, national or international market? Sally's Sandwiches operates locally. In contrast, a micro-business selling greetings cards could reach national and international markets through the internet. If you don't know who your customers are, you could waste time and money trying to reach the wrong people with the wrong messages.

Make the grade

P1 **P3** To meet the requirements of P1, you need to apply a range of marketing concepts in creating a marketing plan for a micro start-up business. The sorts of concepts that you need to apply are segmentation, targeting, identifying the benefits customers are looking for, the nature of market research and the marketing mix, and sales promotion and sales forecasting. Draw up a list of the concepts that you want to include in your plan and then cross them off the list as you build them into your plan. This will then allow you to assess your own business proposition using marketing concepts.

To meet the requirements of P3 you are required to produce a marketing plan for a micro-business. The template provided in Figure 34.1 shows you the sorts of section headings that you should create for your micro-business. In addition, you will benefit from reading the supporting notes that follow below.

Most markets are divided into a number of clear segments. So set out in the marketing plan which segments you are targeting. As we saw in the previous chapter, segments consist of consumers who are broadly similar. So clarify which specific segments of the total market you are aiming for. Are they male or female or both? Are they young or old, rich or poor, frequent purchasers or irregular purchasers, fashionable or conservative? And so on.

You will need to demonstrate that there is a clear demand for the product. This is where some form of testing always helps. If you have tested your product and seven out of ten people said they liked it and they are prepared to pay for it, then you are on to a good thing. If you have letters confirming definite orders this will certainly help.

Activity

Set out who your target market consists of and what particular segments of the total market you are aiming for and how you chose these segments.

1. Market definition and opportunity	Here Sally will define the market – that it consists of local businesses that do not have canteens and are located away from retail centres.
2. Proposed target market segments	Here Sally will show that the market for sandwiches consists of a number of segments in her local town. Different customers are looking for different qualities of sandwich and different types of bread – ranging from healthy eating options, e.g. wholemeal bread and salad, to standard white bread with ploughman's (cheese and pickle) fillings. The business segment is a discrete segment of the total market.
3. Demand for product/service	Sally will need to demonstrate that there will be a demand for her product. In part this will be based on showing that she has a **unique selling proposition** (USP). She will need to identify the numbers of sandwiches she expects to be able to sell based on her market research. She should show what percentage of the total market she will be able to capture.
4. Competition	Here Sally needs to show who the closest competitors are and how her sandwiches and other benefits that she provides are different from the competition.
5. Other external influences	Sally needs to mention any external factors that are likely to affect her business. An important part of this will be identifying trends – for example, are people buying in sandwiches or having them made at home? Is there a growing trend towards people buying from a supplier like Sally? Published market research will help with this.
6. Marketing tactics	In this section Sally needs to set out how she is going to use the marketing mix. She should explain each of the components – product, price, place and promotion – and how they will be integrated. For example, if she is producing top-of-the range sandwiches with expensive bread and fillings, then she should be charging a premium (high) price to reflect the quality of the product.
7. Market research	This is an important section of any marketing plan. Readers of the plan need to feel reassured that the writer of the plan is not just making things up. If a questionnaire or interviews were used, this needs to be explained. How big a sample of customers were interviewed? What were the key findings of the market research? A copy of the questionnaire and any other primary data should be shown in the appendices to the marketing plan.
8. Sales forecasts	The sales forecast enables Sally to show how she will respond to the demand for the product. How many sandwiches will she make each week and how many of these does she expect to sell? Refer back to the market research.
9. Support materials	Here Sally should include letters of support, e.g. from firms agreeing to allow Sally's sandwiches to be sold from their premises. In addition, industry studies might be helpful that show how other suppliers elsewhere have supplied businesses with a similar service.
10. Measuring success	Finally, Sally should outline how she proposes to measure the success of her marketing activities.

Figure 34.1 Market plan for Sally's Sandwiches

Did you know...

A common cause of business failure results from planners not having a clear idea of who their customer is. They may base their view of the customers on their own beliefs about who should want the product or on what they like themselves. The best way to get a clear picture of who the customer is, is to carry out market research.

The competition

Businesses that don't know who the competition is and what the competition offers are likely to fail. List your main competitors and briefly describe their main strengths and weaknesses. Show how what you have to offer is superior to that of your rivals.

Activity

Identify the main competitors for your micro-start-up. Identify strengths of competitors and show how your product or service is superior.

Other external influences

There will be a number of changes taking place that your business has little or no control of. Some of these changes relate to trends. For example, for Sally's Sandwiches an important trend is that more women are going out to work and people are living busier lives, which has led to an increased demand for ready-prepared food. Although this trend is external to Sally's business, she can use this trend in her favour by talking to customers and finding out what sorts of sandwiches they are looking for, and when and where they buy them.

In addition, you need to identify other external factors that are likely to affect your business. Obvious examples are new consumer protection laws, environmental, and health and safety legislation.

Activity

Identify the key external influences likely to impact on your micro-business.

Marketing tactics

Marketing tactics are the means by which businesses find out about customers and then provide them with what they want. The main marketing tactics involve market research and use of the marketing mix.

Market research

Market research should be the starting point in planning the business.

You need to decide on the methods that you will use to carry out your market research. For example, will you use questionnaires, interviews, focus groups or a mixture of these methods? You also need to decide on the scale of the research. How many people are you going to ask? Who will they be? The important thing is to use a big enough sample to get meaningful results. The sample needs to be representative of your target market. Questionnaires are the best way of getting lots of results. However, make sure that you don't ask too many questions. The more questions you ask, the more difficult and time consuming it will be to analyse the results.

Did you know...

A common fault of questionnaires is that they often do not produce helpful results because the questions are badly worded. It is only after the results come to be analysed that this fault comes to light. The way round this is to pilot the questions to find out what sorts of answers people give to the questions and to see if they make sense.

Market research for Innocent

The founders of Innocent Smoothies came up with the idea of producing Smoothies made from 100% pure fruit drink. However, they first needed to be sure that their idea would be popular with potential customers. The market research they initially carried out was simple. They set up a display of their Smoothies on a stall at a music festival. They asked people who bought the Smoothies to give them some feedback. They had set up two containers. They asked consumers to put the empty drinks containers into one of two containers. One container was for those who liked the product and would buy it again. The other was for those who didn't like the drink. By the end of the festival, the first container was full and the other was empty. They knew that they had a winning idea. Since then they have used more detailed market research to find out what types of flavours people like and how much they are prepared to pay.

1. Can you develop a simple market research method to identify whether the product or service of your micro-business would be popular?
2. How do you plan to record the results of your research?
3. What questions do you want answering in your research?
4. How much evidence would you need to know whether the business idea would be a success or not?

Always pilot your questions first to see if people understand them. Piloting also helps you to see if you are getting useful data. A pilot survey is a small survey designed to trial your questions. When you are happy with your questions, you can then carry out more detailed research.

Having carried out your research, you will have a lot of data to analyse. Analysing the results involves looking for patterns. If the research is on a small scale, set out the results in numbers e.g. 15 people said they would buy the product; 5 said they would not buy the product; and 5 were undecided. If you have carried out a larger-scale survey with lots of potential customers, then you can use percentages.

Finally, when you have analysed your results you will be able to draw up key conclusions or recommendations. The conclusions will relate to the original questions that you set out to answer: Is there a market for your product or service? Who makes up the target audience? How often would they be prepared to purchase? Where will they purchase from?

Activity

Create a plan for and carry out market research for a micro-enterprise. Decide what the key questions are that you are seeking answers to. Decide how you will conduct the research. What sort of sample will you use? What methods of research will you employ? Then pilot your research methods to see if they are likely to be successful. Then adjust your research methods in the light of the success of the pilot. Conduct your research; analyse the results; and set out your conclusions.

The marketing mix

The marketing mix that you plan should be based on the findings of the market research. Make sure that you are clear about the product and the key benefits that it offers. Set this out in a way that is easy to understand by potential customers.

You will also need to choose an appropriate pricing strategy for the goods and services that you offer. Think about what competitors are charging as well as how much customers are prepared to pay. Don't neglect to cover the cost of producing or supplying the good or service.

In thinking about the place element of the marketing mix, you need to consider how you will get your product or service to customers. This needs to be informed by the market research findings.

Promotion is covered in more detail below in the separate section on the promotion plan.

Activity

Set out and justify a marketing mix plan for your micro-business. Show how the choice of marketing mix results from market research.

Make the grade

M1 To achieve M1, you are required to explain how marketing principles have been used to develop a marketing mix for a micro start-up business You need to demonstrate ways in which you have applied the marketing mix in your marketing plan for your micro-business and its products and services. Make sure that you consider how each of the elements of the marketing mix fit together to project a consistent mix.

Image

Image in business is as important as the product or service. The image is the picture in the mind of your customers of what the business stands for. There are all sorts of ways that you can project a suitable image – in the name chosen for the business; the look of the products or services; the way in which people that work for the business interact with customers; the nature of the advertising, and so on.

Task

What image do you want customers to have of your business? Explain how you will project this image, e.g. through the name chosen, look of the logo, location of premises, etc.

Sales forecasts

Accurate sales forecasts are an essential part of the marketing plan. You need to get these right because so much else is dependent on them. A sales forecast sets out your expected sales each month. From the sales forecast, you can then predict how much you need to order in terms of raw materials and supplies, how much labour you will need, and other factors. If you exaggerate your sales, then your costs will be too high because you will be left with unused stocks. If you underestimate your sales, that will be almost as bad because you may find that you don't have enough resources to meet the sales requirement.

Task

Set out a monthly sales forecast for the first year of operating your business. Base these figures on sound market research information.

Support materials

A well-constructed marketing plan will enable you to convince potential investors or providers of loans to your business that it will be a success. So back it up by supporting materials that will convince them that your idea is a good one. For example, include letters of support – such as a letter from a customer setting out their intention to buy given quantities of your product. In addition, use industry studies that show that the market sector on which your business is based is a growing one.

Measuring the success of the marketing

Creating a marketing plan and preparing marketing activities take time and resources. You need to be able to demonstrate that these efforts have been worth it. Your marketing plan should therefore briefly set out how you will measure the success of the marketing activity. What measures will you use to measure the success? Examples could include the sales of the good or service, customer awareness of the brand, and of course the profit that the business will generate.

Promotion plan

Promotion is part of the marketing mix. However, in terms of marketing planning, it is helpful to treat the promotional plan as a section on its own because it is so important.

The promotional plan needs to be coordinated with other elements of the marketing mix. For example, if your product is an exclusive and expensive one, then you will want to promote your product through advertising media that put this message of exclusivity across. If you were promoting a top-of-the-range women's perfume, you would be wiser to advertise in *Vogue* magazine rather than in *OK!* or *Bella*, which are aimed at a mass audience.

The image to be developed

Think carefully about the image that you want to promote for your micro-business. An important aspect of the image relates to the segment of the market you are hoping to capture.

Possible market segments

Upmarket	Mid-market	Downmarket
Exclusive and expensive	Above average price and quality	Cheap and affordable to a mass audience

There are other aspects of the product that you will want to promote related to **unique selling propositions**. For example, you may want to project a 'hip' and up-to-date image, or an environmental image, or an alternative image, or a safe, conservative image, and so on.

Activity

What sort of image do you want to create for your micro-business and its products? Working with a small group of students, see if you can generate some statements that reflect your business that can be incorporated in the promotional materials. For example, 'safe and secure', 'convenient and accessible', 'original and new' etc.

Did you know...

It is very difficult to change a 'bad image' of a company. People tend to remember things such as poor service or a bad experience with a product. So make sure that, right from the start, you create and maintain a good image for your business.

Costs

In the previous chapter we identified some of the costs of promotional activity. Costs will vary with:

- the media used
- the length of the promotional campaign (days, weeks or months)
- the extent of the promotion (local, regional or national).

Task

When you have decided on the types of promotions that you want to carry out, then research the costs. The important thing is to make sure that the costs are acceptable in the light of the likely sales revenues that result from the promotional activity.

Schedule for promotional campaign

You will need to prepare a timeline setting out the schedule of promotional activity. For example, Sally's Sandwiches used the following schedule:

Timeline of promotional activity for Sally's Sandwiches

- **Two months before launch**: Flyer to all local businesses to tell them about the new business venture.
- **One month before launch**: Posters sent to local businesses, to be placed in a prominent position advertising the service.
- **One month before launch**: Sally contacted each of the businesses individually by phone to explain the service.
- **Two weeks before launch**: Advert in the local paper for the service.
- **Launch day**: Feature in the local newspapers about Sally and the sandwich service.
- **Launch day**: Meal-deal offers to customers – providing them with a free drink and snack bar along with their sandwiches.
- **Post-launch**: Ongoing leafleting of new businesses advertising the service.
- **Post-launch**: Questionnaires for customers encouraging them to suggest ways of improving the service.

Activity

Create a schedule of promotional activities to get your micro-business off the ground.

Types of promotional material

The next section of your promotional plan should set out the types of promotional materials that you will use. For example, you may want to use posters, leaflets, advertisements or your own website. You need to explain carefully why you are choosing particular types of promotion. Key considerations are cost and suitability for the target market. It will be helpful therefore to carry out some local research to find out what the costs will be. For example, how much will it cost to have a poster designed by a local graphic designer? How much would it cost to print the number of copies of the poster that you are thinking of using? Promotional costs do not have to be expensive.

Task

What types of promotional materials will you use? How much will they cost?

Make the grade

P2 To show evidence for P2, you are required to justify the promotional methods that you use in your marketing plan. Explain why each method is appropriate, in terms of being cost effective and likely to reach the targeted audience. Show how the methods you have chosen are likely to achieve the best results for a micro-business drawing on evidence of success or failure in the marketplace.

SALLY'S
SANDWICHES
Delivered to your place of work
Save yourself the time and trouble of making your own sandwiches
Sally's Sandwiches offers professionally produced sandwiches based on customer demand
We will deliver direct to your place of work. To start with, we are producing 15 types of sandwiches – with different types of bread – white, brown and wholemeal.
There will be a range of popular fillings and we are always open to suggestions for new popular varieties. In addition, we will supply drinks and snacks and anything else that you care to mention.
Look out for Sally's. Our service starts on 15 June with a bumper meal-deal offer whereby we will provide you with a free drink and snack in addition to your chosen sandwiches.

Flyer for Sally's Sandwiches

Nature of promotional materials

You need to describe the promotional materials that you are going to use in more detail. Here you should mention the colours, visual features and type of text that you will use. The promotional materials will need to carry the name of the product/service and the company. You will also need to set out the brand and logo of the company on the promotional materials.

Innocent promotions

Innocent is a good example of a company that keeps its promotional costs down. They believe that the best way of promoting the business is through 'word of mouth'. A satisfied customer will pass the message on that Innocent provides enjoyable and healthy fruit drinks.

The television adverts that the company produces simply involve a cheap, hand-held video camera and pictures of the products in a natural setting, e.g. in a green field, with a voiceover.

1. What are the advantages of keeping promotional costs low?
2. How could you keep the promotional costs low for your micro-business?
3. What methods of promoting your business could you use?
4. How could you encourage the local press to take an interest in your micro-business and hence supply you with free advertising?

Task

Describe how you will lay out and design your promotional materials. Sketches and diagrams will help. You may want to produce some of the materials in finished form, e.g. posters and/or leaflets, providing the logo of the company, the product name, illustrations of the product or service, etc. Set them out using the company colours.

Website design and functionality

If you are going to create an online e-business, then this will involve the creation of a website. You will need to describe the design and functionality of the website. The functionality is what the website will actually do – e.g. display products, provide advice about products, enable customers to view products, make purchases, etc.

Activity

Describe the design and functionality of your website.

How the success of these promotions will be measured

Finally you need to outline how the success of the promotions will be measured. There are various ways of doing this. For example, if you are sending out a leaflet with a competition attached to it, you could measure the number of people entering the competition in relation to number of leaflets. If you are advertising your product, you can measure the number of people who can remember seeing your advert or recall what it was about.

Activity

Decide how you will measure the success of your promotional activity. Is it possible to create a measure of how successful it was?

Make the grade

M2 To show evidence for M2, you are required to produce a cost-effective promotional plan that communicates consistent messages. Your promotional plan will need to include the following headings:

- image to be developed
- costs
- promotional schedule
- type and nature of promotional materials, and
- measuring the success of the promotional plan.

Show how each of these elements will provide a consistent message about the business.

Make the grade

D1 To achieve a Distinction grade, you need to provide a cost-effective marketing and promotional plan that is designed to meet the needs of the targeted market sector. The important thing is that the various elements of these plans are coordinated – i.e. they fit together. A good way of doing this is to regularly cross-reference the various components, e.g. the product to the price, the product to the promotion, etc. You need to demonstrate to the readers of your plan that you have a crucial idea of your targeted market segment – and the price, promotion, place and product that are most suitable.

Key words

Benefits – What customers are looking for when they buy goods and services – i.e. what they expect the good or service to do for them.

Buyer decision-making process – The steps involved in making a buying decision.

Demographic segmentation – Identifying groups of customers who are similar as a result of age, race, gender or some other aspect of population characteristic.

Market-based pricing – Basing prices around those offered by the competition.

Marketing mix – Combination of price, product, place and promotion designed to relate to customer requirements.

Marketing plan – A plan setting out the marketing activities that a business will carry out.

Marketing tactics – Short-term and medium-term marketing actions designed to find out what customers want and then to provide them with an appropriate marketing mix.

Psychographic segmentation – Identifying groups of customers with similar lifestyles and behaviour patterns.

Sales forecast – Prediction of likely sales in a given future period.

Sales promotion – Methods used to encourage customers to buy.

Segmentation – Identifying groups of customers who are broadly similar and who behave in similar ways.

Targeting – Focusing products and marketing activities on specific groups of potential or actual customers.

Unique selling proposition – Individual aspects of a business or product that can be used to distinguish the firm or its products from those of rivals.

Assignment

Chapter 34 shows you how to create a marketing plan for a business building on the principles outlined in Chapter 33. The grid below shows you what you need to do to gain particular grades.

Create a marketing plan for a micro-start up business of your choice. In the plan use a range of marketing concepts (such as marketing segmentation and marketing mix). A useful template for creating your marketing plan is that provided for Sally's Sandwiches on page 407. Use a similar format for your own marketing plan. The key sections will be:

- Market definition and opportunity
- Proposed target market segments
- Demand for the product/service
- Competition
- Other external influences
- Marketing tactics
- Market research

▶

- Sales forecasts
- Support materials and
- Measuring success

1. Produce a marketing plan for a micro start-up business. Cover each of the areas listed above and shown on page 407 for Sally's Sandwiches. **(P3)**
2. Explain how marketing principles have been used to develop a marketing mix for a start-up business. Make sure that you cover the marketing principles explained in Chapter 33. In each case relate the principle to your own business idea. **(M1)**
3. Produce a workable promotion plan that communicates consistent messages to prospective customers. Identify what promotional methods you will use. In each case make it clear why that method is appropriate to your micro-business. Remember that an important constraint will be the marketing budget available. You want to have the maximum promotional impact for each pound spent on promotion. **(M2)**
4. Develop a coordinated marketing mix and promotion plan to meet the needs of a defined target market. Make sure that you explain how your marketing mix and the promotion plan is relevant to your chosen target market. For example, if you were targeting affluent females then you would need to target the media that they are most likely to read, see or hear about. The tone of the promotion needs to be aligned to their aspirations and self-image. You also need to make it clear how your chosen promotional plan is carefully co-ordinated with the selected marketing mix. Think about ways in which the promotional media and messages chosen coordinate with the price, product and place aspects of the marketing mix. **(D1)**

To achieve a pass grade you need to:	To achieve a merit grade you need to:	To achieve a distinction you need to:
P1 assess own business proposition using marketing concepts	**M1** explain how marketing principles have been used to develop a marketing mix for a micro start-up business	**D1** develop a cost-effective coordinated marketing mix and promotion plan to meet the needs of a defined target market
P2 justify types of promotion for a micro start-up business drawing on evidence of success or failure in the marketplace	**M2** produce a cost-effective promotion plan that communicates consistent messages to prospective customers	
P3 plan marketing for a micro start-up business that is relevant to customer needs		
P4 plan costed promotional activity for a micro start-up business that is appropriate for customer groups		

INDEX

Page numbers in **bold** indicate key term definitions.